T0328984

Intangible Flow Theory in Economics

The dominant economic explanations of the 20th century are not comprehensive enough to describe the complexity of economy and society and their reliance on the biosphere. *Intangible Flow Theory in Economics: Human Participation in Economic and Societal Production* outlines a new theory that challenges both economics and the relativism conveyed in social constructivism, poststructuralism and postmodernism.

To mainstream economics and Marxism, monetary flows transform us humans into commodities. To this new theory, flows of economic elements as physical goods or money are consummated by intangible flows that cannot yet be precisely appraised at an actual or approximate value, for instance, workflows, service flows, information flows or communicational flows. The theory suggests a systematic alternative to refute the human commodity framework and interrelated conjectures (e.g., human capital, human resources, human assets). Furthermore, it exhibits that economic and societal production is fully integrated on the biosphere. Conversely, contemporary relativism argues for the end of theory development, suspension of evidence and entrenchment of knowledge validity among local systems (named as paradigms, epistemes, research programs, truth regimes or other terms). Thus, relativism tacitly supports dominant theories such as the human commodity framework because it preventively sabotages the creation of new theoretical explanations. Disputing relativist theses, intangible flow theory demonstrates that innovative theoretical explanations remain possible.

This book is of significant interest to students and scholars of political economy, economic sociology, organization, economics and social theory.

Tiago Cardao-Pito is an assistant professor at ISEG, Universidade de Lisboa (University of Lisbon), Portugal.

Routledge Frontiers of Political Economy

For more information about this series, please visit: www.routledge.com/books/series/SE0345

Intangible Flow Theory in Economics

Human Participation in Economic
and Societal Production

Tiago Cardao-Pito

Routledge
Taylor & Francis Group

LONDON AND NEW YORK

First published 2021
by Routledge
2 Park Square, Milton Park, Abingdon, Oxon OX14 4RN

and by Routledge
52 Vanderbilt Avenue, New York, NY 10017

Routledge is an imprint of the Taylor & Francis Group, an informa business

British Library Cataloguing-in-Publication Data
A catalogue record for this book is available from the British Library

Library of Congress Cataloging-in-Publication Data
A catalog record for this book has been requested

ISBN: 978-1-138-29865-1 (hbk)
ISBN: 978-1-315-09849-4 (ebk)

Typeset in Bembo
by Apex CoVantage, LLC

Contents

Figures

Tables

About the author

Tiago Cardao-Pito is an assistant professor at ISEG, Universidade de Lisboa (University of Lisbon), Portugal. He has been invited as a guest lecturer to several academic programs such as those of the Massachusetts Institute of Technology in Portugal (MIT in Portugal), University of Strathclyde and the Portuguese Military Academy. He also has experience working at the Portuguese Ministry of Finance and Public Administration, the Portuguese Ministry of Health and the private sector.

Part 1

Introduction

1 A new theory, economics and relativism

1.1 Social sciences, the human condition and a new theory

Why cannot the social sciences try characterizing or even improving the human condition? In other words, why cannot the social sciences attempt to answer questions on matters such as the manner in which our species has lived, where we come from, how we relate to one another, how we may organize our societies, how our species could be perpetuated, or how humankind integrates upon the biosphere? For millennia, human life has undeniably improved, though at a variated progress among different global regions and social groups. Through successive generations, for instance, humans live longer and have further access to water and varied food resources, better health care and sanitation, improved literacy, better means of housing and amenities, improved means of transportation and enhanced technology to address human challenges.[1]

Still, our dynamic interactions and impacts upon the biosphere must be carefully addressed. Our planet's atmosphere, hydrosphere and geosphere[2] can be considered part of the biosphere because they provide requirements for the existence of living beings. Despite technologies such as 24-hour mass media, the internet, cloud computing, robotics or artificial intelligence (which will feel banal or obsolete in a few years, but situate the moment when this book was written), we humans are still vitally integrated upon the precious biosphere from which essential resources for our survival and existence are obtained. In our monetary societies, however, exerting motivations for obtaining and accumulating more money, we observe members of our species depleting non-renewable resources and doing effective damage to the biosphere through the most diverse forms of pollution and extinction. Mother Earth's current biodiversity cannot resist every challenge our species poses to the planet. Although several species may yet resist for longer, our own species' survival is not perpetually assured. Hardly could we resist an eventual destruction of our habitats.

Likewise, to address an ancient ambition for humankind, an important effort is under way to reach beyond into outer space. To date, we have only been capable of transporting a few humans to the nearby Moon. The capacity to inhabit other planets and spatial stations may, in extreme circumstances, reduce our species' extinction risk if our planet's conditions were to become untenable from either human or nonhuman phenomena. That is in a (hopefully very) distant future to come. Why cannot the social sciences participate in these human endeavors, as other scientists help find, for example, more efficient renewable-energy sources, food supplies, means of travel, storage or accommodation, new medicines or software? Even machine intelligence is, in some cases, allowed to address human problems, for instance, in water supply systems, transit networks, medical diagnosis and new medicines.

This work provides a defense for scientific methods based upon reason and logic to address the human condition as a subject of study. It is not a manifest to transform the social sciences into a demagogue voice of the people, which could replace the need for political and societal organization or decide human populations' views for them. On the contrary, scientific discipline and rigor can control for populist, demagogue and irrational statements that so often have caused societal catastrophes and disasters. With tested mechanisms, social sciences might formulate and debate ideas, theories, hypotheses, methods, systems and so forth. Within these efforts, novel solutions can be discussed regarding our condition's difficulties. Traditions and beliefs can be either reinforced or contested. Patently, the social sciences must not be expected to always find proper solutions for our many difficulties. Dramatic misgivings will continue to occur. Plenty of historical examples exhibit scientific failures and unsound scientific explanations. Yet, many technologies produced by non-social sciences, which have been quite beneficial to humankind, have also been used to militarily engage in highly destructive wars that have killed many human beings. Science can indeed be captured by political regimes and thus instrumentalized to produce supportive proto-evidence and citizen control mechanisms. Moreover, scientists themselves can create structures in their profession that enforce specific types of research and neglect, boycott or forbid others from expression. Status, roles, resources and accreditations might be allocated to specific scientific programs to the detriment of others. As a result, some dissident yet talented scientists may continue to face long degradation rituals of their reputation.[3]

However, the resilience of scientific testing enables persistence that leads towards new theories and explanations, which may improve previous ones. Furthermore, social structures of science can be amended, as current ones need not be maintained in place forever. Why should they be? We must not equate science with its own worst abuses.[4] Researchers, organizers and regulators can come up with enhanced governance and control mechanisms for scientific activity and its scrutiny, in the same manner we humans have been able to address many difficult problems of our condition. Rankings and prizes to research departments and publications will carry weight until scientists accept to be guided by them. Yet, a social scientist who was currently to admit that he/she is trying to improve the human condition would face the perils of becoming an object of severe disparagement. It could only be made worse if he/she were to admit considering other living humans as his/her brothers and sisters, despite all the DNA evidence that connect us as a species.

The new theory presented in this book addresses two major argumentative blocks against having the social sciences attempt to improve or at least characterize, the human condition. One of these blocks is the discipline of economics, or perhaps mainstream economics,[5] which nevertheless has exported many concepts and methodological frameworks to other social sciences. The other block entails relativist views for the social sciences (or the possibility of science in general), which are often identified under different names such as social constructivism, poststructuralism or postmodernism (or post-postmodernism, post-poststructuralism and so forth).[6] A great array of positions, ideas and highly heterogeneous groups of authors can and often are described under these terminologies, some of whom may not be relativists, and others are not concerned with scientific affairs. To develop our argument, we will be focused on positions and authors who are undeniably relativist (or anti-realist), even if they could themselves swear to be otherwise. We will of course explain why they are relativist. Importantly, economics and relativist perspectives are not opposite stances, but allied argumentative sets.[7] Not least, they both sabotage knowledge production purposed to advance life and the existence we humans may have.

The discipline of economics glorifies money as some sort of mystical commodity. Moreover, it treats humans and our contributions to economic and societal production as commodities (often also with the form of assets or capital or resources) to be traded by monetary flows. Human-related flows not reflected on monetary flows are to be discarded or neglected, even if they could greatly contribute to improve the human condition. Relativism in the social sciences has different versions gathering around the outline that we cannot even be certain of facts, for even facts would be socially constructed. To adapt Kukla's (2000, p. 4) typology,[8] relativism can be as follows: (i) *metaphysical* (transcendental) for doubting that there exists a real world (of, say, objects, properties and relations[9]) outside our social and bio-mental[10] constructions; (ii) *epistemological* (or scientific) for advocating that science cannot have empirical instruments to describe a real world besides our human constructions; and (iii) *semantic* for suggesting that human languages cannot describe a real world besides our human constructions. Semantic relativism may also entail claims over how institutions and social arrangements enable discourses into being.

An adopter of epistemological and/or semantic relativist arrangements may not entirely be a metaphysical relativist. For instance, someone who doubts that we have adequate scientific methods or language vehicles to capture reality may still accept that reality exist beyond our human constructions.[11] Nonetheless, all these three forms lead to relativist results, thereby providing arguments to contest that a definition of the human could be possible, let alone a characterization of our frail human condition. Any account of reality in science would be social constructed, for either (i) reality would not exist outside our individual and social selves or (ii) it would be constructed by scientific methods and/or language molds.[12]

As a result, the framework for the human, or human societies in economics would not need to be strongly contested. Not because those usages would not be constructed by economic methods and human languages, but because any alternative would be a mere *metanarrative* or *grand narrative*[13] to be also deconstructed. Therefore, relativism implicitly allies to mainstream economics' human commodity framework, for at least it (i) does not persuasively work to produce an alternative theory (and indeed several of its proponents adopt concepts formulated in economics) and (ii) preventively sabotages efforts to produce alternative theories.

Intangible flow theory[14] is one such effort. It suggests a new description for human participation in economic and societal production. However, the new theory seeks also to address these two blocks that work against scientifically characterizing the human condition. As for economics, intangible flow theory presents an alternative to replace the human commodity framework where we humans are prevented from being treated as commodities (or assets, capital or resources). Furthermore, it contests the characterization of money as a metaphysical/mystical commodity, which leads to the neglect or obfuscation of flows that are vital for economic and societal production and yet are not reflected upon monetary flows. Moreover, the new theory presents a demonstration that human survival and existence are fundamentally reliant upon the biosphere, which cannot be accomplished by economics' current research technologies.

As for the relativist block, intangible flow theory assumes that there is a reality that does not depend on humans to be created, a position that aligns with transcendental realism.[15] With this standpoint, the new theory does not aim to invoke the unknown and untestable to bring forward metaphysical claims. Instead, it intends to oppose narcissist egotism claiming we humans could have entirely built (constructed) our world merely out of scientific methods and human languages. At the relativist views opposed by the new theory, instead of being constrained by an existing world, alternative universes were ours to make into being. We humans would be as consumers choosing among different realities we could prefer. Indeed, the new theory's alignment to transcendental realism might be contentious, for the existence of a reality beyond ourselves is still an ongoing debate. Nonetheless, relativists have never demonstrated that reality does not exist beyond us humans. For thousands of years, their argumentation has been fundamentally based on decomposing methods and language forms used to claim reality would exist outside human formulations.[16] Thus, it still seems quite safe to assume a reality not depending upon us humans to be authorized to exist.[17]

Furthermore, the new theory accepts that scientific explanations can be partially or totally deconstructed because they have been socially and bio-mentally constructed by human methods and language vehicles. In formulating our explanations, we humans are influenced by many phenomena such as emotions, social context, social structures, temperaments, institutions, biological processes and constraints, and so forth. Indeed, the representation of an object by humans is not necessarily an objective representation of such object.[18] Human reason and logic are products of our bodies and the environments we are situated within. Yet, the understanding that for instance our body, senses, emotions, unconscious bio-mental processes or social constraints may mislead us in capturing reality is no demonstration that reality does not exist beyond ourselves.[19] A specific human society is necessarily constructed by the humans who can be connected to that society, yet such a society may still exist.[20] Although perhaps many explanations have been socially and bio-mentally constructed, we may still achieve explanations that reach empirical and semantic precision in capturing reality beyond ourselves. Our failing in dealing with such reality cannot be presented as evidence that reality does not exist.[21]

The activity of deconstruction has great relevance for relativist approaches.[22] Initially relaunched as a tool for analyzing texts (discourses) whereby tools of literary analysis would be employed,[23] it would later be used to discuss specific scientific methods.[24] Still, without reference to an external reality beyond human constructions, scientific texts cannot be clearly distinguished from works of fiction or poetry.[25] Consequently, deconstruction as employed in this manner may lead to the destruction envisaged by Nietzsche[26] and Martin Heidegger,[27] who had troubling connections to Hitler and his Nazi party.[28] These connections are far from unproblematic, for while constructivists, poststructuralists and postmodernists greatly appreciate speculating about origins of the scientific ideas of others, their own genealogy of ideas is often overlooked.[29]

Without attending to an external reality that could originate materials regarding objects, properties and relations to build upon, observers cannot have raw elements for producing new ideas, theories, technologies and solutions. In this manner, therefore, social constructivists, poststructuralists and postmodernists necessarily obtain relativist results through their analyses, no matter how firmly they could swear to not be relativists themselves. Moreover, given the prominence of relativist perspectives of science, we could expect that the meaning of deconstruction activity should be quite clear. However, relativists are generally against setting proper definitions and explanations for themselves, preferring deconstructing definitions and explanations of others.[30] As a result, the meaning of deconstruction as followed by relativists can be itself rather diffuse.[31]

Nevertheless, deconstruction need not be under a monopoly of relativist practices. By associating the activity of deconstruction with that of analysis, we may accomplish a formulation that is compatible with metaphysical, empirical and semantic realism. Besides including analysis of scientific texts (discourses), we may suggest also integrating the systematic analysis of methods and languages used to make scientific claims either in isolation or as a nexus of claims. Manifestly, these analyses must be made with reference to the situational circumstances where claims have been produced, as for instance social, personal, institutional, historical and so forth. Undeniably, many claims can indeed be deconstructed, for instance, those produced out of human delusion, ignorance or lack of skill or those others produced out of political alliances, jealousy, Machievalism or stupidity. And those many other claims based upon unsustainable grounds regarding reason, logic and evidence.

As described in this manner, however, deconstruction can be connected to ancient scientific and philosophical practices.[32] Instead of something new, analyses of scientific theories, concepts, methods, explanations or language molds could be found in the ancient world where our knowledge was quite a bit more rudimental. Yet, these activities have frequently been used to attempt better explanations that could replace previous ones. What becomes highly problematic with relativist approaches that currently have a large impact upon social sciences is the implicit idea that out of (relativist) deconstruction (destruction), no scientific proposition could survive. Hence, no longer would the role of scientists be to develop innovative theoretical explanations that could replace preceding ones. Nor should scientists much care to find adequate methods for testing prevailing theories, for such efforts would be doomed before the start. In the absence of any connection to reality beyond our social and individual constructions, either verification or refutation regarding scientific claims could be deconstructed until the infinite. Thus, verification or refutation proofs would be of little relevance.[33]

However, if reason and logic were mere social constructions, what could prevent irrational and illogical explanations to be as binding as explanations formulated according to tested standards of reason and logic?[34] Without adequate scientific scrutiny in place, what could prevent science to be the playground for psychopaths, Machiavellians or malignant narcissists to boost their egos, while eventually deluding and/or harming other humans?[35] Why would science not be a mere tool for reproducing the status quo in contemporary human societies, as any alternative explanation could be preventively undermined through irrationality?

Therefore, relativism brings serious risks of allowing irrationality to be at the same level in science and philosophy as reason and logic. Hence, it may condone unethical and harmful practices to us humans.[36] Yet, arguably, it may be quite difficult to convince many a relativist to abandon his/her relativism. Nevertheless, realist theories must do more to explain processes through which phenomena can be captured by standards of reason and logic.[37] Indeed, the study of how things come into being (ontology) in the social sciences is of uttermost importance.[38] However, ontological explanations may still be seized by ontological relativist (or anti-realist) frameworks.[39] For instance, a relativist proponent could suggest that any other ontology would be equally acceptable at a different social group.[40] Furthermore, epistemological relativists could claim there would not be adequate empirical methods capable of explaining how reality comes into being. Moreover, semantic relativists could claim that there are no language forms to explain reality beyond ourselves. Indeed, realists need to better explain processes through which objects, properties and relations previously unknown to humans can be captured by human science. That is, how can what is unknown to us but exists outside ourselves (what

Kant and ancient philosophers calls the noumenoun[41]) become perceptible to us (and according to Kant and ancient philosophers become a phenomenon[42])? Furthermore, realists need to explain better the difference between phenomena and pseudo-phenomena. A pseudo-phenomenon is a different concept to that of reification we can find in Karl Marx and Friedrich Engels[43] or in Berger and Luckman (1966, p. 106). Reification refers to reporting of a human phenomenon as if it was a thing, that is, as having nonhuman or possibly suprahuman terms. For instance, a certain human activity was described as if it was something else that resulted outside human production for having been originated in nature, cosmic laws or divine entities. On the other hand, a pseudo-phenomenon is a nonexistent phenomenon that is employed as demonstrated and verified. Besides better distinguishing phenomena from pseudo-phenomena, realists must be better able to classify phenomena according to their level of tangibility.

To contribute to these challenges, intangible flow theory suggests the existence of a tangible flows hypothesis. Tangible flows are defined as flows that can be identified with precision after they have occurred in a specific time and place[44] (not yet occurred flows cannot be considered tangible). A non-tangible (intangible) flow that has been perceived is a somehow apparently discernible phenomenon that cannot be measured or captured with precision. Yet, it is not something we did not perceive (noumenoun). A non-tangible flow that has not been perceived by us humans remains part of the noumenoun. Nonetheless, when a previously intangible flow can be measured with precision, it is no longer an intangible flow because a process of tangibilization has occurred. The intangible flow theory is not a dialectic theory that could be summarized by the formula thesis-antithesis-synthesis. An intangible flow will remain intangible only until we humans can figure out manners to identify it with precision. However, intangible flows are highly heterogeneous and, in most cases, we do not know why we cannot measure them with precision (otherwise we would). Therefore, intangible and tangible flows cannot be seen as some sort of thesis and antithesis, for an intangible flow is not the opposite of a tangible flow. It is instead a flow we cannot identify with precision in specific space and time.[45]

Scientific descriptions of intangible flows can (and should) be deconstructed. Many of them might be fake and/or fictitious human constructions, hence, to be describing pseudo-phenomena. Furthermore, tangible flows can be inspected and verified. They cannot be deconstructed not because they have not yet been constructed.[46] They cannot be further deconstructed because they can be identified with precision in a specific time and space, even when they are socially constructed as in our human societies' day-to-day existence. Thus, humans may find precise methods and language vehicles to communicate and discuss tangible flows.

Curiously, tangible flows can be communicated among nonhuman beings. For instance, they are communicated when other animals such as ants, elephants or dolphins[47] inform other members of their species about the path they have taken to reach food sources. Moreover, tangible flows can be communicated

in interactions between humans and machines, or among machines themselves, for instance, through artificial intelligence processes. Apparently, some
advanced machines appear to start being able to identify flows that are tangible
to those machines but intangible to us humans.[48] At some point, machines may
become more intelligent than us humans and eventually escape our control or
even dominate us humans.[49] These possibilities pose future risks to us as a species.[50] But let us not by now further complicate this discussion with another
existential human threat. The case is that, if tangible flows exist in that they
are phenomena that can be identified with precision in a specific time and
place after they have occurred, even when socially constructed, then there is an
actual limit for relativism in science. This boundary may enable us to attempt
characterizing the human condition, while creatively displacing economics'
human commodity framework.

Observe, for example, the case of monetary flows. Even opponents to strong
forms of relativism accept that money is socially constructed.[51] To our current knowledge, we seem to be the only species on the planet using monetary
technologies. It is indeed a considerable societal construction that a piece of
paper, a plastic card, a mobile phone, one's face[52] or a number in a digital
account could function for someone ordering goods and services from others
or organizations. Several dimensions of money, for instance, its meaning, refer-
ent, symbols, limit, origin, social space, enforcing mechanisms and institutional
background can and should be deconstructed. Nevertheless, monetary flows
have a specific property in that they are highly tangible after they have occurred
in a specific time and place. For instance, they can be identified when someone
examines a bank account or an organization produces an annual cash flow statement. The traditional physical modalities of money such as coins, paper money
and written checks are now being partially replaced by digital means, such
cards, digital accounts and mobile transactions. Yet, occurred monetary flows
remain highly tangible when they can be identified with precision in time and
space. Thus, although monetary flows might indeed be socially constructed, as
money as an object cannot be identified with precision, monetary flows have
components that are tangible flows and therefore avert further deconstruction. Thus, we can attempt characterizing how those tangible monetary flows
flowed. From where? And to where?

1.2 Economics and its human commodity framework

Indisputably, the discipline of economics could be characterizing the human
condition because in our contemporary societies many flows necessary for
human survival and existence are associated with monetary flows. Examples
are flows of food, machines, raw materials or digital contents; flows that allow
one to have a shelter for himself/herself and his/her family; or communication, transport, or many other human workflows. Moreover, economics could
further aid us in understanding the role of money in human societies.

However, economics is founded on a human commodity framework, which is generally taken for granted. It regularly treats us humans as commodities in the form of assets, capital, or resources. Furthermore, economics entails a massive glorification of money as some sort of mystical commodity. Money is described as having magical powers of creating/defining commodities. Things that are somehow related to monetary flows would mysteriously be defined as commodities. Economics uses these pseudo-phenomena to construct us humans and our contributions to economic and societal production as commodities. These pseudo-phenomena do not result from reification processes. Economics is not describing human phenomena as if they would be nonhuman, for instance, as natural, cosmic or divine phenomena. Instead, economics describes pseudo-phenomena (because they do not exist) as if they had been demonstrated and verified.

Furthermore, money has another mystical property in economics, which arises from another pseudo-phenomenon: that of being able to measure the intangible. To intangible flow theory, human-related intangible flows cannot be defined with precision, for instance, many workflows or knowledge flows. However, according to economic reasoning (or unreasoning), a monetary flow establishing (so-called equilibrium) price associated even remotely with an intangible flow would also measure the intangible flow value, which ought to be treated as akin to a commodity.

From here ensues an allegory where production and use of products by humans (say consumption) would match at the same instant, as in the mystical supply and demand constructions, economics' market parable. This dominant description fundamentally disregards how products are produced. It disregards the many tangible and intangible flows necessary for a product to reach the humans who would make end-use of such a product. Furthermore, economics' description overlooks the connection between production and the biosphere, where many vital resources are obtained. Imagine, for example, how the supply and demand constructions fail to capture so many workflows and transformations received by a simple pineapple that reaches a supermarket shelf stripped within a can. Or those many other flows required for other products to reach supermarket shelves. Indeed, although supermarkets are generally treated as service businesses, their business models are deeply reliant upon physical good flows. Many other examples could be presented. See, for instance, how economics ignores many flows required for obtaining and transforming raw materials into a finished jacket sold online over the internet. Generally in economics, the jacket would simply materialize with its mystical supply and demand. This is also the case with the many workflows required to produce a movie and display it in theaters or on digital machines worldwide. Recurrently, economics ignores how money and physical goods flow, from where and to where. It disregards non-monetary social relations established among participants on those flows. It pays little attention to institutional frameworks. It fails to take account of many flows that are not reflected upon monetary flows, which are however vital for economic and societal production.

Karl Polanyi (1944, 2001) has identified that economics conveys a self-regulating market myth: the mystification that through monetary intermediation, markets could solve most if not all necessities of our human condition.[53] Markets are treated as disembedded from the rest of society, an imposture because markets result from societies where they have been created. For instance, transaction of commodities by money require physical infrastructures, humans to work, or transport systems to eventually move workers, clients, raw materials, products and so forth. Monetary operations require governments, regulations and tribunals, physical and digital infrastructures and so on. Furthermore, Polanyi has identified that economics' explanations are based upon three fictitious commodities (thus, pseudo-phenomena, although he did not use this term), namely, work, land (nature) and money. However, human societies would quite conceivably collapse were any of these elements to be let alone to market devices. Therefore, Polanyi describes a double movement whereby when the market view is taken to extremes (the first movement, the market movement), societies need to find manners and mechanisms to contain market excesses to avoid collapsing risks (the second movement in reaction to the first).

For instance, in contemporary monetary societies, waged work is vital for many humans' survival because without the money they receive as wages they could not provide food and amenities for themselves and eventually their families. Treatment of workflows as mere commodities would allow markets to simply discard those humans who cannot work because they are sick or old or their skills have become obsolete. Or simply let die human beings who cannot find work and thus money and thus food (ignore by now other amenities) in countries facing economic crisis. Or wait for those humans to immigrate to richer countries or to organize and revolt, causing societal havoc. As were several economists from the 19th century, when referring to land, Polanyi is considering nature. The purpose of attaining unconstrained monetary profits through nature could lead some humans to obtain profits by simply burning forests down or causing boundless pollution to the air, land, rivers or the sea. Life would become unbearable. Likewise, although money is treated in economics as a natural commodity, it is neither natural nor a commodity. Without disentangling or clearly noticing them, Polanyi is alluding to both a reification and a pseudo-phenomenon. Indeed, this example helps distinguishing between the two. Treatment of money as something natural instead of inherently human is a reification, whereas treatment of money as a commodity is a pseudo-phenomenon. Hardly could money be a simple output of nature because it requires human phenomena such as governments, legislation, coordination, banks and many other societal mechanisms to function. Furthermore, the treatment of money as a mere commodity would lead to monetary expansions and contractions that would be similar to fires and droughts in nature. These contractions and expansions would wreck countless businesses and lives. In contemporary societies, money is rarely allowed to function without any supervision from governments and/or central banks.

However, Polanyi was not able to explain why work, land and money had not become commodities in monetary societies. Consequently, he recurrently treats work, land and money as if they had been transformed into commodities when somehow associated with monetary flows. Thereby, Polanyi falls upon similar pseudo-phenomena as the economists. He was not able to identify the construction that money would define/create the commodity, which implicitly supposes monetary flows entail commodity trading. Money would be some sort of a King Midas turning everything into a commodity, just for flowing somewhere. However, only in rare circumstances does money flow anywhere without association with human-related flows. This pseudo-phenomenon can also be found in Marxism, maybe the major alternative to mainstream economics during the 20th century. Curiously enough, it can also be found in several postmodernist and poststructuralist writers, who accept this mystical property of money without feeling the need to deconstruct it.

The three fictitious commodities (pseudo-phenomena) identified by Polanyi are three key components of labor theories of value, production and existence. Currently, Karl Marx is perhaps the most famous proponent of labor theories. However, Adam Smith, David Ricardo and several writers who were concerned with social relations of production and existence formulated some form of labor theory before Marx (and Engels). Labor theories can be tracked down at least to the great ancient philosopher Aristoteles, who presupposed a separation between the natural (use) purpose and the nonnatural (exchange) purpose of money. The former, connected to use value, was intended for necessities of existence and harmonious life in the human community (*pollis*). The latter, connected to exchange value, would be related to using of money for the aims of exploiting others and enriching oneself. For writers connected to labor theories, the utility of things is generally related to their usefulness.[54] For instance, water is useful to enable life, be drank upon, rain on plants, flow on rivers, enable travelling by ship, do one's hygiene, and so on. For these motives, various motivated astronomers are trying to find water on planets outside the solar system.

Aristoteles saw with disdain what he called nonnatural use of money. For instance, he was against any form of usury. Back then in ancient Greece, usury was simply defined as lending money with interests, contrarily to our contemporary definitions that see it as lending money at high interest rates.[55] A negative view of usury (deemed as a sin) was dominant in Europe during the Middle Ages and in Scholastic Christian philosophy. Several contemporary Islamic finance banks still follow provisions against usury, which is considered as lending money with interests. In the 18th century, Adam Smith, who is frequently considered the founding father of contemporary economics, lived through different times where lending money with interests was more acceptable. However, Smith was still in favor of mandatorily setting a maximum interest rates to prevent abuses of lenders over borrowers. Thus, hardly could Smith be in favor of having a self-regulating market to conduct monetary affairs by itself.

Derived partially from Aristoteles's ideas, Smith has presented an economic system based upon a work-based theory of production, value and existence, which observes human toil necessary to produce things. However, it treats human work as a commodity through which labor value is expressed in money. Smith's system employs key features that we still find in economics, for instance, the capacity of money to measure intangible value of labor (or of its power), treatment of our human contributions as commodities when reflected somehow in monetary flows, or a glorification of money as the purveyor of the human commodity framework. These attributes can also later be found in Marxism. Before Marx's (and Engels's) writings, however, a hedonist theory of value and production had been formed that would take over mainstream economics in the 20th century and the beginning of the 21st century. While Marx's writings generally appear after 1840,[56] some key hedonist writings appeared before Marx was even born. Regrettably, Polanyi did not realize the importance of this hedonist theory for the self-regulating market myth.

This dominant hedonist theory was drawn after Jeremy Bentham's utilitarianism. Bentham was a contemporary to Adam Smith. Curiously, Bentham was also inspired by ancient philosophers, and particularly the hedonist Epicurus.[57] Nonetheless, Bentham's hedonism is much cruder than that of some ancient hedonist philosophers. Bentham developed a form of quantitative hedonism that according to him would explain human action and societies. After Bentham, hedonist economic theory was developed by 19th-century political economists such as James Maitland,[58] Jean-Baptiste Say, Nassau Senior, Thomas Malthus and John Stuart Mill. While maintaining components of Smith's system, these writers tended to share some extent of aversion towards labor theories of production, value and existence, such as the one in Smith's system. Marxism, it is important to notice, did not yet exist. In utilitarianism, the meaning of the word utility is no longer defined by usefulness, as we have seen water could be useful. Utility becomes *hedonist utility*, for it is defined in terms of pleasure and pain, as for instance, a diamond could (allegedly) give pleasure to its owner. As recommended by Bentham, money would become the tool for hedonist calculus, supposedly measuring pleasure and pain units. The self-regulating market myth claims that monetary flows would be able to compute this hedonist calculus. Interferences with hedonist markets, for instance, government regulations, taxes or communitarian production, would obstruct hedonist equilibrium. In effect, the hedonist theory of value and production is paired to a hedonist quantitative theory of money, which serves as a scapegoat when markets fail, causing crises, misery, diseases, wars and deaths. Although governmental and communitarian production can also be seriously inefficient and fail, in mainstream economics they are not protected by a scapegoat monetary theory.

In monetary societies, to be sure, a negative relation between products' prices and quantity traded was known much before hedonist economic theory was formed. Indeed, not all products have a negative relation between prices and quantities. Some status and luxury goods (for example, expensive sport cars or watches) can increase their business with an increase in prices.[59] Moreover, some products can vary little in trading with small variations in price (for instance, basic goods such as water or bread). Generally, however, most products have a negative price–quantity relation, which was well known before (as some merchants got rich on this knowledge). Such a relation is not necessarily automatic. Nonetheless, utilitarians have abusively taken this empirical relation between prices and quantities as a demonstration of their hedonist moral philosophy. What is worse, they have explained an actual empirical phenomenon with pseudo-phenomena of quantitative hedonism based upon money.

For hedonist utilitarianism, human society would not exist beyond cumulative calculus of individual pleasures and pains. Instead of generation and delivery of flows of products by themselves, production would be generation of hedonist utility, either final, as to the final consumer, or intermediate as incorporated into intermediary materials and products. Supply would describe production of hedonist utility, while demand would represent moneyed individuals looking out for final or intermediate consumption of hedonist utility. Allegedly, production would become matched with consumption through mystical hedonist supply and demand that could compute hedonist calculus. As in labor theories, human contributions reflected upon monetary flows are still treated as commodities (or assets, capital or resources). To utilitarianism, however, human contributions become servient to the generation of hedonist utility to the final consumer or incorporated on intermediate products and materials.

Implicitly, mainstream economics asserts that the market parable could solve every need of our human condition and relation to the biosphere. The myth of a self-regulating market as developed by hedonist utilitarianism maintains that if let alone to their own devices (that is, mystical supply and demand), markets would be the social mechanism able to compute hedonist calculus through its tool, namely, money. A particle of labor theories could be invoked by writers such as John Stuart Mill, Alfred Marshal and economists deemed as neoclassical, who described costs including wages as a constraint to supply (producers would not supply if prices were to be lower than costs). However, in hedonist markets the so called free competition would drive prices to costs, and demand to utility, for then costs would match hedonist utility at the margins. With slight variations in mathematical descriptions, hedonist explanations have survived mostly unchallenged until contemporary mainstream economics. This is true even though this hedonist theory promotes the narcissism of the consumer and puts moneyed individuals at the center of the description regarding economic activity.

One can notice that several other research frameworks have been trying to display this description of markets in economics as incomplete: for instance, as we will see in this book, several missing elements have been exposed such as the relevance of private property, institutional frameworks, geographical and spatial aspects, behavioral aspects, social relations among participants and cultural and symbolic interactions. However, the major drive has been to add further components, while by and large there tends to be acceptability towards the underlying hedonist description. Or at best, there is sparse contestation that money could be a metaphysical measure capable of computing hedonist calculus at the mystical market or that money could be used to measure the intangible. Yet, hedonism tends to ignore the passage of time, human age and life cycles, social relations and our obligations towards others. It tends to neglect human contributions to economic and societal production not reflected in monetary flows (thus hedonist calculus). Its supply and demand constructions are focused on the magical moment of the monetary flow. Such a murky description disconnects us from the biosphere in which we humans are integrated.

Undeniably, money is an important social technology through which we organize our contemporary societies. Indeed, money has become the basis for many instances of production, allocation of products, and incontestably many of our social relations.[60] The term monetary society is preferable to that of capitalism. The latter rests on a concept of capital with dubious meaning. Before Smith, capital meant indeed money invested or investable in business. After Smith, in economics and many other social sciences, capital became what creates wealth,[61] a lose term, and tautological explanation: capital creates wealth because it is what creates wealth. Anything with an incidental relation to generation of monetary flows could thus become capital: under this framework, capital would soon include also us the humans,[62] which is an application of the human commodity framework. Curiously, these definitions are promoted in other social sciences. We can also find several social constructivists, postmodernist or poststructuralist, happily adopting these conceptions regarding capital or capitalism.[63] For exactitude, in intangible flow theory we use the term monetary society to implement a return to the anterior meaning of the word capital (money invested or investable in organizational activity). Furthermore, we will study monetary flows without the pseudo-phenomena we find in economics and other social sciences, such as that (i) money creates/defines commodities, (ii) money can measure the intangible, and (iii) hedonist calculus could be conducted through money.

We humans as a species are quite inventive in creating new methods of economic and societal production. Take, for example, technologies developed in what is frequently called Industry 4.0 (to imply a fourth industrial revolution we are living through since the 18th century).[64] Formidable technologies they are indeed, such as artificial intelligence (including machine learning), advanced robotics, 3-D printing, cloud computing, satellite-driven geolocation, smart sensors, the internet of things, big data processing, quantum computing and biotechnologies (once again, these technologies may feel obsolete in a few years). We are evolving to a hyperconnected existence, mixing humans and technology via our portable internet-connected machines. Yet, economic and societal production are still fundamentally dependent upon the biosphere, which we are quite far from completely controlling, let alone understanding.

Monetary technologies have allowed humans to solve difficult coordination problems, for example, those of what are called global value chains across the planet. Through monetary integration it is possible for instance to manufacture hi-tech machines in Vietnam and Bangladesh with raw materials obtained from Southern Europe and design from Japan. Later, with coordination of storage, security and transport systems along the way, those machines can be sold in China or the US. However, glorification of the micro moment of the monetary flow and treatment of human beings as commodities may become unhelpful to understand these intricate production and delivery processes.[65]

Instead, there are many phenomena we can study regarding monetary technologies and their connections to production and existence. Those phenomena include, for instance, structures that enable the existence of monetary societies, or the behavior of humans regarding money-related decisions. Monetary technologies have depended upon states/governments, banks and other financial institutions, laws and regulations, armed forces, sanction systems, legitimacy and acceptance, cultural and symbolic elements, and so forth. Nonetheless, one can ask whether by explaining money, economists can also be creating social facts about money. That predicament could be connected to the concept of performativity, which has been frequently employed in relativist poststructuralism or postmodernism. This concept implies that while using language to describe reality, scientists (or other observers) also create facts about that reality with effects on action and change (that is, scientists and other observers perform reality).[66] Indeed, studies have shown that economic theory has been relevant in designing the trading infrastructure for option derivatives and other risk-related financial assets.[67] These are, however, minor components in the entire economic and societal production required for the existence of financial markets. It would be attributing miraculous powers to economists (or scientists and observers in general) to be able to create the entire reality regarding monetary phenomena.[68] This relativist view of things would make the use of human languages (discourses) made by scientists (and observers in general) more capable of interfering in human societies and interconnected biospheres than they actually are.[69] Once again, this further relativist formulation implicitly supports dominant theories, which obviously applies to mainstream economics.[70] The biosphere precedes us humans and our languages. For realists, the ability of scientists in constructing facts about reality must be bounded by the existence of a reality outside our social and bio-mental constructions.

Indisputably, in monetary societies the treatment of money as a mystical commodity (or its relativization) benefits those humans who hold and/or control the direction of large monetary flows. Ironically, they can thus use monetary flows to promote economic theories that support and legitimize their own societal position. Indeed, just because someone holds and/or controls the direction of large monetary flows, he/she does not become automatically integrated into a homogeneous class of individuals.[71] Similarly, lack of monetary funds does not incorporate someone automatically into another homogenous human category.[72] Every human being is a unique and distinguishable individual. Societal positions and monetary flows are dynamic and may change. Indeed, some moneyed humans can actually be concerned with improving the human condition. For instance, when in his will Alfred Nobel created the Nobel prizes, he declared that those prizes should be attributed to those who "*have conferred the greatest benefit to mankind.*"[73] He predicted five prizes, namely, chemistry, literature, peace, physics and physiology or medicine. Nobel died in 1896, and the first prizes were attributed in 1901.

Yet, other individuals who have controlled the direction of large monetary flows have used monetary flows to further support their societal position as money bearers. In 1968 the Bank of Sweden decided to generate monetary flows to support a *"prize in economic sciences in memory of Alfred Nobel."* Since first attributed only in 1969, the popular press commonly treats it as just another Nobel prize category. Year by year, however, this prize has been used to promote mainstream theory treating money as a mystical commodity and us humans as commodities and enhancing the societal position of moneyed persons. Similarly, substantial monetary flows have been directed by moneyed individuals to schools, departments, grants, research centers, think tanks, economic journals, television channels, or websites defending mainstream economics.[74] Likewise, in monetary societies, moneyed persons can make monetary contributions to political parties and politicians who defend their interests[75] or use money to qualify and support their children's studies in expensive universities, after which they later can obtain high-level money-generating social positions.[76] Procedures such as these can undermine rival explanations to mainstream theories. Economics' glorification of money as a divine entity (pseudo-god) is also promoted by substantial (tangible) monetary flows. Thereby, theories that do not support persons who hold large amounts of money can be similarly downgraded for lack of resources in comparison to economic theories (or ideologies) that by mystifying money endorse those who control large monetary resources. Nonetheless, this application of money to promote theories that defend the societal position of those who have money generate structures, organizations, information flows, signs, symbols, service flows and other flows, which might cause tangible consequences upon human populations and our bio-habitats.

There could hardly be a doubt that money, as a social technology, has helped us humans to solve some very difficult problems for our survival and existence. Yet, monetary technologies can be improved and enhanced. In ancient Greece, coins substitute nonstandard and heavy forms of money. Later in Medieval Europe and previously in China, checks and paper notes replaced the need, burden and insecurity of travelers having to carry heavy loads of coins over long, isolated routes. Paper money had been linked to reserves of precious metals, and such connections were later abandoned during several periods, including our own.[77] Digital money and credit cards do without the need of coins, paper money, heavy wallets or safes full of cash. Digital machines and body recognition systems can currently serve as means of payment. New institutional frameworks have been set to organize, support and eventually profit from modification in monetary technologies. Generally, money has functioned with reference to an authority as a state, sovereign or government, which supervises and controls it but also collects taxes through monetary means.[78] Powerful means of controlling what citizens or organizations do with digital money have been given to those in charge of powerful digital money modalities.

Nonetheless, we must not take our current monetary technologies as a given or historical determination. Historical examples demonstrate that monetary technologies can be reformulated and eventually improved. Likewise, we need to be open to the possibility of finding better social technologies than money to address many difficulties of our survival and existence. Although alternative social technologies might only be created in a faraway future, contemporary monetary technologies are not necessarily eternal.

Still, economics' hedonist market allegory rejects solutions that are not implicit in its own framework, where money is an instrument of hedonist calculus and we humans are treated as commodities (or capital, assets or resources). A proper example can be found in the human-caused emissions regarding carbon dioxide (CO_2) and toxic particles to the atmosphere. Besides potential problems associated with the climate and global warming, excessive emissions impact the quality of the air and thus health and life-spans of humans and other living beings.[79] Many a mainstream economist can perhaps agree that excessive emissions of CO_2 and toxic particles are pollution. An externality of the production process is a term frequently used by mainstream economists to describe pollution. According to their theory, however, hedonist calculus in money would provide the solution for such pressing human problems. When addressing the issue,[80] economists generally have two monetary solution sets to offer, namely, to either tax polluting organizations or increase their pollution costs with some sort of tradable pollution permits (these permits would be equivalent to market prices of polluting).[81] The second solution is (hedonist) market-based. Nonetheless, although the first solution involves governments' taxes, it is still a hedonist solution claiming to solve pollution through some extension of monetary pain. Still, pollution and biosphere destruction continue as many polluters pay taxes and permits, others disrespect the law, and others yet move production to more lenient countries. Furthermore, a substantial part of the costs is transferred to customers via product prices. Moreover, many governments might to a large degree financially benefit from pollution and biosphere destruction through taxes, permit sales and related economic production. Deluded cost-benefit analyses, merely based upon money (hedonist calculus), are also likely to fail because, currently, tangible monetary flows are at the root of pollution and biosphere destruction.

Yet, non-monetary factors have little role in mainstream economic debates. Apparently, hedonist calculus would be capable of addressing every human challenge. However, to significantly reduce toxic emissions to the biosphere we may need to develop innovative non-monetary technologies, reorganize our economic and societal production, and terminate highly profitable organizational activities, which provide extraordinary tax revenues to governments around the world. Rarely are these themes addressed by mainstream economists. Thus, the hedonist economic framework can indeed peril humankind by theoretically disconnecting us from the biosphere. Mainstream economics and its set of pseudo-phenomena pose an obstacle to the characterization (and improvement) of our fragile human condition.

1.3 Relativism's gaslighting of our human condition

Different forms of relativism (or anti-realism) have been discussed since the ancient world.[82] This work engages with relativism in the sense of it being an obstacle to characterize (and eventually improve) the human condition in the social sciences. As noted, relativism implicitly supports the human commodity framework in economics because besides not working to produce feasible alternatives, it proactively sabotages attempts to build them.

Nevertheless, if relativists were bounded by reason and logic, they would be easily overcome, that is, were they to apply their relativism to their own discourse.[83] There are two simple problems relativists cannot solve, nor can metaphysical, epistemological or semantic relativism solve either of these two problems. The first problem has to do with the claim that all things (for instance, objects, properties and relations) are relative, namely, the thesis of global relativism. However, if all things are relative, it therefore follows that relativism is also relative; thus, some things are not relative. Hence, relativism is not credible or coherent. Global relativism is illogical, unreasonable and self-refuting when applied to itself.[84]

The second problem connects to the local relativism thesis (also referred to as subjectivism): the claim from relativists that truth could only be established in relation to a local system of validity formed by a specific group of human beings. That is, the standard of truth would be subjective because it could only be local and standard specific or internal to the discourse within which that standard is itself proposed, defined or elaborated by a group of human beings.[85] Different names have been attributed to formulations that can be connected to the idea of local systems of validity, such as paradigm,[86] episteme,[87] research program,[88] final vocabulary[89] and regime of the production of truth.[90] Accordingly, as truth would be relative to local systems (and thus subjective), it would be merely a manifestation of the power of the individuals who control knowledge—power relations.[91] Truth would be contingent to the interests that prevail among the social defined "expert" community.[92]

This hyperbolic relativist position has led famous relativists to defend that Galileo's assertions regarding the Earth and the Sun were as compelling as those of Cardinal Bellarmine who in 1616 headed the charges against him at the Inquisition trial.[93] The deduction would be that Galileo and Bellarmino's arguments could only be established in relation to their own local systems of validity. However, why was Galileo's life then in danger at that trial? Why should the Inquisition and Galileo care about their opponents' account of the truth? It is rather illogic that relativists are generally against accepting independent concepts and definitions because they allege that human methods and languages could not provide those, but then several relativists can claim to precisely identify what would be a local system of validity as if addressing non-relativist descriptions. It would be highly questionable that local systems of validity could be identified without relation to any external reality and in absolute disconnection to previous explanatory systems. For instance, it is not a different sun, but the same tangible sun that has enlightened Galileo, Cardinal Bellarmino and also Copernicus, Giordano Bruno, Newton, Einstein, Friedrich Miescher and all of us who have lived upon this Earth. Different explanations refer and address the same sun. Although disruptive breaks with past explanations certainly exist, it is difficult to identify complete ruptures among explanatory systems, methods and language molds.[94]

Still, local relativism (subjectivism) can function as a rhetoric defense for dominant theories because it implicitly suggests that new theories cannot demonstrate that previous theories would be wrong. Allegedly, new theories would operate according to different systems of local validity. Furthermore, this relativist formulation offers manners to openly smear scientists who work on new theoretical explanations. Accordingly, scientific innovators would only be self-serving to selfish interests as those of obtaining prestige, publishing, advancing their careers, obtaining research grants, and gaining other forms of monetary income and so forth.[95] Therefore, relativism once again allies to the dominant theoretical explanations such as the human commodity framework in economics. Yet, the association to economics runs deeper. Local relativism seems to have implicit the idea that scientific theories would operate according to some sort of hedonist market, where scientists would be driven merely by hedonist goals of obtaining more status and money. Money, once again, would be a measurement tool for success regarding scientific theories (and thus of the intangible and hedonist calculus).[96] These theses can be connected to the hedonist self-regulating market parable. Appropriately, Norris has described this thesis as *laissez-faire* relativism.[97]

However, the local relativism thesis also faces a yet unsolvable problem: if truth could only be established in relation to a local system of validity (say a paradigm, episteme, research program, final vocabulary or regime of truth), then relativism could only be considered adequate in relation to such a local system of validity. Therefore, different local systems of validity could expose relativism as a fake or charlatan philosophy. Hence, the local relativism thesis is also illogical and unreasonable when applied to itself.[98] Still, seldom can we testify that relativists accepting that these two systematic problems might have defeated their relativism.[99] Not only are many relativists not constrained by reason and logic, but in many instances they try to sabotage them as a rhetorical strategy.[100] Indeed, few persons may accept to be a relativist, for the position can be self-defeating. However, statements regarding oneself cannot be the only standard to demonstrate relativism. We can for instance inquire writings, ideas or deeds. Otherwise, we would be tantamount to a position of accepting that someone would be declared innocent in court on the grounds that he/she has declared to be innocent, despite contradictory evidence. Relativism is not and should not be a crime. We are merely elucidating the burden of the proof required to identify relativism.

As explained earlier, intangible flow theory supports systematic analysis of texts, discourses, scientific methods or societal and bio-mental contexts of scientific practices. They can be used to destroy former ideas, theories and hypotheses and build new ones, as Joseph Schumpeter advocates that in monetary societies new business ventures innovate, address new needs and destroy traditional business models of incumbent firms. Thus, new business ventures can create more efficient and effective social and technological production and delivery processes.[101] In the present, although one may construct and reconstruct tangible flows or eliminate means regarding their verification, he/she cannot deconstruct and destroy tangible flows that have already occurred in a specific time and place.[102] He/she can, however, deconstruct and destroy present or future flows or methods and language vehicles to capture tangible flows. Thus, the very ancient ideas of creative destruction and destructive creation provide examples where deconstruction and destruction can be used as the basis for highly productive realist purposes. Undeniably, realists need to be open to the new, the different, and the event that had never been observed before, the occurrence that challenges all former explanations, the unpredictability of the future, the many things we do not know how to explain, or the contingency of human, social and biophysical phenomena. However, none of these factors eliminate the possibility of the existence of a reality beyond our social and bio-mental constructions.

Conceivably, a major hindrance with relativism is the attempt to eliminate links to a possible reality beyond our social and bio-mental constructions. Generally, evidence is provided on the grounds that relativists say so. However, without the possibility of connection to an external reality, no responsibility for knowledge creation (or destruction) can be imputed. Hence, relativist endeavors can indeed be used to attempt the destruction of science (and discourse) based on reason and logic, which is very dangerous. It can openly support the advancement of the most diverse forms of unreason, narcissism and tyranny in human societies.[103]

Perhaps there is no point in trying to persuade relativists to abandon their relativism. Without standards of reason and logic, or reference to an independent truth, relativists may freely misconstrue opponents' points of view to support their own and/or assume an attitude in which they always win every argument.[104] For instance, when arguments are found that undeniably contradict relativists, they may say they have won for this would demonstrate that everything is relative.[105] Or they may claim their interpretation has aesthetical privileges. Throughout this book, we will have the opportunity to provide further examples. However, to the extent that it is possible, we will try henceforth to follow the advice of not trying to persuade relativists to abandon their relativism. Curiously, some psychologists give similar advice to someone who in his/her life must deal with a narcissist who cannot feel empathy, shame or regret: the no-contact rule to the extent that it is possible.[106] Peculiarly, it has been established that there is a large amount of narcissism in social constructivism, postmodernism and poststructuralism where the interpreter of the world would be somehow the center of the universe.[107] It has certainly not been demonstrated that no relativist can ever feel empathy, shame or regret.

Still, unless relativists can come up with any new demonstration that reality does not exist beyond our social and bio-mental constructions, we need not engage in a perpetual repetition of the demonstration that global and local relativism have been defeated by reason and logic. Moreover, reason and logic can seldom argue with unreason and illogic. The latter generally do not want to hear. We must, however, attempt to diminish the damage caused to the social sciences by several relativists. We need to deconstruct their claims that truth would not exist, and it would be merely an instrument of power. We need to deconstruct their implicit support for irrationality. We need to deconstruct their underlying support for the maintenance of dominant theories and status quos. We need to tackle their systematic gaslighting towards legitimate attempts to identify, describe and understand reality. Gaslighting has been defined as a conscious or unconscious form of psychological abuse that occurs when a perpetrator distorts information and confuses an individual or a group, triggering the victims to doubt their memory and sanity.[108] It involves, for instance, verbal (rhetorical) attacks, persistent denial (of, for instance, flagrant evidence), misdirection, misleading ingratiation, contradiction between actions and words, isolating targets, or blatant lying to destabilize victims and delegitimize their needs, assurances, feelings and beliefs.[109] In the UK, gaslighting has already been typified as a crime in the context of intimate relationships under coercive control legislation, which displays how serious it can be.[110]

What is more, to address the human condition in the social sciences, no authorization from relativism is required. Relativism has been defeated by reason and logic, has no commitment to an independent truth, and does not systematically work to produce new theories. Furthermore, relativists hardly concede defeat no matter how preposterous their claims could be. Thus, intangible flow theory does not offer new arguments to deal with relativism; as explained, this effort could be pointless. However, the new theory offers methodologies, concepts and frameworks to protect realists against the regular gaslighting conducted by many a relativist. Hence, the new theory provides support to produce social sciences working with reference to a reality beyond our social and bio-mental constructions and, thus, social sciences that can address (and eventually improve) our frail human condition.

1.4 Organization of the first volume of *Intangible Flow Theory*

Including this introduction, the book contains three parts. The second and third parts further present the intangible flow theory and several of its concepts, formulations and frameworks. This new theory should not be understood as the path's end, but the demonstration of the feasibility regarding the creation of new scientific theories at the social sciences. This theory aims towards the replacement of the human commodity framework in economics and the removal of excessive barriers that relativism is fashioning against new contributions based upon reason and logic, which could address the human condition.

The third part makes a realist deconstruction of the origins of human commodity framework in mainstream economics and Marxism, which is partially based upon in the new theory presented in this Introduction, but not entirely dependent upon it.

Notes

1 See, for instance, Norberg (2016) or Pinker (2019).
2 Geosphere refers to the solid parts of our planet, for instance, Earth's soil and undersoil.
3 Thérèsea and Martin (2010).
4 For instance, "its exploitative, its purely instrumental, or technocratic forms" (Norris, 1997, p. 1).
5 Though, some perspective generally defined as heterodox economics carry similar concepts and terminologies.
6 The term post-postmodernism was obtained in McHale (2015).
7 Jameson (1993) and Harvey (1990, 2007) connect postmodernism/poststructuralism to cultural support for late forms of capitalism. However, they do not yet describe relativism as allied to mainstream economics in sabotaging scientific descriptions (or eventual improvement) of our human condition.
8 This adapted typology has been used by Kukla to characterize constructivism. Albeit strong affinity, constructivism is not always synonymous to relativism. However, a similar classification suits us well.
9 Khlentzos (2016).
10 In using the word mental, is in the sense that constructions somehow reach the human mind. We are not suggesting that the human mind reaches intellectual formulations in isolation, as the mind is fully integrated in the human body and interacts with the surrounding environment.
11 Khlentzos (2016), Kukla (2000). Likewise, metaphysical realism must not be confused with empirical realism. While the former suggests that what is real need not be experienced by us humans to come into being, the latter can only suggest that what is real is what has been scientifically demonstrated (Bhaskar, 1975, 1997, 1998; Lawson, 1994, 2019).
12 Semantic relativism is frequently adept in language games.
13 To use the expression in Lyotard (1984, p. xxiv).
14 This new theory had its initial formulation in three previous papers, namely Cardao-Pito (2012, 2016, 2017). Chapter 2 was partially derived from Cardao-Pito (2012), Chapter 4 was partially derived from Cardao-Pito (2016) and Chapter 5 was partially derived from Cardao-Pito (2017). I appreciate and acknowledge authorization to use these materials in those chapters. Some arguments were revised, and others were added. Furthermore, new empirical tests were conducted in Chapter 5.
15 Or metaphysical realism (Bhaskar, 1975, 1997, 1998; Lawson, 1994, 2019; Sayer, 2000; Kukla, 2000).
16 Bhaskar (1975, 1997, 1998), Boghossian (2015), Kukla (2000), Lawson (1994, 2019), Norris (1997), Sayer (2000).
17 Idem.
18 Merleau-Ponty (1945, 2014), Schutz (1967), Berger and Luckman (1966), Brown (1992).
19 Idem.
20 Schutz (1967), Berger and Luckman (1966), Durkheim (1895, 1966).
21 Bhaskar (1975, 1997, 1998), Boghossian (2015), Kukla (2000), Lawson (1994, 2019), Sayer (2000).
22 Deconstruction is a form of analysis with great relevance for constructivism, postmodernism and poststructuralism (Boghossian, 2015; Burr, 2015; Butler, 2002; Ellis, 1989; Kukla, 2000; Sayer, 2000).

23 The term was popularized by Derrida (1974, 1997), and his approach is followed by many constructivists, postmodernists and poststructuralists.

24 Boghossian (2015), Butler (2002), Ellis (1989), Knorr-Cetina (1981), Kukla (2000), Latour and Woolgar (1979), Norris (1997), Sayer (2000). The activity of deconstruction appears sometimes with other names such as critical discourse analysis, of Foucauldian discourse analysis in reference to Michel Foucault (Burr, 2015, pp. 20–21). However, the term discourse may seem quite illusive and ambiguous, for it appears to be associated to semantic concerns and is yet related also to institutions and social arrangements where semantic forms appear. As defined by Foucault (1972, p. 49): discourse would be *"practices which form the objects of which they speak."* Practices can, nonetheless, mean an infinity of things. Given the ambiguity and semantic relativism in Foucault's sense of discourse, the term deconstruction appears preferable. Unambiguously, deconstruction applies not only to texts/discourses but also to scientific methods.

25 Which is rather convenient for experts in literary analysis who do not wish to understand the scientific claim being discussed.

26 Nietzsche advocates a philosophy of destruction (with a hammer in the title) towards metaphysical concepts (see, for instance, Nietzsche, 1888, 1990; Kellner, 1991; Siemens, 1998).

27 *Destruktion* is the terms used by Heidegger. He, however, claims that his destruction activity was positive: "its negative function remains unexpressed and indirect" (Heidegger, 1927, 1962, p. 44).

28 After his death, many of Nietzche's ideas would be adopted by members of the Nazi party, such as the myth of the superhuman (Ubermensch) (see, for instance, Brinton, 1940; Santaniello, 2012). Heidegger was a supporter of Hitler and member of the Nazi party. After the end of the Second World War, he claimed that his support for the Nazi party had been merely instrumental (Sheehan, 2010, pp. 44–45; see also Sluga, 1993).

29 Derrida (1970, 1993, pp. 223–225) recognizes Heidegger, Freud and Nietzsche as precursors of his conception of deconstruction: "I would probably cite the Nietzschean critique of metaphysics, the critique of the concepts of being and truth, for which were substituted the concepts of play, interpretation, and sign (sign without truth present); the Freudian critique or self-presence, that is, the critique of consciousness, subject, of self-identity and of self-proximity or self-possession; and, more radically, the Heideggerean destruction of metaphysics, of onto-theology, of the determination of being as presence." However, Derrida criticized them for still using metaphysics to destroy metaphysics: "But all these destructive discourses and all their analogues are trapped in a sort of circle. This circle is unique. It describes the form of the relationship between the history of metaphysics and the destruction of the history of metaphysics." Hence, Derrida suggests eliminating the need towards any connection to metaphysics or of the signifier over the significant, which is an even more relativist position.

30 Boghossian (2015), Butler(2002), Ellis (1989), Kukla (2000), Putman (1981, 1996), Sayer (2000), Stove (2017).

31 Let us listen to Derrida (1983, 1988, pp. 4–5) himself describing the concept of deconstruction: "To be very schematic I would say that the difficulty of defining and therefore also of translating the word 'deconstruction' stems from the fact that all the predicates, all the defining concepts, all the lexical significations, and even the syntactic articulations, which seem at one moment to lend themselves to this definition or to that translation, are also deconstructed or deconstructible, directly or otherwise, etc. And that goes for the word deconstruction, as for every word. . . . What deconstruction is not? everything of course! What is deconstruction? nothing of course! I do not think, for all these reasons, that it is a good word [un bon mot]."

32 Ellis (1989).

33 The problem of infinite regress of constructions has been presented by Niiniluoto (1991) and Collin (1993). Although Kukla (2000) argues that infinite regress would not be an inner challenge for the constructive stance, it is an actual problem when a solution is required to address a pressing human problem.

34 Boghossian (2015), Habermas (1985, 2007), Kukla (2000), Norris (1997), Stove (2017).
35 In here, a reference is made to the dark triad of personality. These three categories overlap in some aspects but are distinct categories (see Paulhus and Williams, 2002; Furnham, Richards, and Paulhus, 2013).
36 Boghossian (2015), Habermas (1985, 2007), Kukla (2000), Norris (1997), Putman (1981, 1996).
37 Khlentzos (2016).
38 Lawson (1994, 2019).
39 See, for instance, Foucault (1984), Goodman (1975), Quine (1992).
40 See, for instance, Goodman (1978) or Latour and Woolgar (1979).
41 Kant (1781, 1999).
42 Idem.
43 Marx and Engels (1846, 1970), Marx (1990).
44 Assuming that time and space do not depend on us humans to exist, even if we may have different human perceptions about them. Relativists, however, may assume that time and space are social constructions, which nonetheless render them incoherent positions (Kukla, 2000; Evans, 2018; Butler, 2002). For instance, Ankersmith (1994, pp. 33–34) declared that historical time was "recent and highly artificial invention of western civilization" (later at the service of capital). However other civilizations as the Chinese, Persian, Ancient Mesopotamian, Muslim, or Mayan civilizations have developed sophisticated methods to account for the passage of time (Evans, 2018, p. 142). Another form of being incoherent with the time is to claim that when researchers discover something not known before, as for instance a process related to a human hormone or organ or new records describing events from the Roman Empire or French Revolution, relativists claim that those researcher have created those discoveries at that moment as if they did not exist before (Kukla, 2000; Evans, 2018; Butler, 2002). However, the very expressions postmodern and poststructuralist make reference to previous periods (Evans, 2018, p. 142). One could hardly be aware of any relativist who had given up on travelling or the clock, or could escape his/her circadian rhythm. As put by Evans (2018, pp. 156–157): "In the end, therefore, time does pass, a fact we experience only too painfully in the process of human ageing to which we are all subject ourselves, and we cannot simply declare it, as Ankersmith does, that there is no difference between the fourteenth century and the twentieth, or that time is merely a collection of unrelated presents, or that the textuality of the world abolishes the principle of cause and effect. To argue that we can only know causes from their effects, and that therefore the effect is the origin of the cause, as some postmodernists have done, is to mistake the process of enquiry for its object."
45 Thus, we can avoid Hegel's (1807, 1977) and Marx's dialectic methods that are intransigently opposed by several relativist postmodernists and poststructuralist as Deleuze, Derrida, Foucault and Lyotard, even though they have strong links to Marx's work, and in some cases claim to reinvent their own Marx (see for instance Choat, 2010). Undeniably, Marx makes use of dialectic methods: "we have thesis, antithesis and synthesis. For those who do not know the Hegelian language, we shall give the ritual formula: affirmation, negation and negation of the negation" (Marx, 1847, online).
46 For instance, Derrida (1990, 2002) alleges, perhaps abusively that justice cannot be deconstructed because it has not yet been constructed, which clearly opens the door for relativist views of justice.
47 Von Frisch (1974) claims to have discovered that to inform other bees about the location of food sources, bees returning to their hive perform movements in the air (which he calls dances) with reference to the Sun.
48 For instance, Facebook's artificial intelligent computers were shut down after they started talking in a language they created themselves and humans did not fully understand (Griffin, 2017). After some extent of human guidance, a computer self-trained at the game of Go to beat the human champion (Koch, 2016).

49 Bostrom (2016), Ford (2015), Russel (2019), Wiener (1950, 1989).
50 Bostrom (2016), Russel (2019), Wiener (1950, 1989).
51 Boghossian (2015), Kukla (2000), Searl (1997).
52 A few firms in China are already accepting digital face recognition as means of payment.
53 This idea from Polanyi (1944, 2001) has been adapted to the problem of the human condition discussed here.
54 Hence, their use value.
55 Dupont (2017).
56 Marx obtained his PhD in 1841.
57 Bentham (1789)
58 Earl of Lauderdale, often referred to as Lauderdale, but referred in here as Maitland.
59 Veblen (1899), Bagwell and Bernheim (1996), Trigg (2001).
60 Simmel (1907, 2004), Bandelj, Wherry, and Zelizer (2017), Ingham (1996).
61 Cannan (1921), Hodgson (2014).
62 Smith's definition of capital included circulating capital with a provision for the elements required for workers' survival. As we will see in this book, later, many economists would simply refer to workers as human capital, human resources or human assets.
63 For instance, Bourdieu (1985), Deleuze and Guattari (1977), Lyotard (1984, 1997).
64 For instance, Lasi et al. (2014) or Popkova, Ragulina, and Bogoviz (2019).
65 Furthermore, throughout human history, money has had different forms such as that of food, coins, paper money, bank accounts, digital money, or even cryptocurrencies. These forms are not irrelevant and cannot be captured by mainstream economics, which generally treats money as a homogenous commodity.
66 Austin (1970), Butler (2010), Derrida (1988), Lyotard (1984, 1997).
67 Callon (2007), MacKenzie and Millo (2003), Millo and MacKenzie (2009).
68 Jackson (2019, p. 92), Miller (2002), Santos and Rodrigues (2009). Evans (2018, pp. 206–207) makes a similar argument against the claim from postmodernists that historians could only by themselves create the past and public perception about it. Spencer (2020) makes this point in relation to performativity in economics.
69 Idem.
70 Idem.
71 As the owners of the means of production, or bourgeoisie in Marxism. Furthermore, as we will see later, the idea of ownership of means of production precede Marx's. Similarly, the proletariat was a concept present in ancient Rome, which was restored by Sismondi (before Marx) to describe poor wage-workers who had little else than their family proles.
72 Typification of humans into homogenous classes in relation to their wealth, ownership of assets, income or dependence on wages to survive are pitfalls in labor theories of production, value and existence. A basic inspection of such groups could find the most diverse individuals. Every human being is a distinguishable and unique individual.
73 Economist (2019, p. 73).
74 Appelbaum (2019, p. 14): "The economists provided the ideas and the corporations provided the money: underwriting research, endowing universities chairs, and funding think [tanks] like the National Bureau of Economic Research, the American Enterprise Institute, and the Hoover Institution at Stanford University." It would be more correct to say that specific and identifiable executives at specific and identifiable corporations have provided the money, as certainly not all corporations and managers were involved in this funding.
75 Brown, Drake, and Wellman (2014), Boushey (2019), Saez and Zucman (2019), Ovtchinnikov and Pantaleoni (2012).
76 Markovits (2019), Reay (2017), Walpole (2003).
77 When the US declared they could no longer endorse the Bretton Wood System created after World War II, which had put the US dollar at the center of that system.
78 See, for instance, Ingham (2013), Lawson (2016), Peacock (2017), Skidelsky (2018).

79 See, for instance, Kinney (2008) or Dimanchev et al. (2019).
80 Perhaps less frequently than such a pressing matter requires.
81 Andrew, Kaidonis, and Andrew (2010), Denicolo (1999), Goulder (2013), Nordhaus (2007), Norregaard and Reppelin-Hill (2000), Requate (1993).
82 See, for instance, Baghramian (2004), Swoyer (2015).
83 Boghossian (2015), Evans (2018), Habermas (1985, 2007), Kukla (2000), Norris (1997), Stove (2017).
84 Boghossian (2015), Habermas (1985, 2007), Kukla (2000), Norris (1997). In the ancient world, the problem of relativism being self-refuting was demonstrated by Plato. In Theaetetus (Plato, 2013), the figure of Socrates raises this problem to Protagoras's and sophists' relativism (see also, for instance, Chappell, 2019; Baghramian, 2004; Burnyeat, 1976a; Zilioli, 2016).Moreover, in ancient philosophy, the self-refutation problem was also demonstrated by Democritus, Aristoteles and several Stoic philosophers (Burnyeat, 1976b; Lee, 2005). As relativists have not been able to solve this problem, their strategy tends to be attempting to minimize the problem, declaring the invalidity of evidence or questioning the acceptance of reason and logic.
85 Adapted from Norris (1997, p. 12).
86 Kuhn (1970).
87 Derrida (1970, 1993), Foucault (1966, 2005).
88 Lakatos (1968).
89 Rorty (1989).
90 Foucault (1980).
91 Yet both power and knowledge are generally very diffusely defined in relativism, operating also as some sort of mystical entities.
92 Adapted from Norris (1997, p. 58).
93 For instance, Feyerabend (1971) or Rorty (1979, p. 328). Feyerabend (1975, 1993, p. 127) "The trial of Galileo was one of many trials. It had no special features except perhaps that Galileo was treated rather mildly, despite his lies and attempts at deception." Moreover, Kuhn (1970) claims extensively that Galileo's case provides him with evidence for his local relativism thesis of paradigm change. See also Boghossian (2015) and Machamer (1973).
94 Boghossian (2015), Norris (1997).
95 Boghossian (2015), Habermas (1985, 2007), Kukla (2000), Norris (1997). The local validity relativism fails to recognize that the quest for truth carries its own ethical imperative (Norris, 1997, p. 1).
96 Several relativists go so far as claiming that scientists would be looking out for some sort of (tautological) capital as in economics. Latour and Woolgar (1986, pp. 197–198) compare "scientists' credibility to a cycle of capital investment." Bourdieu (1975, 1988) claims that the "*homo academicus*" operates in the context of "*scientific capital*."
97 Norris (1997, p. 3). The expression *laissez-faire* is commonly used to describe those positions that defend markets operating without any type of external intervention.
98 Boghossian (2015), Habermas (1985, 2007), Kukla (2000), Norris (1997).
99 Kukla (2000, p. 127) admits we was himself a relativist who abandoned his previous ways after investigating matters further.
100 Boghossian (2015), Habermas (1985, 2007), Kukla (2000), Norris (1997), Stove (2017).
101 Harvey (1990, p. 17) and Reinert and Reinert (2006) claim that when Schumpeter (1942) introduced the concept of creative destruction in economics he had benefited from the use of the formulation previously presented by Nietzsche. Reinert and Reinert (2006) further add that the German economist Werner Sombart preceded Schumpeter in using the concept, while openly acknowledging the influence from Nietzsche. Furthermore, the roots of creative destruction come from a very old idea, which appear, for instance, in ancient Egyptian and Greek myths of the phoenix reborn from the ashes or at foundational Hinduism where Shiva the God of Destruction would also enable Creation. From Indian philosophy, the idea entered the German literary and

philosophy tradition. Thus, the idea of creative destruction also precedes Nietzsche's conception of philosophical destruction by thousands of years (see Reinert and Reinert for more details).

102 The removal of information or intangibilization of a flow is not the destruction of a flow that has already occurred in a specific time and place.

103 Boghossian (2015), Habermas (1985, 2007), Kukla (2000), Norris (1997).

104 Boghossian (2015), Habermas (1985, 2007), Kukla (2000), Norris (1997).

105 "There's no way that an adherent to this logic can ever be bought to admit defeat" (Kukla, 2000, p. 123).

106 Regarding the advice of no contact with narcissists see, for instance, Sarkis (2016), Malkin (2015) or O'Reilly, Doerr, and Chatman (2018). Sometimes the no contact approach is not possible, as for instance when a divorced person still needs contact with his/her narcissist former spouse because of their children.

107 To replace the Earth before Copernicus and Galileo. See, for instance, Evans (2018), Hutcheon (2013), Levin (2008) or Norris (1997) on narcissism in social constructivism, poststructuralism and postmodernism.

108 See, for instance, Dorpat (1994), Kivak (2017), Moore (2019), Sarkis (2018), Sweet (2019), Tormoen (2019).

109 Idem.

110 Moore (2019). See also Sweet (2019).

References

Andrew, J., Kaidonis, M. and Andrew, B. (2010). Carbon tax: Challenging neoliberal solutions to climate change. *Critical Perspectives on Accounting*, 21(7), 611–618.

Ankersmith, F. (1994). *History and Tropology. The Rise and Fall of the Metaphor*. Berkeley, CA: University of California Press.

Appelbaum, B. (2019). *The Economists' Hour: False Prophets, Free Markets, and the Fracture of Society*. New York: Little, Brown and Company.

Austin, J. (1970). Performative utterances. In Austin, J. (Ed.) *Philosophical Papers*. London: Oxford University Press.

Baghramian, M. (2004). *Relativism*. Oxon: Rutledge.

Bagwell, L. and Bernheim, B. (1996). Veblen effects in a theory of conspicuous consumption. *American Economic Review*, 86(3), 349–373.

Bandelj, N., Wherry, F. F. and Zelizer, V. A. (2017). Advancing money talks. In Bandelj, N., Wherry, F. F. and Zelizer, V. A. (Eds.) *Money Talks: Explaining How Money Really Works*. Princeton, NJ: Princeton University Press.

Bentham, J. (1789, 1838–1843). Objections to the principle of utility answered. In Bowring, J. (Ed.) *The Works of Jeremy Bentham*, 11 vols. Volume 1. Edinburgh: William Tait.

Berger, P. and Luckman, T. (1966). *The Social Construction of Reality*. London: Penguin.

Bhaskar, R. (1975, 1997). *A Realist Theory of Science*. London: Verso.

Bhaskar, R. (1998). *The Possibility of Naturalism: A Philosophical Critique of the Contemporary Human Sciences*. London: Routledge.

Boghossian, P. (2015). *O medo do conhecimento: Contra o relativismo e constructivismo*. Lisboa: Gradiva.

Bostrom, N. (2016). *Superintelligence: Paths, Dangers, Strategies*. Oxford: Oxford University Press.

Bourdieu, P. (1975). The specificity of the scientific field and the social conditions of the progress of reason. *Information (International Social Science Council)*, 14(6), 19–47.

Bourdieu, P. (1985). The social space and the genesis of groups. *Theory and Society*, 14(6), 723–744.

Bourdieu, P. (1988). *Homo Academicus*. Stanford: Stanford University Press.

Boushey, H. (2019). *Unbound*. Boston: Harvard University Press.

Brinton, C. (1940). The national socialists' use of Nietzsche. *Journal of the History of Ideas*, 1(2), 131–150.

Brown, H. (1992). Direct realism, indirect realism, and epistemology. *Philosophy and Phenomenological Research*, 52(2), 341–363.

Brown, J., Drake, K. and Wellman, L. (2014). The benefits of a relational approach to corporate political activity: Evidence from political contributions to tax policymakers. *The Journal of the American Taxation Association*, 37(1), 69–102.

Burnyeat, M. F. (1976a). Protagoras and self-refutation in Plato's Theaetetus. *The Philosophical Review*, 85(2), 172.

Burnyeat, M. F. (1976b). Protagoras and self-refutation in later Greek Philosophy. *Philosophical Review*, 85(1), 44–69.

Burr, V. (2015). *Social Construction*. 3rd Edition. Oxon: Routledge.

Butler, C. (2002). *Postmodernism: A Very Short Introduction*. Oxford: Oxford University Press.

Butler, J. (2010). Performative agency. *Journal of Cultural Economy*, 3(2), 147–161.

Callon, M. (2007). What does it mean to say that economics is performative? Do economists make markets? On the performativity of economics. In MacKenzie, D., Muniesa, F. and Siu, L. (Eds.) *Do Economists Make Markets? On the Performativity of Economics*. Oxford: Princeton University Press.

Cannan, E. (1921). Early history of the term capital. *Quarterly Journal of Economics*, 35(3), 469–481.

Cardao-Pito, T. (2012). Intangible flow theory. *American Journal of Economics and Sociology*, 71(2), 328–353.

Cardao-Pito, T. (2016). A law for the social sciences regarding us human beings. *Journal of Interdisciplinary Economics*, 28(2), 202–229.

Cardao-Pito, T. (2017). Organizations as producers of operating product flows to members of society. *SAGE Open*, 7(3), July–September, 1–18.

Chappell, S. (2019). Plato on knowledge in the Theaetetus. In Zalta, E. N. (Ed.) *The Stanford Encyclopedia of Philosophy*, Winter. Online at: https://plato.stanford.edu/archives/win2019/entries/plato-theaetetus/. https://oll.libertyfund.org/titles/bentham-works-of-jeremy-bentham-11-vols.

Choat, S. (2010). *Marx Through Post-Structuralism: Lyotard, Derrida, Foucault and Deleuze*. London: Continuum.

Collin, F. (1993). Social constructivism without paradox. *Danish Yearbook of Philosophy*, 28, 24–46.

Deleuze, G. and Guattari, F. (1977). *Anti-Oedipus: Capitalism and Schizophrenia*. New York: Viking.

Denicolo, V. (1999). Pollution-reducing innovations under taxes or permits. *Oxford Economic Papers*, 51(1), 184–199.

Derrida, J. (1970, 1993). Structure, sign, and play in the discourse of the human sciences. In Derrida, J. (Ed.) *Writing and Difference*. Chicago: Chicago University Press.

Derrida, J. (1974, 1997). *Of Grammatology*. Baltimore: John Hopkins University Press.

Derrida, J. (1983, 1988). Letter to a Japanese Friend. In Wood, D. and Bernasconi, B. (Eds.) *Derrida and Difference*. Evanston, IL: Northwestern University Press.

Derrida, J. (1988). Signature, event, context. In Derrida, J. (Ed.) *Limited, Inc.* Evanston, IL: Northwestern University Press.

Derrida, J. (1990, 2002). Force of law: The mystical foundation of authority. In Derrida, J. (Ed.) *Acts of Religion*. Edited by Anidjar, G. New York: Routledge.

Dimanchev, E., Paltsev, S., Yuan, M., Rothenberg, D., Tessum, C., Marshall, J. and Selin, N. (2019). Health co-benefits of sub-national renewable energy policy in the US. *Environmental Research Letters*, 14(8), 085012.

Dorpat, T. (1994). On the double whammy and gaslighting. *Psychoanalysis and Psychotherapy*, 11(1), 91–96.

Dupont, B. (2017). *The History of Economic Ideas: Economic Thought in Contemporary Context*. Oxon: Routledge.

Durkheim, E. (1895, 1966). *The Rules of the Sociological Method*. New York: Free Press.

Economist. (2019). The 2019 Nobel Prizes: Supercharged. *Economist*, October 12.

Ellis, J. (1989). *Against Deconstruction*. Princeton, NJ: Princeton University Press.

Evans, R. (2018). *In Defense of History*. Croydon: Granta Books.

Feyerabend, P. (1971). Problems of empiricism II. In Colodny, R. (Ed.) *The Nature and Function of Scientific Theories: Essays in Contemporary Science and Philosophy*. Pittsburgh: University of Pittsburgh Press.

Feyerabend, P. (1975, 1993). *Against Method*. London: Verso.

Ford, M. (2015). *Rise of the Robots: Technology and the Threat of a Jobless Future*. New York: Basic Books.

Foucault, M. (1966, 2005). *The Order of Things*. Oxon: Routledge.

Foucault, M. (1972). *The Archeology of Knowledge*. London: Tavistock.

Foucault, M. (1980). Truth and power: Interview with Alessandro Fontana and Pasquale Pasquino. In Foucault, M. (Ed.) *Power/Knowledge: Selected Interviews and Other Writings, 1972–1977*. London: Vintage.

Foucault, M. (1984). What is Enlightenment? In Rabinow, P. (Ed.) *The Foucault Reader*. Harmondsworth: Penguin.

Furnham, A., Richards, S. C. and Paulhus, D. (2013). The dark triad of personality: A 10 year review. *Social and Personality Psychology Compass*, 7(3), 199–216.

Goodman, N. (1975). Words, works, worlds. *Erkenntnis*, 9(1), 57–73.

Goodman, N. (1978). *Ways of World Making*. Cambridge, MA: Hackett Publishing Co.

Griffin, A. (2017). Facebook's artificial intelligence robots shut down after they start talking to each other in their own language. *Independent*, July 31. Online at: www.independent.co.uk/life-style/gadgets-and-tech/news/facebook-artificial-intelligence-ai-chatbot-new-language-research-openai-google-a7869706.html.

Goulder, L. H. (2013). Markets for pollution allowances: What are the (new) lessons? *Journal of Economic Perspectives*, 27(1), 87–102.

Habermas, J. (1985, 2007). *The Philosophical Discourse of Modernity: Twelve Lectures*. Cambridge: Wiley-Blackwell.

Harvey, D. (1990). *The Condition of Postmodernity: An Inquiry into the Origins of Cultural Change*. Oxford: Basil-Blackwell.

Harvey, D. (2007). *A Brief History of Neoliberalism*. Oxford: Oxford University Press.

Hegel, G. (1807, 1977). *Phenomenology of Spirit*. Oxford: Oxford University Press.

Heidegger, M. (1927, 1962). *Being and Time*. New York: Harper and Row.

Hodgson, G. (2014). What is capital? Economists and sociologists have change its meaning: Should it be changed back? *Cambridge Journal of Economics*, 38(5), 1063–1086.

Hutcheon, L. (2013). *Narcissistic Narrative: The Metafictional Paradox*. Ontario, Canada: Wilfrid Laurier University Press.

Ingham, G. (1996). Money is a social relation. *Review of Social Economy*, 54(4), 507–529.

Ingham, G. (2013). *The Nature of Money*. Cambridge: Polity Press.

Jackson, W. (2019). *Markets: Perspectives from Economic and Social Theory*. Oxon: Routledge.

Jameson, F. (1993). *Postmodernism, or, the Cultural Logic of Late Capitalism*. London: Verso.

Kant, I. (1781, 1999). *Critique of Pure Reason*. Cambridge: Cambridge University Press.

Kellner, D. (1991). Nietzsche and modernity: Critical reflections on twilight of the idols. *International Studies in Philosophy*, 23(2), 3–17.

Khlentzos, D. (2016). Challenges to metaphysical realism. In *Stanford Encyclopedia of Philosophy*. Online at: https://plato.stanford.edu/entries/hedonism/.

Kinney, P. (2008). Climate change, air quality, and human health. *American Journal of Preventive Medicine*, 35(5), 459–467.

Kivak, R. (2017). *Gaslighting*. Hackensack, NJ: Salem Press.

Knorr-Cetina, K. (1981). *The Manufacture of Knowledge*. Oxford: Pergamon Press.

Koch, C. (2016). How the computer beat the go master. *Scientific American*. Online at: www.scientificamerican.com/article/how-the-computer-beat-the-go-master/.

Kuhn, T. (1970). *The Structure of Scientific Revolutions*. 2nd Edition. Chicago: University of Chicago Press.

Kukla, A. (2000). *Social Constructivism and the Philosophy of Science*. Oxon: Routledge.

Lakatos, I. (1968). II-Criticism and the methodology of scientific research programmes. *Proceeding of the Aristotelian Society*, 69, 149–186.

Lawson, T. (1994). A realist theory for economics. In Backhouse, R. (Ed.) *New Directions in Economic Methodology*. Oxon: Routledge.

Lawson, T. (2016). Social positioning and the nature of money. *Cambridge Journal of Economics*, 40(4), 961–996.

Lawson, T. (2019). *The Nature of Social Reality: Issues in Social Ontology*. Oxon: Routledge.

Lasi, H., Fettke, P., Kemper, H. G., Feld, T. and Hoffmann, M. (2014). Industry 4.0. *Business and Information Systems Engineering*, 6(4), 239–242.

Latour, N. and Woolgar, S. (1979). *Laboratory Life: The Social Construction of Scientific Facts*. London: Sage.

Latour, N. and Woolgar, S. (1986). *Laboratory Life: The Construction of Scientific Facts*. 2nd Edition. Princeton, NJ: Princeton University Press.

Lee, M. (2005). *Epistemology after Protagoras: Responses to Relativism in Plato, Aristotle, and Democritus*. Oxford: Oxford University Press.

Levin, D. (2008). *The Opening of Vision: Nihilism and the Postmodern Situation*. Oxon: Routledge.

Lyotard, J.-F. (1984, 1997). *The Postmodern Condition: A Report on Knowledge*. Minneapolis: University of Minnesota Press.

Machamer, P. (1973). Feyerabend and Galileo: The interaction of theories, and the reinterpretation of experience. *Studies in History and Philosophy of Science*, 4(1), 1–46.

MacKenzie, D. and Millo, Y. (2003). Constructing a market, performing theory: The historical sociology of a financial derivatives exchange. *American Journal of Sociology*, 109, 107–145.

Malkin, C. (2015). One simple way to protect yourself from narcissists: How to preserve your self-esteem when leaving isn't an option. *Psychology Today*. Online at: www.psychologytoday.com/us/blog/romance-redux/201508/one-simple-way-protect-yourself-narcissists.

Markovits, D. (2019). *The Meritocracy Trap*. New York: Penguin.

Marx, K. (1847). *The Poverty of Philosophy*. Online at: www.marxists.org/archive/marx/works/1847/poverty-philosophy/ch02.htm.

Marx, K. (1990). *O capital-Livro 1-Tomo 1*. Lisbon: Edições Pogresso/Avante.

Marx, K. and Frederick, E. (1846, 1970). *The German Ideology*. New York: International Publishers.

McHale, B. (2015). *The Cambridge Introduction to Postmodernism*. Cambridge: Cambridge University Press.

Merleau-Ponty, M. (1945, 2014). *Phenomenology of Perception.* Oxon: Routledge.

Miller, D. (2002). Turning Callon the right way up. *Economy and Society*, 31(2), 218–233.

Millo, Y. and MacKenzie, D. (2009). The usefulness of inaccurate models: Towards an understanding of the emergence of financial risk management. *Accounting, Organizations and Society*, 34, 638–653.

Moore, A. (2019). Abuse prevention: How to turn off the gaslighters. *The Guardian*, Saturday March 2. Online at: www.theguardian.com/lifeandstyle/2019/mar/02/abuse-prevention-how-to-turn-off-the-gaslighters.

Nietzsche, F. (1888, 1990). *The Twilight of the Idols and the Anti-Christ: Or How to Philosophize with a Hammer.* New York: Penguin.

Niiniluoto, I. (1991). Realism, relativism and constructivism. *Synthese*, 89, 132–162.

Norberg, J. (2016). *Progress: Ten Reasons to Look Forward for the Future.* London: Oneworld.

Nordhaus, W. (2007). To tax or not to tax: Alternative approaches to slowing global warming. *Review of Environmental Economics and Policy*, 1(1), 26–44.

Norregaard, M. and Reppelin-Hill, M. (2000). *Taxes and Tradable Permits as Instruments for Controlling Pollution: Theory and Practice.* Washington, DC: International Monetary Fund. Working Paper.

Norris, C. (1997). *Against Relativism: Philosophy of Science, Deconstruction and Critical Theory.* Oxford: Basil-Blackwell.

O'Reilly, C., Doerr, B. and Chatman, J. (2018). "See you in court": How CEO narcissism increases firms' vulnerability to lawsuits. *The Leadership Quarterly*, 29(3), 365–378.

Ovtchinnikov, A. and Pantaleoni, E. (2012). Individual political contributions and firm performance. *Journal of Financial Economics*, 105(2), 367–392.

Paulhus, D. and Williams, K. (2002). The dark triad of personality: Narcissism, Machiavellianism, and psychopathy. *Journal of Research in Personality*, 36(6), 556–563.

Peacock, M. (2017). The ontology of money. *Cambridge Journal of Economics*, 41(5), 1471–1487.

Pinker, S. (2019). *Enlightenment Now: The Case for Reason, Science, Humanism, and Progress.* London: Penguin.

Plato. (2013). *Theaetetus: Translated by Benjamin Jowett.* The Project Gutenberg EBook. Online at: https://www.gutenberg.org//files/1726/1726-h/1726-h.htm.

Polanyi, K. (1944, 2001). *The Great Transformation: The Political and Economic Origins of Our Time.* Boston: Beacon Press.

Popkova, E., Ragulina, Y. and Bogoviz, A. (Eds.) (2019). *Industry 4.0: Industrial Revolution of the 21st Century.* London: Springer.

Putman, H. (1981). *Reason, Truth and History.* Cambridge: Cambridge University Press.

Putman, H. (1996). Irrealism and deconstruction. In McCormick, P. (Eds.) *Realism, Antirealism, Irrealism.* Boston: MIT Press.

Quine, W. (1992). *Pursuit of Truth.* Cambridge, MA: Harvard University Press.

Reay, D. (2017). *Miseducation.* London: Policy Press.

Requate, T. (1993). Pollution control in a Cournot duopoly via taxes or permits. *Journal of Economics*, 58(3), 255–291.

Reinert, H. and Reinert, E. (2006). Creative destruction in economics: Nietzsche, Sombart, Schumpeter. In Backhaus, J. G. and Drechsler, W. (Eds.) *Friedrich Nietzsche (1844–1900). The European Heritage in Economics and the Social Sciences.* Volume 3. Boston: Springer.

Rorty, R. (1979). *Philosophy and the Mirror of Nature.* Princeton, NJ: Princeton University Press.

Rorty, R. (1989). *Contingency, Irony, and Solidarity.* Cambridge: Cambridge University Press.

Russel, S. (2019). *Human Compatible: AI and the Problem of Control.* New York: Allen Lane.

Saez, E. and Zucman, G. (2019). *The Triumph of Injustice*. New York: W. W. Norton & Company.

Santaniello, W. (2012). *Nietzsche, God, and the Jews: His Critique of Judeo-Christianity in Relation to the Nazi Myth*. New York: SUNY Press.

Santos, A. and Rodrigues, J. (2009). Economics as social engineering? Questioning the performativity thesis. *Cambridge Journal of Economics*, 33(5), 985–1000.

Sarkis, S. (2016). How to leave a narcissist for good how to get out with your pscyhe intact. *Psychology Today*. Online at: www.psychologytoday.com/us/blog/here-there-and-every where/201606/how-leave-narcissist-good.

Sarkis, S. (2018). *Gaslighting: Recognize Manipulative and Emotionally Abusive People – And Break Free*. Boston, MA: Da Capo Press/Lifelong Books.

Sayer, A. (2000). *Realism and Social Science*. London: Sage.

Schumpeter, J. (1942). *Capitalism, Socialism and Democracy*. New York: Harper and Row.

Schutz, A. (1967). *The Phenomenology of the Social World*. Chicago: Northwestern University Press.

Searl, J. (1997). *The Construction of Social Reality*. New York: Free Press.

Sheehan, T. (2010). *Heidegger: The Man and the Thinker*. Piscataway, NJ: Transaction Publishers.

Siemens, H. (1998). Nietzsche's hammer: Philosophy, destruction, or the art of limited warfare. *Tijdschrift voor filosofie*, 60(2), 321–347.

Simmel, G. (1907, 2004). *The Philosophy of Money*. Oxon: Routledge.

Sluga, H. D. (1993). *Heidegger's Crisis: Philosophy and Politics in Nazi Germany*. Boston: Harvard University Press.

Skidelsky, R. (2018). *Money and Government: A Challenge to Mainstream Economics*. Milton Keynes: Penguin.

Spencer, D. (2020). Economics and 'bad' management: The limits to performativity. *Cambridge Journal of Economics*, 44(1), 17–32.

Stove, D. (2017). *Scientific Irrationalism: Origins of the Postmodern Cult*. Oxon: Routledge.

Sweet, P. (2019). The sociology of gaslighting. *American Sociological Review*, 84(5), 851–875.

Swoyer, C. (2015). Relativism. In Zalta, E. N. (Ed.) *Stanford Encyclopedia of Philosophy*, Summer Edition. Online at: https://plato.stanford.edu/archives/sum2015/entries/relativism/.

Thérèsea, S. and Martin, B. (2010). Shame, scientist! Degradation rituals in science. *Prometheus: Critical Studies in Innovation*, 28(2), 97–110.

Tormoen, M. (2019). Gaslighting: How pathological labels can harm psychotherapy clients. *Journal of Humanistic Psychology*. https://doi.org/10.1177/0022167819864258.

Trigg, A. (2001). Veblen, Bourdieu, and conspicuous consumption. *Journal of Economic Issues*, 35(1), 99–115.

Veblen, T. (1899, 1994). The theory of the leisure class. In *The Collected Works of Thorstein Veblen*. Volume 1. London: Routledge, 1–404.

Von Frisch, K. (1974). Decoding the language of the bee. *Science*, 185(4152), 663–668.

Walpole, M. (2003). Socioeconomic status and college: How SES affects college experiences and outcomes. *The Review of Higher Education*, 27(1), 45–73.

Wiener, N. (1950, 1989). *The Human Use of Human Beings: Cybernetics and Society*. London: Free Association.

Zilioli, U. (2016). *Protagoras and the Challenge of Relativism: Plato's Subtlest Enemy*. Oxon: Routledge.

Part 2

Intangible flow theory

2 Introducing intangible flow theory[1]

2.1 Introduction

Let us first define intangible, flow, and intangible flow. The word intangible means not tangible. According to Merriam-Webster's dictionary, the term tangible can defined as "capable of being perceived especially by the sense of touch," "capable of being precisely identified or realized by the mind" and "capable of being appraised at an actual or approximate value." Because it is one of the characteristics that distinguish goods from services, intangibility has been often studied in organizational studies. There are very few products that are pure physical goods or pure services.[2] Most products have tangible and intangible components. However, the degree of product intangibility could be classified according to a continuum.[3] A distinction between two major approaches to intangibility identifies two types: (i) Physical intangibility: a product is intangible if it is not palpable or cannot be touched. It is roughly the first definition on Merriam-Webster that comes from the Latin origin of the word. Nonetheless, immateriality must not be confused with imperceptibility. Music is the perfect example of a perceptible yet immaterial reality.[4] Even if the element has no material body, it is possibly perceptible by one of the four other human senses. (ii) Mental intangibility, where the product cannot be grasped mentally.[5]

In intangible flow theory, we will use the concept of intangibility without necessarily relating it to the sense of touch, but to the faculty of being identified with precision, that is, capable of being precisely identified or realized by the mind and capable of being appraised at an actual or approximate value.[6] Hence, although music is non-corporeal, it can be identified with precision by those who understand music coding. Under the precision definition of tangibility, therefore, music is tangible for the knowledgeable listener who can describe it with precision and intangible otherwise.

Besides human services, intangibility can be used to describe other important economic elements such as information. Some mathematicians and statisticians are aware that much information is intangible[7] and yet try to devise quantitative methods to study it.[8] Yet, here we attain the paradox of quantifying intangibility or aporia of quantifying intangibility, which applies to intangible elements. The elements of previous intangibility for which scientists can find quantitative methods to attribute well-defined quantities that, therefore, can be precisely appraised at an actual or approximated value have properties of tangibility, whereas the other dimensions remain intangible. *Tangibilization* is the term given in intangible flow theory to the process of being able to precisely capture dimensions that were previously intangible.

Unfortunately, the use of quantitative methods is not a enough of a condition to achieve tangibility. Furthermore, those methods can be used to produce pure metaphysical speculation and imaginary projections of future scenarios that could not be reached with precision. Scientists support their work on concepts that are themselves highly intangible. There is a distinction between pattern recognition and pattern prediction, and for scientists to recognize complex patterns they must make (intangible) conceptual predictions of those patterns.[9]

Semantics would be a macro set where the dimensions of information that cannot be described through a well-defined mathematical function would be put. Hence, for the purpose of scientific knowledge, the use of mathematical analysis can only capture certain dimensions of information. A simple distinction among data, information and knowledge might already bring many difficulties.[10] The conceptual formulation that there is a symbolic interaction between members of society mediated by symbols and significations, where the meanings attributed evolve with processes of stimulus and response,[11] would not be reachable merely through mathematical reasoning. Nevertheless, the failure of mathematical reasoning to capture them would not imply the nonexistence of symbols, meanings and significations. In an apparently simple nearby communication between two human beings, not only are semantic words and language (discourse) exchanged but a full range of highly heterogeneous interactions such as body movements and gestures,[12] facial expressions,[13] postures,[14] eye gaze[15] or paralinguistic sound of the voice[16] are communicated even without the need for words.

By flow we understand the movement of an element deriving from a source, which implies that an element that is not flowing should be considered as static. A human-related intangible flow is therefore the movement of an element, deriving from a person or group of persons, which cannot be precisely identified or realized by the mind and cannot be appraised at an actual or approximate value. This book focuses on intangible flows that are also human-related and thus of direct interest to the social sciences (such as workflows, service flows, communication flows and information flows). Yet, the intangible flow concept could be embraced by the natural sciences because not all intangible flows are human-related. For instance, flows of light or atoms could not be precisely perceived by the human senses, but scientists have figured ways of studying them.[17]

As occurs with the human-related intangible flows, the nonhuman-related intangible flows can be integrated in dynamic sets comprising both tangible and intangible flows. As in the example of Heraclitus's river passing by into which one can step only once, the flow of the river may contain both tangible and intangible components. Most importantly, intangible flows referred to in this theory have an instrumental property that makes them from the field of phenomena: they can be verified, even if through an imprecise description. Intangible flows that cannot be demonstrated are from the domain of metaphysics and thus not a subject of discussion in this book.

2.2 Two examples of human-related intangible flows

Two examples of human-related intangible flows that can be demonstrated are service flows and information flows. Products (outputs) such as services have properties that distinguish them from tangible physical goods. Previous studies suggest that products can be classified according to their level of intangibility.[18] A suggested scale ranges from most tangible (such as clothes and furniture) to most intangible products (pure services such as consulting or teaching). In the middle of the scale are the products combining tangible and intangible components. For example, meals in restaurant chains mix tangible food and drinks with intangible services and marketing. Several academic textbooks on the marketing of services adapt a definition of services that could be traced back to Rathmel (1966: 33). *Services are "acts, deeds, performances, or efforts," and physical goods are "articles, devices, materials, objects, or things."* There are very few products that are purely services or purely physical goods. The most tangible of goods requires services to be sold/delivered to customers, and the most intangible of services are generally associated with elements of tangibility (for example: the paperwork).

A survey of research in organization studies identified four characteristics that distinguish services from physical goods: intangibility, heterogeneity, inseparability of production and consumption of many services, and perishability.[19] Lovelock and Gummeson tried to replace these distinctions.[20] They recognize that service intangibility is the most widely acknowledged and amply taught distinction in academic textbooks. Another characteristic was suggested: the non-ownership of the services. Although the customer has the right to consume the service through a rental or access fee, he/she cannot own the service as he/she would be able to own a physical good. Nonetheless, the non-ownership of services seems to derive from the same properties identified earlier and, particularly, the intangibility from which the other key goods–services distinctions may emerge.[21] Intangible, heterogeneous and perishable products such as services, normally consumed when produced, are not owned as physical goods may be or reported on the balance sheet as assets (or capital), unlike physical goods or other assets (or capital) such as cash. Other specific characteristics of services include the active participation of the customer in the production of many services, contrary to what generally happens with physical goods,[22] as well as other specific features.

Services are much more difficult to identify with precision than physical goods. Therefore, service flows are much harder to capture merely with

mathematical/quantitative tools. To some extent, engineering progress or artificial intelligence may be employed to do the tangibilization of some previous
intangible dimension on services, for instance, in customer relations or storage
handling. However, the other dimension will remain intangible, as explained
through the paradox[23] of trying to measure intangibility.

Likewise, non-codified information also has characteristics that distinguish
it from material elements because several of its dimensions cannot be precisely
appraised at an actual or approximate value. Therefore, intangible information
flows cannot be considered equivalent to flows of economic material elements
such as physical goods or cash, which can be precisely quantified. Currently,
it would be easily accepted that information is imperfect and that there are
costs to obtain information and information asymmetries, which are affected
by individuals and organizational actions. Accordingly, mainstream economics'
market economy characterization would be deeply affected by such findings.

Nevertheless, mainstream economics sees information as signals, which separate information from cognition and make a distinction between meaningful
signals and noise, with the latter being understood as a lack of determined patterns.[24] The movement of information would be similar to that of signals circulating on a circuit board. Therefore, the mainstream economic understanding
about information might yet be very poor. Because it ignores the intangibility
of information, it could not notice that intangibility distinguishes information
from physical goods. Furthermore, information may not verify the same conditions of scarcity observed in other resources. The oil or gold reserves of our
planet are limited, whereas a good idea can be downloaded on the internet as
many times as possible. Thus, mainstream economics misses the sociocultural
element of the analysis because scarcity could be inherent to the human use
of that resource. Moreover, resources are not always scarce. They can also be
enough or abundant, as it occurs with information, which poses serious difficulties to the mainstream analytical framework based on assuming the scarcity
of all resources.[25]

Although some mainstream economic studies about information may propose concepts as those of lack of scarcity or non-rivalry in the use of information, those studies are referring to information as a special type of good and
thus a special type of intangible asset.[26] Because information has properties that
distinguish it from physical goods, for purposes of precision, intangible flow
theory restricts the concept of good to that of a clearly identifiable physical
good. Hence, information is not necessarily considered a good and/or an asset.

What is worse, the logic of mainstream economics is to capture information through mathematical tools. However, if information, knowledge and
relations would be assets, such formulation would imply that many of those
so-called assets are inside of human beings' brains. Hence, those alleged assets
cannot be separated from the respective human and his/her cognition and
affectivity. For millenniums in philosophy, an unsolved debate of what is in
fact knowledge (and information) has subsisted. However, taking a shortcut,
mainstream economics already makes monetary valuations of knowledge and

information without knowing what and where they are. One could suggest that first it would be necessary to understand them. The work with knowledge and information is not static. It is dynamic, as it is the work with relationships and of what are called social assets. A relationship must be dynamized to exist.

2.3 Introductory case study

Let us observe a case study where facts could be gathered: a conversation between two human beings (A and B) that would be associated with an apparently simple economic activity: the selling of a restaurant's lunch for two. A dynamic interaction between intangible and tangible flows can be identified, which in the theory is called intangible flow dynamics. (i) The choice of the restaurant: imagine that A becomes interested about the place after reading a positive review in a website publication. Here an intangible element moves from the newspaper to A's cognition, leading him to have an action that he would not have otherwise. (ii) B will be convinced by A to attend that restaurant through an intangible telephonic conversation; otherwise, she would not be aware of that restaurant's existence. (iii) They arrive in the restaurant, and in comes another human being, C, the server, smiling and delivering an intangible service; she will soon indicate the table and bring the menu. (iv) When A and B study the menu, the intangible information moves from the menu to their cognition. The choice will be discussed and communicated to C. (v) The tangible food and drinks arrive through the intangible service of C and required also the intangible work produced by staff in the kitchen, those who produced and sold the items, and the manager, or other staff members. (vi) The communication between A and B does not involve only semantic words and language but also body movements, gestures, expressions, postures, eye gaze or paralinguistic sounds. Communicators are, at one and the same time, senders and receivers of messages.[27] After the dessert and coffee, it is time to ask C for the bill. (vii) The intangible information regarding the bill to pay is printed on a tangible piece of paper. (viii) A is always forgetting his wallet at home. B pays the bill with her bank card. The cash flow will be reported in both bank accounts.

In the case here, note that although the transaction was implemented through a bank card in (viii), thus containing intangible elements, the respective monetary flow has tangible characteristics, as B, the restaurant and the banks can precisely quantify the monetary flow. Therefore, the cash flow can be considered a material flow. Note also the intangible flow dynamics in (i) through (vii) that lead to the occurrence of the material cash flow in (viii). The non-occurrence of some intangible flows would necessarily result in the non-occurrence of the material cash flow: (i) if the website had not published the restaurant's reference; (ii) if B had not answered her phone (neither the messages); or (iii) if the restaurant was closed. A similar reasoning is applicable to the material flow of food and drinks in (v).

2.4 Enter the intangible flow theory

We start with the tangibility of concrete material elements. Physical goods, such as cars or clothes, are tangible elements which to large extent can indeed be quantifiable with precision. The same applies to long-term fixed investments such as property, equipment and plant. However, what about money, which can take several forms, such as notes and coins, checks, credit cards, digital money or online accounts? The intangible flow theory will define that monetary flows, that is, flows of money and its equivalents, are tangible because they can be precisely quantified at an exact value. This applies either to physical coins or to cryptocurrencies that only exist online. The material practice of money is one of its defining properties, even if related to distinct symbolic referents and social systems.[28] Money is not a neutral medium of exchange, and money can have different forms, which interfere with its conception and practices,[29] for instance, forms of coins, notes, credit cards, bank accounts, checks, government bonds, discount coupons, cryptic currencies and so on. Furthermore, people may attribute different perceptions and meanings according to distinct origins and applications of money. Yet, monetary flows can be quantified with precision after they have occurred in a precise time and space. That is, although money can have several social roles and meanings, under discussion by social scientists, it also has a pragmatic nature in modalities of exchange and circulation.[30] Whichever form a monetary flow may assume, human beings are able to know the exact amount of money that has been moved. In the same manner, through the cash flow statement, a corporation presents a precise report of its complete cash movements during each fiscal period.

Therefore, through their research tools that require mathematical/quantitative modeling,[31] mainstream economists can observe the cash flows, and they can also quantify several empirical variables that are materialized in monetary values, such as prices, profits, growth, capital structures, interest rates or financial deficits. When mainstream economists call people and their contributions human capital or human assets, they are presupposing that people and their contributions can be owned, manipulated and accumulated as physical goods or money. Denominations of humans as commodities, assets, capital or resources are, however, pseudo-phenomena. Instead of representing an external reality, they take as given something that has never been demonstrated. People would be commodities, assets, resources or capital because economists call them this, not because there is any empirical that we behave like property, equipment, merchandizing, loans or stock market shares in society. Besides the serious ethical issues in placing people at the same level as nonhuman material things, the economic framework, as currently understood and practiced, is profoundly flawed because it fails to understand the complexity of people and our intangible activities.

The intangible flow theory will proceed as follows: First, one defines monetary flows as tangible flows because they represent concrete monetary transactions that are precisely identifiable after they have occurred in a specific time and space. Second, one postulates that nonhuman resources such as information (and knowledge), physical goods and machines should be considered generally static in the generation of monetary flows if they are not dynamized by mainly human-related flows, which cannot be precisely appraised at an actual or approximate value. Although human beings are not intangible, some of our contributions can be intangible (such as workflows, service flows, information flows, knowledge flows and communicational flows).

Hence, we can now reach the fundamental proposition: In human society, the occurrence of material tangible flows, as flows of physical goods or money, is associated to intangible flows inherent to human actions that are necessary to the prosecution of those material flows. The monetary flows cannot be considered intangible flows because even when they have a non-touchable form, they have properties of tangibility. They are precisely quantifiable at an actual or approximate value. Thus, analyses and decisions related to tangible material flows must consider the more relevant intangible flows that are necessary for material flow consummation.

According to the theory, the intangible flows with effects on monetary flows can be of various types, such as service flows, relationship flows, communication flows, information flows, knowledge flows and data flows. Although they could not be precisely quantified, they are necessary for the occurrence of tangible material flows, such as the flows of money and physical goods. The intangible flows require an abstract formulation specifically because of their inherent intangibility. Therefore, an abstraction is a necessary description for their study and understanding. Nevertheless, this theoretical formulation can be corroborated by empirical tests that prove the association of intangible flows with concrete monetary flows.

2.5 Five corollaries to be associated with the new theory

In the developing of and with reference to this theory, the following five corollaries are proposed, the first corollary is that associated with the occurrence of the tangible flows. There can be a very vast and complex conjunct of intangible flows, in which, inclusively, some of those intangible flows can be very difficult to identify. This first development appears to explain that this is not a motive for the concept of intangible flows not to be recognized or scientifically systematized, nor is it a motive for the concept of intangible flows not to be considered. What is complex and what is simple depends on our knowledge and understanding and changes over time. Scientists may devise precise methods to capture currently intangible dimensions. However, the existing dimensions that scientists would not be capable to precisely identify, realize or appraise at an actual or approximate value will remain intangible.

The second corollary is that it is not necessary for a temporal coincidence to exist between intangible flows and tangible flows for intangible flows to impact tangible flows (for example, the training of the personnel may take some time to have effects on the productivity of the organization or the marketing campaigns might take some time to have intangible consequences that will be reflected in the organization's money inflows). Inclusive cash flows, as they are part of a dynamic process, might have effects on intangible flows and the latter again will have influence on other cash flows of the organization (for instance, the expenses with publicity or branded merchandizing collocated near potential clients).

The third corollary is that the non-occurrence of economic material flows can also be a consequence of intangible flows that have a negative effect on their consummation (such as advertising campaign from a competitor, poor quality services and cost reduction policy). Similarly, intangible flows exist that might worsen the monetary flows of an interested person or group (for example, staff absenteeism and political effects).

The fourth corollary is that the tangibility of tangible flows refers to tangible flows (e.g., monetary flows) that occur within a specific time and space. Not yet verified tangible flows cannot be considered already materialized. This corollary establishes a difference between those tangible flows that can be precisely quantified, for they have taken place in a specific time and place, and those that despite an appearance of measurability might not be precisely quantifiable because their occurrence is uncertain. For instance, when mainstream economics requires projections of future cash flows to operate their concepts of "discounted future cash flows value" or "utility maximization under pareto optimality," the non-verified monetary flows cannot be considered already materialized and thus their quantification might be the object of speculation and/or imagination. For instance, mainstream economists claim to have done a mathematical synthesis of Keynes's thinking, but Keynes himself (1936: 149) was aware that our knowledge of factors that will govern the yield of an investment some years hence is usually very slight and often negligible.[32] The mainstream futurology can bring much harm to the social sciences because it may assure an appearance of certainty to rather unknown outcomes.

The fifth corollary is that although mathematical/quantitative research tools can be used to precisely measure tangible material flows, they are insufficient to research and capture intangible flows and their relationships with the tangible material flows. This corollary explains why mathematical/quantitative methods, which are highly relevant for science, are insufficient for studying and understanding the intangible flow dynamics of concrete empirical phenomena observed in economy and society and why mainstream economists who profess a metaphysics of mathematics (which refuses to accept non-mathematical/quantitative forms of scientific inquiry) cannot reach complex human-related intangible flows that are necessary for the consummation of precisely quantifiable tangible material flows.

2.6 The challenge of testing the theory

As currently formalized, the intangible flow theory is stated for subsequent testability. Therefore, the challenge is to identify intangible flows and establish concrete associations with tangible material flows, as done in the case study earlier. Figure 2.1 exemplifies the complexity of several intangible flows with influence in the monetary flows of an organization.[33] It represents a simplified visual model with a dynamic network of intangible flows that could be used later for testing the intangible flow effects on an organization's cash flows. The figure's purpose is to express evidence of the intangible flows, not to represent the complete set of relevant intangible flows.

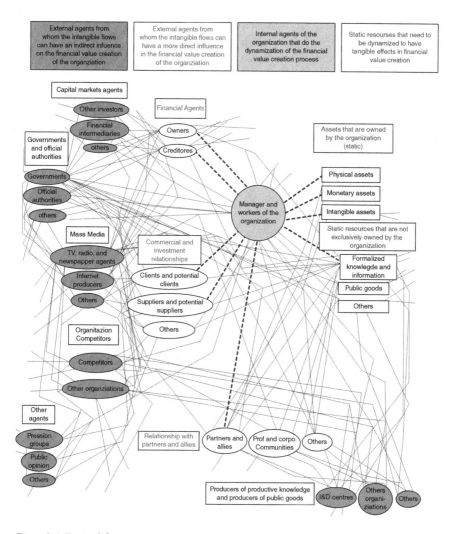

Figure 2.1 Exemplification of intangible flow dynamics with implications on an organization's monetary flows

Source: Adapted from Cardao-Pito (2004, 2012).

A first component of the model includes the manager and the workers of an organization, those persons who with their intangible flows of work, services, communication, information, knowledge or others contribute to the active consummation of the organization cash flows.

The model includes also resources considering that they need to be dynamized to have material effects in the organization's cash flows. Without the dynamical effect of the human-related intangible flows, the resources would be static, with no material effects in generating cash flows. Two types of resources are distinguished: first, assets that are exclusively owned by the organization such as physical assets, monetary assets or intangible assets and, second, static resources that are not exclusively owned by the corporation, such as formalized knowledge and information or public goods.

External agents from whom the intangible flows can have a more direct influence in the cash flow include commercial and investment relationships such as with clients and suppliers, relationships with partners and allies, and relationships with financiers of the firm, which include owners and debt holders.

Nonetheless, one must not forget external agents from whom intangible flows can have an indirect influence in the cash flow generation of the organization, such as governments and official authorities, capital markets agents, mass media, or competitors.

2.7 Conclusion

The idea that the Earth has a spherical shape is not compatible with the idea that the Earth is flat and rests on top of a cube, regardless of what calls to action, devices, discourses and analytical/practical descriptions could be used to argue any of those possibilities.[34] The form and location of Earth in space precedes human discourses by billions of years. Several societal phenomena, traditionally studied by mainstream economics and Marxism, can be addressed by alternative explanations, such as human survival and existence, growth, profits, inflation, financial decisions and financial crisis. Likewise, we can suggest alternative explanations for human participation in economic and societal production. Scientists outside the realm of mainstream economics should accept the challenge of studying those same phenomena, even if this means entering direct confrontation with the dominant explanations derived from its metaphysics of mathematics and money.

The explanations for the occurrence of material flows and other empirical phenomena might benefit from knowledge obtained from quite distinct fields such as heterodox economics, sociology, anthropology, organization studies, accounting, history, philosophy, or interdisciplinary studies. However, we should not argue for the substitution of a tyranny of explanations for others, as this would be repeating the intolerance of many mainstream economists (and some Marxists) to other forms of reasoning. Nevertheless, to reach new explanations, we cannot simply deconstruct previous explanations, we must come forward with new ones.

Although mathematical/quantitative tools are insufficient to describe and understand intangible flows, they must not be disdained. On the contrary, those methods are quite relevant for empirical analysis of hypotheses and samples, and the natural sciences can give very precious help in providing methods for quantifying several dimensions of current intangibility and in exposing the metaphysics of mathematics as professed by mainstream economists. Scientific work bases itself on highly intangible concepts, and the concept of natural intangible flow may also be of use for the natural sciences.

Intangible flow theory, it must be observed, does not offer a totalizing explanation for all natural and biosocial phenomena. It instead offers a realist approach that allows addressing the new, the different, events that challenge previous explanations, the ruptures in understanding, while at the same time providing the boundary of tangibility that limits the deconstruction of phenomena that can be identified with precision.

Notes

1 This new theory had it is initial formulation in three previous papers, namely Cardao-Pito (2012, 2016, 2017). Chapter 2 was partially derived from Cardao-Pito (2012), Chapter 4 was partially derived from Cardao-Pito (2016) and Chapter 5 was partially derived from Cardao-Pito (2017). I appreciate and acknowledge authorization to use these materials in those chapters. Some arguments were revised, and others were added. Furthermore, new empirical tests were conducted in Chapter 5.
2 Rathmel (1966) and Shostack (1977).
3 Shostack (1977).
4 Flipo (1988, p. 287).
5 Bateson (1979), which is similar to the definition in the Merriam-Webster dictionary.
6 Just as the passenger who reaches the train station just a few seconds too late does not need to touch the train to know precisely that he has just missed it.
7 Such as Soofi (1994) or Cover and Thomas (2005).
8 "[T]he notions of information consist of a spectrum ranging from semantic to technical. In the semantic context, the term information is used in an intuitive sense. It does not refer to a well-defined numerical quantity that can be used for measuring the extent of uncertainty differentials due to changes in the states of nature. In the technical sense, information is referred to as a well-defined function that quantifies the extent of uncertainty differentials"(Soofi, 1994, p. 1243).
9 Hayek (1967). As in Popper (1959, 2008), Hayek defends a fact-based scientific work, where scientific predictions must be formulated with the possibility of refutation/falsifiability.
10 Boisot and Canals (2004).
11 Blumer (1962, 1969); Perinbanayagam (1985).
12 See, for instance, Montepare et al. (1999); Kendon (1984).
13 See Ekman and Friesen (1975)
14 See Heller (1997).
15 See Knapp and Hall (1997); Richmond and McCroskey (2000).
16 See Scherer (1979); Wigboldus, Spears, and Semin (1999).
17 For instance, modern physics and cosmology have been developed assuming that the speed of light was a constant value c, but a recent theory, the variable speed of light theory, suggests that the velocity of light might be variable due several factors, which would imply the need to rewrite everything that previously assumed a constant speed of light c (see Magueijo, 2003).

18 Shostack (1977).
19 Zeithmal, Parasuraman, and Berry (1985); Zeithaml, Bitner, and Gremler (2006); Hoffman and Bateson (2006). The property of perishability suggests that services cannot be saved, stored, resold or returned as physical goods. Some of these features of services had, however, already been identified by Say (1821), who concluded that monetary flows paid to obtain services would make services akin to commodities, setting the precedent that still rules in mainstream economics. See Chapter 14 for more details.
20 Lovelock and Gummesson (2004).
21 Bateson (1979), Zeithmal, Parasuraman, and Berry (1985).
22 Hubbert (1995); Meuter and Bitner (1998); Meuter et al. (2000). Note, however, that although the final user participates in the production of several services (for instance, ordering the meal at a restaurant), he/she does not necessarily participate in the production of every service.
23 Or aporia.
24 Volmer, Mennicken, and Preda (2009).
25 Daoud (2010), Lee and Keen (2004).
26 See, for instance, Romer (1990), Haskel and Westlake (2018).
27 Hargie and Dickson (2004, p. 14).
28 Gilbert (2005).
29 Bandelj, Werry, and Zelizer (2017), Morduch (2017), Zelizer (1994).
30 As put by Maurer (2006, p. 30), "representational flaw does not mean representational failure, either for money or for anthropological (and other social science) accounts of it" or, as put by Callon and Muniesa (2005, p. 1245), "Economic calculation is not an anthropological fiction, precisely because it is not a purely human mechanical and mental competence; it is distributed among human actors and material devices."
31 Lenger (2019).
32 Keynes (1936, p. 149): "If we speak frankly, we have to admit that our basis of knowledge for estimating the yield ten years hence of a railway, a copper mine, a textile factory, the goodwill of a patente medicine, an Atlantic liner, a building in the City of London amounts to little and sometimes to nothing; or even five years hence. In fact, those who seriously attempt to make any such estimate are often so much in the minority that their behaviour does not govern the market."
33 Adapted from Cardao-Pito (2004, 2012).
34 Formulation in Caliskan and Callon (2009, 2010).

References

Bandelj, N., Werry, F. and Zelizer, V. (2017). Advancing money talks. In Bandelj, N., Werry, F. and Zelizer, V. (Eds.) *Money Talks: Explaining How Money Really Works*. Princeton, NJ: Princeton University Press.

Bateson, J. (1979). Why we need service marketing. In Ferrell, O. C., Brown, S. W. and Lamb, C. W. Jr (Eds.) *Conceptual and Theoretical Developments in Marketing*. Chicago: American Marketing Association, 131–146.

Blumer, H. (1962). Society as symbolic interaction. In Rose, A. (Ed.) *Human Behavior and Social Process: An Interactionist Approach*. New-York: Houghton-Mifflin.

Blumer, H. (1969). *Symbolic Interactionism: Perspective and Method*. Berkeley, CA: University of California Press.

Boisot, M. and Canals, A. (2004). Data, information and knowledge: Have we got it right? *Journal of Evolutionary Economics*, 14(1), 43–67.

Caliskan, K. and Callon, M. (2009). Economization, part 1: Shifting attention from the economy towards processes of economization. *Economy and Society*, 38(3), 369–398.

Caliskan, K. and Callon, M. (2010). Economization, part 2: A research programme for the study of markets. *Economy and Society,* 39(1), 1–32.

Callon, M. and Muniesa, F. (2005). Economic markets as calculative collective devices. *Organization Studies,* 26(8), 1229–1250.

Cardao-Pito, T. (2004). *Contributo para uma teoria dos fluxos intangiveis na criacao de valor financeiro.* Lisbon: ISEG, Technical University of Lisbon. Approved Academic Thesis.

Cardao-Pito, T. (2012). Intangible flow theory. *American Journal of Economics and Sociology,* 71(2), 328–353.

Cardao-Pito, T. (2016). A law for the social sciences regarding us human beings. *Journal of Interdisciplinary Economics,* 28(2), 202–229.

Cardao-Pito, T. (2017). Organizations as producers of operating product flows to members of society. *SAGE Open,* 7(3), July–September, 1–18.

Cover, T. and Thomas, J. (2005). *Elements of Information Theory.* 2nd Edition. New York: Wiley-Blackwell.

Daoud, A. (2010). Robbins and Malthus on scarcity, abundance, and sufficiency. *American Journal of Economics and Sociology,* 69(4), 1206–1229.

Ekman, P. and Friesen, W. (1975). *Unmasking the Face: A Guide to Recognizing Emotions from Facial Cues.* Upper Saddle River, NJ: Prentice Hall.

Flipo, J. (1988). On the intangibility of services. *Service Industries Journal,* 8(3), 286–293.

Gilbert, E. (2005). Common cents: Situating money in time and place. *Economy and Society,* 34(3), 357–388.

Hargie, O. and Dickson, D. (2004). *Skilled Interpersonal Communication: Research, Theory and Practice.* 4th Edition. London: Routledge.

Haskel, J. and Westlake, S. (2018). *Capitalism without Capital: The Rise of the Intangible Economy.* Princeton, NJ: Princeton University Press.

Hayek, F. (1967). The theory of complex phenomena. In Kegan, P. (Ed.) *Studies in Philosophy, Politics and Economics.* London: Routledge, 22–42.

Heller, M. (1997). Posture as an interface between biology and culture. In Segerstrale, U. and Molnar, P. (Eds.) *Nonverbal Communication: Where Nature Meets Culture.* Mahwah, NJ: Lawrence Erlbaum Associates.

Hoffman, K. D. and Bateson, J. (2006). *Essentials of Services Marketing.* 3rd Edition. New York: Thomson-South Western.

Hubbert, A. R. (1995). *Customer Co-Creation of Service Outcomes: Effects of Locus of Casuality Attributions.* Doctoral dissertation. Arizona State University. Temple, Arizona. Cited by Wilson, A., Zeithmal, V., Bitner, M. and Gremler, D. (2008). *Services Marketing: Integrating Customer Focus Across the Firm.* McGraw-Hill International, European Edition, EUA, 299–305.

Kendon, A. (1984). Some use of gestures. In Tannem, D. and Saville-Troike, M. (Eds.) *Perspectives on Silence.* New York, NY: Norwood-Ablex.

Keynes, J. (1936). *The General Theory of Employment Interest and Money.* London: Macmillan St Martin's Press.

Knapp, M. and Hall, J. (1997). *Nonverbal Communication in Human Interaction.* 4th Edition. Fort Worth: Harcour Brace College Publishers.

Lee, F. and Keen, S. (2004). The incoherent emperor: A heterodox critique of neoclassical microeconomic theory. *Review of Social Economy,* 62, 169–199.

Lenger, A. (2019). The rejection of qualitative research methods in economics. *Journal of Economic Issues,* 53(4), 946–965.

Lovelock, C. and Gummesson, E. (2004). Whither services marketing? In search of a new paradigm and fresh perspectives. *Journal of Services Research,* 7(1), 20–41.

Magueijo, J. (2003). *Faster than the Speed of Light: The Story of a Scientific Speculation*. Cambridge, MA: Perseus Books Group.

Maurer, B. (2006). The anthropology of money. *Annual Review of Anthropology*, 35, 15–36.

Meuter, M.L., Ostrom, A.L., Roundtree, R.I. and Bitner, M.J. (2000). Technologies: Understanding customer satisfaction with technology-based service encounters. *The Journal of Marketing*, 64(3), July, 50–64.

Meuter, M. and Bitner, M. J. (1998). *Self Service Technologies: Extending Service Frameworks and Identifying Issues for Research*. In Grewal, D. and Pechmann, C. (Eds.). American Marketing Association Winter Educators' Conference, 12–19.

Montepare, J., Koff, E., Zaitchik, D. and Albert, M. (1999). The use of body movements and gestures as cues to emotions in younger and older adults. *Journal of Nonverbal Behaviour*, 23, 133–152.

Morduch, J. (2017). Economics and the social meaning of money. In Bandelj, N., Werry, F. and Zelizer, V. (Eds.) *Money Talks: Explaining How Money Really Work*. Princeton, NJ: Princeton University Press.

Perinbanayagam, R. (1985). *Signifying Acts: Structure and Meaning in Everyday Life*. Carbondale: Southern Illinois University Press.

Popper, K. (2008). *The Logic of Scientific Discovery*. 12th Edition, 1st Edition, 1959. London: Routledge.

Rathmel, J. (1966). What is meant by services. *Journal of Marketing*, 30(5), 32–36.

Richmond, V. and McCroskey, J. (2000). *Nonverbal Behaviour in Interpersonal Relations*. Boston: Allyn and Bacon.

Romer, P. (1990). Endogenous technological change. *Journal of Political Economy*, 98(5), 71–102.

Scherer, K. (1979). Acoustic concomitants of emotional dimensions: Judging affect from synthesized tone sequences. In Wetiz, S. (Ed.) *Nonverbal Communication: Readings with Commentary*. New York: Oxford University Press.

Shostack, G. (1977). Breaking free from product marketing. *Journal of Marketing*, 41(2), 73–80.

Soofi, E. (1994). Capturing the intangible concept of information. *Journal of the American Statistical Association*, 89, 1243–1254.

Volmer, H., Mennicken, A. and Preda, A. (2009). Tracking the numbers: Across accounting and finance, organizations and markets. *Accounting, Organization and Society*, 34(5), 619–637.

Wigboldus, D., Spears, R. and Semin, G. (1999). Categorizing, content and the context of communicative behaviour. In Ellemers, N., Spears, R. and Doosje, B. (Eds.) *Social Identity*. Oxford: Basil-Blackwell.

Zeithmal, V., Bitner, M. and Gremler, D. (2006). *Services Marketing: Integrating Customer Focus Across the Firm*. New York: McGraw-Hill Companies.

Zeithmal, V., Parasuraman, A. and Berry, L. (1985). Problems and strategies in services marketing. *Journal of Marketing*, 49(2), 33–46.

Zelizer, V. (1994). *The Social Meaning of Money*. New York: Basic Books.

3 Monetary flows and commodities

3.1 Introduction

Throughout the last century and currently, the dominant economic view has been to treat human contributions to economic and societal production as if they were commodities, for instance, to treat workflows, service flows, knowledge flows, or communication flows as commodities when they are somehow related to monetary flows. This approach is lectured to thousands of students in economic and business schools each year and has influenced other social sciences, which frequently employ related metaphors (e.g., human capital, human assets, human resources or social capital). Curiously, last century's major alternative to mainstream economics, namely, Marxism, is also derived from a human commodity framework.

Different conceptions of market fundamentalism exist arguing that markets would solve most if not all requirements for human life and existence.[1] These conceptual endeavors are generally well served by treating human contributions to production as a form of capital, which can be metamorphosed into commodities that may be bought and sold. Such views argue for a larger influence of markets on human life, an approach that has resulted in further inequality and fewer national-state or communitarian production activities, besides hurting human communities.[2] However, it has never been demonstrated that humans and our contributions to economic and societal production are similar to commodities. We may observe therefore a pseudo-phenomenon process in which an abstraction of work is defined as a commodity as though it were the real thing, but without supporting evidence. A pseudo-phenomenon must be distinguished from the reification of a phenomenon.[3] Reification refers to describing of a human phenomenon as if it was a thing, that is, as having nonhuman or possibly suprahuman terms. Invoking a reification would be for instance to describe the treatment of us humans as commodities as a social phenomenon, which would had been misconstrued as a natural phenomenon. Intangible flow theory suggests that this treatment is instead a pseudo-phenomenon, for there is no evidence to demonstrate we humans are commodities (assets, capital or resources). For economists, labor in an organization or at home is only considered to be work if it involves some form of monetary payment (wage). Vital work for human survival and existence, such as educating children, voluntary service to the community or even preparing food, is otherwise ignored.[4] Thus, economics is not fit to theorize human relations or even work.[5]

Karl Polanyi (1886–1964) has noted that the dominant economic view is built upon a formulation based upon what he has described as three fictitious commodities, namely, humans (work), money and land (nature).[6] Correctly, Polanyi has identified three important pseudo-phenomena in economics, though he did not use this term. However, he could not explain why capitalism (monetary society) has not transformed humans, money and nature into commodities, admitting that market societies may have just done that.[7] Furthermore, we will see that Polanyi's definitions are to some extent underdeveloped. Work is not the same as humans. Through intangible flow theory, humans can be distinguished from their work and other intangible flows. Money can in some instances be a commodity and in others not be so. And nature is far broader than land. Intangible flow theory argues that economic and societal production is fundamentally based upon the biosphere and the biophysical world, which are vital for human survival and existence.

In economic sociology and related fields prevails the notion that economic phenomena are embedded in social relations. This is an important idea that has been advanced in Polanyi's work.[8] Our comprehension of social relations in production has been expanded to include the study of institutions, environment, assets, contingencies, rules, interdependency, networks and micropolitical and cognitive cultural dimensions of agency.[9] Nonetheless, we have been unable to challenge the status quo of mainstream economics.[10] On the other hand, contemporary Marxists claim to have the long-needed alternative to mainstream economics.[11] However, although Marx referred to the alienation and reification of workers in productive processes,[12] he also promoted human commodity framework explanations.

Using the intangible flow theory, we may build a valid alternative whereby humans cannot be constructed as commodities, assets, capital or resources. Contrarily to Polanyi's formulation,[13] we humans can indeed be distinguished from our work. Human-related intangible flows explain how to distinguish us humans from our intangible flows and to distinguish both humans and work-flows from commodities. Furthermore, within and outside monetary societies, human work exists regardless of an eventual association with monetary flows. To clarify that every economic phenomenon is also a social phenomenon is quite important, albeit not enough. We need to develop a persuasive explanation of mainstream economics' structural failure to capture human participation in economic and societal production. If human contributions to productive processes are not commodities, what are they? To answer this question, intangible flow theory proposes a challenging perspective that is not an end in itself. This theory does not have a totalizing view aiming at fully explaining the biosphere and human societies, for it is open to the new, the different, the event that has never been detected and/or observed before.

Furthermore, it embraces interdisciplinary contributions and dialogues with other perspectives.[14]

What kind of problems do mainstream and Marxist theories fall into when they conceptualize human participation in production on par with commodity inputs, and how does the intangible flow theory address those specific problems? Mainstream economics and Marxism's research methodologies are not technologically prepared to capture the intangible flow dynamics of economic and societal phenomena. Therefore, human-related intangible flows such as workflows, service flows, knowledge flows or communication flows become unobservable or inextricable from tangible flows as monetary or physical-good flows. Thus, the distinction between humans and commodities falls beyond reach. Therefore, a better solution cannot be attained than to describe human contributions to economic production as commodities (or assets, capital, resources) and humans as mere commodity-like production factors. Intangible flow theory can identify the intangible flow dynamics of economic and/or societal phenomena and establishes a distinction between humans and commodities. Furthermore, the new theory demonstrates how economic and societal production relies not only on social relations but also on the biosphere and physical world. Natural resources that are required for human survival and existence cannot be fully controlled by human beings. Thus, the new theory provides a foundation for research technologies capable of addressing phenomena that are mystified through the human commodity framework and the pseudo-phenomenon that monetary flows make/define commodities. Monetary flow occurrences need themselves to be explained. Moreover, the new theory may deal with human-related flows not necessarily connected to monetary flows.

3.2 Myth of a self-regulating market

Remarkably, Polanyi has also identified the self-regulating market myth: a self-functioning market would address most if not all human needs for existence and survival, to the point of a market, or interconnected markets, becoming the center of human societies.[15] Local and international societies would operate mainly by barter and exchange principles, that is, through buying and selling, as adjusted by the price mechanism.[16] Accordingly, a human society would not require other institutions to function besides the market. This claim would render as unnecessary, for instance, governments, regulations or protections for dispossessed persons and communities.

Polanyi described this view as "*the economic superstitions of the nineteenth century*"[17] because it was promoted by many economists after Adam Smith. To a large extent, this myth is still quite alive in the 21st century because it has been promoted in contemporary mainstream economics. Even when many contemporary mainstream economists observe that markets have failed and need intervention from governments, they still hold to the idea of an economy (and society) based upon self-equilibrating markets.[18] Thus, this myth has concrete effects upon national and international policies. Many contemporary governments follow mainstream economists' advisement in deregulating, removing the state from economic and societal production and expanding the market outreach.[19]

At his time, Polanyi (1944) observed what he has supposed to be consequences of such myth: great wars, economic crises, distress, revolts and revolutions. To him, the ongoing expansion of an uncontrolled market would put at risk the fabric of human communities and societies. Without basic conditions for survival and dignity, an unstable human society will be prone to unrest, for instance, by lack of food, social integration, housing, support for family existence or security. Thus, for Polanyi the self-regulating market myth comes along as a double movement. It is a utopia, which when implemented results in extreme negative consequences. Thus, human societies must find manners to protect human life and existence.

On one hand, the market can never function by itself, as alleged in the myth. The market is embedded in human society. It is the government/sovereign state that creates legislation allowing markets to operate. It is the government/ state that provides judiciary systems required to support and supervise market operations. Education of the population and many infrastructures as road and transport systems are required by markets. However, part of those activities is conducted outside market transactions.[20] Furthermore, markets exist because humans participate in them. On the other hand, the idea of allowing the market mechanism to be the "*sole director of the fate [of] human beings and their natural environment*"[21] creates harsh outcomes, for instance, the inoccupation of large parts of the population, deprivation, hunger and even diseases, or environmental disasters. Human societies need to react, because, otherwise, human life may become unbearable, thus, Polanyi's hypothesis of a second/counter movement resulting from the self-regulating market utopia.

The counter movement can have different forms. Such is the case of Roosevelt's new deal implemented in the US from 1933 to 1937, after the devastation of the post-1929 crisis.[22] Nonetheless, Polanyi has claimed that Marxist revolutions and fascist/populist power grabbing could also be rooted in a "*market society that refuses to function.*"[23] This is an issue that then "*radiate[s]to almost any field of human activity whether political or economic, cultural, philosophical, artistic, or religious.*"[24] For Polanyi, Marxism follows the same basic framework as the "*liberal creed*" framework in Adam Smith and John Stuart Mill.[25] The same applies to Marx's followers such as Lenin, who led the Soviet Revolution.[26] As for populist movements with fascist autocratic tendencies, Polanyi notes that they can have many different forms in distinct national contexts.[27] They represent a social force that remains latent for some time and then will grow again according to the "*the condition of the market system.*"[28] Making coalitions with disparate forces and promoting simple popular ideas as necessary to gain power, Polanyi sees populist fascist movements as growing when the market system is in peril. Fascist support expands with their promise of restoring law and order as to keep "*the market system going,*" even if for that purpose democracy and constitutional liberties must be sabotaged or suspended.[29]

At the last century's culmination, after the fall of the Berlin Wall and collapse of the Soviet sphere, the end of human history was being declared by Fukuyama, which might have been another manner to promote the self-regulating market myth.[30] Then, perhaps the hypothesis of a double movement could be doubted. Indeed, Callon noted in 1998 "*that the market seems triumphant everywhere.*"[31] However, history did not simply end there. Once again, we have social unrest and the rise of populist political forces in the US, Europe, Asia, Africa and Latin America. Around the globe, extreme rhetoric gains further traction with the special assistance of social media over the internet. The reformed communist state of China is in the running to be the largest and most technologically advanced economy in the world. Although this book is not focused upon Polanyi's double movement hypothesis, one cannot fail to see that this hypothesis cannot yet be abandoned. Nevertheless, Polanyi's identification of the self-regulating market myth is of great importance to our discussion.

3.3 Embeddedness

Perhaps Polanyi's most referred to concept on economic sociology is the already-mentioned embeddedness.[32] He can sometimes be relatively vague about it.[33] However, the concept in Polanyi seems not entirely identical to the version currently used in economic sociology.[34] The latter has more to do with market transactions depending on trust, mutual understanding, legal enforcement of contracts, institutions, environment, assets, contingencies, rules, interdependency, networks and micro-political and cognitive cultural dimensions of agency.[35] As explained by Block, Polanyi is interpreted as claiming that with the rise of capitalism in the 19th century, the market economy was successfully disembodied (disentangled) from the rest of the human society and came to dominate it. On the contrary, Polanyi has wished to demonstrate that a market can never be separated from the society in which it functions. Although yet partial, the former interpretation of the concept of embeddedness has promoted a relatively successful agenda in economic sociology.[36]

Granovetter (1985) reintroduced the embeddedness term, however, with non-coincidental meaning to Polanyi's. The former justifies the term's reintroduction with long debates regarding explaining human action in terms of either human agency or social structures.[37] Human agency explanations are based upon how individuals interact, formulate their identities and present themselves to others.[38] Structure-based explanations are focused on social institutions and their constraining power over individuals.[39] Previously, Giddens (1976, 1979) had suggested the need for a theory integrating both structure and agency explanations because while individual actions are shaped by social structures, systematic patterns in social structures are the result of these individual actions.[40] For Granovetter, the usual account based on human agency in economics provide an "*undersocialized*" or atomized-actor explanation of human action. On the other hand, those who attempt to bring social structures back in do so in an "*oversocialized*" manner.[41] Thus, Granovetter uses the concept of embeddedness to try integrating human agency in structures of social relations. He attempts eliminating structure–agency dichotomies, as to avoid over-/ undersocialized human action perspectives. As a result, market processes traditionally studied by economics would be amenable to sociological analysis, which could reveal central features of these processes.[42] Nevertheless, while Polanyi uses the concept of embeddedness to refute dominant economic theory, Granovetter is much less critical towards economics. Instead, Granovetter tries to assimilate economics and sociology along with market research.

As in mainstream economics, the reformed concept of embeddedness takes the market as the centerpiece of analysis.[43] The market is described as a coordinating device, where agents pursue their own self-interests either by competing or cooperating.[44] In several studies, market participants are described by expressions such as *"calculative agencies"* or *"calculative agents,"*[45] which are not very far from the economic textbook. Accordingly, an agent calculation would not be related to his *"inherent selfishness or altruism, nor is it due to the nature of the relationships in which it is engaged (a market transaction or, by contrast, love, friendship or the family)."*[46] Even disinterested human gifts could be seen as calculative when they expect return in a short time.[47] Therefore, by describing human interactions as mostly transactional and calculative, these sociological authors plainly risk assisting mainstream economists in expanding market mythologies.

Many studies in network analysis follow this lead when explaining markets. They try to combine human agency and social structures alongside a market network background, where calculative agencies take care of their self-interests. Actors and networks are tentatively defined as the same, both agency and structure.[48] Operations are framed to be from the market in order to enable calculative technologies. Therefore, they would be disentangled from the rest of society.[49] Economists contribute to disentangle markets from the rest of society with concepts, devices and calculative technologies. That is, instead of being simple observers, economists are *performing* the market because their work has impact upon market operations.[50] Nonetheless, market activities cannot be completely disentangled, for they generate externalities or *"overflowing"* from the frame of the market.[51] Clearly, however, the market as the center of human activity is not questioned in a broad section of contemporary economic sociology. As in economics, the market is somehow the explanation for economic and societal production.

On the contrary, Polanyi uses the expression embeddedness in trying to refute, or at least reveal, mainstream economics. For him, the concept cannot be separated from the self-regulating market myth. Polanyi implies that the economy is not autonomous from the rest of society, as suggested by economic theory. The economy must be subordinated to several societal components and institutions such as politics, religion, the state or social relations.[52]

Although our knowledge about institutions has advanced, important debates remain about their change and stability and on whether they result from the agency of human beings or the societal structure or both.[53] Still, for Polanyi, economists are not just performing markets in the sense offered by constructivists, postmodernists and poststructuralists, that is, formatting calculative agencies by providing required calculative tools or by framing what can be entangled in the market.[54] Economists explain market operations through a description based upon three fictitious commodities, namely work, money and land, which are treated as actual commodities. However, markets cannot be separated from societies. Although this conception of fictitious commodities (hence, pseudo-phenomena) is quintessential for Polanyi's argument, many contemporary debates about embeddedness tend to avoid these important themes.[55]

3.4 That monetary flows do not make or define commodities

Polanyi intended to demonstrate that a separation of the economy from other societal spheres can only be artificial. It would be based on reducing to buying and selling several elements that are not actual commodities.[56] No doubt societies must have a system of some kind to ensure production and distribution of elements necessary for human life and existence. However, in previous tribal, feudal and mercantile societies, the *"economic order is a function of the social order."*[57] The same ought to happen in a market economy, which can only exist in a society based upon markets.[58]

For Polanyi, a commodity is something that has been produced for sale in a market.[59] Work, money and land are fictitious commodities because they have not been produced for sale:

> Labor is only another name for human activity which goes with life itself, which in its turn is not produced for sale but for entirely different reasons, nor can that activity be detached from the rest of life, be stored or mobilized; land is only another name for nature, which is not produced by man; actual money, finally, is merely a token of purchasing power which, as a rule, is not produced at all, but comes into being through the mechanism of banking or state finance. None of them is produced for sale. The commodity description of labor, land and money is entirely fictitious.[60]

However, Polanyi notes that work, money and land are crucial components of economic systems. Moreover, work, money and land are organized as markets in a market society because they seem to be bought and sold.[61] Thus, the commodity fiction would provide the organizing principle bearing on human institutions on which market society rests.

The market myth implementation leads to extreme aftereffects. Humans as commodities detached from their physical, psychological and moral dimensions, and cultural institutions could be entrapped by vice, perversion, crime and starvation. Nature can be destroyed in the voracity for food, raw materials and profits. And the market administration of purchasing power would periodically liquidate organizations for shortages and surfeits of money as floods and droughts would create mayhem in primitive societies. Although work, land and money are essential for a market economy, no human society could resist if they were simply let be according to the rules of a market economy. Some form of societal protections, safeties and guarantees must be in place to protect society from extreme consequences of markets.[62]

However, Polanyi has no alternative as to imply that markets and economic theory have somehow transformed work, land and money into commodities. Even if they might be artificial commodities, they still pertain some commodity outline because they appear to be bought and sold in actual markets. Taking great lengths in his work, Polanyi tries to determine the specific point where economists have contributed with their theories, proposals and writings to create a market for work.[63] He goes into less detail regarding land and money, but a similar reasoning would apply. According to him, the creation of a market for work occurred when classical economic thinkers such as Jeremy Bentham, John Stuart Mill, David Ricardo and Thomas Malthus campaigned to abolish poor laws in England, which forced parishes to provide outdoor relief to poor members of the population.

The Spenhamland Law (or Berkshire Bread Act) was implemented in 1795 as an amendment to the Poor Relief Act implemented in 1601. It came in the tradition of the better-off in society taking responsibility for the poor and dissolute citizens. It resulted from England's war with France. It should have compensated the poor for price increases in bread and other essential goods. Polanyi and Canning claim that this act may have prevented England from a revolution in the spirit of the French Revolution.[64] Naturally, historical phenomena are complex and have many intricate causes. One must be careful with providing simple explanations to complex historical events. Furthermore, societal transformation can also be implemented gradually. Britain observed great transformations in the 19th century. The political system in England was not comparable to the French system at the dawn of the revolution. In the previous centuries, England also had episodes of violent revolts.

However, at an active period of the Industrial Revolution, this amendment to the Poor Relief Act appeared to be inhibiting the creation of a labor market in England.[65] After the economists' campaign, the Spenhamland Act was abolished in 1834 in an abrupt manner.[66] At that point, those who were able-bodied and wealthless must fit some form of paid work to survive and/or provide for their families. Hence, according to Polanyi: *"whatever the future had in store for them, working-class and market economy, appeared in history together."*[67]

> The traditional unity of a Christian society was giving place to a denial of responsibility on the part of the well-to-do for the condition of their fellows. The Two Nations were taking shape. . . . The mechanism of the market was asserting itself and clamouring for its completion: human labor has to be made a commodity."[68]

Therefore, for lack of alternative or concession, Polanyi still raises the possibility that at some point in the 19th century, work was transformed into a commodity by economists, governments, regulations, investors and other forces. The same applies to nature and money. One can argue that this view has indeed some resemblance to those who currently use the concept of embeddedness after Granovetter,[69] such as those economic sociologists who discuss markets where calculative agencies participate or those who claim that economists could perform, frame, entangle and disentangle markets and their operations. The reasoning is so far that in pragmatic terms, calculation of wage payments transforms work into a commodity.[70] Commodities are still defined in terms of potential monetary flows as in mainstream economics' market framework.[71]

However, economists and sociologists are in many cases simple observers to economic and societal production. Money might flow in markets. However, there are also flows of elements assuring human life and existence without entailing monetary flows, for example, flows of food, constructions, services, communication, shelter, transportation or appliances, which happen much before or after monetary flows take place or even without relation to any cash flow. Polanyi has identified an important problem in economic theory. Yet, he did not formulate the possible solution currently attempted by intangible flow theory.

Polanyi has noted Adam Smith's fallacy of primitive societies being simply based upon barter and exchange of one thing for another.[72] Hence, primitive societies were also some sort of market societies, as if a self-regulating market would be at the center of human societies since the dawn of time.[73] Polanyi's position came to form the substantive position, which opposes the formalist and economists' position that human society must have always had the form of a market society.[74] Although some exchange may have existed since long ago, primitive barter may have been related to very particular goods that did not exist in specific communities, thus compelling interactions with other human communities. Polanyi identifies other forms of providing for the necessities of life, which were present in ancient human societies. One way or another, they still exist. These forms are reciprocity, redistribution and householding. In reciprocity, humans act in a pattern of symmetry, giving and receiving things, dividing work as necessary. In redistribution, a hierarchical system such as a kingdom, an empire, a ruler, or a hierarchical structure decide on the provisions of life and existence, as well on the division of labor. In some cases, to obtain resources that are vital for survival, hierarchical systems may entail aggressive conflicts against other human communities. In householding, forms of reciprocity and redistribution operate in a family/domestic context.[75] Indeed, this classification can strike us as simplistic. Nonetheless, it comes in a tradition of classifying large chunks of human history into ad-hoc stages.

Though, let us not lose sight of Polanyi's proposition that human societies need not be based upon barter. Polanyi saw Smith's proposition that human societies have always been utopian market societies as a form of market determinism.[76] However, Polanyi did not completely grasp the impact of the barter metaphor. In his own reasoning, therefore, he has adopted some components of economists' market myth. A case in point is when commodities are defined in terms of buying and selling, hence, in terms of being exchanged by money in a potential market. Although a reference to banking and state finance is made, he unfortunately takes on board economists' perspective that money in a market becomes as a commodity that could be exchanged by other commodities. Hence, Polanyi cannot explain why economists and markets have not actually transformed human work into commodities, why money can be a commodity in some cases and not in others, or why commodity production is utterly dependent upon natural resources and the biophysical world.

Another important fallacy in economics (and interconnected social sciences) is the pseudo-phenomenon that the monetary flow makes or defines the commodity, that is, the misrepresentation that the occurrence of a monetary flow implies the transaction of a commodity. When Polanyi defines a commodity as something that has been produced for sale in a market, he still associates the commodity with the occurrence of a monetary flow (the sale) in a market. Without noticing, Polanyi has also taken on board this peculiar assumption from mainstream economics (and Marxism). The purpose of the commodity in Polanyi still is to be lent or sold, hired or purchased.[77] Hence, without being clear about it, Polanyi has still allowed economists to provide the framework of the market. How do monetary flows flow, and to where? How are flows of products produced and delivered? These questions must not be taken for granted.

3.5 The market as a micro moment: Tangible flows of money and physical goods not to be taken for granted

Intangible flow theory rejects the pseudo-phenomenon whereby monetary flows would make and/or define commodities. Monetary flows are phenomena that need themselves to be explained. Money can flow for a myriad of reasons, which do not necessarily imply commodity flows. For instance, cash can be a gift or be used to create an intangible flow or repay a debt. Likewise, a commodity can flow without the need for a monetary flow. A young mother can go to a supermarket to buy fruit and bread, where she transfers monetary means to the supermarket. However, when she arrives home with the food, the fruit and bread no longer need to be associated with further monetary flows to be eaten by her family members. Likewise, if she takes her family to see a show at the festival, she may pay some money to obtain tickets, but the perishable show they will see is not a commodity.

Economics supposes that nonphysical elements are commodities when somehow peripherally linked to monetary flows. However, these suppositions have never been demonstrated. For empirical precision in intangible flow theory, the concept of commodity is restricted to a clearly identifiable physical good, which can have different states of matter (e.g., solid, liquid, gas or plasma) if precisely identifiable. Moreover, as described further later, in intangible flow theory human beings cannot be considered commodities (assets, capital or resources). For example, knowledge that cannot be separated from a human being and is not converted into a physical good cannot be considered a commodity.[78] Flows of commodities do not necessarily imply flow of money, and flow of money does not necessarily imply commodity flows. Commodities must be defined in relation to human survival and existence, not in relation to eventual markets. Flows of commodities and money are phenomena that cannot be taken for granted, as in the market myth. Distinguishing humans from commodities, we can see that seldom has a commodity generated monetary flows by itself without human intervention. Even robots making payments and trades are somehow related to human beings. In rare occasions such as natural disasters, monetary flows can occur without human intervention (for instance, money in a safe). However, most rarely money flows without any human intervention.

When Polanyi defines work as human activity, he equates work as both human beings and workflows. Therefore, one can understand his trouble in explaining why economists have not transformed us human beings into commodities. He can observe correctly that human work has been associated with monetary flows. Moreover, he is also correct that many humans require those monetary wages to survive and exist in monetary societies. However, Polanyi has not yet observed the concept of intangible flow, which distinguishes us human beings from our intangible activities. Although our intangible flows might be necessary for the occurrence of flows of money and commodities, our intangible flows are not commodities. The new theory takes this argument further by claiming that no evidence demonstrates that we human beings are commodities, assets, capital or resources in economic and societal production, a problem not addressed in Polanyi's important work.[79]

Fixation with the moment of the monetary flow and less attention to flows necessary for human life and existence led Polanyi to a yet undeveloped understanding of the role of nature and the biosphere in economic and societal production. He simply defines land as *"only another name for nature, which is not produced by man."*[80] However, when one defines commodities in terms of physical goods instead of monetary flows, he must observe that most if not all commodities are reliant upon natural resources and the biophysical world. Even the production of intangible flows from one human being to another (for example, a lecture or storytelling) requires elements obtained in nature. Both human beings need food, water, energy, shelter, and so forth to survive and exist.

Indeed, human beings require the biosphere to survive and exist. Therefore, market societies have an ecological embeddedness.[81] Polanyi is correct that most of nature is not produced by man. Man (and woman) sometimes deludes himself (herself) that he (she) can completely control natural forces. However, physical goods need not be produced by human beings to have critical relevance for human survival and existence. Polanyi does not yet observe that by eliminating the pseudo-phenomenon that the monetary flows make/define commodities, and by separating us humans from commodities, economic and societal production results as highly reliant upon the biosphere. Commodity flows required for human survival and existence would not be possible without natural resources and the biophysical world. A central thesis in the new theory is that economic and societal production is vitally reliant upon nature, natural resources and the biophysical world.

As for the pseudo-phenomenon that money would be a commodity, Polanyi is appropriate in identifying that in economics after Adam Smith money is considered as a commodity. However, Polanyi does not go as far as he could in trying to understand why. Moreover, in some cases money can be a commodity. Coins and notes have a physical-good form. In Part 3, we will further explain better why money is considered a commodity in economics. Adam Smith has used the ancient Greek philosopher Aristoteles's (384–322 BC) concept of money, in whose time physical coins where a relatively recent technology. Coins have the form of physical goods. They have replaced other commodities used as money, for instance, metal ingots of gold or silver, food or arrows.

Aristoteles could not envisage monetary forms we find somehow banal, such as paper money, digital money, bank accounts, credit cards, mobile phones or cryptocurrencies. Likewise, the concept of fiat (fiduciary) money was not known to him. Fiat money is a currency without intrinsic value, which has been established as money, often by government or sovereign regulations. As noted by Polanyi, contemporary money requires the mechanism of banking and state finance. The currencies of many countries have a fiat money configuration. Smith has observed fiat money but decided to go along with Aristoteles's commodity theory of money. It is from there that the barter theory of societies arises. Money is not just considered a commodity, but somehow the perfect commodity for trading purposes, the commodity that can be traded/exchanged by any other commodity and the commodity that attributes value to the other commodities. This pseudo-phenomenon that the money commodity would make/define commodities appears both in mainstream economics and Marxism.

We can observe some tangible and intangible features of money. Indeed, notes and coins have properties of physical goods (thus, commodities), as gold and silver are commodities. However, digital money, bank accounts or credit card transactions do not have those properties.[82] Yet, the previous chapter has explained that although value tends to be intangible because it cannot be identified with precision, monetary flows occurring in a precise space and time are highly tangible. That is, although money might be a social construction, flows of money are highly tangible.[83]

Yet, tangibility of money flows does not transform them into commodities. Money is not the perfect commodity for exchange claimed in economics, but instead a powerful social technology developed by us human beings. By rejecting the fallacy that the monetary flow creates/defines the commodity, and by observing that economic and societal production is fundamentally dependent upon nature and the biophysical world, intangible flow theory may offer a better understanding of the tangible flows of commodities (physical goods) and money.

Notes

1 And of neoliberalism (Flew, 2014).
2 Smart (2003), Harvey (2007), Sandel (2012), Desan (2014), Piketty (2014).

3 We can find in Berger and Luckman (1966, p. 106) or Marx and Engels (Marx and Engels, 1846, 1970; Marx, 1990).

4 In the widely popular observation, if a man marries his housekeeper or his cook, then the gross national product is diminished (Pigou, 1932).

5 Abbott (2014).

6 Polanyi (1944, 2001), Block and Somers (2014), Bockman (2014), Cahill (2014), Dale (2011), Fraser (2014).

7 Idem.

8 Granovetter (1985), Callon (1998a, 1998b), Dale (2011).

9 Ingham (1996), Manning (2008), Heidenreich (2012).

10 Krippner (2002, 2011), Krippner and Alvarez (2007), Crouch (2011), Spicer (2012), Lafferty (2013).

11 Braverman (1998), Fleetwood (2001), Bryer (2006), Adler (2009), Marens (2009), Thompson and Smith (2009), Hudson (2011), Beilharz (2012), Marzec (2013), Buzgalin and Kolganov (2015).

12 See Meszaros (2005), Brook (2009).

13 Polanyi (1944, 2001), Block and Somers (2014), Bockman (2014), Cahill (2014), Dale (2011), Fraser (2014).

14 For reasons of space, this book focuses on comparing the conception of intangible flow theory to those of mainstream economics and Marxism. Other theoretical frameworks should be addressed elsewhere in more detail. Furthermore, although making connections to the treatment of money and nature as commodities, this book will be focused on studying the human commodity framework.

15 Polanyi (1944, 2001).

16 Polanyi (1944, 2001), Block (2001)

17 Polanyi (1944, 2001, p. 59).

18 Block (2001, p. xxiii).

19 Block and Somers (2014), Bockman (2014).

20 See also Mazzucato (2018).

21 Polanyi (1944, 2001, p. 76).

22 More than 3,000 banks went bankrupt and unemployment and deprivation run havoc in the US (Reinhart and Rogoff, 2009; Michie, 2006). The American government decided to limit the extent to which markets would serve the basis of human societies. The American currency was removed from the gold standard. Supervision, restrictive regulations and programs of public constructions and activities were implemented to provide means of survival and occupation to a large portion of the population.

23 Polanyi (1944, 2001, p. 248).

24 Idem.

25 Polanyi (1944, 2001, pp. 26, 88, 131, Chapter 13).

26 Polanyi (1944, 2001, pp. 24, 26).

27 Polanyi (1944, 2001, pp. 244–247).

28 Polanyi (1944, 2001, p. 250).

29 Polanyi (1944, 2001, p. 247).

30 Fukuyama (1992).

31 Callon (1998b, p. 1).

32 Polanyi (1944, 2001, pp. 24, 26).

33 Block (2003).

34 Block (2001, pp. xxiv, xxv).

35 Block (2001, pp. xxiv, xxv), Ingham (1996), Manning (2008), Heidenreich (2012).

36 Block (2001, 2003). At least in terms of the number of papers published.

37 Giddens (1976, 1979), Granovetter (1985), Scott (2006).

38 Idem.

39 Giddens (1976, 1979), Scott (2006).

40 See also Scott (2006, pp. 131–132)

41 Granovetter (1985, pp. 481, 483–484), Dennis (1961).

42 Granovetter (1985, p. 505)
43 Caliskan and Callon (2009, 2010), Granovetter (1985).
44 Caliskan and Callon (2009, 2010), Callon (1998a and b, pp. 3–4), Guesnerie (1996), Hawkins (2011), McFall (2009), Muniesa, Millo, and Callon (2007).
45 Idem.
46 Callon (1998b, p. 15).
47 Callon (1998b, pp. 12–17), Bourdieu (1997).
48 Callon (1999), Latour (2005), Law (2008).
49 Thomas (1991), Callon (1998a, 1998b). As explained by Callon (1998b, p. 17): "Framing is an operation used to define agents (an individual person or a group of persons) who are clearly distinct and dissociated from one another. It also allows for the definition of objects, goods and merchandise which are perfectly identifiable and can be separated not only from other goods, but also from the actors involved, for example in their conception, production, circulation or use. It is owing to this framing that the market can exist and that distinct agents and distinct goods can be brought into play. Without this framing the states of the world can not be described and listed and, consequently, the effects of the different conceivable actions can not be anticipated."
50 You can find more about the concept of performativity or performation in economics at Callon (1998b, pp. 23–32), Cochoy, Giraudeau, and McFall (2010), Esposito (2013), MacKenzie (2006), Maki (2013).
51 Callon (1998a, 1998b).
52 Block (2001, p. xxiv).
53 See Bouilloud et al. (2019).
54 Callon (1998b).
55 With notable exceptions as Block (2001, 2003), Block and Somers (2014).
56 Polanyi (1944, 2001, pp. 74–76).
57 Idem.
58 Idem.
59 Block (2001, 2003), Idem.
60 Polanyi (1944, 2001, pp. 75–76). Note also that this conception is very different from the concept of commodity fetishism in Marxism, which only distinguishes commodities' use value from exchange values, while accepting the concept of labor as a commodity. You may also see Keen (1993). We will return to this theme.
61 Polanyi (1944, 2001, pp. 75–76).
62 Idem.
63 Polanyi (1944, 2001, Chapters 7–10).
64 Polanyi (1944, 2001, p. 97).
65 Polanyi (1944, 2001, p. 81).
66 Polanyi (1944, 2001, Chapters 7–10).
67 Polanyi (1944, 2001, p. 105). In a strict sense, this is not entirely correct. Labor unions were authorized by the repel of the Combinations Law in 1824, which is before the repeal of the Poor Law in 1834 (Backhouse, 2002).
68 Polanyi (1944, 2001, pp. 106–107).
69 For instance, Callon (1998a and b) agrees that economists have created a market for labor.
70 Callon (1998b, p. 2), for instance, agrees with the idea that economists have established a labor market.
71 As Polanyi, Callon (1998b, p. 19) and Thomas (1991) define a commodity in relation to a potential monetary flow: "Commodities are here understood as objects, persons, or elements of persons which are placed in a context in which they have exchange value and can be alienated. The alienation of a thing is its dissociation from producers, former users, or prior context."
72 Smith (1977 [1776]).

73 You may also see Polanyi, Arensberg, and Pearson (1957).
74 Granovetter (1985), Jongman (2013).
75 Polanyi (1944, 2001, Chapter 4).
76 Polanyi (1947), Thomasberger (2012).
77 To use Senior's (1854) formula in his definition for (exchange) value.
78 When Burawoy (2015) claims that knowledge is a fictitious commodity, he is simply following Polanyi's reasoning.
79 Perhaps if Polanyi had presented a conclusive argument to explain why we humans are not commodities, the problem of we humans being considered as assets, capital or resources would never exist. However, in the last decades there has been a proliferation of texts in the social sciences (not just economics), considering us human beings as commodities, assets, capital or resources.
80 Polanyi (1944, 2001, pp. 75–76).
81 Whiteman and Cooper (2000).
82 They still require a physical infrastructure to be accomplished, however.
83 If registered.

References

Abbott, K. (2014). Why labour economics is inadequate for theorizing industrial relations. *Journal of Interdisciplinary Economics*, 26(1–2), January and July, 61–90.

Adler, P. (2009). Marx and organization studies today. In Adler, P. (Ed.) *The Oxford Handbook of Sociology and Organization Studies: Classical Foundations*. Oxford: Oxford University Press.

Backhouse, R. (2002). *The Penguin History of Economics*. London: Penguin.

Beilharz, P. (2012). Labour's utopias revisited. *Thesis Eleven*, 110(1), 46–53.

Berger, P. and Luckman, T. (1966). *The Social Construction of Reality*. London: Penguin.

Block, F. (2001, 1944). Introduction. In Polanyi, K. (Ed.) *The Great Transformation: The Political and Economic Origins of Our Time*. Boston: Beacon Press.

Block, F. (2003). Karl Polanyi and the writing of the great transformation. *Theory and Society*, 32(3), 275–306.

Block, F. and Somers, M. (2014). *The Power of Market Fundamentalism: Karl Polanyi's Critique*. Cambridge, MA: Harvard University Press.

Bockman, J. (2014). The power of market fundamentalism: Karl Polanyi's critique. *Thesis Eleven*, 125(1), 157–161.

Bouilloud, J. P., Pérezts, M., Viale, T. and Schaepelynck, V. (2019). Beyond the stable image of institutions: Using institutional analysis to tackle classic questions in institutional theory. *Organization Studies*. doi:10.1177/0170840618815519.

Bourdieu, P. (1997). *Meditations Pascaliennes*. Paris: Le Seuil.

Braverman, H. (1998). *Labor and Monopoly Capital: The Degradation of Work in the Twentieth Century*. New York, NY: Monthly Review Press.

Brook, P. (2009). The alienated heart: Hochschild's emotional labour thesis and the anti-capitalist politics of alienation. *Capital and Class*, 33(2), 7–31.

Bryer, R. (2006). Accounting and control of the labour process. *Critical Perspectives on Accounting*, 17(5), 551–598.

Burawoy, M. (2015). Facing an unequal world. *Current Sociology*, 63(1), 5–34.

Buzgalin, A. and Kolganov, A. (2015). Critical political economy: The 'market-centric' model of economic theory must remain in the past – Notes of the post-soviet school of critical Marxism. *Cambridge Journal of Economics*. doi:10.1093/cje/beu080.

Cahill, D. (2014). The power of market fundamentalism: Karl Polanyi's critique. *Thesis Eleven*, 125(1), 152–157.

Caliskan, K. and Callon, M. (2009). Economization, part 1: Shifting attention from the economy towards processes of economization. *Economy and Society*, 38(3), 369–398.

Caliskan, K. and Callon, M. (2010). Economization, part 2: A research programme for the study of markets. *Economy and Society*, 39(1), 1–32.

Callon, M. (1998a). The embeddedness of economic markets in economics. In Callon, M. (Ed.) *The Laws of Markets*. London: Wiley-Blackwell, 1–57.

Callon, M. (1998b). Introduction: The embeddedness of economic markets in economics. *The Sociological Review*, 46(1 suppl), 1–57.

Callon, M. (1999). Actor-network theory – The market test. *The Sociological Review*, 47(S1), 181–195.

Cochoy, F., Giraudeau, M. and McFall, L. (2010). Performativity, economics and politics: An overview. *Journal of Cultural Economy*, 3(2), 139–146.

Crouch, C. (2011). *The Strange Non-Death of Neoliberalism*. Cambridge: Polity Press.

Dale, D. (2011). Social democracy, embeddedness and decommodification: On the conceptual innovations and intellectual affiliations of Karl Polanyi. *New Political Economy*, 15(3), 369–393.

Dennis, W. (1961). The oversocialized conception of man in modern sociology. *American Sociological Review*, 26(2), 183–193.

Desan, M. (2014). Bankrupted Detroit. *Thesis Eleven*, 121(1), 122–130.

Esposito, E. (2013). The structures of uncertainty: Performativity and unpredictability in economic operations. *Economy and Society*, 42(1), 102–129.

Fleetwood, S. (2001). What kind of theory is Marxist labour theory of value? A critical realist inquiry. *Capital and Class*, 25(1), 41–77.

Flew, T. (2014). Six theories of neoliberalism. *Thesis Eleven*, 122(1), 49–71.

Fraser, N. (2014). Can society be commodities all the way down? Post-Polanyian reflections on capitalist crisis. *Economy and Society*, 43(4), 541–558.

Fukuyama, F. (1992). *The end of History and the Last Man*. London: Penguin.

Giddens, A. (1976). *New Rules of Sociological Method*. London: Hutchinson.

Giddens, A. (1979). *Central Problems in Social Theory*. London: Macmillan.

Granovetter, M. (1985). Economic action and social structure: The problem of embeddedness. *American Journal of Sociology*, 91(3), 481–510.

Guesnerie, R. (1996). *L'économie de marché*. Dominos, Paris: Flammarion.

Harvey, D. (2007). *A Brief History of Neoliberalism*. Oxford: Oxford University Press.

Hawkins, G. (2011). Packaging water: Plastic bottles as market and public devices. *Economy and Society*, 40(4), 534–552.

Heidenreich, M. (2012). The social embeddedness of multinational companies: A literature review. *Socio-Economic Review*, 10(3), 549–579.

Hudson, R. (2011). Critical political economy and material transformation. *New Political Economy*, 17(4), 373–397.

Ingham, G. (1996). The new economic sociology. *Work Employment and Society*, 10(3), 549–564.

Jongman, W. (2013). Formalism-substantivism debate. In *The Encyclopedia of Ancient History*. Wiley Online Library.

Keen, S. (1993). Use-value, exchange value, and the demise of Marx's labor theory of value. *Journal of the History of Economic Thought*, 15(1), 107–121.

Krippner, G. (2002). The elusive market: Embeddedness and the paradigm of economic sociology. *Theory and Society*, 30(6), 775–810.

Krippner, G. (2011). *Capitalizing on Crisis: The Political Origins of the Rise of Finance*. Cambridge, MA: Harvard University Press.

Krippner, G. and Alvarez, A. (2007). Embeddedness and the intellectual projects of economic sociology. *Annual Review of Sociology*, 33, 219–240.

Lafferty, G. (2013). Book review essay: Dominance by default: Neoliberalism's continuing ascendancy. *Work Employment and Society*, 27(1), 178–185.

Latour, B. (2005). *Reassembling the Social: An Introduction to Actor-Network-Theory*. Oxford: Oxford University Press.

Law, J. (2008). Actor network theory and material semiotics. In *The New Blackwell Companion to Social Theory*. Hoboken, NJ: Blackwell Publishing, 141–158.

MacKenzie, D. (2006). Is economics performative? Option theory and the construction of derivatives markets. *Journal of The History of Economic Thought*, 28(1), 29–55.

Maki, U. (2013). Performativity: Saving Austin from MacKenzie. In *EPSA11 Perspectives and Foundational Problems in Philosophy of Science*. Cham: Springer, 443–453.

Manning, S. (2008). Embedding projects in multiple contexts – A structuration perspective. *International Journal of Project Management*, 26(1), 30–37.

Marens, R. (2009). Its not just for communists any more. In Adler, P. (Ed.) *The Oxford Handbook of Sociology and Organization Studies: Classical Foundations*. Oxford: Oxford University Press.

Marx, K. (1990). *O Capital-Livro 1-Tomo1*. Lisbon: Edições Pogresso/Avante.

Marx, K. and Frederick, E. (1846, 1970). *The German Ideology*. New York: International Publishers.

Marzec, W. (2013). Reading polish peripheral Marxism politically. *Thesis Eleven*, 117(1), 6–19.

Mazzucato, M. (2018). *The Entrepreneurial State: Debunking Public vs. Private Sector Myths*. London: Penguin.

McFall, L. (2009). Devices and desires: How useful is the 'new' new economic sociology for understanding market attachment? *Sociology Compass*, 3(2), 267–282.

Meszaros, I. (2005). *Marx's Theory of Alienation*. London: Merlin.

Michie, R. (2006). *The Global Securities Markets: A History*. Oxford: Oxford University Press.

Muniesa, F., Millo, Y. and Callon, M. (2007). An introduction to market devices. *The Sociological Review*, 55(2_suppl), 1–12.

Pigou, A. (1932). *The Economics of Welfare*. London: Macmillan.

Piketty, T. (2014). *Capital in the Twenty-First Century*. Cambridge, MA: Belknap Press.

Polanyi, K. (1944, 2001). *The Great Transformation: The Political and Economic Origins of Our Time*. Boston: Beacon Press.

Polanyi, K. (1947). On belief in economic determinism. *The Sociological Review*, 39(1), 96–102.

Polanyi, K., Arensberg, C. and Pearson, H. (1957). *Trade and Market in the Early Empires*. New York: Free Press.

Reinhart, C. and Rogoff, K. (2009). *This Time is Different: Eight Centuries of Financial Folly*. Princeton, NJ: Princeton University Press.

Sandel, M. J. (2012). *What Money Can't Buy: The Moral Limits of Markets*. London: Macmillan.

Senior, N. (1854). *Political Economy*. 3rd Edition. London: Richard Griffin and Co. Online at: https://oll.libertyfund.org/titles/senior-political-economy-1850-ed.

Smith, A. (1977, 1776). *An Inquiry into the Nature and Causes of the Wealth of Nations*. Chicago: University of Chicago Press.

Smart, B. (2003). *Economy, Culture and Society: A Sociological Critique of Neo-Liberalism* Buckingham: Open University Press.

Scott, J. (2006). *Social Theory: Central Issues in Sociology*. London: Sage.

Spicer, A. (2012). Book review: The strange non-death of neoliberalism. *Organization Studies*, 33(9), 1257–1259.

Thomas, N. (1991). *Entangled Objects: Exchange, Material Culture and Colonialism in the Pacific*. Cambridge, MA: Harvard University Press.

Thomasberger, C. (2012). The belief in economic determinism, neoliberalism, and the significance of Polanyi's contribution in the twenty-first century. *International Journal of Political Economy*, 41(4), 16–33.

Thompson, P. and Smith, C. (2009). Labour power and labour process: Contesting the marginality of the sociology of work. *Sociology*, 43(5), 913–930.

Whiteman, G. and Cooper, W. H. (2000). Ecological embeddedness. *Academy of Management Journal*, 43(6), 1265–1282.

4 New scientific law

We humans are not commodities, assets, capital or resources

4.1 Human participation in production according to the intangible flow theory

The new theory's intangibility concept is not linked to the sense of touch, but to precision. The paradox (or aporia) of attempting to measure intangibility is that intangibility cannot be precisely measured. At best, intangible dimensions can be transformed into measurable tangible elements when humans find quantitative methods to assign an actual or approximate value to them. The unmeasurable elements remain intangible.

Concerned with distinguishing tangible from intangible flows in economic and societal production, the intangible flow theory avoids the post–Adam Smith concept of capital that we will study with greater detail later. Intangible flow theory defines capital as money investable or invested in human organization. Money is not transformed into other forms of capital. For instance, money that is used to buy a machine or pay a salary is not transformed into physical capital, human capital or labor power. In fact, money expended in a precise moment in time can be measured with precision, instead of being lost in a self-vanquishing intangible concept of capital.

In mainstream economics, Marxism and Polanyi's work, the existence of commodities is the main explanation for why monetary flows occur. That is, when a monetary flow occurs, a commodity, which could encompass any element, has been traded. However, no evidence shows that we human beings are akin to commodities, assets, resources or capital in economic and societal production. These are mere pseudo-phenomena that the new theory intends to eliminate. Likewise, to consider human emotions, services, conversations and knowledge flows as commodities,[1] even if they have some influence on the occurrence of cash flows, entails further pseudo-phenomena.

The occurrence of a cash flow can be a very complex phenomenon. It may be associated with many tangible and intangible flows, which might display substantial time lags (corollary 2 and 3). Some of these intangible flows can be very difficult to identify; however, that difficulty is not a motive for not scientifically systematizing and considering the intangible flow concept (corollary 1). A monetary flow does not necessarily imply transaction of a commodity. Human contributions to production that cannot be captured with precision can be considered as intangible flows but not as commodities. Intangible flows can be very complex and are not restricted to workflows. We, as humans, may participate in the generation of economic revenues through dynamic intangible contributions that we provide to production processes. Human work might be necessary to consummate and transform dynamic flows of raw materials, physical goods and monetary flows, but it must not be construed as a commodity. Intangible flows have several characteristics preventing them from being considered as assets, capital or resources.

For example, when a human job is replaced by a machine, both mainstream and Marxist economics describe this event as the human commodity (i.e., human being or his/her labor power) being replaced by another commodity (i.e., a machine) to increase the future cash flows or surplus value that owners/shareholders could capture. In the intangible flow theory, commodities must be defined in relation to human users or, more broadly, to humankind. Thus, when humankind produces high-precision machines capable of performing tasks that previously could only be performed by humans (e.g., robots capable of producing cars, artificial intelligence capable of hearing complaints), the intangible flow theory explains this phenomenon by stating that humans have transformed previously intangible flows into tangible tasks that can be performed with precision by robots/machines. The production process undergoes "tangibilization," which does not necessarily imply an end to organizations, industries and operating product flows, but rather a change in production methods. An intangible flow is not the opposite of a tangible flow, to which one could simply apply the dialectic formula of thesis-antithesis-synthesis.[2] Intangible flows will remain intangible only until we humans can figure out ways to identify them with precision. However, we do not always know why intangible flows are intangible; otherwise we would in many cases be capable of identifying them with precision in a specific time and space.

4.2 Defining human being in the intangible flow theory

Until this point, a key concept has not been presented, explicitly, what are human beings to whom intangible flows are related, indeed quite a relevant problem. On one hand, an alternative is intended for the human commodity framework followed in economics. On the other hand, it is necessary to tackle relativistic constructivist, postmodernist and poststructuralist stances claiming that we could not reach precise definitions for us human beings or humankind (or any definition at all for that matter). Explanations would be relative and could only be formed in relation to local validity systems as paradigms, epistemes or systems of truth. This relativist attitude implicitly supports dominant explanations (as the human commodity framework in economics), for although it does not work to build feasible alternatives, it works to sabotage attempts to build alternative explanations.

The new theory requires a precisely demonstrable (thus, tangible) concept. Indeed, a human being is verifiable in intangible flow theory through the same burden of proof that would be required in a law courtroom prepared to test evidence. For the new theory, a human being is a living homo sapiens who is recognizable through his/her human deoxyribonucleic acid (DNA).[3] Contemporary equipment is advanced to the point of being capable to trace every human being's specific DNA with a high degree of confidence. In a tribunal, this technology can be used to solve legal conflicts (for instance, paternity tests or forensic evidence). It can also be employed in the social sciences. Unambiguously, human beings are quite tangible. The definition of human beings as homo sapiens allows integrating such different disciplines studying this subject matter as history, sociology, anthropology, philosophy, biology or others. Hence, this definition allows questioning the contemporary strange state of affairs where economics presents itself as an isolated and at the same time dominant discipline. Furthermore, this definition can be used to contest relativism claims that we cannot define a human being or humankind. This definition of the human is neither geography-centric nor culture-centric. It is not done in binary opposition, where the human need to be defined in relation to what is not human (opposite). It encompasses all beings that are described by this definition. However, it asserts no privilege of human beings towards other living beings. This definition integrates human beings in the biosphere, while it allows to precisely identify them (us).

Human beings comprise complex inner systems such as digestive systems, cardiovascular systems, brain cells, feelings and consciousness (besides interactions with our microbiome). Nonetheless, elements that can be distinguishable from human beings, for not being described by this definition, are not human beings. In intangible flow theory, external intangible flows are those flows that can be separated from the human organism; that is, they flow outside the human being, in his/her interactions with the exterior world (e.g., a service, a communicational flow, a conversation, a text). Human beings die, while their outputs may keep existing. As noted in another context, the concept of a person or his/her work can be distinguished from the human organism.[4] For instance, when a famous author/writer dies, collective memory of his/her works and the conception of his/her person may have flowed out of him/her and keep subsisting in part of the living human population. Internal intangible flows that cannot be separated from a human being (e.g., inner information flows that remain within the body or intangible intercellular communication) remain part of what that human being is.

The proposed law advanced in this theory is that human beings are not commodities and, therefore, human beings are not assets, capital or resources in economic production. This law is to be applicable even in the extreme case when a human being is treated as a slave, where there is still no demonstration that he/she is a commodity. When Hodgson (2014), who himself criticizes the post-Smith capital concept, or Piketty (2014) argue that human beings can be capital when they are treated as slaves, they are victims of a fallacy based upon a pseudo-phenomenon explained before. Their reasoning is that slaves are commodities because they can be sold (exchanged by money) as collateral. Hence, Hodgson and Piketty define the commodity in relation to the potential monetary flow. Likewise, in Polanyi a similar reasoning is present when he contends that because many humans need wage payments to survive in market societies, their human activities gain commodity form because they receive cash flows in the form of wages. Even when he calls work as a fictitious commodity, Polanyi does not explain how to distinguish work from actual commodities. As many economists and sociologists, these authors have tumbled upon considering that the occurrence of the monetary flow creates/defines the commodity. The pre-Smith concept of capital used in intangible flow theory is restricted to means of money invested or investable in organizations. Further uses and flows of that money are not necessarily commodities, assets, capital or resources.[5]

However, what about nonhuman sentient beings or transhuman beings; should they be considered commodities in productive processes? This additional question is not solved here. The expression "sentient beings" refers to beings capable of experiencing feelings, perception and conscience.[6] Recent scientific evidence confirms that many animals (e.g., dolphins, dogs, elephants, cats, gorillas, crows) have inner consciousness, perception and feelings that are akin to humans'.[7] Those findings dismiss a long-established common sense (especially in the West) that human beings would be the only creatures capable of sensing conscientiousness and complex feelings.

Transhumanism referred initially to the enhancement of the human condition through sophisticated technology, which could modify human bodies to improve intellectual, physical and psychological capabilities.[8] When a living human body is still involved, intangible flow theory's law is straightforwardly applicable. However, posterior developments argue for a radical modification of human bodies through technology, which was called post-humanism.[9] Furthermore, robots and artificial intelligence beings might also reach a post-human stage and become sentient.[10] These latter cases are more difficult to address. Seemingly, nonhuman or post-human sentient beings might be distinguishable from human beings, while sharing features that are common in humans. Indeed, a law defining that humans are not commodities does not define whether other sentient beings are commodities in economic and societal production.

4.3 Example of phenomena addressable by the intangible flow theory

Economics and interrelated social sciences require research tools to distinguish tangible from intangible flows and human beings from commodities. Two examples are presented about how intangible flow theory can address phenomena that are currently outside the scope of mainstream economics' research technologies.

4.3.1 Observing economic and societal production

The peculiarities through which outputs are produced and delivered are not irrelevant to understand their societal relevance (or even monetary trading and surplus). Consider for instance a supermarket. For many persons' survival and existence, the supermarket may provide food and other vital supplies. Hence, how those products are actually produced and reach supermarkets' shelves are pertinent problems to understand those persons' lives (or other people's such as the supermarket's employees, suppliers, owners and neighbors).

We cannot advance our understanding of human participation in economic and societal production when social scientists are advised to focus on monetary surplus and avoid concrete underpinnings of production. While claiming to describe economic production, mainstream economics and Marxism lack technological tools to understand human participation in productive processes. Furthermore, a human being's life is not only restricted to be a production factor. The all-encompassing commodity description fails to acknowledge human existence not reflected on monetary flows. Social phenomena need to be understood in relation to, but not reduced to, their biological and psychological substrates.[11]

The intangible flow theory is applicable not only to capitalist/market forms of organizations but to all organizations that deliver flows of operating products to members of society, which also include NGOs, governmental organizations and hybrid forms. After all, markets are themselves human organizations.[12] A methodology to quantify equilibrium market prices (for transaction values) has been elusive because such prices are social constructs embedded in structures of social relations.[13] Indeed, there might be no adequate quantitative methodology to find equilibrium prices because these prices are dependent on complex intangible flows that cannot be measured with precision.

4.3.2 The occurrence of cash flows: To where do cash flows flow?

Intangible flow theory suggests that we must pay greater attention to tangible flows of economic material elements occurring at specific moments, which can be identified with a relevant degree of accuracy. Instead of chasing intangible concepts of value based upon projections of future monetary flows or abstract labor values as in mainstream economics and Marxism, we should understand what happens to the tangible monetary flows generated by organizations through sales of operating products.

To where do monetary flows actually flow? A model[14] to address this question is formulated in Figure 4.1. Money generated through sales can (i) remain in the organization and be reinvested in operations, (ii) flow to the owners of the firm, either through dividends or stock (equity) buy backs, (iii) flow to the top-level managers/executive deciders, (iv) flow to debt holders in the form of interest and repayments, (v) flow to the organization's workers,[15] (vi) be used to pay the accounts of suppliers and other creditors, (vii) flow to national governments in the form of taxes and other legal obligations, (viii) be used in donations and

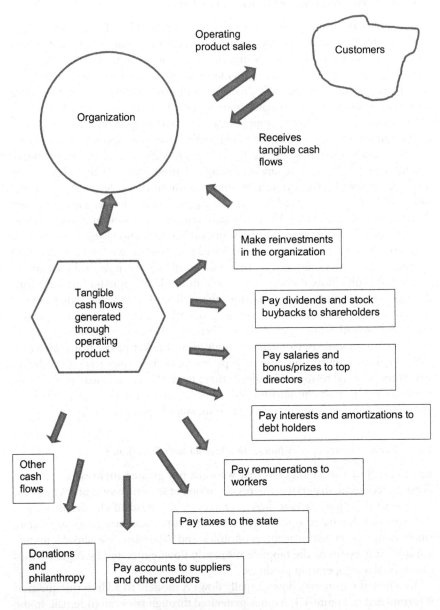

Figure 4.1 To where do monetary flows generated by organizations flow?

philanthropy, or (iv) be used in other cash flows. Hence, the mainstream and Marxist approach of treating economic production as a commodity-consuming box fails to capture the complexity of the cash flow generation process. Furthermore, their value approach implies that after exploiting all commodities (including human commodities), the appropriated value goes solely to the owners of enterprises. In reality, the situation is not nearly so simple, and sales-generated monetary flows are allocated to many people.

For instance, consider markets for automatic guns, tobacco and alcohol, in the sense that these items are traded by money among different persons and entities. Money from these businesses flows not only to corporate shareholders but also to workers, lenders, suppliers and government taxes. Regardless of whether a worker of a related enterprise has any alternative for employment, in order to earn a wage for him-/herself, the employee is responsible for producing intangible flows that might eventually cause lethal gunshots or tobacco- and alcohol-related diseases.

Within the intangible flow theory framework, workers (and their representatives) are, as human beings, the owners of firms' equity. As suggested by mainstream economics and Marxism, many capitalists/investors may participate in the productive process to increase their monetary flows. However, the intangible flow theory refuses the abstract category of capital as a homogeneous group of people, preferring the tangible identification of human beings. Owners of financial resources may control monetary stocks and be very different among themselves. A group of workers who could gain control of a firm's capital become owners themselves. Owners of an organization's equity can also be workers. Existence of rent-maximizing investors does not imply that human societies allow human organizations to exist merely for that purpose. Furthermore, workers cannot be excused for causing harm to society merely because they would be allegedly alienated and reified in the productive process, as suggested by Marxism. As another example, an elected politician might be willing to legislate against automatic gun trades or tobacco/alcohol sales, but to do so, he/she would face a decrease in tax revenues and an increase in unemployment due to the closing of factories and shops. Although cash generated by operating product sales can be used to support many important philanthropic projects, it can also be used to finance lobby organizations and to support campaigns and media outlets that promote the election of lobby-friendly politicians or politicians who would reduce taxes and therefore enable further cash flows to owners of productive means.

After the tangibilization of productive process occurs, money that otherwise would flow to workers either can be distributed or partially captured by those in control of the productive process.[16] In industrialized societies, those in control of the productive process generally refer to owners, financiers and managers/directors of large corporations.[17] By no coincidence, these are the persons who, by virtue of being situated in the top of the income ladder, have seen increases in their real incomes in recent decades, in contrast to almost everybody else.[18]

4.4 Deconstructing and destroying the human commodity framework but also building foundations for systematic alternatives

Mainstream economics and Marxism define commodities in terms of an association to monetary flows (sales), which leads to the human commodity framework. It is also present in relativistic writings. Undeniably, several market transactions are relevant. Nevertheless, when compared with all flows necessary for a product to be delivered to a human being, most markets as described in economics are merely micro moments where monetary flows might eventually occur. Thus, per se markets could not explain economic and societal production. Moreover, tangible flows of money and commodities must not be taken for granted.

Intangible flow theory rejects the pseudo-phenomenon whereby commodities would be defined in terms of monetary flows. To the new theory, commodities are defined as precisely identifiable physical goods and distinguished from human beings. There is no systematic evidence proving that we human beings are commodities in economic and societal production and, hence, can be considered as capital, assets or resources. Monetary flows do not necessarily define the existence of commodities because monetary flows are phenomena that need themselves to be explained. Money can flow without association with commodities. Commodities can be transformed and flow without being associated with monetary flows. However, seldom do commodities generate monetary flows by themselves unless associated with a human-related intangible flow dynamic. It is not, as supposed by Polanyi, that work is a fictitious commodity, with still some commodity features in market societies. Human work can be distinguished from the humans who produces the work and from commodities.

Money can have commodity form (e.g., coins and notes) and non-commodity form (e.g., bank accounts or credit card transactions). In contemporary societies, it is to a large extent created and enabled by governments and banking. Nonetheless, registered flows of money that have occurred in a specific period are highly tangible. Human beings frequently create flows of economic material elements through human-related intangible flows, which cannot be identified with precision. Through tangibilization of economic production, previously intangible dimensions can be turned into tangible processes, and machines may gain the skills necessary to replace human work or perform new tasks. The tangible money generated or saved by machines that enhance productive processes' tangibilization may tend to flow to the human beings who own and/or control these productive processes.

We humans have concrete survival and existence needs associated with physical goods (commodities). In human societies, production is fundamentally dependent upon natural resources and the biosphere. Besides being socially and ecologically embedded, human survival and existence would not be possible without sourcing nature and the biophysical world, which we humans can harm but are from being able to control. Theories do not explain phenomena we are certain of. It is the other way around. Theories exist to explain phenomena we do not completely understand. The two greatest economic theories of the 20th century, namely mainstream economics and Marxism, contain an important misunderstanding. They consider humans and our contributions to economic and societal production as commodities (assets, capital or resources). In contrast, the intangible flow theory aims to establish a law for the social sciences: explicitly, that *we human beings are not commodities, assets, capital or resources.* A human being is defined as a living homo sapiens who is recognizable through his/her human DNA.[19]

This new law deconstructs and indeed destroys the manner in which we humans are described in both mainstream economics and Marxism. However, this law is not determinist and predictive of the future (teleological). The future remains uncertain and contingent to human actions, the biosphere and bio-physical world we humans are integrated upon. Furthermore, this law brings not a relativistic destruction that would be ungrounded on a reality existing beyond our social and bio-mental constructions. It is accompanied by a systematic definition for human being that allows integrating several disciplines studying this subject matter such as history, sociology, anthropology, philosophy and biology. In summary, this new law tackles two major argumentative blocks against having the social sciences addressing (and eventually improving) the human condition: the human commodity framework in economics, and the relativism that currently has a great bearing upon the social sciences.

The proposed law is applicable not only to capitalist/market organizations but to all organizations that deliver flows of operating products to members of society. Therefore, this law encompasses NGOs, governmental organizations, hybrid organizations, communal production and other forms of economic organizations, including those not yet invented by humankind. It bids a manner to build systematic alternative explanations for human participation in economic and societal production. This theory will not be consensual. However, those who, knowingly or not, treat human contributions to the productive process as akin to commodities will need to have better explanations for this approach than the flawed explanations presented to date. Only through their failure can the proposed scientific law thrive.

Notes

1 See, for instance, Brook (2009), Hochschild (2003 [1983], 2003, 2004).
2 Thus, we can avoid fowling upon dialectic methods used by Hegel, Marx and Engels (see, for instance, Hegel, 1807, 1977; Marx, 1847, online) which are disparaged by some relativist constructivists, postmodernists, and poststructuralists, who, however, out of semantic relativism, want to reinterpret Marx without what Marx writes and advocates (see, for instance, Choat, 2010).
3 Or a subsequent methodology.
4 Roth (2013).
5 Furthermore, a complex relationship in a society, which may lead one human being to claim to own another could not be captured simply by a tangible cash flow.
6 The conception of sentient being is present in several ancient religions as Hinduism, Buddhism, Sikhism, and Jainism. For instance, in Buddhism, sentient beings hold five aggregates, or skandhas, namely: matter, sensation, perception, mental formations and consciousness.
7 See, for instance, Economist (2015).
8 More and Vita-More (2013), Ranisch and Sorgner (2014); Porpora (2017).
9 More and Vita-More (2013), Ranisch and Sorgner (2014).

10 Clark (2016).
11 Jenks and Smith (2013).
12 Ahrne, Aspers, and Brunsson (2015).
13 Beunza, Hardie, and MacKenzie (2006).
14 Adapted from Cardao-Pito (2016).
15 In contemporary monetary societies, organizations are the principal sources of monetary income to many human beings. There are several organizational practices that impact upon these forms of monetary income such as hiring, role allocation, promotion, compensation and organizational structuring (Amis, Mair, and Munir, forthcoming). Nonetheless, these income forms are mostly derived from the revenues organizations generate by delivering flows of products to members of society.
16 Also applicable in cases where corporations outsource work overseas for less money than it would cost to hire nationals to do service production.
17 Kristal (2013).
18 Excluding some artists, Hollywood actors, TV show hosts and sport stars.
19 As explained before, the scientific law proposed here at no point specifies whether non-human sentient beings are akin to commodities in economic production.

References

Ahrne, G., Aspers, P. and Brunsson, N. (2015). The organization of markets. *Organization Studies*, 36(1), 7–27.

Amis, J. M., Mair, J. and Munir, K. (Forthcoming). The organizational reproduction of inequality. *Academy of Management Annals*. Online at: https://journals.aom.org/doi/10.5465/annals.2017.0033.

Beunza, D., Hardie, I. and MacKenzie, D. (2006). A price is a social thing: Towards a material sociology of arbitrage. *Organization Studies*, 27(5), 721–745.

Brook, P. (2009). The alienated heart: Hochschild's emotional labour thesis and the anti-capitalist politics of alienation. *Capital and Class*, 33(2), 7–31.

Cardao-Pito, T. (2016). A law for the social sciences regarding us human beings. *Journal of Interdisciplinary Economics*, 28(2), 202–229.

Choat, S. (2010). *Marx Through Post-Structuralism: Lyotard, Derrida, Foucault and Deleuze*. London: Continuum.

Clark, A. (2016). *Surfing Uncertainty: Prediction, Action, and the Embodied Mind*. Oxford: Oxford University Press.

Economist. (2015). Animal minds: Animals think, therefore. . . . *Economist*, December 19. Online at www.economist.com/printedition/2015-12-19.

Hochschild, A. (2003, 1983). *The Managed Heart: Commercialization of Human Feeling*. Berkeley, CA: University of California Press.

Hochschild, A. (2003). *The Commercialization of Intimate Life: Notes from Home and Work*. Berkeley, CA: University of California Press.

Hochschild, A. (2004). The commodity frontier. In Alexander, J., Marx, G. and Williams, C. (Eds.) *Self, Social Structure and Beliefs: Essays in Sociology*. Berkeley, CA: University of California Press.

Hodgson, G. (2014). What is capital? Economists and sociologists have changed its meaning: Should it be changed back? *Cambridge Journal of Economics*, 38(5), 1063–1086.

Jenks, C. and Smith, J. (2013). Reshaping social theory from complexity and ecological perspectives. *Thesis Eleven*, 114(1), 61–75.

Kristal, T. (2013). The capitalist machine: Computerization, workers' power, and the decline in labor's share within U.S. Industries. *American Sociological Review*, 78(3), 361–389.

Marx, K. (1847). *The Poverty of Philosophy*. Online at: www.marxists.org/archive/marx/works/1847/poverty-philosophy/ch02.htm.

More, M. and Vita-More, N. (Eds.) (2013). *The Transhumanist Reader: Classical and Contemporary Essays on the Science, Technology, and Philosophy of the Human Future*. Hoboken, NJ: Wiley-Blackwell.

Piketty, T. (2014). *Capital in the Twenty-First Century*. Cambridge, MA: Belknap Press.

Porpora, D. (2017). Dehumanization in theory: Anti-humanism, nonhumanism, post-humanism, and trans-humanism. *Journal of Critical Realism*, 16(4), 353–367.

Ranisch, R. and Sorgner, S. (Eds.) (2014). *Post- and Transhumanism. An Introduction*. New York, NY: Peter Lang/GmbH, Internationaler Verlag der Wissenschaften.

Roth, S. (2013). Dying is only human. The case death makes for the immortality of the person. *Tamara: Journal for Critical Organization Inquiry*, 11(2), 37–41.

Sandel, M. J. (2012). *What Money Can't Buy: The Moral Limits of Markets*. London: Macmillan.

5 Operating product flows enhancing human survival and existence

5.1 Introduction

According to standard economic and financial textbooks, organizations exist to increase the wealth (value) of their owners/shareholders, and therefore financial, investing and operating decisions would be independent. Several developments based upon this view have won Nobel prizes in economics. Many major economic concepts support the view that organizations exist to increase the wealth of their owners, as if an investment decision could be detached from economic and societal production. The intangible flow dynamics of economic and societal phenomena was to be put inside a box used to represent the organization and ignored there as irrelevant or negligible. We can exemplify with several mainstream theoretical outlines, such as the Coase theorem that firms are merely substitutes to market operations,[1] the theory of the firm as a nexus of contracts (based on expectations of future cash flows discounted by a rate),[2] a resource-based view of the organization,[3] behavioral economics[4] or the human capital concept.[5]

To the intangible flow theory, on the other hand, the major purpose of organizations might be to deliver operating product flows to members of society. Furthermore, economic and societal production is fundamentally dependent upon natural resources and the biophysical world. Even if some persons and entities may invest in organizations mostly with pecuniary aims, or create structures as mere vehicles of wealth,[6] most human organizations have specific societal roles and are dependent upon the biosphere.

The new theory is not restricted to monetary societies. However, most organizations may aim at delivering flows of operating product flows to their customers, which require resources obtained from the biophysical world and biosphere. For example, the major drive of a coffee shop may not be to make money payable to owners/shareholders per se, as would be suggested by mainstream economics or financial economics,[7] but to deliver flows of coffees, teas, cakes and other products to customers who, as a consequence, will generate cash flows. Likewise, a textile manufacturer may aim to produce flows of clothes and related products to be delivered to members of society, while managing productivity and suitable technologies. According to the intangible flow theory, monetary inflows to organizations occur because organizations address their main purpose of delivering products to members of society.[8]

This chapter explains a new system to classify firms according to the tangibility of their operating product flows, namely, the level of operating intangibility. It will be used to classify large sets of listed firms from China, Germany, Japan, the US and the UK during the time period 2000 through 2017.[9] The total sample includes 14,270 clearly identifiable organizations. The new classification system allows observing how organizations' operating, financing and investing decisions seem to interrelate. Generally, operating product flows delivered to members of society seem to be essential to explain organizations' being.

Moreover, we will observe that the organizations with the largest monetary revenues in the sample are not based upon pure intangible flows. Instead they are delivering flows of products that are highly reliant upon natural resources and the biosphere. Usually, the largest monetary flow–generating firms are delivering either commodities (that is, physical goods requiring therefore natural resources obtained in the bio/physical world), have mediating access to highly tangible resources (as defined in the last chapters), and/or employ a great number of people (who, as we have seen in the last chapters, are neither resources nor intangible, but require physical resources to survive and exist). Even organizations mostly based upon delivering intangible flows require natural resources obtained in the biosphere for survival and existence of their human members.

Thus, we may need to abandon the dismal hypothesis that organizations exist merely to increase the wealth of their owners/shareholders, as advocated by mainstream economics. In contemporary societies, human organizations enable economic and societal production required for human life and existence. Furthermore, organizations mediate the interaction among human society, resources and the biophysical world. Such interactions would not be possible merely through uncoordinated market activities. Indeed, markets are themselves human organizations operating within organized human societies.[10] Human organizations and markets are fully integrated upon the biosphere.

5.2 The challenge from intangible flow theory

In recent years' economic and organizational research, the word intangibles (plural) as related to organizations has usually been employed to describe both intangible assets and intangible capital, which are interlinked through the same expression.[11] The concepts of asset and capital have origins in accounting, where they are traditionally used to report financial transactions. In economics and sociology, these terms convey different meanings from their earlier accounting notions. For economists and sociologists, intangibles are generally understood to be drivers of growth/wealth creation (translated somehow into money) payable to owners/shareholders, which have the property of intangibility. The dominant conception of intangible asset is derived from mainstream economic theory, namely, that organizations exist to increase the wealth of their owners/shareholders. Clearly, we are in the presence of a tautology, as intangible assets would create wealth because they are what creates wealth (similar to the tautology represented by capital). Furthermore, some sort of magical explanation over a pseudo-phenomenon through which something that is not clearly defined allows investors/shareholders to become richer, reinforcing the conception that organizations exist to make them richer.

The current chapter's debate is centered not on intangibility of assets, but on tangibility of operating product flows. For such, we do not need to assume that organizations exist to increase shareholders'/investors' wealth. A human-related intangible flow such as pure human service may have been necessary to generate flows of cash in economic and societal production. However, neither the human nor intangible contribution can be considered as commodities, assets, capital or resources. Under the new theory, commodities are restricted to physical goods. As described earlier, there are several reasons to restrict commodities to physical goods and to distinguish numerous outputs of the production process from commodities. However, there are very few products which are pure physical goods (commodities) or pure services.[12] Most products have tangible and intangible components. Degree of output intangibility can be classified according to a continuum.[13] At one extreme are pure physical goods, for instance, salt or furniture, and at the other are products that are mostly intangible, such as pure services (e.g., teaching or consulting). In the middle are products that are semi intangible or hybrid products themselves. For example, a restaurant meal includes tangible food and drinks and intangible services as cooking or attending.

Intangible products have concrete properties that distinguish them from tangible physical goods. Intangible flow theory suggests that the generation of monetary flows cannot be simply explained by commodities, that is, through the pseudo-phenomenon where everything that originates monetary flows would be defined as a commodity. Although determinant for monetary flow generation, human beings are not commodities, assets, capital or resources, according to the new law proposed earlier.

5.3 Operating (in)tangibility: The classification of organizations according to the tangibility of their operating product flows

To intangible flow theory, a product is an output that results from the productive process and commodities are physical goods. Hence, a product can be, but is not necessarily, a commodity. A purely intangible product is a product that is not associated with any commodity (e.g., a pure service such as legal advisement[14]). A hybrid product is an output of economic production that integrates one or more commodities with intangible flows such as service flows, communication flows or knowledge flows. As earlier, an example of a hybrid product might be a restaurant meal.

Operating intangibility aims at inferring the tangibility of operating product flows produced by organizations. It is inferred by the component of an organization's operating cost structure not directly related to the costs of commodities (i.e., physical goods) or tangible fixed assets (e.g., equipment, property, or plant). The level of operating intangibility (LOI) framework intends to describe the degree to which an entire organization is reliant on intangible inputs and outputs (e.g., the LOI can approximately determine whether the product flows of Microsoft and Coca-Cola are more intangible-intensive than the product flows of Toyota and BP). LOI (ζ) is equal to one minus the expenses directly related to commodities and tangible fixed assets (ϕ) divided by the total operating costs ($\aleph$). Thus, by approximation, the LOI framework identifies the directly observable tangibility to infer the intangibility through the absence of observable tangibility.

It is never too much to emphasize that intangibility, by definition, cannot be measured with precision because previous intangible elements that can be measured with precision become tangible. As explained earlier, intangible flow theory is not a dialectic theory with the form thesis-antithesis-synthesis, where a tangible flow would be the opposite of an intangible flow. Intangible flows are highly heterogeneous, and we do not know how to identify them with precision (otherwise we would). Therefore, intangibility needs to be inferred from precisely identifiable tangible elements such as monetary or physical good flows that are associated with intangible elements. This system does not measure intangible flows. It measures the tangible monetary transferences to infer that they might be related to intangible flows. Likewise, when several authors claim to use accounting to measure intangible assets, what they suggest is to measure tangible monetary flows, which would be eventually related to intangible assets.[15] They cannot measure intangible assets per se. The LOI framework uses a similar process to try and capture intangible flows, that is, producing inferences through tangible monetary flows. However, this is done without holding the illusion of being able to measure intangibility with precision, as most intangible asset literature does.

A method is required to infer expenses that are directly related to commodities and tangible fixed assets (ϕ). For this book, the method is related to the database used (thus, the evidence available). The current methodology can be improved in future research (see the section on limitations). Refinitiv's Datastream Worldscope database subdivides operating costs into four rubrics: the cost of goods sold (α), amortizations (Λ), depreciations (ς) (amortizations and depreciations are computed together in this database), selling, general and administrative expenses (Ω), and other operating costs (Θ) :

$$\aleph = \alpha + \Lambda + \varsigma + \Omega + \Theta \tag{5.1}$$

For practical purposes, one must choose among information available in the database, even if such information is known to be imperfect. A proxy to identify a firm's operating intangibility is defined in the following manner:

$$\zeta^{\Delta} = 1 - \frac{\alpha + \Lambda + \varsigma + \Theta}{\aleph} = \frac{\Omega}{\aleph} \tag{5.2}$$

Accordingly, the LOI is quantified as equal to one minus the ratio of the sum of the cost of goods sold, amortizations and depreciations of fixed assets, and other operating costs to the total operating costs. Thus, the database allows computing LOI as the selling, general and administrative expenses divided by the total operating costs. Far from perfect, yet useful for our practical purposes, this solution should be improved in future research.

The LOI puts commodity (physical good)–intensive firms (e.g., producing and selling automobiles or relying heavily on physical infrastructures, such as hotel chains or airline companies) at one end of the scale and intangible product–intensive firms (e.g., firms producing software and pure services) at the other. At the middle of the scale are firms that supply a mixture of physical goods and intangible products in their core business model, as well as firms that offer products that are themselves mixed. For example, whereas one may consider a soft-drink firm as a company focused mainly on the sales of physical goods, such a firm may invest massively in marketing and brand awareness, as Coca-Cola and PepsiCo do. Therefore, its mean LOI can be much higher than that of supermarkets, which are fundamentally based in delivering physical goods to consumers. However, supermarkets would have been traditionally classified as intangible service providers and heavy-advertisement soft-drink companies as tangible physical good/manufacturing companies. The LOI systems demonstrates that the operating product flows of the latter are much more intangible that those of the former. Likewise, a hotel network or an airline company would traditionally be considered as pure service firms. However, they rely intensively on physical commodities or tangible fixed resources when generating monetary flows through product flows. For instance, the hotel network requires all the tangibility associated to physical infrastructure of the buildings and constructions. The airline company requires the undeniably physical objects as planes, jet fuel (or alternative combustion systems) and airports.

5.4 Exemplifying with relatively well-known organizations

The total sample contains five country samples. Many factors distinguish the five countries studied as society, historical path, political systems, economy, legislation, accounting practices and so forth. Therefore, the observations were not tested together, but divided by their respective country, creating five subsamples: China (36,790 observations; 3,520 organizations); Germany (10,648; 968); Japan (58,115; 4,563); the UK (29,748; 3,115) and the US (29,948; 2,104). Appendix A describes with more detail the data obtained from the Refinitiv Datastream database. It covers only the specific period from 2000 to 2017 for Germany, the UK, and the US and from 2002 to 2017 for China and Japan (for which 2000 and 2001 data were unavailable). It is quite possible that in the future some of the studied firms will evolve, change business operations or even cease to exist altogether. One must understand the impermanence of things and be open to the new, the different, the event that challenges previous explanations. The analysis in this chapter refers only to this specific period.

Figure 5.1 orders several relatively well-known firms according to the materiality of their product flows (outputs) as identified by their mean level of operating (in)tangibility. Furthermore, it provides information about those organizations' mean revenues in their national currency (billions) over the sample period (computed at 2010 value, for comparison[16]). As expected, car

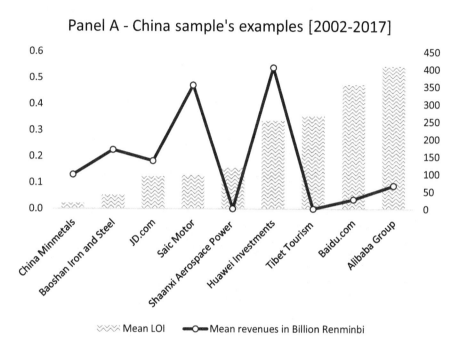

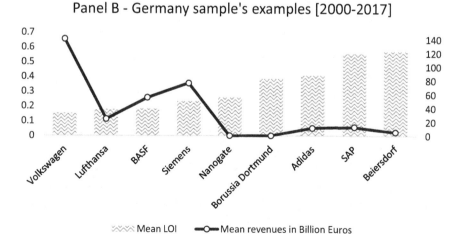

Figure 5.1 Example of organizations in the five country samples classified by mean revenues and mean LOI

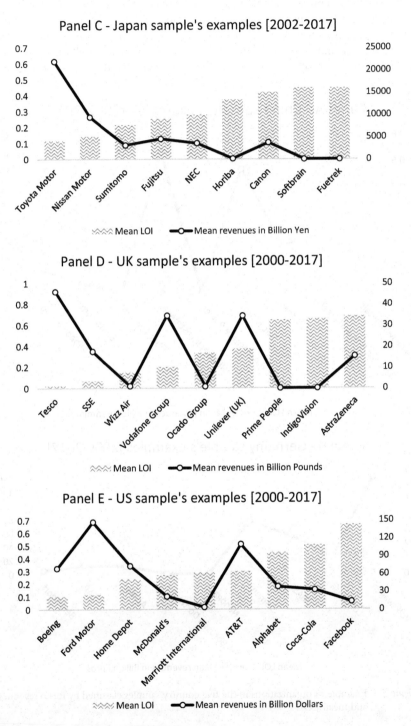

Figure 5.1 (Continued)

manufacturers have been found to have low levels of operating intangibility. Commodity-intensive, car makers are sustaining their operations in highly physical product flows. Examples are SAIC Motor (in China), Volkswagen (in Germany), Toyota and Nissan (in Japan), or Ford Motor Company (in the US). Other organizations heavily relying on natural resources to produce flows of commodities are also classified as having low levels of operating intangibility. In those are organizations such as China Minmetals, a mining company; Baoshan Iron and Steel (in China); Basf, a chemical company (in Germany); SSE, an energy company (in the UK); or Boeing (in the US).

Digital platform companies are firms enabled by the advent of the internet.[17] As expected, they have been found to have high levels of operating intangibility. Their business operations are fundamentally dependent upon intangible flows.[18] Quite often, platform firms' operations may involve physical structures not owned by them. Likewise, their operations may also entail commodities not produced, owned or stored by them. Thus, they are platforms enabling the digital framework for operating non-owned physical infrastructures and commodity flows. See, for instance, how Airbnb does not own the rooms and houses they help renting or Uber does not own the cars used by drivers registered in their databases. Examples in Figure 5.1 are Alphabet (Google parent company), Facebook (in the US) and Alibaba and Baidu.com (in China). Likewise, software and internet application firms such as SAP (in Germany), Fuetrek (in Japan) or Indigo Vision (in the UK) also have high levels of operating intangibility. Moreover, pharmaceutical and cosmetic companies such as AstraZeneca (in the UK) or Beiersdorf (in Germany) that rely heavily on R&D, patents, marketing and brand awareness in their product flows have been found to have relatively high LOIs.

Classified somewhere in the middle of the LOI scale are organizations that deliver a mixture of physical goods and intangible products in their primary business model as well as organizations that offer products themselves mixed, for example, firms that have a mixture of software and hardware technologies, besides heavily relying on R&D and/or marketing. Other examples are companies delivering communication flows, which involve high degree of physical structure but also technology and marketing efforts, such as AT&T (in the US), Vodafone (in the UK) or Huawei (in China), or organizations that would traditionally be classified as industrial manufacturing firms, but have a significant component of their cost structure based upon highly intangible advertisement, marketing interactions with their potential customers, and/or R&D. These firms include Siemens (in Germany), Fujitsu and Canon (in Japan), and Unilever (in the UK). Observe, for instance, Coca-Cola (in the US) or Adidas, a sport apparel maker (in Germany), which could traditionally be considered as pure manufacturing companies. However, their operating intangibility level identifies how their cost structure has a significant intangible flow component related to factors such as brand awareness, product conception and customer relationship.

The new system allows to identify possible misconceptions in previous studies. For instance, supermarkets and airline companies would traditionally be considered as service companies and therefore supposedly contributing to the "*intangible economy*." However, supermarket chains such as Tesco (in the UK) or Walmart (in the US; see Figure 5.1) have very low operating intangibility. Similarly, airline organizations as Lufthansa (in Germany) or Wizz Air (in the UK) have low LOIs. Indeed, supermarkets deliver systematic flows of physical goods (commodities) to their customers. Likewise, airlines have a high degree of tangibility in their physical planes, which consume expensive (and polluting) tangible jet fuel. They also require a high degree of tangibility to depart, fly and land planes at physical airports.

Although some organizations seldom have physical shops, through online sales they deliver commodities that they own and store. Thus, they should have relatively lower LOIs than pure platform companies. Commodity flows should be captured by the LOI framework. It happens, for example, with JD.com, a large Chinese online retail site, and Ocado, an online supermarket in the UK. On the other hand, organizations that could be traditionally classified as intangible-intensive for being based upon services require substantial levels of tangibility to produce their product flows. For instance, the restaurant chain McDonald's or the Marriott International hotel chain (US sample) rely on the physical structure and components necessary to produce the product flows they deliver to members of society.

5.5 Association between operating tangibility and monetary flows: A systematic approach

A lower LOI does not immediately imply larger revenues, and thus more monetary flow generation, in comparison to a higher operating intangibility level. A simple corner shop can have a very low LOI while generating relatively little revenue. However, there is something puzzling in Figure 5.1. Currently, Alphabet, Facebook and Baidu are perhaps some of the largest platform firms in the world. SAP is perhaps one of the largest software makers in the world. Borussia Dortmund is one of the most well-known football teams in Germany. These organizations are conceivably some of the most prominent organizations in comparison to others who would try to produce similar product flows. However, the size of their average revenues is rather small if compared with commodity flow–intensive firms such as carmakers Volkswagen or Ford Motor Company or supermarkets like Tesco or the mining company China Minmetals. Indeed, the time period of the sample (2002–2017) for China and (2000–2017) for the US may not capture recent growth of internet-based major companies such as Alphabet, Facebook and Baidu. However, these companies' recent growth in monetary flow generation has been accompanied by the tangibilization of their business operations both in physical infrastructures (e.g., buildings, offices, IT machinery and artificial intelligence servers) and number of workers. At the end of 2018, Alphabet had 98,771 full-time employees,[19] Facebook had 35,587 employees,[20] and Baidu had 42,267 employees.[21] Thus, a significant tangibilization of their operations has occurred along with the growth in monetary flow generation.

Undeniably, technology will impact the car industry, for instance, through online renting, self-driving cars or operating systems powered by artificial intelligence. Likewise, technology and digital-based companies will impact the manner in which groceries could be delivered to humans or extractive organizations operate. However, cars, groceries and minerals will remain tangible and dependent upon nature and the biophysical world to be produced and delivered. If an intangible-intensive organization was to start producing and delivering cars, groceries or minerals, then that organization would necessarily become less intangible-intensive. It would rely more upon physical structures and commodities.

An empirical connection between operating intangibility and size of organizational cash flows might be suggested in the samples studied. The variable commonly identified in economics as size, or firm size, describes the magnitude of the monetary turnover (revenue) generated through the delivery of products to customers.[22] Although in several cases there might be a temporal lag between revenues and monetary flows, the latter can be considered tangible flows because they can be precisely quantified in a specific time and place. Regardless of the form that a monetary flow may assume, the exact amount of money that has been moved is knowable when verified.

This reasoning is congruent with the enduring concept of break-even.[23] As is well known, a firm accomplishes the break-even point when its revenue function equals its cost function, that is, the point where the revenues cover all costs. A firm is unable to survive if it remains below the break-even point for many years, due to insolvency. Physical good–intensive firms may thus require larger economies of scale to function and be sustainable in the long run. Although higher operating intangibility will not always imply a smaller firm size, this empirical association may be observable in samples with many firms, as is the case of the five samples studied.

Figure 5.2 displays the scatterplot of all organizations in the five samples by their mean LOI and mean revenues at their national currency (in billions). Each point corresponds to a perfectly identifiable organization. That is, we no longer need to speculate about the abstract fantasy firm in the standard economic textbook. The smoother line shows a tendency curve among the data. The shadow situated bellow the line gives the 95% confidence interval.[24] Each graph informs about the number of organizations, mean LOI and mean size of revenues (at 2010 values) for the entire country sample.

In all samples, there are many more firms on the left-hand side of the graph, namely, the lower LOI side. Therefore, there is a much broader number of organizations requiring resources obtained from nature and the biophysical world to organizations that could be identifiable as intangible product flow–intensive. However, even intangible-intensive organizations still depend on biophysical resources to function, as humans need food, water and shelter and

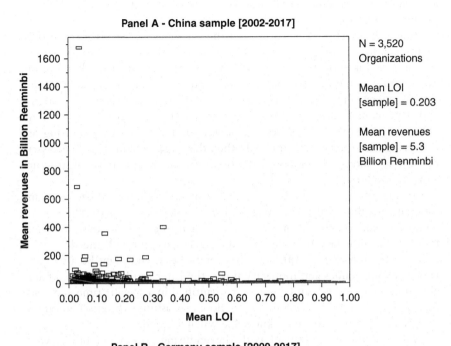

Panel A - China sample [2002-2017]

N = 3,520
Organizations

Mean LOI
[sample] = 0.203

Mean revenues
[sample] = 5.3
Billion Renminbi

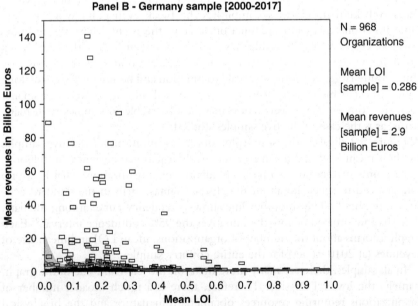

Panel B - Germany sample [2000-2017]

N = 968
Organizations

Mean LOI
[sample] = 0.286

Mean revenues
[sample] = 2.9
Billion Euros

Figure 5.2 Scatterplot of all organizations in sample by mean size of revenues and mean level of operating intangibility

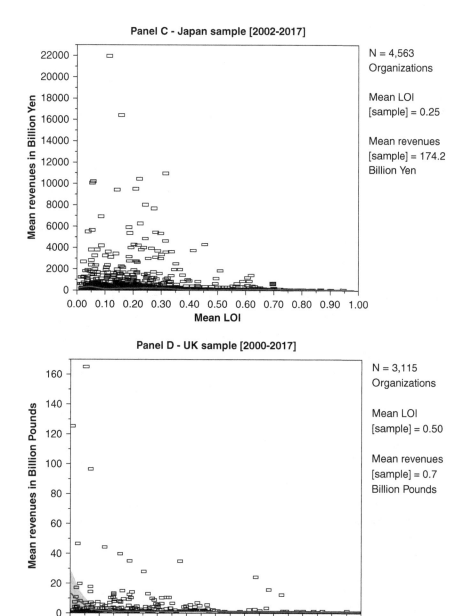

Figure 5.2 (Continued)

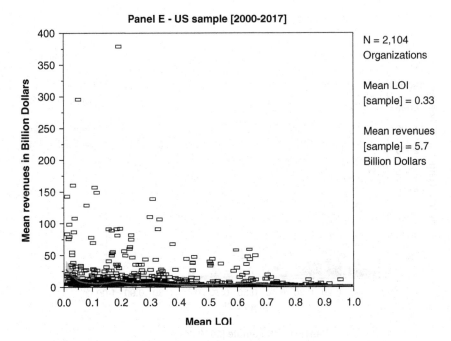

Figure 5.2 (Continued)

other amenities to survive and exist. The smoother line identifies an association between tangibility of product flows and monetary flow generation. As emphasized, not all organizations with low LOI are larger cash generators. Still, organizations with lower LOI tend to be larger than those with higher operating intangibility. This association was confirmed in statistical tests including control variables and including or excluding outlier observation. Results are displayed in Appendix C.

5.6 Observing the largest cash flow–generating organizations' operating product flows

As displayed in Figure 5.2, the organizations generating the largest monetary flows in all samples seem to be generally based upon tangible flows that are highly reliant on natural resources and the biophysical world. The 20 organizations with higher average revenues are identified in Figure 5.3's scatterplots. Furthermore, Table 5.1 makes an approximate classification of those 100 organizations by their major activities.

Although these organizations' operating cash inflows are obtained from around the planet, their average revenues represent a large proportion of their

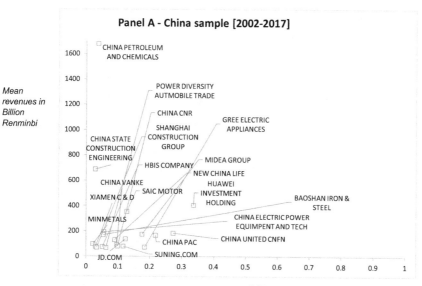

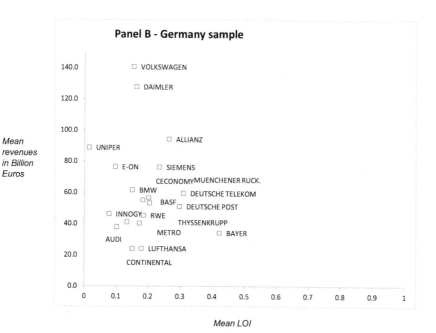

Figure 5.3 Scatterplot of the largest 20 organizations in each sample by their mean size of revenues

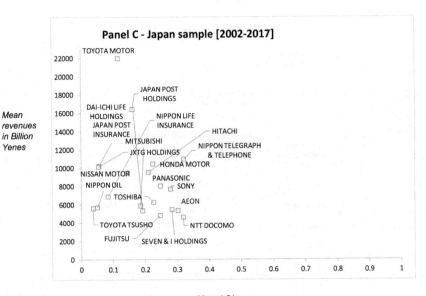

Mean revenues in Billion Yenes

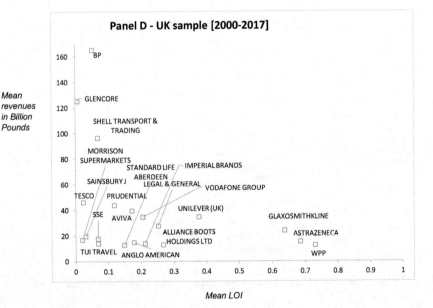

Mean revenues in Billion Pounds

Figure 5.3 (Continued)

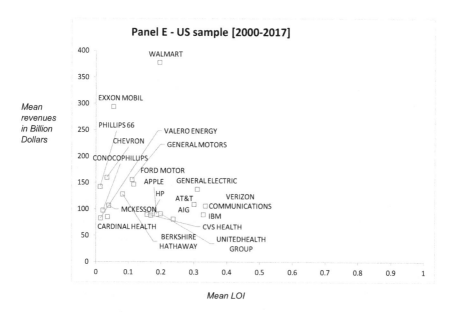

Figure 5.3 (Continued)

country's average GDP.[25] In Germany, average revenues of the largest 20 organizations represent 48% of the average GDP; in China, 12%[26]; in Japan, 35%; in the UK, 51%; and in the US, 19%. Hence, these are organizations generating substantial monetary flows. By studying them, we may better appreciate monetary flow phenomena.

The largest cash flow generators in each subsample in the studied period are as follows: two companies related to energy, extractive and chemical operations, namely, China Petroleum and Chemicals and BP in the UK; two car manufacturers, namely, Toyota in Japan and Volkswagen in Germany; and a large supermarket chain highly based upon physical good (commodity) flows, namely, Walmart in the US. Clearly, all these firms produce highly tangible flows of products. With very few exceptions, the largest money generators tend to be organizations with relatively low LOI (higher product flow tangibility).

In all samples, there are several organizations related to energy, extractive and chemical manufacturing, which require natural physical resources to produce and deliver their product flows. This finding seems to demonstrate the reliance of contemporary societies on energy, minerals and raw materials obtained, transformed, transported, stored and delivered by these organizations. All five samples contain conglomerates with physical manufacturing operations in the largest monetary flow generators. An organizational form also present in every sample are organizations connected to enhancing human communication and

Table 5.1 Approximate classification by major activities of the 20 firms with higher average revenues in each sample

	China sample	Germany sample	Japan sample	UK sample	US sample
Airline and travel companies		Lufthansa		TUI Travel	
Automobile and transport machinery manufacturers	SAIC Motor, China CNR	Volkswagen, Daimler, BMW, Audi, Continental	Toyota Motor, Honda Motor, Nissan Motor, Mitsubishi		General Motors, Ford
Communication firms involving commodities and physical structure	China United Communication Network	Deutsche Telekom, Deutsche Post	Japan Post, Nippon Telegraph and Telephone, NTT DoCoMo	Vodafone Group	AT&T, Verizon Communications
Construction and building structures related organizations	China State Construction and Engineering, China Vanke, Xiamen C&D, Xanghai Construction Group				
Energy related, mining/extractive and chemical companies	China Petroleum and Chemicals, Minmetals, China Electric Power Equipment and Technology;	Uniper, E-ON, Basf, Innogi, Rwe, Bayer	JXTG Holdings, Nippon Oil	BP, Glencore, Shell Transport and Trading, SSE, Anglo American	Exxon Mobil, Chevron, Philips 66, ConocoPhiips, Valero Energy
Insurance organizations	China Pac, New China Life	Allianz, Muenchener Ruck	Japan Post Insurance, Nippon Life Insurance, Dai-ichi Life Holdings	Prudential, Aviva, Legal and General, Standard Life Abeerdeen WPP	AIG
Intangible-intensive companies					
Other industrial manufacturing and conglomerates with several manufacturing operations	Baoshan Iron and Steel, HBIS Company	Siemens, ThyssenKrupp	Hitachi	Unilever, Imperial Brands	General Electrics, Berkshire Hathaway
Physical machines and appliances manufacturers	Huawei Investment, Midea Group, Gree Electric Appliances		Panasonic, Sony, Toshiba, Toyota Tsusho, Fujitsu		Apple, IBM, HP
Producers and distributers of health related products				GlaxoSmithKline, AstraZeneca, Alliance Boots	McKesson, United Health Group, CVS Health, Cardinal Health
Retailers and intermediaries storing and delivering physical goods (commodities)	JDCom, Suning.com, Power Diversity Automobile Trade	Ceconomy, Metro	Seven & I Holdings, Aeon	Tesco, Sainsbury, Morris Supermarkets	Walmart

internet services, such as Vodafone in the UK, Deutsche Telekom in Germany and NTT Docomo in Japan. Although human communication and internet flows can to a large extent be intangible, geographically distant communication and internet require commodities and hard physical infrastructures to be possible. Moreover, apart from the UK sample, all samples contain highly tangible car manufacturer organizations in the largest monetary flow generators, organizations such as SAIC in China, Nissan in Japan or Ford in the US.

China, Japan and US samples contain several physical machine and appliance manufacturers in the largest monetary flow–generating firms, for instance, the Gree Electric Appliance Group, Toshiba or Apple. China is the only sample containing organizations directly related to construction and building structures in the top 20 largest cash flow–generating firms. The UK and the US are the two samples having firms connected to human health, which might not be unrelated with their domestic health systems, for instance, organizations producing health services, which therefore require highly tangible hospitals, machines, furniture and ambulances. Another example is pharmaceutical companies such as GlaxoSmithKline and AstraZeneca, which are connected to some degree of intangibility in R&D, patents or marketing, which is reflected in a higher average LOI. Still, medicines and medical machines have a physical form and commodity properties.

Among the largest monetary flow generators, a few organizations could traditionally be classified as intangible-intensive. Nonetheless, intangible flow theory explains why they are highly reliant upon tangibility for their product flows. There is an airline (Lufthansa in Germany) and a travel company that also owns planes, besides hotels (TUI Travel in the UK). These two could traditionally be classified as mere service providers. However, as explained before, airways are highly dependent on tangible jet fuel, planes, airports, and so forth. Likewise, hotels require highly tangible physical structures such as buildings, furniture and machines.

Similarly, organizations based upon storing and delivering physical goods could also traditionally be classified as mere service providers and thus intangible-intensive. As a matter of fact, their product flows are based upon commodities. Therefore, their product outflows are highly tangible, for example, supermarket and retail stores chains such as JD.Com, Suning.com and Power Diversity Automobile Trade (in China); Ceconomy (in Germany); Seven & I Holdings and AEON (in Japan); Tesco, Sainsbury and Morris Supermarkets (in the UK); and Walmart (in the US). Other examples are gross traders delivering goods to supermarkets, retailers and other shops as Metro (in Germany).

In all samples, there is at least an insurance company in the largest cash flow generator set. Clearly, a key resource for insurance organizations is money. Monetary flows are highly tangible. Furthermore, insurance contracts can be classified between (human) life (as over health, pensions, etc.) and non-life (as over property such as houses, cars and factories). Thus, most insurance contracts involve tangible fixtures and conditions.

The one organization in these 100 firms that might be producing product flows with higher intangibility is WPP, a giant advertising and communication company (in the UK). Indeed, this firm has a relatively high average LOI. However, its operations are far from being entirely intangible. According to its 2017 annual report, that year the organization had 203,000 people working with them at 3,000 (physical) offices in 112 countries around the world. These people require highly tangible physical flows to survive and exist, let alone to work.

Therefore, Figure 5.3 and Table 5.1 further confirm the association between monetary flow generation and tangible flows, which are reliant upon natural resources and the biophysical world. Furthermore, those tangible flows require human-related intangible flow dynamics to be produced and delivered.

5.7 Robustness procedures and limitations

The LOI methodology was used to classify organizations according to the tangibility of operating product flows they deliver to members of society. While trying to empirically identify connection among different firms' characteristics, one needs to be aware that firms' decisions do not only dependent upon the firms themselves. These decisions are impacted by a multitude of other factors. Furthermore, firms' characteristics change along different historical periods, stages of the country development or firm life, environmental interactions, and so forth.

Similar results to those shown earlier were obtained via alternative statistical tests and following different econometric specifications. Furthermore, all tests have been repeated after outlier observations have been excluded for the five country samples. The exclusion of outliers did not produce substantially different findings. Likewise, the tests were conducted in five additional country samples from the Refinitiv Datastream database, which has resulted in similar findings. These five country samples included listed firms from Australia, Canada, Malaysia, Singapore and South Korea.[27]

Perhaps useful and interesting, these findings are a descriptive analysis. No claim is made as to the direction of causation between the studied economic characteristics. These findings merely reflect the samples and period under study. Furthermore, organizational managers or stakeholders must not make automatic and non-reflected decisions related to operating intangibility, size, capital expenditures, or debt leverage. Any major organizational decision must be carefully considered and chosen according to the specific characteristics, resources, and environment of the organization. Within the circumstance of the limitations and cautions mentioned earlier, the intangible flow theory may contribute to form a new perspective from which to observe real-life organizations.

Despite a battery of empirical tests, there were still some imperfections in this study, both conceptually and empirically. As explained by the intangible flow theory, intangible flows cannot be measured with precision. By definition, a proxy cannot measure intangible flows exactly because this would imply tangible flows. Therefore, we need to use tangible flows for quantitatively inferring intangible flows. The proxies are mere estimates. For the large sample used, the proxies seem to be statistically significant and congruent. However, they are approximations, not precise measurements of intangible flows. Furthermore, the item "selling, general and administrative expenses" in the database incorporates a diverse agglomerated expense set. Most of these expenses seem to be related to intangible flows, such as work and service production, marketing, R&D and legal expenses. However, some firms may incorporate items that are not intangible flow–related into their selling, general and administrative expenses. Moreover, the use of different accounting policies among firms, years, and countries may influence the results, although the econometric robustness procedures address samples with panel data characteristics. Additionally, some issues with the proxy can only be solved by accounting authorities, as only accounting norms have the power to mandate that companies discriminate expenses with more detail in their financial statements.

If fewer observations had been used, there would be a greater risk that the result would be because of a small sample size. All the proxies that were used are related to operating expenses and, therefore, operating decisions, which is one of the major issues under study in this article. Nevertheless, this chapter reports preliminary testing whereby operating intangibility proxies have been used in the context of identifying the tangibility of a firm's product flows. As such, the behavior of operating tangibility is still not fully understood. A proxy for operating intangibility that is computed with publicly available information must always rely on a sensible balance between inferring immeasurable intangible flows with reasonably quantifiable tangible elements.

5.8 Discussion and conclusions

Intangible flow theory is not a mere criticism to mainstream economics, Marxism and relativism. It offers new concepts, ideas, methods and tools that were not previously available. In this chapter, the new theory makes two claims. The first is that organizations exist to deliver operating product flows to members of society. The second is that most operating product flows are highly reliant upon natural resources and the biosphere (which can consider including atmosphere, geosphere and hydrosphere providing for living beings). These two claims have been accompanied by a new system to classify organizations according to the tangibility of their operating product flows.

Hence, the theory attempts to measure a characteristic of organizations that has not been observed by previous frameworks. At one extreme of the classification systems are organizations delivering tangible physical goods. At the other are organizations delivering highly intangible products. At the middle of the scale are firms delivering mixed products, which combine, for instance, physical goods and intangible services, or hybrid products themselves.

This new system allows exhibiting that firms partially organize themselves according to operating needs associated with the tangibility of the flows of operating products (outputs) delivered to customers, who are members of human societies. Firms that produce and deliver physical goods/commodities (e.g., cars or planes) may inherently have different economic characteristics compared to firms that deliver intangible products (e.g., consulting or advertising). Indeed, an association between operating intangibility and monetary flow generation has been identified. However, this association appears as a trend in five large samples over a specific time period. It is not automatic. Lower LOI does not inevitably imply larger monetary flow generation.[28] Moreover, one must be aware that organizations' decisions are not only dependent upon themselves. For example, such decisions are impacted by other organizations, human societies and the environment they are integrated within.

Nevertheless, we can address previous misconceptions. For instance, although organizations such as airline companies, supermarkets, online platforms selling physical goods, and hotel chains have in the past been considered as producers of intangible products and/or intangible-intensive, actually these organizational forms deliver to their costumers flows of physical goods (e.g., as flows of goods in supermarkets or jet fuel in airplanes) or products that heavily rely on tangible long-term fixed assets (as hotel buildings, airplanes or airports). Moreover, several of these organizations hire a substantial number of people who, as we have seen the previous chapters, are not intangible. Furthermore, we humans require physical goods to survive and exist. Likewise, some organizations that would be traditionally classified as physical good–intensive firms are in fact highly reliant on intangible-related expenses in R&D, marketing or brand awareness (as for instance some soft-drink, cosmetic product and sports companies). These misconceptions are present when one reads extraordinary claims about intangible assets addressing physical and biological human needs or replacing tangible product flows.

Some individuals, institutional investors and financial entities may indeed invest in organizations with the purpose of increasing their own wealth. However, organizations do not merely exist to increase their financial investors' wealth, as argued by both mainstream economics and Marxism (and implied by relativism in their implicit support of dominant theories). Furthermore, organizations are not just "*huge fictitious bodies*," as suggested by several writers, including Polanyi.[29] Organizations are not fictious because they entail actual and demonstrable phenomena. They produce and deliver actual flows of products, which are essential for human survival and existence. These organizations are in many cases structured as hierarchical distributive systems in relation to natural resources and the biophysical world. Operating product flows would not be observable were one to be absorbed by the micro moment where the monetary flow moves from the buyer to the seller, as in the market parable in mainstream economics from which Polanyi could not yet escape. From a flow perspective, the monetary flow is just a micro moment in relation to all flows necessary that go from obtaining natural resources at the biosphere to delivering a finished product to a human being.

The mere forces of market supply and demand would not be able to produce several highly complex product flows delivered by organizations to members of society through complex human-related intangible dynamics. Human organizations are not merely replacements to market operations. On the contrary, markets are also a form of human organization.[30] We have closely observed the largest cash flow–generating organizations in this five-country sample from 2000 to 2017 or 2002 to 2017. Clearly, those are organizations that produce and deliver flows of physical goods and/or products that intensely rely on tangible long-term fixed assets and/or employ many people. For instance, major internet-based organizations'[31] recent growth has been accompanied by a substantial growth in the number of tangible and identifiable workers and physical infrastructures. Thus, large internet-based organizations are quite far from being classifiable as merely intangible-intensive.

Organizations contemporarily mediate human societies' integration upon the biosphere and the biophysical world in a manner that non-coordinated market activities could not achieve. Only by identifying the relevance of operating product flows to human survival and existence, one may inquire what could be the best manners to produce and deliver them. The pseudo-phenomenon that the cash flow makes/defines the commodity might avert us to observe how economic and societal production is fundamentally dependent upon biophysical resources. It might prevent us to look at the biosphere beyond any representation in terms of monetary flows. These pseudo-phenomena may make us unconscious as to understand the impact our economic and societal production might be having. Undeniably, money has been an important social technology for human societies. It has allowed to solve important problems regarding production and allocation. However, by obsessing with monetary flows, we may inattentively risk and cause damage, disasters and catastrophes to the biosphere in which our species is integrated.

Notes

1 Markets would be replaced by firms essentially due to transaction costs of trading through markets; otherwise markets would suffice for every economic transaction (Coase, 1937, 1960; Callon, 1998a, 1998b).
2 See, for instance, Grossman and Hart (1986), Hart and Moore (1990); Williamson (1975, 1985, 1989).
3 Wernerfelt (1984); Barney (2001); Kraaijenbrink, Spender, and Groen (2010); Barney, Ketchen, and Wright (2011).
4 See, for instance, Thaler (1997)
5 Becker (1962, 1964, 2008); Schultz (1961).
6 Soener and Nau (2019).
7 See, for instance, Damodaran (2011), Brealey and Myers (2003), Koller, Dobbs, and Huyett (2011), Geddes (2011).
8 Cardao-Pito (2004, 2010, 2012a, 2012b, 2016, 2017).

9 For Japan and China, the sample comprises the period 2002 to 2017 because the data points in 2000 to 2001 were not in the national currency.

10 Ahrne, Aspers, and Brunsson (2015), Callon (1998a, 1998b).

11 See, for instance, Cañibano, Garcia-Ayuso, and Sanchez (2000), Cardao-Pito (2015), Edmans (2011), Haskel and Westlake (2018), Johanson, Mårtensson, and Skoog (2001), Lev (2001), Sewchurran, Dekker, and McDonogh (2018).

12 Rathmel (1966) and Shostack (1977).

13 Shostack (1977).

14 It is difficult to find an entirely intangible product out of an organization, as even these examples can be associated with tangible forms and receipts.

15 Haskel and Westlake (2018), Lev and Gu (2016), Lev (2001).

16 Monetary values were compared through the World Bank's Consumer Price Index statistics.

17 See, for instance, Parker, Van Alstyne, and Choudary (2016).

18 Sometimes, some platform operations may involve physical structures not owned by them. It may also entail commodities not produced, owned or stored by them. Thus, they are platforms enabling the digital framework for operating those physical infrastructures and moving those commodities. For instance, Airbnb does not own the rooms and houses they help renting and Uber does not own the cars used by the drivers registered at their databases.

19 Alphabet (2019, p. 6).

20 Facebook (2019, p. 7).

21 Baidu (2019, p. 117). These employees were divided into: "21,774 employees in research and development, 13,324 employees in sales and marketing, 4,926 employees in operation and service, and 2,243 employees in management and administration. As of December 31, 2018, we had 25,845 employees in Beijing, 16,080 employees outside of Beijing but within China, and 342 employees outside of China. We also hire temporary employees and contractors from time to time."

22 In this chapter, we do not address the size of market capitalization. As will be explained later, dominant economic theory claims market capitalization is identical to (unpredictable) future cash flows discounted by a rate. However, no evidence has so far been presented that could support the dominant view.

23 See, for instance, Dean (1948); Charnes, Cooper, and Ijiri (1963).

24 In a few cases, the shadow representing the 95% confidence interval is so small, one can barely see it.

25 At 2010 values for comparison.

26 The sample contains only organizations listed in stock markets. Although 12% of Chinese GDP is still a very impressive figure, the lower proportion when compared to the other samples might be related with state owned enterprises not listed on stock exchanges and producing a substantial activity in this reformed communist state.

27 You can see also Cardao-Pito (2017).

28 In the same manner, other economic characteristics may also be impacted upon by the tangibility of product flows such as the financial structure and the investment policy manifested in capital expenditures. Larger organizations require more complex financial endeavors to organizations with little collateral and requiring little investment, in some cases almost self-financed through revenues. (Rajan and Zingales, 1995; Fama and French, 2002; Frank and Goyal, 2009; Booth et al., 2001; Kurshev and Strebulaev, 2007; Öztekin, 2015). Likewise, it might be fair to assume that a large proportion of firms' investments is directed to the production of operating product flows to be delivered to members of society. Even if no quantitative difference could be found, a qualitative difference in the investment made should be easily demonstrated. For instance, even though the proportional quantity of investment would be the same among them, a hotel chain network could invest in new hotels, a car manufacturer in new car plants, and a digital company in new online platforms. (Ahrne, Aspers, and Brunsson, 2015; Simon, 1991).

29 Polanyi (1944, 2001, p. 176).
30 Ahrne, Aspers, and Brunsson (2015) and Simon (1991).
31 For instance, Alphabet or Baidu.

References

Ahrne, G., Aspers, P. and Brunsson, N. (2015). The organization of markets. *Organization Studies*, 36(1), 7–27.

Alphabet, Inc. (2019). *Annual Report Pursuant to Section 13 or 15(d) of the Securities Exchange act of 1934: For the Fiscal Year Ended December 31, 2018.* Alphabet. Online at: https://abc.xyz/investor/static/pdf/20180204_alphabet_10K.pdf?cache=11336e3.

Baidu, Inc. (2019). *Annual Report Pursuant to Section 13 or 15(d) of the Securities Exchange act of 1934: For the Fiscal Year Ended December 31, 2018.* Baidu. Online at: http://ir.baidu.com/static-files/4ce88b07-60fe-4561-9cc9-2b0e0ec9dfd6.

Barney, J. (2001). Resource-based theories of competitive advantage: A ten-year retrospective on the resource-based view. *Journal of Management*, 27(6), 643–650.

Barney, J., Ketchen, J. and Wright, M. (2011). The future of resource-based theory: Revitalization or decline? *Journal of Management*. March Online First.

Becker, G. (1964). *Human Capital.* New York: Columbia University Press.

Becker, G. (2008). *Human Capital: The Concise Encyclopedia of Economics.* Library of Economics and Liberty. Online at: www.econlib.org/ library/Enc/HumanCapital.html.

Booth, L., Aivazian, V., Demirguc-Kunt, A. and Maksimovic, V. (2001). Capital structures in developing countries. *Journal of Finance*, 56, 87–130.

Brealey, R. and Myers, S. (2003). *Principles of Corporate Finance.* New York: Mcgraw-Hill Companies.

Callon, M. (1998a). Introduction: The embeddedness of economic markets in economics. *The Sociological Review*, 46(S1), 1–57.

Callon, M. (1998b). An essay on framing and overflowing: Economic externalities revisited by sociology. *The Sociological Review*, 46(S1), 244–269.

Cañibano, L., Garcia-Ayuso, M. and Sanchez, P. (2000). Accounting for intangibles: A literature review. *Journal of Accounting literature*, 19, 102–130.

Cardao-Pito, T. (2004). *Contributo para uma teoria dos fluxos intangiveis na criacao de valor financeiro.* Portugal: ISEG, UTL.

Cardao-Pito, T. (2010). *The Level of Operating Intangibility and the Economic Characteristics of Firms.* Paper presented to the American Accounting Association Annual Conference, San Francisco, July 31–August 4.

Cardao-Pito, T. (2012a). *Intangible Flow Theory, Operating Intangibility, and Other Economic Characteristics of Firms.* Ph.d thesis, University of Strathclyde, Glasgow, Scotland (British Library: Ethos Electronic Theses Online Services).

Cardao-Pito, T. (2012b). Intangible flow theory. *American Journal of Economics and Sociology*, 71(2), 328–353.

Cardao-Pito, T. (2015). Intangibles. In Werry, F. and Schor, J. (Eds.) *Sage Encyclopedia of Economics and Society*. Volume 4. Thousand Oaks, CA: Sage, 948–950.

Cardao-Pito, T. (2016). A law for the social sciences regarding us human beings. *Journal of Interdisciplinary Economics*, 28(2), 202–229.

Cardao-Pito, T. (2017). Organizations as producers of operating product flows to members of society. *SAGE Open*, 7(3), July–September, 1–18.

Charnes, A., Cooper, C. and Ijiri, Y. (1963). Breakeven budgeting and programming to goals. *Journal of Accounting Research*, 1(1), 16–43.

Coase, R. (1937). The nature of the firm. *Economica*, 416, 386–405.

Coase, R. (1960). The problem of social cost. In *Classic Papers in Natural Resource Economics*. London: Macmillan, 87–137.

Damodaran, A. (2011). *Corporate Finance: Theory and Practice*. Hoboken, NJ: Wiley-Blackwell.

Dean, J. (1948). Cost structures of enterprises and break-even charts. *American Economic Review*, 38(2), 153–164.

Edmans, A. (2011). Does the stock market fully value intangibles? Employee satisfaction and equity prices. *Journal of Financial Economics*, 101(3), 621–640.

Facebook, Inc. (2019). *Annual Report Pursuant to Section 13 or 15(d) of the Securities Exchange act of 1934: For the Fiscal Year Ended December 31, 2018*. Facebook. Online at: http://d18rn0p25nwr6d.cloudfront.net/CIK-0001326801/a109a501-ed16-4962-a3af-9cd16521806a.pdf.

Fama, E. and French, K. (2002). Testing trade-off and pecking order predictions about dividends and debt. *Review of Financial Studies*, 15(1), 1–33.

Frank, M. and Goyal, V. (2009). Capital structure decisions: Which factors are reliably important? *Financial Management*, 38(1), 1–37.

Geddes, R. (2011). *An Introduction to Corporate Finance Transactions and Techniques*. Hoboken, NJ: Wiley-Blackwell.

Grossman, S. and Hart, O. (1986). The costs and benefits of ownership: A theory of vertical and lateral integration. *Journal of Political Economy*, 94(4), 691–719.

Hart, O. and Moore, J. (1990). Property rights and the nature of the firm. *Journal of Political Economy*, 98(6), 1119–1158.

Haskel, J. and Westlake, S. (2018). *Capitalism without Capital: The Rise of the Intangible Economy*. Oxford: Princeton University Press.

Johanson, U., Mårtensson, M. and Skoog, M. (2001). Mobilizing change through the management control of intangibles. *Accounting, Organizations and Society*, 26(7–8), 715–733.

Koller, T., Dobbs, R. and Huyett, B. (2011). *Value: The Four Cornerstones of Corporate Finance*. Hoboken, NJ: Wiley-Blackwell.

Kraaijenbrink, J., Spender, J. and Groen, A. (2010). The resource-based view: A review and assessment of its critiques. *Journal of Management*, 36(1), 349–372.

Kurshev, A. and Strebulaev, I. (2007). *Firm Size and Capital Structure*. In AFA 2008 New Orleans Meetings Paper. New Orleans: American Finance Association.

Lev, B. (2001). *Intangibles*. Washington, DC: Brookings Institution Press.

Lev, B. and Gu, F. (2016). *The End of Accounting*. New York: Wiley-Blackwell.

Öztekin, Ö. (2015). Capital structure decisions around the world: Which factors are reliably important? *Journal of Financial and Quantitative Analysis*, 50(3), 301–323.

Parker, G., Van Alstyne, M. and Choudary, S. (2016). *Platform Revolution: How Networked Markets Are Transforming the Economy – and How to Make Them Work for You*. New York. W. W. Norton & Company.

Polanyi, K. (1944, 2001). *The Great Transformation*. Boston: Beacon Press.

Rajan, R. and Zingales, L. (1995). What do we know about capital structure? Some evidence from international data. *Journal of Finance*, 50, 1421–1460.

Rathmel, J. (1966). What is meant by services. *Journal of Marketing*, 30(5), 32–36.

Sewchurran, K., Dekker, J. and McDonogh, J. (2018). Experiences of embedding long-term thinking in an environment of short-termism and sub-par business performance: Investing in intangibles for sustainable growth. *Journal of Business Ethics*, 1–45.

Schultz, T. (1961). Investing in human capital. *American Economic Review*, 51(1), 1.

Shostack, G. (1977). Breaking free from product marketing. *Journal of Marketing*, 41(2), 73–80.

Simon, H. A. (1991). Organizations and markets. *Journal of Economic Perspectives*, 5(2), 25–44.

Soener, M. and Nau, M. (2019). Citadels of privilege: The rise of LLCs, LPs and the perpetuation of elite power in America. *Economy and Society*, 48(3), 399–425.

Thaler, R. (1997). Irving fisher: Modern behavioral economist. *American Economic Review*, 87(2), 439–441.

Wernerfelt, B. (1984). A resource-based view of the firm. *Strategic Management Journal*, 5(2), 171–180.

Williamson, O. (1975). *Markets and Hierarchies*. New York: Free Press.

Williamson, O. (1985). *The Economic Institutions of Capitalism*. New York: Free Press.

Williamson, O. (1989). Transaction cost economics. *Handbook of Industrial Organization*, 1, 135–182.

Appendix A Description of observations used from Refinitiv Datastream database

	China sample	Germany sample	Japan sample	UK sample	US sample	Total sample
Observations with LOI available and between [0;1]	37,822	11,148	59,195	31,647	30,080	169,892
Keeping organizations with 4 or more observations	36,790	10,648	58,115	29,748	29,948	165,249
Number of organizations	3,520	968	4,563	3,115	2,104	14,270

Notes:

1) Germany, UK and US samples cover the period 2000–2017. China and Japan samples cover the period 2002–2017, as observations in national currency were not available for 2000–2001.
2) The variables are described in Appendix B.
3) The final sample contains observations for organizations with at least four observations.

Appendix B Computing the variables in the Refinitiv Datastream database

Variables	Description	Mnemonics in the database
Testing variables		
LOI	The level of operating intangibility (LOI) is equal to one minus the ratio of the sum of the cost of goods sold, amortizations and depreciations of fixed assets, and other operating costs to the total operating costs. The Datastream Worldscope database allows computing LOI as the selling, general, and administrative expenses divided by the total operating costs.	(WC01101/ (WC01001- WC01250))
SIZE	Logarithm of the sales, after the sales values have been deflated by the consumer price index produced by the World Bank (with reference to 2010). For the purpose of computing econometric regressions, a logarithm was computed at this variable.	WC01001⋆ CPIfactor
CAPEX_PPE	Capital expenditures in the tangibles property, plant, and equipment expressed as a fraction of total revenues.	(WC04601/ WC01001)
DEBT_ LEVERAGE	Book value of total liabilities divided by total assets.	(WC03351/ WC02999)

(*Continued*)

Appendix B (Continued)

Variables	Description	Mnemonics in the database
Control Variables		
PROFITABILITY	Net income divided by the total assets. In robustness procedures, the ratio of operating income to total assets is also tested.	(WC01250/ WC02999)
MARKET_TO_ BOOK[Equity]	Market value divided by the book value per equity shares at close date.	(MTBV)

Appendix C Regression findings

Panel C.A– LOI as independent variable

	China Sample	Germany Sample	Japan Sample	UK Sample	US Sample
Intercept	1.067	0.623	1.270	0.910	1.116
	(37.85)★★★	(12.50)★★★	(70.38)★★★	(26.50)★★★	(33.13)★★★
LOG_SIZE	−0.060	−0.032	−0.054	−0.064	−0.028
	(−80.98)★★★	(−13.96)★★★	(−72.15)★★★	(−49.45)★★★	(−26.76)★★★
CAPEX-PPE	0.001	−0.000	−0.002	0.000	−0.000
	(3.57)★★★	(−0.75)	(−1.59)	(0.09)	(−4.80)★★★
DEBT_ LEVERAGE	0.027	−0.047	−0.005	−0.044	−0.005
	(7.27)★★★	(−4.37)★★★	(−1.85)★	(−6.30)	(−1.03)
PROFITABILITY	0.028	0.008	0.002	−0.001	0.008
	(7.17)★★★	(5.58)★★★	(2.13)★★	(−0.53)	(1.58)
MARKET_TO_ BOOK	0.000	0.000	−0.000	0.000	0.000
	(−4.20)	(0.36)	(−0.65)	(0.27)	(−0.48)
R-Squared	0.793	0.704	0.922	0.833	0.908
Fixed Effects by Year	YES	YES	YES	YES	YES
Fixed Effects by Organization	YES	YES	YES	YES	YES
Number of Observations	25 699	8 184	52 576	19 833	23 831
Number of Organizations	2 330	765	4 171	2 128	1 696
Years	[2002–2017]	[2000–2017]	[2002–2017]	[2000–2017]	[2000–2017]

Notes:
1 The variables are defined in Appendix B. The variable *LOG_SIZE* is the natural logarithm of the variable *SIZE* described in Appendix B.
2 Observations with missing values in the variables *CAPEX_PPE* and *MARKET_TO_BOOK* were removed.
3 Panel A contains all useful observations. Panel B excludes outlier observations from the tests.
4 The regression models are controlled by the fixed effects of organizations and years.
5 β = regression coefficient.
6 In parentheses () appear the *p* value = Prob > |r| under H0: Rho = 0.
7 Notation after the parentheses: ★*p* value of at least 10%. ★★*p* value of at least 5%. ★★★*p* value of 1% or better.
8 In all regression tests, there is a very strong statistical association between *LOI* and *LOG_SIZE* and therefore the size of monetary revenues, despite of the many control variables used.
9 Similar results were found when removing outlier observations (not reported for space motives).

6   Non-deconstructable flows and countering relativism

6.1 Introduction

Intangible flow theory is metaphysical realist. It assumes a real world of objects, properties and relations, which does not require contingent human authorizations to exist.[1] It does not aim to appeal to the unknown and untestable to bring forward metaphysical claims. Instead, it intends to oppose the narcissist stance that we humans could have entirely built (constructed) our world merely out of scientific methods and human languages. This new theory likewise exhibits that we are we far from having scientific methods and language forms to fully capture this world beyond our social and bio-mental constructions. Many phenomena are yet intangible to humankind. Along the way, we create pseudo-phenomena, fake formulations and misguided reporting that are unmatched by actual objects, properties and relations. Furthermore, there must be many things we do not have any awareness about. The new theory endorses inquiries and eventual deconstructions towards scientific methods and language forms. However, this endorsement aligns with finding better methods and language vehicles to account for the reality we humans are immersed in.

By indicating partial tangibility beyond our human constructions, the new theory suggests that there are phenomena we humans may identify with precision. Along the biosphere and biophysical world, we can likewise find tangible phenomena in human societies. As explained in previous chapters, occurred monetary flows are examples of social and yet tangible phenomena. While money is socially constructed and has several intangible dimensions, monetary flows that have occurred in a specific time and space are quite tangible. Their social construction does not imply nonbeing. However, monetary flows are consummated by many intangible and not yet perceivable flows. Thus, we cannot hitherto precisely explain their occurrence or predict future monetary flow phenomena with certainty.

Furthermore, the new theory brings on the concept of tangibilization: when humans find methods and language forms through previously intangible dimensions that can be identified with precision (tangible). We humans can analyze and deconstruct but also improve, renew and innovate scientific methods and language vehicles. Therefore, intangible flow theory might be compatible with substantial evidence that over thousands of years in the most diverse areas of our existence, we humans have advanced our knowledge and skills. As in Socrates' formulation described (and probably created) by Plato,[2] the major obstacles are not from an ignorance aware of its fragility, but the self-assurance of an apparent knowledge.

6.2 Addressing relativism in the social sciences with intangible flow theory

By adopting the outlook summarized earlier, the new theory must address the relativism that in the last decades has been rampant in several academic departments around the planet.[3] Indeed, significant disdain for the truth and inconsideration for evidence can bring upon negative, yet unpredictable consequences to the human sciences.[4] Categorically, one may ask what would be the point of having scientists for performing the role of claiming they cannot explain anything with reference to reality. Without the burden of evidence, apparently anyone could do the job of denying reality. In such a hypothetical scenario, what would universities be for besides collecting monetary flows from students, moneyed sponsors, moneyed investors and eventual governments?

Relativist positions have been described as social constructivism, poststructuralism or postmodernism. However, these terms are misleading and unhelpful to our intents. Frequently, they are employed in aesthetical and artistic areas such as writing, cinema, painting, architecture and sculpture. When somehow employed in connection to scientific matters, these terms may pertain to large and heterogeneous sets of authors, a few of whom may not hold relativist stances. Moreover, these terms generally are poorly defined. In different reviews, the same writer can be described as a social constructivist, poststructuralist or postmodernist.[5] Moreover, poststructuralism and postmodernism terms could give the mistaken impression that the preceding structuralism and modernism they allude to have been properly defined. It is not the case.[6] For example, two writers who have been classified as poststructuralist may have rather different positions regarding structuralism. While one can imply poststructuralism to be a continuation of structuralism,[7] the other may assert to be anti-structuralism.[8] The same happens to two writers who have been classified as postmodernists. One writer may define himself to be doing the history and critique of modernity,[9] therefore presuming somewhat that modernity or modernism have existed at least at one society after the enlightenment (also poorly defined).[10] The other writer could claim that we humans have never been modern, hence, implying that modernism has never existed.[11] These are just a few examples.

Instead of adopting broad and poorly defined expressions, we specifically tackle the issue of relativism. That is, we address relativist writers who may or may not have been classified as social constructivists, poststructuralists or postmodernists. We define relativism by adapting Kukla's (2000, p. 4) interrelated typology[12]: (i) *Metaphysical* (or transcendental) *relativism* questions the existence of a real world (of say objects, properties and relations[13]) outside our social and bio-mental[14] constructions. (ii) *Epistemological* (or scientific) *relativism* argues that science cannot have empirical instruments to describe a real world besides our human constructions. (iii) *Semantic relativism* suggests that human languages cannot describe a real world besides our human constructions. Semantic relativism can also entail wide-ranging proclamations on institutions and social arrangements enabling discourses into being.

An adopter of epistemological and/or semantic relativist arrangements may claim to not be a (full) relativist on the grounds of not sanctioning metaphysical relativism. For example, a writer who doubts we have adequate scientific methods or language vehicles to capture reality may still accept that reality exists beyond our human constructions.[15] Nonetheless, all these three forms can lead to relativist assertions that accounts of reality would be merely social constructed. Either (i) reality would not exist outside our individual and social selves or (ii) it would be constructed by scientific methods and/or language molds.

Despite their seeming recent success, relativists hold peculiar argumentative positions because they cannot coherently admit to present evidence to debate. Obviously, valid evidence on a specific matter would demonstrate that relativist theses would be incoherent. Evidently, however, to present an argument, sooner or later, relativists must invoke some supporting substantiation. However, they must not openly admit doing so. Hence, relativists' aims easily become to undermine others' evidence legitimacy and/or openly smear social groups and scientists themselves. For this purpose, they may create self-referring research bubbles. Alternatively, relativists could claim that everything exists only inside one's head (solipsism) without of course defining what a head is or how the head integrates into the human body and the body in the biosphere. However, solipsism is unattainable when one claims that reality would be social constructed. Social construction requires at least two human beings interacting.

Sooner than later, relativists need to present some evidence to argue with. However, they cannot admit it for being contradictory to their stance. However, without openly providing valid evidence, hardly could relativists produce new theories and hypotheses to replace dominant ones. Hence, ironically, relativism generally reinforces dominant theories and likewise dominant social groups. Promises of liberation of speeches and conversations, effusion of ideas, empowered human communities, universal liberty, and auspicious futures soon become hollow because relativists cannot provide legitimate accounts to substantiate alternative explanations. Indeed, relativism effectively sabotages formation of new theories. Included are, of course, explanations for human participation in economic and societal production, as the dominant human commodity framework in economics and interrelated sciences we will further study in the next part.

What then could prevent scientific discourses from falling into insidious forms of narcissism whereby proto-scientists would delude themselves into having created the universe by arts of discourse, methodologies and social construction? Then again, what could prevent scientific departments falling upon tribal/gang mentalities, where mere attainment of status and financial resources would be at stake? What is worse, those in powerful societal positions would no longer have to put up with any serious contestation because no evidence could contest their theories and arguments. Science is itself a case study. Relativism ends up protecting those who have high academic status by controlling prestigious scientific departments, high-ranked journals, financial resources and much else. Relativism cannot clearly dissociate the law of the jungle to reason and logic. Without commitment to the truth, reason or logic, a few humans may stick to lying, cheating, manipulating, mobbing, threating, harassing and so forth. Although relativists might appear to deconstruct dominant theories, they seldom have means for presenting alternative theories given that they deny binding connections to a reality beyond our social and bio-mental constructions. Paradoxically, thus, relativism reinforces dominant theories and social groups.

Intriguingly, however, many contemporary relativists repeat arguments and debates that were heard in ancient monetary societies of Greece and Rome. Contemporary relativists have very much in common to olden Sophist and Skeptic philosophies.[16] By the term Skeptic we are not referring the healthy dose of skepticism one needs to have in life affairs, but to ancient relativist schools named as such. Their opponents, remarkable ancient philosophers as Plato, Socrates (narrated by Plato), Aristoteles, Democritus and diverse Stoics took great pains to demonstrate perils of relativism and furthermore to exhibit that relativism is illogical and unreasonable when applied to itself.

Nevertheless, an apparently innocuous relativism of knowledge can easily fall into insidious moral relativism. Ancient philosophers who opposed relativism did not demise it as a frivolous philosophy. They understood important consequences it could have on human societies. As Socrates narrated by Plato notes,

> when they speak of justice and injustice, piety and impiety, they are confident that in nature these have no existence or essence of their own – the truth is that which is agreed on at the time of the agreement, and as long as the agreement lasts; and this is the philosophy of many.[17]

Written around the 4th and 5th centuries before Christ, these words remain impressively on spot to describe many contemporary relativists. After one declares that truth would be relative, he/she would have found a rhetorical strategy whereby nothing he/she could say could be contradicted. Although such might not be purpose of the relativist, his/her reasoning assists in justifying manners of abuse and evil.[18] Thus, relativism is far from harmless.[19]

Relativizing the truth suited well Protagoras, a leader among Sophist philosophers. In ancient Greece, they made a living by receiving money for their expensive lessons. They would lecture moneyed persons and their descendants to develop rhetorical skills to defend themselves in court and other venues.[20] Protagoras was famous for declaring that among every two competing arguments, he could make the weakest argument defeat the strongest or make the worse appear the better cause.[21] He had another famous proposition, declaring man to be the measure of all things (*"of the existence of things that are, and of the non-existence of things that are not"*[22]). Approximately, this view could apply to current versions where all things would be socially constructed. The interpretative community would be the measure of all existing and nonexisting things.

Nonetheless, Plato, Socrates (as narrated by Plato), Aristoteles,[23] Democritus and several Stoic philosophers have demonstrated that relativism is not credible or coherent.[24] As a summary, we can note that if all things are relative, it therefore follows that relativism is also relative; thus, some things are not relative. Hence, relativism is not credible or coherent. Global relativism is illogical, unreasonable and self-defeating when applied to itself.[25] A similar demonstration can be applied to the thesis of local relativism (or subjectivism), that reality exists only (or is subjective) in relation to a social group of local interpreters. Identifications of the social group's members and their interpretation require at least two truth assertions (which contradict relativism).[26] Thousands of years ago as currently, however, as relativists have no commitment to the truth, reason, logic and evidence, they would have little motif to accept defeat. For many years, these debates continued in Ancient Greece and later in Ancient Rome. Skeptic philosophers would create the leading relativist schools.[27] On the other hand, Stoic, Platonic and Peripatetic (after Aristoteles) philosophers would become perhaps their major opponents. In the endnote, you can find a summary of the Stoics' case against relativism as described by a leading Skeptic from the 3rd and 2nd centuries BC.[28] This Skeptic would try addressing the objections with similar schemes to recent relativists, who we will observe later.

Unfortunately, relativists seldom apply their relativism to their own work. Contemporary and ancient relativists alike have used strategies of suspending judgement over evidence and contesting criteria and proofs presented by non-relativists.[29] However, relativism is unreasonable and illogical, as displayed a thousand years ago to no avail. Yet, many relativists have kept loudly arguing. Nowadays, openly or covertly, they have endeavored undermining and smearing science based upon reason and logic. Perhaps in the absence of new evidence, arguing with relativists should be avoided. Otherwise, relativists may freely misconstrue opponents' points of view to support their own.[30] They may assume an attitude where they always win every argument through denying the legitimacy of evidence presented against their arguments. As follows from their lack of commitment to the truth, reason or logic, relativists can freely claim that they have won every discussion, even when flagrantly they did not.[31] Or they may claim privileges (e.g., aesthetical). Norris (1997, p. 214)[32] suggests shifting the burden of the proof to relativists. Indeed, relativists most often try sabotaging evidence presented by others. Still, most relativist claims, including the quite extravagant ones, are argued without clearly assuming supportive evidence to back them up. If relativists do not admit supportive evidence, why should we care to believe or entertain them? There is no need to constantly repeat that global and local relativism (subjectivism) have been defeated by reason and logic thousands of years ago. Moreover, reason and logic would have the hardest time arguing with unreason and illogic.

Nevertheless, another substantial issue must be addressed: Through massive colonization of social science departments, relativists have become ever more powerful in academia. They control departments, academic journals, other publications, research funding, research rankings, and many other mechanisms of academic power. Along the way, many relativists have been establishing abusive and toxic relationships with both the truth and science based on reason and logic. Consequently, the very possibility of having social sciences studying, and eventually improving, the human condition has been systematically opposed by relativist writers, who, in some cases, are proud to declare their anti-science stance.

Gaslighting is part of their abusive and toxic activities. It consist of conscious or unconscious forms of psychological abuse that occur when a perpetrator distorts information and confuses an individual or a group, triggering victims to doubt their memory and sanity.[33] Gaslighting involves, for instance, verbal (rhetorical) attacks, persistent denial (of, for instance, flagrant evidence), misdirection, misleading ingratiation, contradiction between actions and words, isolating targets, or blatant lying to destabilize victims and delegitimize their needs, assurances, feelings and beliefs.[34] As relativists have great difficulty in providing evidence that reality does not exist, for evidence of something is itself contradictory to relativism, they very often adopt gaslighting strategies. Intangible flow theory makes several contributions to address the systematic gaslighting that many relativists have been practicing towards the truth and science based upon reason and logic.

6.3 Examples of prominent relativists gaslighting the truth and science

6.3.1 Condescending word salads: Claiming privileged access to language

To provide evidence, this section exhibits notorious examples of gaslighting committed by foremost writers in contemporary relativist movements. These examples are not exhaustive. Moreover, not all relativists have exerted the exact same gaslighting activities, as these events can be quite heterogeneous. Furthermore, we do not conduct a complete review of relativism in human sciences. The aim is to provide evidence that, in recent decades, gaslighting has been at the core of foremost relativist projects.

A common gaslighting tactic is for relativists to cast doubt on others' use of language while themselves using language forms that would be excused by some sort of privileged status regarding the employment of language. Undeniably, scientific use of language is quite relevant. It must be studied and better understood. In many cases, it may need to be deconstructed, replaced and improved. However, for this purpose, we do not need to fall upon semantic relativism whereby human language vehicles would have lost any possible connection to reality beyond human constructions.

Implicitly, or explicitly, several semantic relativists acknowledge Ferdinand Sassure (1857–1913), who however is invoked out of convenience, without due regard for his proposals, and ignoring several difficulties therein. The formation of structuralism in linguistics is often attributed to Saussure.[35] Thus, the term poststructuralism could be apparently related to him. However, his reference book barely uses the term structure, preferring instead system(s).[36] He aimed promoting a scientific discipline of linguistics, which could better understand the formation of words and their relationships. He contested a view of words as direct representative of things[37] ("*a list of words, each corresponding to the thing that it names*"[38]). Instead, he created a theory of signs of language (later evolved into semiotics),[39] basically, making a distinction among two elements of the sign, (i) the significant or abstract concept (for example, the concept of a tree or a horse), and (ii) the signifier or sound (sound of the word to express a tree or a horse, which Saussure referred to as acoustic image).[40] Saussure then proposed studying relationships of signs and their evolution out of historical, cultural, geographic and other factors that to some extent might be quite arbitrary.[41] His proposals, while far from being entirely accepted in linguistics,[42] have expanded to other social sciences. Often it is noted that signs may not be restricted to words.[43]

However, Saussure did not claim that signs could not represent any reality. At one hand, the signifier required the significant. Thus, he supposes therefore that some significands might be real, and precede signifiers, whereas other might be created by signifiers. Moreover, signifier–significant demonstrations can often be highly speculative. On the other hand, Saussure invokes actual phenomena of sensory demonstrability in humans.[44] Furthermore, use of language vehicles to describe objects, properties and relations is not evidence of their nonexistence. One must carefully avoid describing Saussure's work as either relativism or gaslighting. He has presented relevant concerns regarding language use, made appreciable connection to objects and demonstrable extra-linguistic psychological states, and displayed appreciation for scientific work.

However, several relativists who claim to address Saussure's reasoning are engaging in gaslighting activities. For instance, while claiming to follow Nietzsche and Heidegger,[45] Derrida wishes to question the tendency of Western science and philosophy to regard language as a manner of expressing an actual external reality, which he deems as "*logocentrism*."[46] Saussure's semiotic and his followers were made targets. Derrida would wish to eliminate residues of that logocentrism. He finds a difference between signifiers and significands at signs. However, he would claim that writing implies language and that in respective (language) games, there would be signifiers of signifiers and significands operating as signifiers.[47] Derrida's relativist deconstruction project is not a mere language analysis project. Instead, he wishes to destroy any possible connection that words, writing and languages could have with that logos representing an external truth: "*it inaugurates the destruction, not the demolition but the de-sedimentation, the de-construction, of all the significations that have their source in that of the logos. Particularly the signification of truth.*"[48] For instead of representing an external reality, speeches would represent simulacrums of reality.[49] In this sense, Derrida's deconstruction approximates the destruction envisaged by Nietzsche[50] and Heidegger.[51] Eliminating, without any evidence, connections to what he calls the logos, Derrida can declare his famous bombastic statement that "*There is nothing outside of the text.*"[52] Perhaps without being aware, Derrida was repeating the argument of ancient relativist Skeptics such as Pyrrhos and Sextus Empiricus. Stoic philosophers had a theory of the sign slightly different to Saussure's. To the former, the sign would roughly be used to describe evidence for something.[53] Ancient Skeptics would claim (without evidence and using words themselves) that no sign could represent external evidence of something, which to a great extent is Derrida's position.

Other semantic (or sign) relativists follow similar gaslighting strategies. Baudrillard would declare that we would be living in an era of simulations ("*hyperreal,*"[54] "*a gigantic simulacrum*"[55]) that replaces signs of the real for the real itself.[56] It would now be impossible to isolate the process of the real or to prove the real.[57] As an example, Baudrillard claims maps would now be confused with territories.[58] Disneyland, an entertainment park, would be his ultimate demonstration.[59] Barthes has decided by himself that text authors were no longer necessary because any interpretation of a text would be possible. Therefore, he has declared the death of the author, which could liberate readers from possible hegemony, dominance and oppression of meaning that authors could wish to establish in their texts.[60] Derrida and Foucault agree in undermining the relevance of connecting a text to who has written it.[61] Foucault moves further in his semantic relativism, claiming that truth could only exist in relation to discourses formed out of regimes of production of truth.[62]

However, these relativists use language vehicles to criticize others for using language vehicles. Although semantic relativists use themselves texts, speeches, grammar and words, they claim a privileged status on such usage, which is not warranted by any form of evidence. How would semantic relativists demonstrate that language forms cannot reach a real world beyond human constructions? By making speeches at conferences or writing books and articles. What they criticize in others, they themselves would be authorized to do. These double standards demonstrate their gaslighting.

Let us observe a few other semantic examples. Rorty claims to abolish a lump/text dichotomy (he himself has created) where a lump would be something that would be a subject of analysis to a natural scientist and a text something that would be interpreted as a subject of analysis in the humanities.[63] He invokes several prejudices according to which neither natural science nor the humanities could ever reach objectivity, adequate meaning or truth statements. How would Rorty provide such demonstration? By writing himself a paper full of truth statements, where evidently, he would use language vehicles.[64] Likewise, Foucault creates a dichotomy between the document and the monument in his *Archeology of Knowledge*.[65] In this book, he makes proposals regarding discovering origins of scientific ideas and discourses, which he will develop in later writings linked to Nietzsche's genealogy.[66] However, Foucault's proposals are not entirely unproblematic because he tends to fail applying genealogy of ideas to his own work, with serious consequences. Still, on others he rejects both appeals to transcendental truths and principles of unity or progress in history.[67] Let us briefly observe Foucault's dialectic between document and monument. Foucault claims that archeology traditionally dealt with monuments, which he defines as *"inert traces, objects without context, and things left by the past."*[68] However, for scientific respectability and acceptance, archeologists have aimed at transforming monuments into (written) documents (where they discuss and report their findings).[69] According to Foucault, a traditional view of history would also be to deal with documents (that is, written texts). However, he would propose the inverse: an archeologist history, which would transform documents into monuments.[70] How would Foucault implement this move from documents into monuments? By debating the matter through authoring books. Hardly could there be an object more suitable to the category of document than a book.

Part of Derrida's deconstruction was identifying binary oppositions and metaphors in reasoning. Binary oppositions pinpoint how the meanings of words could be traced to their opposite meaning instead of to an external reality.[71] By metaphor, Derrida invokes and adapts Nietzsche's theory of metaphor,[72] where relations among words are used to suggest meaning.[73] However, his very close associates pave their statements with both binary oppositions and metaphors of their own making, for instance, Rorty's metaphor and binary opposites of texts and lumps or Foucault's metaphor of archeologist history based upon the binary opposites of monuments and documents. Likewise, by (relativist) deconstruction, Derrida has himself offered a metaphor associated with building physical structures and edifices. Furthermore, the word deconstruction operates as binary opposite to construction. What these relativists criticize in others regarding language would be acceptable to them, which displays their flagrant gaslighting.

6.3.2 Denying evidence: On the grounds they say so

The gaslighting form previously described can also be used to lay into scientific methods. Willard Quine, an ontological relativist, is a good example.[74] He claims that scientific facts could not be separated from their semantic (or linguistic) components.[75] Accordingly, any statement could be made true or false, if we would *"make drastic adjustments somewhere in the system."*[76] This reasoning is dependent on assuming that truth would be drawn only out of a whole system of statements (holism).[77] Thereby, it would not be possible to identify the truth in relation to a world beyond our human constructions, but only in relation to relative statement systems. Quine goes further in explaining nature of reality. He declares that physical objects[78] and abstract entities that are the substance of mathematics (for instance, numbers)[79] would be myths at a similar epistemological level as Homer's gods in the *Odyssey* and *Iliad*.[80] Quine, how-ever, feels entitled to the privilege of writing books to explain all this through plenty of truth statements.

Another gaslighting form is to have relativists describing themselves as abso-lute philosophers of science or sociologists of knowledge. Discarding debates with thousands of years, while using ancient Sophist vests, these relativists claimed they could explain to others what science and knowledge all were about. Yet, while these relativists undermined the validity of evidence, refer-ence to other explanatory systems would no longer be needed. Undeniably, scientists, scientific methods and practices must be studied and integrated in their many contexts such as social, economic, geographic and cultural. Fur-thermore, scientific results must not be taken for granted. Evidence must be thoroughly verified. What we are addressing here, however, is different. It is the severing of links to reality through gaslighting. We will provide evidence with leading self-assigned philosophers of science as Karl Popper, Thomas Khun, Imre Lakatos and Paul Feyerabend. However, these examples could easily be extended to other relativists who have appointed themselves as absolute sociol-ogists of knowledge such as Barry Barnes, David Bloor, Nelson Goodman and Bruno Latour. They likewise claim that what scientists discover or investigate are mere social constructions.[81]

Some readers may find it strange encountering Popper here. After all, he branded himself as a critical rationalist, defender of science. Indeed, he seems quite popular among many scientists. However, Popper's views are frequently aligned to irrationalism and ancient Skepticism.[82] Relativists such as Khun, Lakatos and Feyerabend, despite criticizing Popper, followed his master foot-steps.[83] As indication, you can see the many references Popper makes to the so-called problem of induction presented by David Hume, an 18th-century philosopher.[84] Hume has developed his empirical Skepticism with direct refer-ence to ancient relativists as Pyrrhos and Sextus Empiricus.[85] They claimed that inductive arguments (based on our experience of the world), could not be logi-cally justified, which would be the argumentative dream of ancient relativists. Accordingly, we could not pass judgement due to the preannounced invalidity of all evidence in establishing the truth (suspension of judgment). However, this assertion represents a mega induction. It takes as evidence all inductive arguments ever made by human beings to claim that none would be justified for a single inference. Contrarily to many relativists, nonetheless, Hume, with the maturity of an older age, has abandoned part of his earlier radical Skepti-cism, including his deductivism.[86]

Unfortunately, we have no space to fully address the pathway of ideas. Our aim must be constricted to finding evidence of gaslighting. Although Stove (2017) was not on the lookout for gaslighting, he has identified two activi-ties practiced by these four writers that can be classified as such: The first is to neutralize science's success words. Indeed, success in science consists in the ability of explaining. However, these authors claim (without evidence) that evidence could not be used to demonstrate anything. Hence, they feel entitled to impair words that entail scientific achievement as "*'knowledge,' 'dis-covery,' 'facts,' 'verified,' 'understanding,' 'explanation,' 'solution (of a problem),' and a great many more besides.*"[87] These writers use these words quite freely in historical contexts. However, as part of their relativism, they deny that these words could imply scientific accomplishment, therefore gaslighting the many examples of scientific success.

The second activity consists in sabotaging logical expressions. Stove[88] defines logical expressions as statements establishing the logical relation among two or more propositions. An example of a logical expression is that p implies q, and therefore p does not imply non q. However, these four writers deny the exist-ence of logical relations beyond human deductions that could be definitively confirmed by external evidence (deductivism). Hence, they sabotage valid logical expressions by integrating them in human contexts, generally involving scientists (epistemic contexts). For instance, they reformulate the logical rela-tion that p implies q into something as according to scientists p implies q, or scientists seem to believe that p implies q, regardless of evidence confirming (or contradicting) this relation. However, by integrating logical relations into human contexts, these writers deny the validity of evidence on the grounds that they say so. They are not shy of invoking scientific heroes as Galileo or Einstein[89] to do their sabotaging.

Popper's[90] famous proposal of moving science from verifiability into falsifi-ability is an example of both neutralizing success words and sabotaging logical expressions. According to him, science could not verify the truth of theories or hypotheses as allegedly demonstrated by Hume (it has not been demon-strated).[91] What it could do was to form general propositions in manners that they could be tested to fail (hence be falsified). Thus, from the onset, Popper declares a relativist stance, in that truth could never be attained. The gaslighting in Popper is not the verification of hypothesis and theories, which were done much before him. It is instead his denial of the possibility of scientific success. In a well-known example, a black swan contradicts the claim that all swans are white.[92] However, Popper is forcing scientists to present the general claim that all swans are white as the acceptable scientific statement, where other scien-tific statements could be valid such as that all swans we have found so far are white or we may find more white swans in this region, though our likelihood is intangible.

Furthermore, Popper has sabotaged the important logical expression of refu-tation, a term describing that something has not been verified. For if we are testing whether p implies q and find that it does not, we would have evidence that in this specific test p did not imply q. Thus, p could imply non q at this test. In Popper's example, finding a black swan would confirm that not all swans are white. However, Popper refuses to admit that we could make infer-ences about the truth through scientific refutations. He prefers to invoke a "*relativity of basic statements*"[93] to deny that a refutation could have truth value. Instead, he alleges that refutations would be based on scientists' other theories and hypothesis. However, if p previously implied q, there is no manner in which scientists could have made p to imply q. On the other hand, if scientists have made p to imply q, then, previously, p did not imply q.

Kuhn, Lakatos and Feyerabend criticize instances of Popper's writings. However, their master's denial of connections to an external reality is crucial to their local relativism theses: that truth exists only (and is subjective) in relation to systems of local validity established by specific social groups. Kuhn calls local systems of validity within science paradigms. He claims that such paradigms could not be compared for they would use different meanings of words and were incommensurable among themselves.[94] Scientists working within a paradigm would be working under normal science. When a scientific revolution occurs, a new paradigm could be established. However, it would not be because better understanding of the truth would be possible. It would come down to scientific politics of the relevant community. With slight variations, Lakatos denominates his version of local systems of validity in science as research programs.[95] Feyerabend decides that science is itself a local system of validity that should have no privileged status in relation to other validity systems in contemporary societies' global conversation. Hence, he declares himself against scientific methods[96] and what he calls "*the tyranny of science*" in aiming for the truth, a tyranny that must be resisted.[97]

Thus, ancient Sophists' arguments are repeated: Regarding evidence, we would need to suspend our judgement. Yet, although these relativists deny to others use of evidence to establish the truth, they themselves invoke plenty of substantial evidence. For example, Popper accepts that black, white and swans exist. Moreover, these writers summon large amounts of historical evidence, which when employed by these writers would have a privileged status for them to use.[98] When these writers mention the likes of Galileo, Newton, Einstein and quantum physics theorists, they accept that these scientists and their writings have existed. Their claim that existing local systems of validity could not be comparable is but pure gaslighting nonsense. These writers could not have identified groups of scientists supporting different theories and modifications among theories without plenty of truth statements.[99] Although different theories may make ruptures, they generally have common elements with previous theories, methods and language forms. Thus, we have presented evidence of prominent relativists gaslighting scientific methodologies and evidence.

6.3.3 Smearing: Preventive character assassination of innovators

Several other variations of the local relativism (subjectivism) thesis exist such as Derrida and Foucault's episteme,[100] Rorty's final vocabulary,[101] or Foucault's regime of the production of truth.[102] Lyotard also fits the bill[103]: "*simplifying to the extreme, I define postmodernism as incredulity towards metanarratives.*" He is appealing to local validity systems where "*little narrative [petit récit] remains quite essential.*"[104] Nonetheless, terms such as metanarrative, grand narrative, vocabularies or language games[105] to describe scientific theories imply that scientific theories would be akin to works of fiction. This comment has no lack of appreciation for some magnificent works in literature. Instead, we are observing that scientific writing must have adequate mechanisms to corroborate claims, which are not required by works of fiction. As other relativists, Lyotard would self-contradict if he were to apply his arguments to his own writings. His *"metanarratives"* formulation is itself a theory, which however would assert privileges of not being contradicted.[106]

To sustain local relativism theses, many relativists are on the lookout for points of separation among different theories, which allegedly would demonstrate distinct validity systems, for instance, changes and variance in meaning, incommensurable elements, or differences, events and occurrences that challenge previous explanations. However, relativist explanations simply cannot eliminate many common elements in methods and language vehicles regarding different theories. Furthermore, relativists force rivalries among theories that in many cases address different phenomena.[107] Moreover, they assume theories are generally absolutist and full of certainty, explaining everything or nothing, when rarely this is the case. Moreover, relativists cannot rhetorically eliminate external phenomena theories may try explaining.

Yet, another form of gaslighting results from this: smearing scientific innovators through their character assassination. Supposedly, scientists would not be able to use language forms or scientific methods to investigate reality. Without reference to a world beyond human constructions, even accumulation of knowledge becomes contested.[108] Moreover, the term knowledge would have been neutralized or sabotaged.[109] By declaring the absence of objective truth, ancient and contemporary relativists can serve dominant scientific theories and social groups. Allegedly, new theories or findings could never challenge dominant theories with better evidence or methodological analysis. Hence, scientists doing their work of discovering new phenomena and formulating new explanations would be looking out for something else, as in the vacuous knowledge-power formula we can find in Foucault, without explaining, demarcating or positioning any of them.[110] As the smearing goes, innovators would only be looking for hedonist gratification because knowledge would be never be verifiable human constructions. Thus, scientists could only be after status, career advancements, grants, more money, publications, power, domination over others, and so forth. Just the act of presenting a new theory would be smeared, for example, as incommensurable abnormal science (as in Kuhn), a deluded attempt at metatheory (as in Lyotard) or will to power (as in Foucault following Nietzsche and Heidegger).

Science is therefore confused with its worst abuses.[111] Undeniably, abuses have been practiced by some scientists. They have had effects not only on status, careers, rankings, grants and so forth but on the domination of ideas on human societies. Yet, through relativism these abusive practices became as legitimate as those involving honest pursuit of the truth based on our provisional knowledge. Accordingly, relativists and theory-dominant scientists would be justified in abusing scientists claiming to present new theories, hypotheses, frameworks or findings that could dispute them. The smeared scientists would have been deprived of scientific methods and language vehicles that could contest either relativism or dominant theories. Relativists and dominant scientists could create research bubbles, where they could define who would be the experts authorized to participate in those bubbles, involving, for instance, expert journals, conferences, academic departments, rankings and so forth as well as access to the media, websites, and public discourse. By smearing scientific discovery, the scientific aim would be instead nurturing interpretative communities. However, scientific innovators disputing dominant theories and hierarchies would have suffered preventive character assassination.[112] Likewise, relativism's gaslighting can be employed to smear those who may wish to challenge prevailing individuals and social groups in human societies.

6.3.4 Courting unreason: Campaigning for anti-science

Another gaslighting form is campaigning against science as if it would be a failing project, despite all evidence to the contrary. Undeniably, science has helped us fly machines, build long bridges and tunnels, and better understand the solar system and galaxies beyond or the small world of microbes and atoms, among many other wonders. Likewise, science has helped us address difficult problems of our human condition in food sources, lodgings, health, security and so forth. Nevertheless, relativist anti-science campaigns can be divided into two groups: those who openly do their campaigns and a more dangerous second group who do anti-science campaigns while pretending to be great friends and supporters of science, reason and logic. As before, we are not conducting an integral review. Instead, we are presenting evidence with important references to contemporary relativist projects.

Feyerabend's writings suit well the first group. In books such as *Against Method*,[113] or *Farewell to Reason*,[114] here and there he invokes (and smears) scientific heroes and pretends to be just kidding as an *infant terrible*. However, his propaganda is serious. By pseudo eliminating scientific methods and reason, Feyerabend implies that traditional enemies of science such as clairvoyance or astrology would be at similar levels, if they work. However, given that Feyerabend claims that no objective validity could exist, we could not verify whether science would be better or worse than its traditional enemies. Likewise, Derrida claims his self-imposed disconnection from the logos (without evidence) may requires we abandon the word rationality altogether. Thus, he implies abandoning the possibility of science.[115] Lyotard in *Lessons on Paganism* defends a pagan philosophy against the universality of science.[116] Science, as any discourse, would be narrative. All theory, all politics, all law, would be merely collections of stories.[117] Later, after perhaps being criticized, he seems to have realized what Plato understood thousands of years ago. When one assumes a relativist stance, there cannot be valid criteria for justice or fairness. Hence, in *Just Gaming*[118] (which resembles "just kidding") and at the end of the *Postmodern Condition*, he seems keen in claiming to be a supporter of justice.[119] However, as a relativist, Lyotard necessarily undermines it.

Much worse is the second group who pretend to be great friends of science, reason and logic. An ultimate example is Popper's (1959, 2002) most popular book title: *"The Logic of Scientific Discovery."*[120] Apparently, he seems to commend both logic and scientific discovery. As seen earlier, however, he systematically demoralizes scientific success and sabotages logical expressions. Let us now observer another example involving Foucault. We have no space here to entirely address Habermas's case against him, Derrida, and Georges Bataille.[121] Yet, we can observe that among other serious accusations, Habermas has suggested that writers aligning to postmodernity often endorse relativists and anti-reason stances. Furthermore, they necessarily camouflage truth normative stances under the claim that they do not provide normative stances[122] (again a demonstration that relativism is self-defeating). As others, Habermas would trace origins of contemporary relativism to Nietzsche and Martin Heidegger. Hence, postmodernism would have started in the 19th century with Nietzsche, not at the end of the 20th with recent relativists.

Foucault would onwards ingratiate both Habermas and his Frankfurt School group for their *"most important and valuable"* work, a practice he would repeat at other venues.[123] Despite the flattery, Foucault has gaslighted Habermas's legitimate accusations by trying to persuade us that we should avoid differentiating reason and unreason: *"it is senseless to refer to reason as the contrary entity to nonreason. Last, because such a trial would trap us into playing the arbitrary and boring part of either the rationalist or the irrationalist."*[124] Yet, at the same time, Foucault insinuates that rationalism has given us pathological forms or diseases of power such as fascism and Stalinism.[125] He has proclaimed a relation between rationalization and excesses of political power leading up to the Nazi *"concentration camps."*[126] We could find other relativists smearing reason or realism with Nazism and Stalinism.[127] As explained before, we should not expect relativists to be logical, reasonable or coherent. However, even by these low standards, Foucault's behavior entails strong intellectual dishonesty.

Undeniably, many opponents to fascism and Stalinism have benefited from science, reason and logic. However, Foucault's dishonesty goes much further. Relativists appreciate deconstructing and making genealogies about others' ideas and writings, while systematically failing to analyze their own. Indeed, many relativists repeat arguments advanced by Nietzsche and Heidegger, themselves linked to ancient relativists. Nevertheless, Nietzsche and Heidegger had disturbing connections to Hitler and the Nazi regime in Germany. After his death, many of Nietzsche's ideas would be adopted by members of the Nazi party, such as the myth of the superhuman.[128] In life and before the mental hospice, Nietzsche described himself as an *"immoralist."*[129] Heidegger was a supporter of Hitler and member of the Nazi party. After the end of the Second World War, he claimed at an interview that his support for the Nazi party had been merely instrumental.[130] Yet, it was real.[131]

Despite postwar denazification attempts, during the Third Reich Heidegger tried operating as a self-appointed philosophical Fuhrer, university rector for a spell, notorious professor and party member, radio persona and snitch.[132]

Evidence does not seem to confirm that Heidegger was a non-committed Nazi supporter.[133] However, even if we could accept that to be the case, his relativism would reinforce the dominant social group at the Third Reich, namely, the Nazi elite. What is worse, several relativists camouflage ideas from philosophers with strong links to the Nazi regime. They do so without justification or context, as Foucault does. Then, acting as a drama queen, he irresponsibly blames reason for concentration camps and Holocaust evilness. We could present other examples of relativist writers gaslighting connections amid relativism and the book-burning Nazi regime.[134] Likewise, contemporary relativists may have persuaded many humans that it would be better to avoid reality and disconnect from other humans and that it would be better creating self-referent bubbles denying our common humanity.

6.3.5 Silencing and blaming: The alleged impossibility of describing humans

For space, we will conclude with this gaslighting practice: to blame and try silencing scientists for producing science. It is particularly employed against social scientists. We consider social sciences in relation to intangible flow theory's definition of the human in Chapter 3. We also refer to the ancient characterization in Aristoteles's *Politics* that man is by nature a social animal.[135] Sciences that can study humans in isolation, as for instance specific research in neurosciences, psychology, or medicine, still study homo sapiens identifiable by their specific DNA, who are social animals.

However, several relativists claim that the human could not be defined or known. Thus, sciences addressing the human condition should stop working and instead justify their guilt. This gaslighting must not be confused with legitimate accounts regarding inadequate definitions of the human, as for instance one that is European-centric, religion-centric, and/or ethno-centric and has been used to exploit other humans in colonies at previous centuries[136] or one where the human is man and excludes women,[137] which may importantly renew social sciences. What becomes gaslighting is the crusade against studying humankind. For sure, our understanding is incomplete and rudimental. However, those who admit trying to study the human condition are blamed by relativists with scorn, disdain and even vengefulness. Yet, relativists themselves invoke expressions as man, women or human being, which are expressions that have been used for thousands of years to indicate specific beings. However, relativist would invoke some sort of entitlement in using those expressions. Recurrently, relativism refutes itself.

Heidegger has had great influence in this gaslighting activity. After the Second World War, the Denazification Committee found him guilty of his important position in the Nazi regime; introducing the Führer principle and thereby changing the university structure; engaging in Nazi propaganda; and inciting students against professors who opposed the Third Reich. Therefore, he was forbidden from lecturing at German universities (though he was reinstated in 1951).[138] Moreover, he lost his *"prophet status"* within the Nazi regime.[139] However, although his reputation was tamed in Germany, he started interacting with leading French philosophers, who, oddly, were keen to welcome him.[140]

Along with that, Heidegger bought his and Nietzsche's relativist ideas. Included was an important variation of Protagoras's old doctrine that truth could not be attained because of man being measure of all things. Protagoras was indeed outdated. As Plato explains, Protagoras would claim we could not know whether the weather would be hot or cold, because to one person it could feel chilly and to the other warm.[141] With the advance of human knowledge, this problem is easily solved with a thermometer. Indeed, with approximate accuracy, we can predict next fortnight's temperature, humidity or wind. To update, Heidegger presents a Protagorian variation: The truth could only come from something as humans being out there in the world (*dasein*).[142] That is, the external world would be dependent on man being there. Allegedly, we could not study human beings without defining being.[143]

As other relativists have, Heidegger fails to apply relativism to his work. By mentioning "human," he appeals to previous conceptions. Moreover, he fails to explain what it is "we could not define." We have no space to fully address Heidegger's impact on France, from where his relativist ideas would be re-exported to the rest of the world.[144] Still, he has spread ideas that would instruct further relativist prophets as Derrida, Lyotard, Latour or Foucault. Not happy to declare the death of the author (noted earlier), Foucault would go on to declare the *death of man*.[145] This claim is, as it looks, ridiculous. Foucault presumes entitlements in using the word man to declare its demise but denies to others the use of this word. According to him, man would be a social construction[146] out of a humanist local system of validity (episteme) formed somewhen along the 19th century after the (poorly defined) enlightenment. Foucault makes this extravagant statement because as an epistemological and semantic relativist he denies that methods and language vehicles could capture an external reality. Moreover, he feels no burden towards evidence. For instance, around the year 350 BC, Aristoteles characterized man as a social animal (as mentioned earlier). Or long before 1800, in the Middle Ages and Renaissance, there were several attempts at developing the humanism of ancient philosophers.[147]

Presuming that humans exist only in relation to discourses, Foucault presents his Protagorian variation: Man is both object and subject in knowledge: *"man appeared as an object of possible knowledge (. . .) and at the same time as the being through which all knowledge is possible (subject)."*[148] This pseudo problem only exists because of his epistemological and semantic relativism. Consequently, subjects as men could only be discursively constructed.[149] Hence, discourses and power would be ubiquitous and would define (subjective) validity systems. It is under this reasoning that Foucault creates formulations such as that madmen or criminals would be discursive constructions of reason and science after the enlightenment.[150] Nonetheless, we have, for instance, evidence of madmen throughout human history (e.g., Caligula). Moreover, due to technological advancements, neurosciences can observe malfunctions in brains' structures preceding human methods and languages. We also have evidence of ancient Babylon's Code of Hammurabi. After researching a maximum-security state prison in Maryland, Alford[151] has concluded that the prison's empirical reality proved Foucault to be wrong. Hence, we cannot conclude that subjects are merely discursively constructed. Yet, several relativist movements consider enough to invoke Foucault's authority in establishing that the truth could only be ascertained in relation to discursive systems and power – knowledge regimes of production of truth.[152]

In the last decades, following Heidegger and Foucault, poorly defined words such as human or humanism have been employed to abuse social scientists studying the human condition. We must not confuse this form of abuse with the important studies in transhumanism mentioned before (Chapter 4), which address human beings and our possible biological and technological evolutions.[153] The abuse mentioned here is to implicitly deny that we could study the human condition, as manifested in Foucault's death of man. Likewise, we can be certain that Heidegger's philosophy is anti-humanist because he has admitted as much.[154] In their followers, we can read the most extraordinary distortions such as *"it is almost impossible to think of a crime that has not been committed in name of humanity."*[155] Or likewise to imply that following poststructuralist philosophers we would know that humanism leads to *"colonialism, Auschwitz, Hiroshima and the Gulag – to mention but a few of the horror[s] of modern history."*[156] As explained earlier, relativists have low standards and authorize themselves to make these statements without requiring evidence. Still, this intellectual dishonesty is formidable: Heidegger, founder of contemporary anti-humanism, wrote a memorandum during the Denazification Committee. There, he admitted that one reason for his support to the Nazi Party had been his believe in Nietzsche's conception of *"the universal rule of the Will to Power within global history."*[157] Undeniably, the Nazi Party led to Auschwitz and had colonial aims.

Anti-humanism shares a common relativist framework, although it may appear with different names such as *posthumanism,*[158] *the inhuman,*[159] *ahuman,*[160] or *the non-human turn.*[161] However, although gaslighting the human condition, relativists cannot provide methods and language vehicles for alternative scientific theories and frameworks, that is, unless, they were to abandon their relativism. Hence, for lack of an alternative, relativists end up implicitly supporting dominant theories. See, for instance, Braidotti's (2013, 2019)[162] proposal of creating *"posthuman humanities."* She cannot do better than still using the expression "human" twice. Yet, she abuses others for admitting studying humans and our condition. Likewise, her proposal of post-anthropocentric turn, refers to anthropocentrism, a previous specific term for a geological phase where we humans are causing extreme changes to the planet Earth.[163] However, it is not possible to identify and improve human effects on our current planet without studying human beings and our economic and societal production. Relativism is far from harmless.

6.4 Intangible flow theory and boundaries to scientific relativism

Relativist movements have been gaslighting the truth and science for thousands of years. Dominant theories and social groups have greatly benefited with their practices. As relativists are not constrained by reason, logic or evidence, they have little reason to accept defeat. Nor should they be expected to do so.[164] Albeit quite important, demonstrating that relativism is incoherent and self-defeating is not enough. Scientific scrutiny must improve to defend science from relativism's implicit normalization of abuse, evilness and wrongdoing.

Despite their preaching, the relativists mentioned earlier did not generally commit to relativist lives. As ancient Sophists, they enjoyed status and monetary flows arising from their comfortable academic jobs and publications. They travelled the world to meet other relativists at conferences, seminars and workshops besides personal gatherings. Meanwhile, they knew which planes to take, which hotels to stay in, and which houses to return to. They enjoyed security. Largely, economic and societal production have been taken for granted, which should be ready to attend to their comfortable needs.

Curiously, many relativists take aim at Galileo who, along with others such as Copernicus or Giordano Bruno, has done important work demonstrating that planet Earth, currently our human home, was not the mystical body along which all celestial bodies would gravitate. Yet, relativism advocates a deluded return to the position of man as center of the universe. As reality either did not exist or could not be attained by methods or language vehicles, animal man would have the power of creating alternative realities that could suit him/her better. We humans would be as consumers choosing among different realities we could fancy. Each human would be the measure of all things, as proclaimed long ago by Protagoras. Relativism, thus, is a deeply narcissistic intellectual project. Intangible flow theory can assist in establishing healthy boundaries regarding relativism in the human sciences. These boundaries' non-negligible secondary outcomes might increase self-esteem of scientists and research communities who have had to endure decades of toxic relations with anti-sciences relativists.

The reason and logic defended by the new theory are to be produced by us humans in our many contexts by the life of our bodies, populated with microbes and in systematic interactions with other living beings, and the external environment; by our brains integrated in our bodies with emotions, biological functions, consciousness and many unconsciousness activities; and by us humans in our social and historical situations and with our many biological and social constraints. Reason and logic must be able to be transferred among different persons and social groups, across human generations, and beyond mere local systems of validity. Furthermore, scientific work must be open to the new, the different, and the event that has never been observed before, the occurrence challenging former explanations, the unpredictability of the future, the many things we do not know how to explain, and the contingency of human, social and biophysical phenomena.

As seen earlier, although Popper claims an adequate method for scientific scrutiny, he endorses a relativist agenda. Thus, hardly could his method be fit for the reality we humans are immersed within. As explained by intangible flow theory, scientific descriptions are related to previous methods and language forms. Moreover, they are constrained by tangible and intangible phenomena. Still, scientific scrutiny methodologies must better explain processes through which objects, properties and relations previously unknown to humans can be captured by human sciences. That is, how what is unknown to us but exists outside ourselves (what Kant and ancient philosophers calls the noumenoun) can become perceptible to us (and according to Kant and ancient philosophers become a phenomenon). By understanding better these processes, we may exhibit that previously metaphysical elements may have become perceivable and eventually tangible to us humans.

Figure 6.1 summarizes new proposals. An intangible flow is a someway apparently discernible phenomenon that cannot be measured or captured with precision. Yet, it is not something we did not perceive. A flow that has not been perceived by us humans remains part of the noumenoun. An intangible flow will remain intangible only until we humans could find methods and language vehicles to identify it with precision. However, intangible flows are highly heterogeneous, and in most cases, we do not know why we cannot measure them with precision (otherwise we would). An intangible flow is not the contrary of a tangible flow. It is instead a flow we cannot identify with precision in a specific space and time. But it is no longer part of what we do not know. Scientific descriptions of intangible flows can (and should) be deconstructed. Many of them might be fake and/or fictitious human constructions, which can never become tangible.

Furthermore, intangible flow theory suggests that tangible flows cannot be further deconstructed because they can be identified with precision after they have occurred in a specific time and place. Not yet occurred flows cannot be considered tangible beforehand because dependent on intangible flows and unknown flows. However, when a previously intangible flow can be identified with precision, a tangibilization process has occurred. Tangible flows can be inspected and verified. They cannot be deconstructed because they can be identified with precision, even when they are socially constructed, as in our human societies' existence. Thus, precise methods and language vehicles can communicate and discuss tangible flows. Hence, we have an explanation for the advancement of human knowledge which encompasses conquering previous metaphysical dimensions that in some instances we have turned tangible. For instance, the many things we did not know, that become known to us, from microbes, cells, DNA and atoms to our possibilities of travelling in outer space. Or our use of energy from the sun, the wind and the sea. Or improving human longevity, access to water and food resources, health care and habitation, literacy, transportation, technology and so forth (albeit at different rhythms among regions and social groups). Tangible flows can provide boundaries to scientific relativism and to the gaslighting of the truth.

Panel A- Actual-flows

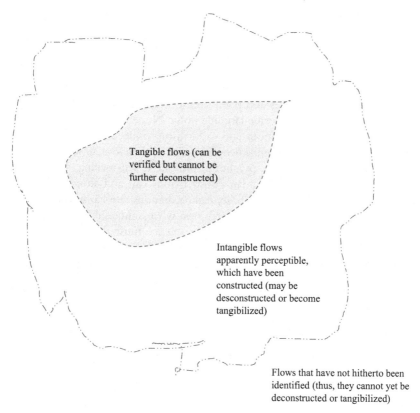

Tangible flows (can be
verified but cannot be
further deconstructed)

Intangible flows
apparently perceptible,
which have been
constructed (may be
desconstructed or become
tangibilized)

Flows that have not hitherto been
identified (thus, they cannot yet be
deconstructed or tangibilized)

Panel B – Pseudo-flows

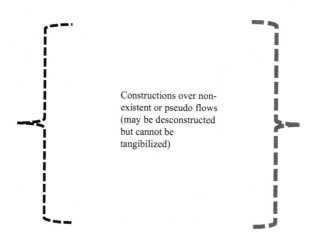

Constructions over non-
existent or pseudo flows
(may be desconstructed
but cannot be
tangibilized)

Figure 6.1 Occurred tangible (undeconstructable), deconstructable and not yet constructed
flows in a precise time and space

Nevertheless, science must not replace the requirement for political and societal organization or decide human populations' views for them. Indeed, science can devise manners to control for what is tangible and what is not, thereby exposing populist, demagogue and irrational statements that so often have caused societal disasters and catastrophes. Undeniably, however, a text may not aim to describe tangible flows. For example, the contents of a poem or work of fiction may not intend to describe an external truth beyond human and social constructions. Hence, those contents are not necessarily bound by tangible flows. Yet, novels, romances and poems exist. Reports about their production and their authors might describe tangible flows. Nonetheless, many texts, messages, speeches, communications and so forth may indeed ambition to capture reality. With reference to tangible flow boundaries, therefore, unfounded, naïve, false, fictitious, manipulative, psychotic, dishonest, self-serving, hallucinated, demented and many other human constructions can and should be deconstructed. Moreover, pseudo tangibility can be demonstrated as flagrant intangibility. Science cannot describe with precision what is intangible and cannot yet be aware of what is unknown. Scrutiny of science must also address attempts of attributing pseudo tangibility to phenomena that remain intangible or to pseudo-phenomena. There are many things of which we are not certain and many more we do not know. Hopefully, may we restore the will to knowledge as a legitimate endeavor and sincerely rejoice with the advancement of science.

Notes

1 This position aligns to transcendental realism or metaphysical realism (Bhaskar, 1975, 1997, 1998; Lawson, 1994, 2019; Sayer, 2000; Kukla, 2000).
2 As reported, for instance, in Plato's (2013) *Theaetetus*. It is quite likely that Plato used Socrates's character in his dialogues to convey his own views (see, for instance, Cornford, 2013).
3 Dennet (2013), Kukla (2000), Norris (1997). As explained by Burr (2015, p. 9): "Social constructionism denies that our knowledge is a direct perception of reality. Instead, as a culture or society we construct our own versions of reality between us. Since we have to accept the historical and cultural relativism of all forms of knowledge, it follows that the notion of "truth" becomes problematic. Within social constructionism there can be no such thing as an objective fact." As explained later, this elucidation would fail if it were to apply its relativism to itself.
4 Boghossian (2015), Habermas (1985, 1998), Kukla (2000), Norris (1997).
5 For instance, Jean-Francois Lyotard is described as postmodernist in McHale (2015), a poststructuralist in Williams (2005) and a constructivist in Kukla (2000).
6 Butler (2002), Harvey (1990), Williams (2005).
7 That is the case of Derrida (1974, 1997). See also Bennington (2004) and Williams (2005).
8 Foucault (1991a, p. 56): "In that sense, I don't see who could be more of anti-structuralism than myself."
9 That is the case of Foucault again, who besides being often classified as poststructuralist is also frequently characterized as a postmodernist. However, perhaps not for his appreciation for he might have preferred to define his work by history and critique of modernity. See for instance Koopman (2010) or Oram (2016).

10 See also Foucault (1991b).

11 Latour (1993, p. 47): "No one has ever been modern. Modernity has never begun. There has never been a modern world. The use of the past perfect tense is important here, for it is a matter of a retrospective sentiment, of a rereading of our history. I am not saying that we are entering a new era; on the contrary we no longer have to continue the headlong flight of the post-post-postmodernists; we are no longer obliged to cling to the avant-garde of the avant-garde; we no longer seek to be even cleverer, even more critical, even deeper into the 'era of suspicion'. No, instead we discover that we have never begun to enter the modern era. Hence the hint of the ludicrous that always accompanies postmodern thinkers; they claim to come after a time that has not even started."

12 This adapted typology has instead been used by Kukla to characterize constructivism. Although having very strong affinity, constructivism is not always synonymous to relativism. However, a similar classification suits us well to describe relativism.

13 Khlentzos (2016).

14 In using the word "mental," it is in the sense that constructions somehow reach the human mind. I am not suggesting that the human mind reaches intellectual formulations in isolation as the mind is fully integrated in the human body and interacts with the surrounding environment.

15 Khlentzos (2016), Kukla (2000). Likewise, metaphysical realism must not be confused with empirical realism. While the former suggests that what is real need not be experienced by us humans to come into being, the latter can only suggest that what is real is what has been scientifically demonstrated (Bhaskar, 1975, 1997, 1998; Lawson, 1994, 2019).

16 Several leading relativists such as Derrida and Foucault claim to follow Nietzsche, whose writings had strong connections to ancient Skeptics' ideas, for instance, those of Sextus Empiricus (see Berry, 2011). Zilioli (2016) establishes connections between contemporary relativist writers such as Feyerabend and Rorty and the ideas of ancient Sophists such as Protagoras. See also Lee (2005). Stove (2017, pp. 99, 108) demonstrates that arguments from Popper, Feyrabend, Kuhn and Lakatos are repetitions of arguments that could be found in ancient Skeptics such as Pyrrho of Elis and Sextus Empiricus, whose arguments were obtained via David Hume. Several other studies connect ancient and recent relativists. See, for instance, Berry (2011) and Crome (2004).

17 Plato (2013, p. 58).

18 Plato (2013). See also Burnyeat (1976a, 1976b) and Lee (2005).

19 Boghossian (2015), Habermas (1985, 1998), Norris (1997).

20 According to Zilioli (2016), Protagoras was perhaps Plato's subtlest enemy.

21 See, for instance, Sesonske (1968) and Zilioli (2016).

22 Plato (2013, p. 45).

23 In *Metaphysics*, Book 4, Aristoteles also discusses the properties that all entities have in virtue of being entities. These include the Law of No Contradiction (an entity cannot exist and not exist) and Excluded Middle (an existing entity cannot be half existing or half nonexisting) (see, for instance, Priest, 1998; Inciarte, 1999). Other ancient philosophers have discussed these themes. Furthermore, Aristoteles has produced a treatise on *Rhetoric* where he addressed the art of persuasion and how one could deal himself/herself with Sophist rhetoric.

24 To acknowledge ancient philosophers' important demonstrations against relativism does not imply the need of accepting their theories of knowledge.

25 See, for instance, Boghossian (2015), Burnyeat (1976a, 1976b), Habermas (1985, 1998), Kukla (2000), Norris (1997).

26 Idem.

27 Sextus Empiricus, noted earlier, was a prominent member of the Skeptic school known as Pyrrhonism. Another leading ancient Skeptic school was known as Academic Skeptics.

28 A summary of the arguments of Stoic philosophers as narrated by Sextus Empiricus, a leading Skeptic, is (Burnyeat, 1976b, p. 51): "(i) If the Skeptic uses a criterion to assert that there is no criterion, 'he will refute himself/be reversed and in asserting that there is no criterion he will acknowledge that he is using a criterion in proof of this assertion' (M 7.440). (ii) If the Skeptic argues for the nonexistence of signs, he produces a sign for the nonexistence of signs and in so doing acknowledges that there is a sign (M 8.282). Thus he who states that there is no sign will be reversed into saying that there is a sign (ibid., 295). (iii) If the Skeptic purports to prove there is no proof, by this very fact he acknowledges that there is proof; the argument which proves there is no proof is a proof that there is. Thus, the thesis of the nonexistence of proof is rebutted/reversed by itself, the very means it uses to abolish proof establishing the reality of proof by self-refutation/reversal (M 8.463 ff.; PH 2.185). (iv) If the Skeptic cites a reason why there is no such thing as a reason [or cause], he refutes himself/is reversed, and in the act of saying there is no such thing as a reason he lays it down that there is (PH 3.19; M 9.204)." Here, PH and M stand for two works by Sextus Empiricus, namely, *Outlines of Pyrrhonism* and *Against the Mathematicians* (Burnyeat, 1976b, p. 51).

29 Boghossian (2015), Burnyeat (1976a, 1976b), Habermas (1985, 1998), Kukla (2000), Norris (1997), Plato (2013), Stove (2017).

30 Boghossian (2015), Habermas (1985, 1998), Kukla (2000), Norris (1997). Let us observe two further examples of relativists misconstruing the demonstration in Plato's *Theaetetus* that relativism is self-refuting: (i) Addressing directly the demonstration in Plato's writings, Gergen (2015, pp. 224–225) does not deny it. Instead, he claims that would be the *"very beauty of constructionism."* Later he claims that when opponents try to undo constructionism they are also practicing constructionism. Evidently, in any manner this solves the problem. Realists are not generally against conducting analysis. What Gergen does is merely to change the subject in order to attempt that serious problems could be ignored by distraction. (ii) To solve the problem identified by Plato, Meiland (1980, p. 121) misconstrues it as a myth. Accordingly, all that relativists would have to do is to say that everything would be relative except relativism itself. Obviously, that would be quite a risible solution. At one hand, Meiland's assertion has at least a truth statement that disproves relativism. On the other hand, if something could be real, why then no other element could also be real? Meiland claims to himself the right of arbitrarily establishing a specific truth, while denying that others could also identify specific truth statements (Bearn, 1986). These two example add to the substantial evidence later that relativist conduct gaslighting activities to conduct their theses.

31 Idem.

32 "That the burden of proof rests squarely with the sceptic than the realist."

33 See, for instance, Dorpat (1994), Kivak (2017), Moore (2019), Sarkis (2018), Sweet (2019), Tormoen (2019).

34 Idem.

35 Bennington (2004), Derrida (1974, 1997), Giddens (1987), Waterman (1956), Williams (2005).

36 Giddens (1987), Normand (2004).

37 Saussure (1916, 1959, pp. 65–68).

38 Saussure (1916, 1959, p. 65).

39 The discussion of signs as representatives of objects is in fact very old. See, for instance, Manetti (1993).

40 Saussure (1916, 1959, p. 67): "I propose to retain the word sign [signe] to designate the whole and to replace concept and sound-image respectively by signified [signifie] and signifier [signifiant].The last two terms have the advantage of indicating the opposition that separates them from each other and from the whole of which they are parts. As regards sign, if I am satisfied with it, this is simply because I do not know of any word to replace it, the ordinary language suggesting no other."

41 Normand (2004).

42 See, for instance, Tallis (2016) or Jackson (2014).

43 See, for instance, Lounsbury and Ventresca (2003) or Bourdieu (1984).

44 Saussure (1916, 1959, pp. 65–66): "We have seen in considering the speaking-circuit (p. 11) that both terms involved in the linguistic sign are psychological and are united in the brain by an associative bond. This point must be emphasized. The linguistic sign unites, not a thing and a name, but a concept and a sound-image. The latter is not the material sound, a purely physical thing, but the psychological imprint of the sound, the impression that it makes on our senses. The sound-image is sensory, and if I happen to call it "material," it is only in that sense, and by way of opposing it to the other term of the association, the concept, which is generally more abstract."

45 See, for instance, Derrida (1974, 1997, p. 7), Derrida (1970, 1993, pp. 223–225).

46 Concept previously found in Ludwig Klages, who has used to describe the Platonic ideal of attaining truth.

47 Derrida (1974, 1997, p. 7).

48 Derrida (1974, 1997, p. 10).

49 Derrida (1974, 1997, p. 240).

50 Nietzsche advocates a philosophy of destruction (with a hammer in the title) towards metaphysical concepts (see, for instance, Nietzsche, 1888, 1990; Kellner, 1991; Siemens, 1998).

51 *Destruktion* is the term used by Heidegger. He, however, claims that his destruction activity was positive: "its negative function remains unexpressed and indirect" (Heidegger, 1927, 1962, p. 44).

52 Derrida (1974, 1997, p. 158). See also, for instance, Hendricks (2016).

53 Burnyeat (1976a, p. 51); Stough (1969, pp. 97–99). See also Manetti (1993).

54 Baudrillard (1983, 2004, p. 366): "It no longer has to be rational, since it is no longer measured against some ideal or negative instance. It is nothing more than operational. In fact, since it is no longer enveloped by an imaginary, it is no longer real at all. It is a hyperreal: the product of an irradiating synthesis of combinatory models in a hyperspace without atmosphere."

55 Baudrillard (1983, 2004, p. 368).

56 Baudrillard (1983, 2004, pp. 365–366).

57 Baudrillard (1983, 2004, p. 373).

58 Baudrillard (1983, 2004, pp. 365–366). Baudrillard uses this example perhaps for yet a lack of appreciation of future GPS technologies.

59 Baudrillard (1983, 2004). Evidently, for making this argument, Baudrillard must assume that Disneyland exists.

60 Barthes (1968, 1996, 1977).

61 Derrida (1974, 1997), Foucault (1969, 1969, 1991).

62 Foucault (1991a).

63 Rorty (1985, p. 8): "Think of a lump as something which you would bring for analysis to a natural scientist rather than to somebody in the humanities or social sciences-something which might turn out to be, say, a piece of gold or the fossilized stomach of a stegosaurus."

64 Rorty (1985), Norris (1997, Chapter 6).

65 Foucault (1972).

66 Bevir (2008), Sax (1989).

67 Idem.

68 Foucault (1972, p. 6). See also Williams (2005) and Walker (2018).

69 Foucault (1972, p. 6): "the document was always treated as the language of a voice since reduced to silence, its fragile, but possibly decipherable trace." See also Williams (2005) and Walker (2018).

70 Foucault (1972, p. 7) "To be brief, then, let us say that history, in its traditional form, undertook to 'memorize' the monuments of the past, transform them into documents, and lend speech to those traces which, in themselves, are often not verbal, or which

say in silence something other than what they actually say; in our time, history is that which transforms documents into monuments." See also Williams (2005) and Walker (2018).

71 Derrida (1974, 1997, p. 33): "is that the opening of the 'image' within it appears as the condition of 'reality'; a relationship that can no longer be thought within the simple difference and the uncompromising exteriority of 'image' and 'reality,' of 'outside' and 'inside,' of 'appearance' and 'essence,' with the entire system of oppositions which necessarily follows from it." The opposition between signifier and significant in Saussure would be one binary opposition among others that Derrida would wish to deconstruct. See also Williams (2005) and Gross (1986).

72 Spivak (1974, 1997, p. XXVII).

73 Derrida (1974, 1997, p. 275): "Metaphor must therefore be understood as the process of the idea or meaning (of the signified, if one wishes) before being understood as the play of signifiers. The idea is the signified meaning, that which the word expresses. But it is also a sign of the thing, a representation of the object within my mind. Finally, this representation of the object, signifying the object and signified by the word or by the linguistic signifier in general, may also indirectly signify an affect or a passion. It is in this play of the representative idea."

74 Kukla (2000), Norris (1997), Quine (1969), Stove (2017).

75 Kukla (2000), Norris (1997), Quine (1953, 1969), Stove (2017).

76 Quine (1953, p. 53, 1951).

77 Quine (1953, p. 53, 1951, 1969). This thesis is presented in conjunction with Duhem (1954).

78 Quine (1951, p. 44).

79 Quine (1951, p. 45).

80 Quine (1951, pp. 44–45).

81 Baghramian (2008, p. 238), Kukla (2000).

82 See, for instance, Collins (2009), Norris (1997), Stove (2017) and Musgrave (1993).

83 Idem.

84 Popper (1959, 2002).

85 Popper (1959, 2002, p. 12 footnote) acknowledges himself the connection between Hume and Sextus Empiricus: "Thus Hume, like Sextus, condemned his own Enquiry on its last page; just as later Wittgenstein condemned his own Tractatus on its last page." See also Chisholm (1941), Olshewsky (1991) or Popkin (1951).

86 (Hume, 1779; Ribeiro, 2009; Stove, 2017, p. 190).

87 Stove (2017, p. 28).

88 Stove (2017, p. 51).

89 Note that Einstein's general relativity theory is not a relativist theory in this context.

90 Popper is the heir of another anti-metaphysical approach, namely, logical empirism/positivism, which contrarily to Popper still accepted making logical inferences from empirical induction.

91 Popper (1959, 2002, p. 5).

92 In latter versions, Popper denies the possibility of even characterizing swans for using a word that transcends experience (1959, 2002, p. 444).

93 Popper (1959, 2002, p. 86): "For any basic statement can again in its turn be subjected to tests, using as a touchstone any of the basic statements which can be deduced from it with the help of some theory, either the one under test, or another. This procedure has no natural end."

94 Kuhn (1970).

95 Lakatos (1968).

96 Feyerabend (1975, 1993).

97 Feyerabend (1996, 2011).

98 Norris (1997, pp. 133–134), Davidson (1984).

99 Muntz (1985, p. 119), Norris (1997, pp. 222–223). Curiously, relativists who address the discipline of history try to relativize it.

100 Derrida (1970, 1993), Foucault (1966, 2005).
101 Rorty (1989).
102 Foucault (1980).
103 Lyotard (1984, 1997, p. xxiv).
104 Lyotard (1984, 1997, p. 60).
105 We have no space to address Ludwig Wittgenstein, who was not necessarily a relativist.
106 Sim (2001).
107 Stove (2017).
108 Baghramian (2008), Stove (2017), Norris (1997).
109 Idem.
110 See, for instance, Foucault (1991a), Fraser (1981), Shiner (1982). Conception partially inspired in (relativist) Nietzsche's theory that most of humans do come from will to power (Habermas, 1998, pp. 266–267).
111 For instance, "its exploitative, its purely instrumental, or technocratic forms" (Norris, 1997, p. 1).
112 Ad hominem.
113 (1975, 1993).
114 (1987).
115 Derrida (1974, 1997, p. 10).
116 Lyotard (1977).
117 Woodward (2020).
118 Lyotard and Thébaud (1985).
119 Williams (2000), Woodward (2020).
120 Stove (2017).
121 See Habermas (1985, 1998), Habermas and Ben-Habib (1981), Burrell (1994), Isenberg (1991), King (2009).
122 Habermas calls this practice cryptonormative (Habermas, 1985, 1998).
123 Foucault (1982, p. 779).
124 Foucault (1982, p. 779).
125 Idem.
126 Idem.
127 For instance, Lyotard (1977, p. 75), Wolfson (2018).
128 Brinton (1940), Santaniello (2012), Whyte (2008).
129 Nietzsche (1968, pp. 136, 202).
130 Bevir (2000), Farias (1989), Norris (1997), Sheehan (2010), Sluga (1993).
131 Idem.
132 Norris (1997, p. 151), Farias (1989), Sheehan (1988), Wolfson (2018).
133 As previous endnotes.
134 See, for instance, Rockmore (1995, pp. 148–168).
135 "Man is by nature a social animal; an individual who is unsocial naturally and not accidentally is either beneath our notice or more than human. Society is something that precedes the individual. Anyone who either cannot lead the common life or is so self-sufficient as not to need to, and therefore does not partake of society, is either a beast or a god" (Aristoteles, 350 BC).
136 For instance, Said (1978, 2004).
137 For instance, Nussbaum (2017).
138 Sheehan (1988).
139 Janicuad (2001, p. 4)
140 As Jean-Paul Sartre, Simone de Beauvoir, Jean Beaufret and Jaques Lacan (Janicuad, 2001; Rockmore, 1995).
141 Plato (2013).
142 Heidegger (1962).
143 Grassi and Walker (1988), Heidegger (1962).
144 Nor his relation to phenomenology or existentialism. You may see Janicuad (2001) or Rockmore (1995).

145 Foucault (1994b, p. 386; published in French in 1966), Ferrando (2013), Gordon (1999); Han-Pile (2010), Moutinho (2004).
146 "Man is an invention of recent date. And one perhaps nearing its end." Idem.
147 Han-Pile (2010); Grassi and Walker (1988).
148 Foucault (1994a, p. 607). Also reference and translation in Han-Pile (2010). See also Gordon (1999).
149 Armstrong (2015).
150 Foucault (1977).
151 Alford (2000).
152 Adapted from Armstrong (2015, p. 29).
153 Ferrando (2013, p. 27).
154 "[T]he thinking expressed in *Being and Time* is against humanism" (Heidegger, 1949 cited by Grassi and Walker, 1988, p. 136). See also Granik (2007) and Rockmore (1995).
155 Davies (1997, p. 141).
156 Braidotti (2013, p. 4).
157 Sheehan (1988); Heidegger (1975–1976, p. 485).
158 Posthumanism as anti-humanism, for instance, in Braidotti (2013, 2019). Not to be confused with posthumanism as synonymous to transhumanism (see earlier).
159 Lyotard (1989).
160 MacCormack (2014).
161 See Grusin (2015).
162 She also misconstrues Protagoras as opponent to relativism.
163 See, for instance, Lewis and Maslin (2015) or Steffen et al. (2011).
164 Though, it may happen.

References

Alford, C. (2000). What would it matter if everything Foucault said about prison were wrong? Discipline and Punish after twenty years. *Theory and Society*, 29(1), 125–146.

Armstrong, P. (2015). The discourse of Michel Foucault: A sociological encounter. *Critical Perspectives on Accounting*, 27, 29–42.

Baghramian, M. (2008). Relativism about science. In Psillos, S. and Curd, M. (Eds.) *Routledge Companion to the Philosophy of Science*. Oxon: Routledge.

Baudrillard, J. (1983, 2004). Simulacra and simulations. In Rivkin, J. and Ryan, M. (Eds.) *Literary Theory: An Anthology*. Oxford: Basil-Blackwell.

Barthes, R. (1968, 1996). Death of the author. In Rice, P. and Waugh, P. (Eds.) *Modern Literary Theory: A Reader*. London: Arnold.

Barthes, R. (1977). *Image-Music-Text*. London: Fontana Press.

Bearn, G. C. (1986). Nietzsche, Feyerabend, and the voices of relativism. *Metaphilosophy*, 17(2/3), 135–152.

Bennington, G. (2004). Saussure and Derrida. In Sanders, C. (Ed.) *The Cambridge Companion to Saussure*. Cambridge: Cambridge University Press.

Berry, J. (2011). *Nietzsche and the Ancient Skeptical Tradition*. Oxford: Oxford University Press.

Bevir, M. (2000). Derrida and the Heidegger controversy: Global friendship against racism. *Critical Review of International Social and Political Philosophy*, 3(1), 121–138.

Bevir, M. (2008). What is genealogy? *Journal of the Philosophy of History*, 2(3), 263–275.

Bhaskar, R. (1975, 1997). *A Realist Theory of Science*. London: Verso.

Bhaskar, R. (1998). *The Possibility of Naturalism: A Philosophical Critique of the Contemporary Human Sciences*. London: Routledge.

Boghossian, P. (2015). *O medo do conhecimento: Contra o relativismo e o construtivismo*. Lisboa: Gradiva.

Bourdieu, P. (1984). *Distinction: A Social Critique of the Judgment of Taste*. Cambridge, MA: Harvard University Press.

Braidotti, R. (2013). Posthuman humanities. *European Educational Research Journal*, 12(1), 1–19.

Braidotti, R. (2019). A theoretical framework for the critical posthumanities. *Theory, Culture & Society*, 36(6), 31–61.

Brinton, C. (1940). The national socialists' use of Nietzsche. *Journal of the History of Ideas*, 1(2), 131–150.

Burnyeat, M. F. (1976a). Protagoras and self-refutation in Plato's Theaetetus. *The Philosophical Review*, 85(2), 172.

Burnyeat, M. F. (1976b). Protagoras and self-refutation in later Greek Philosophy. *Philosophical Review*, 85(1), 44–69.

Burr, V. (2015). *Social Constructionism*. New York: Routledge.

Burrell, G. (1994). Modernism, postmodernism and organizational analysis 4: The contribution of Jürgen Habermas. *Organization Studies*, 15(1), 1–19.

Butler, C. (2002). *Postmodernism: A Very Short Introduction*. Oxford: Oxford University Press.

Chisholm, R. (1941). Sextus empiricus and modern empiricism. *Philosophy of Science*, 8(3), 371–384.

Collins, H. (2009). We cannot live by scepticism alone. *Nature*, 458(7234), 30–30.

Cornford, F. (2013). *Plato's Theory of Knowledge*. Oxon: Routledge.

Crome, K. (2004). *Lyotard and Greek Thought*. London: Macmillan.

Davidson, D. (1984). On the very idea of a conceptual scheme. *Inquiries into Truth and Interpretation*, 183, 183–198.

Davies, T. (1997). *Humanism*. London: Routledge.

Dennett, D. (2013). Dennett on Wieseltier V. Pinker in the new republic: Let's start with a respect for truth. *Edge*, October 19. Online at www.edge.org/conversation/ dennett-on-wieseltier-v-pinker-in-the-new-republic.

Derrida, J. (1970, 1993). Structure, sign, and play in the discourse of the human sciences. In Derrida, J. (Ed.) *Writing and Difference*. Chicago: Chicago University Press.

Derrida, J. (1974, 1997). *Of Grammatology*. Baltimore: John Hopkins University Press.

Dorpat, T. (1994). On the double whammy and gaslighting. *Psychoanalysis and Psychotherapy*, 11(1), 91–96.

Duhem, P. (1954). *The Aim and Structure of Physical Theory*. Princeton, NJ: Princeton University Press.

Farias, V. (1989). *Heidegger and Nazism*. Philadelphia: Temple University Press.

Ferrando, F. (2013). Posthumanism, transhumanism, antihumanism, metahumanism, and new materialisms. *Existenz*, 8(2), 26–32.

Feyerabend, P. (1975, 1993). *Against Method*. London: Verso.

Feyerabend, P. (1987). *Farewell to Reason*. London: Verso.

Feyerabend, P. (1996, 2011). *The Tyranny of Science*. London: Polity Press.

Foucault, M. (1966, 2005). *The Order of Things*. Oxon: Routledge.

Foucault, M. (1969). Qu'est-ce qu'un auteur? *Bulletin de la Société française de philosophie*, 63(3), 73–104.

Foucault, M. (1969, 1991). What is an author? In Rabinow, P. (Ed.) *The Foucault Reader*. New York: Penguin.

Foucault, M. (1972). *The Archaeology of Knowledge and the Discourse on Language*. New York: Pantheon Books.

Foucault, M. (1977). *Discipline and Punish: The Birth of the Prison*. London: Penguin.

Foucault, M. (1980). Truth and power: Interview with Alessandro Fontana and Pasquale Pasquino. In Foucault, M. (Ed.) *Power/Knowledge: Selected Interviews and Other Writings, 1972–1977*. London: Vintage.

Foucault, M. (1982). The subject and power. *Critical Inquiry*, 8(4), 777–795.

Foucault, M. (1991a). Truth and power: Foucault interviewed by Alessandro Fontana and Pasquale Pasquino. In Rabinow, P. (Ed.) *The Foucault Reader*. New York: Penguin.

Foucault, M. (1991b). What is Enlightenment? In Rabinow, P. (Ed.) *The Foucault Reader*. New York: Penguin.

Foucault, M. (1994a). *Dits et Ecrits: 1954–1988*. 4 vols. Paris: Gallimard.

Foucault, M. (1994b). *The Order of Things*. New York: Random House.

Fraser, N. (1981). Foucault on modern power: Empirical insights and normative confusions. *Praxis International*, 1(3), 272–287.

Gergen, K. (2015). *An Invitation to Social Construction*. London: Sage.

Giddens, A. (1987). Structuralism, post-structuralism and the production of culture. In Giddens, A. and Turner, J. (Eds.) *Social Theory Today*. Stanford: Stanford University Press.

Gordon, N. (1999). Foucault's subject: An ontological reading. *Polity*, 31(3), 395–414.

Granik, M. (2007). Theory and practice in Heidegger's "letter on humanism". *Philotheos*, 7, 369–380.

Grassi, E. and Walker, R. (1988). The rehabilitation of rhetorical humanism: Regarding Heidegger's anti-humanism. *Diogenes*, 36(142), 136–156.

Gross, E. (1986). Derrida and the limits of philosophy. *Thesis Eleven*, 14(1), 26–43.

Grusin, R. (2015). *The Nonhuman Turn*. Minneapolis: University of Minnesota Press.

Habermas, J. (1985, 1998). *The Philosophical Discourse of Modernity: Twelve Lectures*. Oxford: Polity Press.

Habermas, J. and Ben-Habib, S. (1981). Modernity versus postmodernity. *New German Critique*, (22), 3–14.

Han-Pile, B. (2010). The "death of man": Foucault and anti-humanism. In O'Leary, T. (Ed.) *Foucault and Philosophy*. New York: Basil-Blackwell.

Harvey, D. (1990). *The Condition of Postmodernity: An Inquiry into the Origins of Cultural Change*. Oxford: Basil-Blackwell.

Heidegger, M. (1927, 1962). *Being and Time*. New York: Harper and Row.

Heidegger, M. (1975–1976). The rectorate 1933/34: Facts and thoughts. Translated by Karsten Harries. *Review of Metaphysics*, 29, 481–502.

Hendricks, G. P. (2016). Deconstruction the end of writing: 'Everything is a text, there is nothing outside context'. *Verbum et Ecclesia*, 37(1), 1–9.

Hume, D. (1779). *Dialogues Concerning Natural Religion*. London: Obtained at Google Books.

Inciarte, F. (1999). Aristotle and Aquinas: The principle of excluded middle. *History of Philosophy and Logical Analysis*, 2(1), 139–148.

Isenberg, B. (1991). Habermas on Foucault critical remarks. *Acta Sociologica*, 34(4), 299–308.

Jackson, L. (2014). *The Poverty of Structuralism: Literature and Structuralist Theory*. London: Routledge.

Janicuad, D. (2001). *Heidegger in France*. Indiana: Indiana University Press.

Kellner, D. (1991). Nietzsche and modernity: Critical reflections on twilight of the idols. *International Studies in Philosophy*, 23(2), 3–17.

Khlentzos, D. (2016). Challenges to metaphysical realism. In *Stanford Encyclopedia of Philosophy*. Online at: https://plato.stanford.edu/entries/hedonism/.

King, M. (2009). Clarifying the Foucault – Habermas debate: Morality, ethics, and normative foundations. *Philosophy & Social Criticism*, 35(3), 287–314.

Kivak, R. (2017). *Gaslighting*. Hackensack, NJ: Salem Press.

Koopman, C. (2010). Revising Foucault: The history and critique of modernity. *Philosophy and Social Criticism*, 36(5), 545–565.

Kuhn, T. (1970). *The Structure of Scientific Revolutions*. 2nd Edition. Chicago: University of Chicago Press.

Kukla, A. (2000). *Social Constructivism and the Philosophy of Science*. Oxon: Routledge.

Lakatos, I. (1968). II-Criticism and the methodology of scientific research programmes. *Proceeding of the Aristotelian Society*, 69,149–186.

Latour, B. (1993). *We Have Never Been Modern*. Cambridge, MA: Harvard University Press.

Lawson, T. (1994). A realist theory for economics. In Backhouse, R. (Ed.) *New Directions in Economic Methodology*. Oxon: Routledge.

Lawson, T. (2019). *The Nature of Social Reality: Issues in Social Ontology*. Oxon: Routledge.

Lee, M. (2005). *Epistemology after Protagoras: Responses to Relativism in Plato, Aristotle, and Democritus*. Oxford: Oxford University Press.

Lewis, S. and Maslin, M. (2015). Defining the anthropocene. *Nature*, 519(7542), 171.

Lounsbury, M. and Ventresca, M. (2003). The new structuralism in organizational theory. *Organization*, 10(3), 457–480.

Lyotard, J. (1977). Lessons in Paganism. In Benjamin, A. (Ed.) *The Lyotard Reader*. Oxford: Basil-Blackwell.

Lyotard, J. (1989). *The Inhuman: Reflections on Time*. Oxford: Basil-Blackwell.

Lyotard, J.-F. (1984, 1997). *The Postmodern Condition: A Report on Knowledge*. Minneapolis: University of Minnesota Press.

Lyotard, J. and Thébaud, J. (1985). *Just Gaming*. Minneapolis: Minnesota University Press.

MacCormack, P. (Ed.) (2014). *The Animal Catalyst: Towards Ahuman Theory*. London: Bloomsbury.

Manetti, G. (1993). *Theories of the Sign in Classical Antiquity*. Indiana: Indiana University Press.

McHale, B. (2015). *The Cambridge Introduction to Postmodernism*. Cambridge: Cambridge University Press.

Meiland, J. (1980). On the paradox of cognitive realism. *Metaphilosophy*, 11, 115–126.

Moore, A. (2019). Abuse prevention: How to turn off the gaslighters. *The Guardian,* March 2. Online at: www.theguardian.com/lifeandstyle/2019/mar/02/abuse-prevention-how-to-turn-off-the-gaslighters.

Moutinho, L. (2004). Humanism and anti humanism. *Natureza humana*, 6(2), 171–234.

Muntz, P. (1985). *Our Knowledge of the Growth of Knowledge: Popper or Wittgenstein*. London: Routledge.

Musgrave, A. (1993). Popper on induction. *Philosophy of the Social Sciences*, 23(4), 516–527.

Nietzsche, F. (1968). *The Will to Power*. New York: Vintage Books.

Nietzsche, F. (1888, 1990). *The Twilight of the Idols and the Anti-Christ: Or How to Philosophize with a Hammer*. New York: Penguin.

Normand, C. (2004). System, arbitrariness, value. In Sanders, C. (Ed.) *The Cambridge Companion to Saussure*. Cambridge: Cambridge University Press.

Norris, C. (1997). *Against Relativism: Philosophy of Science, Deconstruction and Critical Theory*. Oxford: Basil-Blackwell.

Nussbaum, M. (2017). *Martha C. Nussbaum on Humanity and Feminism*. Online at: https://hekmah.org/wp-content/uploads/2017/10/Humanities-and-Feminism-an-interview-with-Martha-Nussbaum.pdf.

Oram, M. (2016). *Modernity and Crisis in the Thought of Michel Foucault: The Totality of Reason*. London: Routledge.

Olshewsky, T. (1991). The classical roots of Hume's skepticism. *Journal of the History of Ideas*, 52(2), 269–287.

Plato. (2013). *Theaetetus: Translated by Benjamin Jowett*. The Project Gutenberg EBook. Online at: https://www.gutenberg.org/files/1726/1726-h/1726-h.htm.

Popkin, R. H. (1951). David Hume: His Pyrrhonism and his critique of Pyrrhonism. *The Philosophical Quarterly*, 1(5), 385–407.

Popper, K. (1959, 2002). *The Logic of Scientific Discovery*. London: Routledge.

Priest, G. (1998). To be and not to be – That is the answer. On Aristotle on the law of non-contradiction. *History of Philosophy and Logical Analysis*, 1(1), 91–130.

Quine, W. (1951). Two dogmas of empiricism. *Philosophical Review*, 60(1), 20–43.

Quine, W. (1953). *From a Logical Point of View*. New York: Harper Torchbooks.

Quine, W. (1969). *Ontological Relativism and Other Essays*. New York: Columbia University Press.

Ribeiro, B. (2009). Hume's changing views on the 'durability' of scepticism. *Journal of Scottish Philosophy*, 7(2), 215–236.

Rockmore, T. (1995). *Heidegger and French Philosophy: Humanism, Antihumanism, and Being*. Oxon: Routledge.

Rorty, R. (1985). Texts and lumps. *New Literary History*, 17(1), 1–16.

Rorty, R. (1989). *Contingency, Irony, and Solidarity*. Cambridge: Cambridge University Press.

Said, E. (1978). *Orientalism*. Harmondsworth: Penguin.

Said, E. (2004). *Humanism and Democratic Criticism*. New York: Columbia University Press.

Santaniello, W. (2012). *Nietzsche, God, and the Jews: His Critique of Judeo-Christianity in Relation to the Nazi myth*. New York: SUNY Press.

Sarkis, S. (2018). *Gaslighting: Recognize Manipulative and Emotionally Abusive People – And Break Free*. Boston, MA: Da Capo Press/Lifelong Books.

Saussure, F. (1916, 1959). *Course in General Linguistics*. New York: Philosophical Library.

Sayer, A. (2000). *Realism and Social Science*. London: Sage.

Sax, B. (1989). Foucault, Nietzsche, history: Two modes of the genealogical method. *History of European Ideas*, 11(1–6), 769–781.

Sesonske, A. (1968). To make the weaker argument defeat the stronger. *Journal of the History of Philosophy*, 6(3), 217–231.

Sheehan, T. (1988). Heidegger and the Nazis. *New York Review of Books*, 35(10), 38–47.

Sheehan, T. (2010). *Heidegger: The Man and the Thinker*. Piscataway, NJ: Transaction Publishers.

Shiner, L. (1982). Reading Foucault: Anti-method and the genealogy of power-knowledge. *History and Theory*, 21(3), 382–398.

Siemens, H. (1998). Nietzsche's hammer: Philosophy, destruction, or the art of limited warfare. *Tijdschrift voor filosofie*, 60(2), 321–347.

Sim, S. (2001). Postmodernism and Philosophy. In Sim, S. (Ed.) *The Routledge Companion to Postmodernism*. London: Routledge.

Sluga, H. D. (1993). *Heidegger's Crisis: Philosophy and Politics in Nazi Germany*. Boston: Harvard University Press.

Spivak, G. (1974, 1997). Translator's preface. In Derrida, J. (Ed.) *Of Grammatology*. Baltimore: John Hopkins University Press.

Steffen, W., Grinevald, J., Crutzen, P. and McNeill, J. (2011). The Anthropocene: Conceptual and historical perspectives. *Philosophical Transactions of the Royal Society A: Mathematical, Physical and Engineering Sciences*, 369(1938), 842–867.

Stough, C. (1969). *Greek Scepticism*. Berkeley, CA: University of California Press.

Stove, D. (2017). *Scientific Irrationalism: Origins of the Postmodern Cult*. Oxon: Routledge.

Sweet, P. (2019). The sociology of gaslighting. *American Sociological Review*, 84(5), 851–875.

Tallis, R. (2016). *Not Saussure: A Critique of Post-Saussurean Literary Theory*. London: Springer.

Tormoen, M. (2019). Gaslighting: How pathological labels can harm psychotherapy clients. *Journal of Humanistic Psychology*. https://doi.org/10.1177/0022167819864258.

Walker, A. (2018). *Monuments of the Present: The Document and Monument in Michel Foucault's Archaeology*. The University of Western Ontario Electronic Thesis and Dissertation Repository, 5743. Online at: https://ir.lib.uwo.ca/etd/5743.

Waterman, J. T. (1956). Ferdinand de Saussure-forerunner of modern structuralism. *Modern Language Journal*, 40(6), 307–309.

Whyte, M. (2008). The uses and abuses of Nietzsche in the third Reich: Alfred Baeumler's Heroic Realism. *Journal of Contemporary History*, 43(2), 171–194.

Williams, J. (2000). *Lyotard and the Political*. London: Routledge.

Williams, J. (2005). *Understanding Poststructuralism*. New York: Routledge.

Wolfson, E. (2018). *The Duplicity of Philosophy's Shadow: Heidegger, Nazism, and the Jewish Other*. New York: Columbia University Press.

Woodward, A. (2020). Jean-François Lyotard (1924–1998). *Internet Encyclopedia of Philosophy*. Online at: https://iep.utm.edu/lyotard/.

Zilioli, U. (2016). *Protagoras and the Challenge of Relativism*. Oxon: Routledge.

Part 3

Origins of the human commodity framework in mainstream economics and Marxism

7 Adam Smith's synthesis and the human commodity framework

7.1 Introduction

7.1.1 Smith as economic system builder[1]

The human commodity framework has bearings for both theory and practice. To study its origins in mainstream economics and Marxism, we start our analysis with reference to Adam Smith (1723–1790) and the influential Scottish enlightenment movement. Our inquiry will be partially informed by the new theory presented in Parts 1 and 2. However, it is not entirely dependent on that new theory. Although we cannot address all relevant economic thinkers and ideas, we will still try to further understand the currently dominant human commodity framework.

Smith is often considered the founding father of contemporary economics or even economics altogether.[2] Indeed, he promoted concepts that still have great impact, such as the concept of capital. However, mainstream economics focus only on a minor part of his work, while the broader part is commonly avoided or forgotten. By starting with Smith, we must leave out remarkable previous thinkers. Certainly, Smith did not launch economic thinking. For instance, the *Oikonomikus* word appears in a work by Xenophon (430–354 BC) who was a Socrates (470–399 BC) disciple and military commander, later concerned with efficient administration of estate and household.[3] Likewise, we will need to leave out of this part several remarkable writers from the period mediating Ancient Greece and Smith's writings. Smith, himself, was very influenced by ancient Greece's philosophers and by Aristoteles (384–322 BC) in particular.[4] As the dominant economic theories of the 20th and beginning of 21st century have been developed at the West, we will tend to focus in this book on Western writers. However, this analysis could later be expanded further.

As frequently acknowledged, several ideas in Smith's *The Wealth of Nations*[5] (1776) were not entirely new.[6] Smith seems to not always give credit where it was due.[7] Schumpeter, for instance, accuses Smith of lack of generosity to his predecessors.[8] Others, such as Rothbard or Rashid, go so far as openly accusing Smith of plagiarism.[9] Nevertheless, Smith has presented an integrated system organizing many disperse ideas, which was perhaps his greatest contribution.[10]

A system to explain the economic sphere of human activity as an integral part of human society, an idea not that distant from the concept of social embeddedness we have discussed before in Part 2. Although others have tried to present systems for the same purpose,[11] it was Smith's version that caught the imagination of his contemporaries.[12] In economics, part of his system still endures.[13]

7.1.2 Are there laws for human society harmony?

Smith was a moral philosopher.[14] During several years he held the Chair of Moral Philosophy at Glasgow University, a post previously held by his Professor Francis Hutcheson (1694–1746), who would have great influence on him. Hutcheson is considered a founding father of Scottish enlightenment.[15] Likewise, his close friend David Hume (1711–1776) would also have great impact on him despite their divergences.[16] John Locke (1632–1704)[17] and Francis Bacon's (1561–1626) empiricism revealed new possibilities for knowledge production. While using mathematical analysis, Isaac Newton (1642–1726/27) had shown that the universe seems to follow specific rules such as the gravity law. Several Scottish enlightenment philosophers were concerned with inquiring whether such rules could exist for human societies. Would there be laws that could lead into harmonious human society functioning?[18]

These questions are still quite relevant for humankind. Relativism's gaslighting of our human condition cannot undermine their relevance. Back then, prominent European writers had presented the case for authoritarianism/absolutism at the hands of a sovereign. Wars were fought to impose or contest sovereign power. Machiavelli (1469–1527), while noticing that no sovereign could rule all times against an entire population, identified several strategies for obtaining and holding power, including lying, manipulation and fearmongering. He saw humans as capricious, weak, false and ready to abandon their sovereign for better interests.[19] Accordingly, it would be better to be feared than loved.[20] Hobbes (1588–1679) argued that a society without a clear sovereign in which anyone would be authorized to do anything would result in a *"war of all against all."*[21] No industry, production, culture, arts or peace could be sustainable without a strong authority as if respected by a social contract. Otherwise, everyone in human society would be in *"continual fear, and danger of violent death; and the life of man, solitary, poor, nasty, brutish, and short."*[22] Smith and others in the Scottish enlightenment group were concerned whether social harmony could exist without the need of being imposed by a strong sovereign, as for instance absolutist kings in France, not yet dethroned by the revolution.

Furthermore, Bernard Mandeville's (1670–1733) fable of the bees needed to be addressed.[23] Although this fable was somehow popular at that time, it was very shocking for Christian and traditional values, thereby deemed as degrading for morality. Mandeville's allegory of a society of bees, akin to a human society, defends that immoralities, luxuries and vicious greed led to invisible cooperation in society. Morality would be a hypocrisy. The selfish prodigal spender buys fancy clothes, wine, food, expensive items and even sexual company that the frugal man would not. Hence, selfish and amoral spenders sustain economic equilibrium by attending their vices.[24] Smith disagrees. He has presented a specific defense of frugality in *Wealth of Nations*. Contrary to what could be inferred by the selfish and individualistic *homo economicus* model, which is dominant in contemporary economics, Smith vehemently criticized greed, selfishness and prodigality.

As Hutcheson, Smith makes an ad-hoc division of history into four periods, namely, (i) hunting, (ii) pasturage, (iii) farming and (iv) commerce.[25] In *Wealth of Nations*, Smith attempts to explain societal harmony in what he considers the final stage, namely, commerce/mercantile/manufacturing society. As frequently pointed out, this book is a continuation of *The Theory of Moral Sentiments (1759)*, a treaty in moral philosophy.[26] In there, Smith does not credit natural human kindness for social harmony, as Hutcheson and Hume would in response to Mandeville.[27] Indeed, Smith observes that humans have a natural sense of benevolence and concern for the fortune of others and their happiness. He calls this sense sympathy towards others or fellow feeling.[28] Although not entirely similar, the concept of fellow feeling has some connection to what we currently understand as empathy.[29] Smith has reformulated the description of this sentiment initially proposed by his friend Hume.[30] Furthermore, Smith noticed that in human society we have a sense of observation and being approved by others.[31] However, Smith claims that feelings of benevolence, sympathy and need of approval towards others are not enough to produce harmony in societies. Smith realizes that humans also have passions and are concerned with improving their own condition. Some human actions and passions may be unsocial or selfish. Hence, systems of justice and morality are required to keep social harmony in check.[32] Undeniably, Smith is quite far from the notion of a self-regulating market capable of addressing all human needs.

7.2 Reinstating Aristoteles's theory of commodity money and value

The publication of *The Wealth of Nations* coincides with the American declaration of independence (1776) and within a period of great wars, for instance, the Austrian war of succession (1741–1748), colonial wars among England, France and Spain (1754–1763), seven year war (1756–63) or Ottoman-Russian wars (1768–1774). A few years later, the French Revolution (1789–1799), would cause wars and great havoc all over Europe until at least 1815. It was also a period of great social and political transformations and technological inventions connected to ongoing industrial revolutions. Among those inventions are Watt's steam engine, Hargreaves's spinning jenny, Cugnot's steam wagon, and Volta's electroscope, electrophorus and discovery of methane gas.[33] Perhaps in part due to the coincidence of time, Smith came to be known as a philosopher of the times to come, the philosopher of a new order under the emergent capitalist industrial revolution.

Yet, a significant component of Smith's conceptual framework was not obtained in the dynamic industrial revolution or from higher finance soon to emerge in full steam.[34] Instead, Smith adopted many ideas discussed already by ancient Greek philosophy. It seems safe to observe that ancient Greek philosophers were not discussing Britain's 18th-century industrial revolution.[35] For instance, a key theme in *The Wealth of Nations* is the division of labor and how cooperation can improve production and distribution. Perhaps Smith would understand what we today refer to as international economic value chains.[36] To produce a tablet computer or a car, many of the globe's regions may participate in the final product with work, materials or investment. For Smith, the division of labor is limited and can be enhanced by the extent of a market. Yet, division of labor was already observed by Xenophon and Plato (428/427–348/347 BC), another Socrates disciple, and by Aristoteles, who has studied under Plato, and later diverged from his master in several aspects. Likewise, in *The Wealth of Nations* Book 1, Smith discusses how private property has evolved in his ad-hoc typology of four-phase human history. He proposes that private property did not exist through the hunting stage. However, when the commercial stage was reached, private property has been fully established. Thousand years before, in *Politics* (Book 2), Aristoteles had presented a defense of private property in comparison to communal property.[37]

Quite importantly, Smith's adoption of Aristoteles's theory of money would persist in economics and other related social sciences. We have already mentioned this theory in Parts 1 and 2. Although monetary societies existed thousands of years before Britain's industrial revolution, metal coins seem to have been a relatively recent technology to ancient Greece. They appear to have been devised in Lydia,[38] under the rule of King Croesus, who would later be defeated by the Persian Empire in 547 BC,[39] thus, just a few centuries before Aristoteles. For the great Macedonian philosopher, money had mostly the form of metal coins. In fact, coins bring several advantages for trading purposes in comparison to commodities previously used as money, such as metal ingots of gold or silver, salt, food, arrows and shells.[40] Coins are easier to store and transport, and they deteriorate much less with time as compared, for instance, to food. However, as physical objects used in ancient Lydia and Athens, coins still very much resemble previous commodity money varieties. Furthermore, coins' transaction value was associated with precious metals that they contained, such as silver or gold.[41] For Aristoteles, money was clearly a tangible, physical thing. Indeed, coins appear like other tradable objects. Here are perhaps some causes of Aristoteles's miscomprehension.

Higher standardization to previous forms of money would allow coins to better perform a key function of money to economists, namely, to be the unity of account,[42] that is, to be able to attribute a (monetary) value for different economic elements. Yet, both Aristoteles and Smith take the unit of account perspective to extremes, as if money could thus be used to measure the intangible which, as seen before, is a paradox (aporia). This problem persists in economics. Money is considered as akin to a perfectly tradable commodity.

Despite being somewhat abundant in ancient Athens where Aristoteles lived a great part of his life, coins were, for instance, seen with suspicion in neighbor and sometimes enemy Sparta[43] or by Plato, who thought only lower classes in society should use them.[44] When Aristoteles formulated his theory of money, he could not imagine monetary forms that today we find somehow banal, as paper money, digital money, or even cryptocurrencies. Likewise, the concept of fiat (fiduciary) money was not known to Aristoteles. Fiat (fiduciary) money is a currency without intrinsic value (for instance, in comparison to precious metals), which has been established as money, often by government or sovereign regulations. However, fiat money is currently the most common monetary form.[45]

Adam Smith has observed paper money, which is addressed at *The Wealth of Nations*.[46] He notes several advantages it may bring, such as convenience for transport, circulation and greater trade among merchants. On page 394, he describes how the major cities in his home country of Scotland, namely, Glasgow and Edinburgh, had significantly increased trade since the formation of banks there.[47] Banks, Smith notes, have not been the only cause for the increase in trade but have definitively contribute to it. However, paper money requires great degree of trust in the issuer. Smith is against fiduciary money:

> The whole paper money of every kind which can easily circulate in any country never can exceed the value of gold and silver, of which it supplies the place, or which (the commerce being supposed the same) would circulate there, if there was no paper money.[48]

Furthermore, Smith advises that paper money should be primarily for traders and manufacturers, not the general public.[49] Clearly, Smith still has difficulty in detaching money from the commodity form. In Smith and economics in general, money appears as a quasi-physical thing. Rarely is a social construction with intangible (but also tangible) components described.

Perhaps this idea of restricting the uses of money to trading purposes is a Western bias of reasoning.[50] In many human societies where money exists or existed, it had religious, statutory and power purposes.[51] Instead, for Aristoteles, as for Smith, money was invented for helping trade and as a form of the division of labor. Although they consider that monetary exchange has replaced barter, the two forms of exchange would be equivalent.[52] Here we have the barter fallacy identified by Polanyi, as described in Part 1 and 2. For instance, one human being specializes in building houses and other in making shoes. Were the shoemaker to buy a house, he would have difficulty in expressing house worth in shoes. Through money, he can sell shoes to receive money and use that money to buy the house.[53] Thus, we have a key foundation for the conception of money as a perfect commodity for trading purposes.

Furthermore, Aristoteles made several distinctions in terms of money with bearing upon Smith's work, for instance, use value and exchange value of a commodity, which we also find in Smith[54]:

> The word value, it is to be observed, has two different meanings, and sometimes expresses the utility of some particular object, and sometimes the power of purchasing other goods which the possession of that object conveys. The one may be called 'value in use' and the other, 'value in exchange.'[55]

Hence, the water and diamond paradox we find in Smith followed Aristoteles's reasoning.[56] Perhaps no other thing might be so precious to human life than water, eventually apart from air. Water can solve thirst or be used in agriculture and manufacturing. Yet, diamonds are much more expensive.

Both Aristoteles and Smith understand utility as usefulness. That is, for instance, water is useful because it can solve human thirst and water the soil. However, according to the intangible flow theory, Aristoteles and Smith's concept of use value is intangible. It cannot be identified with precision. On the contrary, both Aristoteles and Smith consider that the alleged use value could be measured with the perfect tradable commodity, namely, money. Given their conception of money as a commodity, they fail to realize that the value of money may itself be intangible, as it cannot always be identified with precision. They confuse the tangibility of monetary flows that occurred in a specific time and space with the intangibility of monetary value, a recurrent problem in economics.

7.3 Work as commodity and standard of value (expressed in money)

In ancient Greece (and later Rome), the basic form of production was highly reliant on the institution of slavery at home, in agriculture, in industry and even in military activities.[57] Therefore, for Aristoteles and other Greek philosophers, a labor theory of value and prices as we find in Smith would be quite difficult to anticipate.[58] Wages were not paid for most work.[59] Moreover, Aristoteles displayed great disdain for interests paid on monetary loans.

Albeit related, Aristoteles's distinction between natural and nonnatural use of money was not identical to Smith's. To Aristoteles, natural use of money should be for addressing life necessities, for instance, eating, drinking or finding a shelter. Nonnatural use of money should be for reasons of enrichment through trade or usury, namely, selling with unjustifiable profits or lending money while charging interest rates. Nowadays, we see usury as lending money at excessive interest rates, whereas in ancient Greece or the Middle Ages usury simply meant lending money at any interest rate.[60] Furthermore, during many centuries, religious scholars in the West and the Arab world would strongly condemn usury. Aristoteles had great contempt for what he understood as nonnatural use of money.[61] Likewise, human life necessities appear throughout Smith's writings. Many references are made to water, food, shelter, clothes and so forth.[62] However, Smith's distinction between natural and exchange value differs from Aristoteles's. Smith is still concerned with the extortion of usury through high interest rates. However, he does not share Aristoteles's derision for loans with interest. Instead, Smith advises fixing a legal rate to prevent abuses of usury.[63]

Nevertheless, Aristoteles (as Xenophon and Plato) had a view in which some people would have innate characteristics for being slaves, namely, the concept of *"natural slave."*[64] Aristoteles goes so far as to consider that *"the use made of slaves and of tame animals is not very different."*[65] Slavery still existed at Smith's time, and we will get back to that theme. However, an adjacent manufacturing and commercial society would operate through paying wages to workers. It was only a short stretch for Smith to see humans and their work as commodities to be brought about by the money commodity. Property over the slave could be a commodity in ancient Greece and Rome. It is also seen as such by Smith.

Locke has used part of Aristoteles's defense of private property in order to sustain that one's work is also a form of one's property.[66] Smith's friend, David Hume, had presented a species flow theory to argue that money would not really be the source of wealth, but *"the wheels of trade."*[67] Prices would change accordingly to the quantity of money available (quantitative theory of money). If a country has a temporary surplus in precious metals such as silver and gold, prices would adjust in time as to nullify the precious metal surplus. Smith agrees. Following Aristoteles and Hume, Smith sees money as a mean of circulating commodities: *"The sole use of money is to circulate consumable goods."*[68] For Smith, the real wealth of the country is *"the annual produce of its land and labour."*[69] He comments upon the examples of Spain and Portugal. Despite being perhaps the countries with the most productive mines at the time (in their colonies), they could be some of the least developed European countries.[70] Moreover, the discovery of Americas had devaluated gold and silver.[71]

Yet, Smith describes our human contributions to economic and societal production as commodities when linked to monetary flows.[72] Money is a means of expressing the value of things, which can actually be translated into labor, as in the following passage:

> Labour was the first price, the original purchase-money that was paid for all things. It was not by gold or by silver, but by labour, that wall the wealth of the world was originally purchased, and its value, to those who possess it, and who want to exchange it for some new productions, is precisely equal to the quantity of labour which it can enable them to purchase or command.[73]

In mercantile/manufacturing societies, for convenience, commodities are exchanged by money. However, according to Smith, commodities' true value would be labor purchased or commanded.[74]

Smith defines labor as the measure for the value of things, which he conceded may be difficult to identify with precision, for instance, when comparing two different quantities or qualities of labor.[75] The quantity of labor can be an abstract notion, which *"though it can be made sufficiently intelligible, is not altogether so natural and obvious."*[76] Smith implies that such value can be measured in monetary terms by bargaining.[77] Hence, we have again money as the measure for the intangible. Although labor gives the value, such value is expressible in money, the perfect trading commodity. Mainstream economics (and some Marxists) would decades later abandon Smith's labor theory of value. However, economists would still see work and human contributions to economic and societal production as akin to commodities measurable in monetary terms. Concepts of human asset, human capital or human resource results from this framework of human contributions as commodities expressible in money (commodity).

7.4 Manufacturing/mercantile society to Smith

7.4.1 Class-based society established upon wages, profits and rents

Although he has often been considered founder of contemporary economics, Smith's system has addressed many themes that today we tend to associate to its major rival theory, namely, Marxism,[78] for instance, the phasing of human history, class-based society, social relations of production, labor theory of value, declining rate of profit and keeping workers at subsistence levels.[79] Indeed, although we tend to connect the idea of a class conflict between workers and owners/investors of capital (or means of production) to Marxism, namely a conflict between the proletariat and bourgeoisie, we find a society divided into classes in Smith's *Wealth of Nations*. For mainstream economists, the expression *"invisible hand"* in Smith's work is often used to argue that self-interest of market participants would unknowingly lead to social harmony. However, Smith is concerned with conflicts among different social classes in mercantile societies and with natural harmony arising from natural law and the Divine Providence.[80] Thus, quite often a misrepresentation of Smith's ideas is committed.

Once more, Smith was not the first to create a system based on social classes to explain society. For instance, in a previous system attempt by Francois Quesnay (1694–1774) and a group of French thinkers known as the Physiocrats (Physiocracy), land is the significant factor explaining wealth creation.[81] Most Physiocrats were also large landowners, which is perhaps not a coincidence.[82] For them, the activities not related to land, for instance, manufacturing or commerce, were considered nonproductive in terms of wealth creation. Several Physiocrats would go so far as to suggest that taxes should be exclusively based on land. Furthermore, Richard Cantillon (1680–1734) may have anticipated Smith's labor theory of value and production. The former had proposed that although in the short run market prices might be determined by supply and demand, in the long run they should tend to their intrinsic value, which would be based upon land and work necessary for production.[83]

Smith's system replaces land with capital as the key factor for wealth crea-tion.[84] In the process, he has modified the concept of capital (see next sec-tion). Accordingly, there would be three major groups in a mercantile society: workers who work and receive wages, stockholders (capitalists) who invest and expect to receive profits, and landowners who lease their land (or mines or houses) to receive rents. This division of human beings into three classes is an oversimplification, which can be quite incorrect. Within these three groups are many other groups, as different types of workers (say the manager, engi-neer and door attendant) or investor (say the individual small-time investor and hedge fund executive). Moreover, Smith is not contemplating other possible groups. A worker can also be a landowner. A capitalist can also be a worker. And so on. Still, it is important to emphasize that Smith identifies society as different groups interacting. In Smith's system, these three social classes have a natural conflict, which would be resolved in terms of the perfectly tradable commodity: money. From this conflict emerges a natural order, as if under an *invisible hand*.

For Smith, as for Aristoteles, transaction (exchange) price is the price obtained in trading, which is dependent on fluctuations of supply and effec-tive demand.[85] In Smith, effective demand refers to those who can actually buy the commodity in opposition to those who may wish to have the commodity but have no financial means to ever obtain it. Unlike Aristoteles, however, for Smith the natural price is based upon profits, wages and rents. According to him, in the long run the transaction price should orbit towards the natural price, namely, an equilibrium, as if a supposed natural price could gravitate towards the supposed natural movement of profits, wages and rents.[86]

Following his labor theory of production, value and existence, Smith defines that the

> real value of all different component parts of price, it must be observed, is measured by the quantity of labour which, they can, each of them, purchase or command. Labour measures the value not only of that part of price which resolves itself into labour, but of that which resolves itself into rent, and of that which resolves into profit.[87]

Smith considers that wages are kept in equilibrium with workers at their sub-sistence level. Furthermore, profits suffer a declining rate in time.[88] Rents are dependent on profits and wages. Yet, only transaction prices can be identified with precision. Smith's formulation of natural price is highly speculative, at best, if not altogether false.

7.4.2 *Altering the concept of capital to explain wealth creation*

Capital's previous concept of money as investable or invested in business is still used in business and social circles. Since long ago in economics and other social sciences (e.g., sociology), capital implies elements involved in a production process that can be used to increase the wealth of nations or individuals. We do not know when the original meaning was established. Evidence demonstrates that the concept was already used by medieval traders in the western world[89] and Roman jurists.[90] In his "Early History of the Term Capital," Cannan (1921) exhibits that several ancient texts convey the original meaning, as the *Universal Dictionary of Trade and Commerce* (1751), Bank of England's 1697 act of Parliament, Dictionary of the French and English Tongue (1611), or Postlethwayt's *Universal Dictionary of Trade and Commerce* (1751).[91]

On the other hand, the meaning change made by Smith (1776a, 1999, 1776b, 1999)[92] is well documented. Instead of considering capital as a sum of money, which is to be invested or which has been invested in certain elements, Smith makes it the elements themselves, such as machines, land, us human beings and our intangible contributions. This alteration has eliminated the direct association between capital and money. As described by Marshal (1890, 53): "*Adam Smith said that a person's capital is that part of his stock from which he expects to derive an income.*" Indeed, that is the definition we find in Smith:

> When the stock which a man possess[es] is no more than sufficient to maintain him for a few days or a few weeks, he seldom thinks of deriving any revenue from it. He consumes it as sparingly as he can, and endeavours by his labour to acquire something which may supply its place before it be consumed altogether. His revenue is, in this case, derived from his labour only. This is the state of the labouring poor in all countries.
>
> But when he possesses stock sufficient to maintain him for months or years, he naturally endeavours to derive a revenue from the greater part of it; reserving only so much for his immediate consumption as may maintain him till this revenue begins to come in. His whole stock, therefore, is distinguished into two parts. That part which, he expects, is to afford him this revenue is called capital.[93]

For Smith, the stock of any country or society is the same as that of all its inhabitants or members. It is divided into three parts, namely, the component for immediate consumption, fixed capital and circulating capital.[94] The *immediate consumption* proportion is connected to the basic necessities of life, such as food, clothes, housing or household furniture. It is not described as capital because it does not ensure future revenue flows. *Fixed capital* is the component that affords a revenue or profit without circulating or "*changing masters.*" It has been divided into four parts: useful machines, buildings, improvements of land and acquired and useful abilities of all the inhabitants or members of the society.

Circulating capital, according to Smith, affords a revenue only by circulating or "*changing masters.*" Smith divides circulating capital into four parts: (i) money, by means of which all the other parts are circulated and distributed to their proper consumer; (ii) stock and provision that are in possession or merchants and manufacturers, from the sale of which they expect to make a profit; (iii) materials that are in a rude or less manufactured stage; and (iv) work, which Smith treats as capital and a commodity.[95] To Smith, capital is always related to work. Considering money as the *"wheel of circulation"* makes it altogether different from the goods that are circulated by means of it. Money is not where the revenue is generated.[96] Likewise, *"The intention of the fixed capital is to increase the productive powers of labour, or to enable the same number of labourers to perform a much greater quantity of work."*[97]

In describing the capital accumulation as the key factor for wealth creation, Smith makes a further distinction: productive and nonproductive labor. The former enables capital accumulation. The latter does not. For instance, a manufacturer's labor adds generally to the value of materials which he works upon, his maintenance and his master profits. On the other hand, the work of the menial servant, or an actor, or a musician perishes in the instant of production, even when useful and/or pleasant.[98] Productive work would replace and renew capital by increasing revenues, whereas nonproductive work is maintained by revenue and thus consumes the annual produce of labor and land.[99] Evidently, this separation is also problematic because human flows tend to be intangible and perishable, even when later materialized in physical objects and money flows. It is, however, used by Smith to put his new concept of capital at the center of his wealth creation explanation.

Thus, the word capital has been applied by Smith to describe both physical goods and human contributions to the productive process, as long as somehow they may have some lateral effect to increase someone's, some organization's or some country's wealth. It has led to a plethora of related terms, such as reputational capital, organizational capital, cultural capital and intellectual capital.[100] The conceptualization of humans as capital is similar to using formulations such as "human assets"[101] and "human resources,"[102] in that human contributions are seen as instrumental means to increase the wealth of investors. In sociology, a particularly popular leaning uses the expression social capital after Hanifan (1916) and Bourdieu (1977, 1986). Overarching use of the word capital, which can encompass everything with a tangential impact upon wealth creation, including human beings and our intangible contributions, triggers a strong meaning ambiguity. Moreover, it leads to tautological systems with great bearing in economics and other social sciences[103]: Capital explains wealth creation because it is what creates wealth. For precision, intangible flow theory uses the pre-Smith meaning of capital: money investable or invested in business.[104]

7.4.3 Interactions of agents in a productive system

Much commented on is the citation[105]: *"It is not from the benevolence of the butcher, the brewer, or the baker that we expect our dinner, but from their regard to their own interest."* Mainstream economics generally praises Smith's writings about market operations, while mostly ignoring other components of his reasoning. To justify such artificial separation, some scholars claim that markets correspond to the theme of *microeconomics*, whereas other parts would be *macroeconomics* or *institutionalism*.[106] This alleged separation is, evidently, difficult to sustain. Besides the impossible question of when one starts and the others end, how could human beings interact with other humans while switching micro and macro levels and partake from institutions as they go along?

Indeed, we human beings and our contributions are in fact defined as commodities by Smith:

> labour, like commodities may be said to have a real and a nominal price. Its real price may said to consist in the quantity of the necessaries and conveniences of life which are given for it; its nominal price, in the quantity of money.[107]

Smith is attempting to explain equilibrium within a conflict-prone society, while employing a labor theory of value, which sees human work as both capital and commodity.

Smith sees self-love as a governing principle in the intercourse of human society.[108] Thousands of years before Smith, ancient writers had already noted how self-love impacts upon human society.[109] Nevertheless, for Smith, self-love is not the same as selfishness and lack of morality as appears in the model of *homo economicus* currently dominant in economics. As a moral philosopher, Smith praised the sentiments of sympathy/empathy and benevolence. Still, he did not trust those sentiments alone to address human needs in human societies:

> as it is by treaty, by barter, and by purchase that we obtain from one another the greater part of those mutual good offices which we stand in need of, so it is this same trucking disposition which originally gives occasion to the division of labour.[110]

As observed, Smith considers natural price of commodities as resulting from the equilibrium of wages, profits and rents:

> These ordinary or average rates may be called the natural rates of wages, profit, and rent. . . . When the price of any commodity is neither more nor less what is sufficient to pay the rent of land, the wages or the labour, and the profits of the stock employed in raising, preparing and bringing to the market, according to their natural rates, the commodity is then sold for what may be called its natural price.[111]

This form of describing prices as connected to costs or payments is generally described as an objective theory of value, in contraposition to subjective theories of prices and values, which explains value in terms of subjective preferences of users/consumers/acquirers. Despite of the common terminology, this so-called objective theory of value is a rather speculative in describing prices. Smith consider that wages, profits and rents are related to a labor theory of value, which tries to measure the intangible.

On the other hand, for Smith, market (transaction) price is the actual price at which any commodity is sold.[112] The market price would tend to the *natural price* in the long run. In the meanwhile, there would be fluctuations because the market price is regulated by *"the proportion between the quantity which is actually bought to market, and the demand of those willing to pay the natural price, or the whole value of the rent, labour and profit."*[113] This equilibrium of sorts results from a conflict among the classes, where generally working people and landowners desire to receive the highest possible payments and employers and tenants to pay as little as possible.

Wages must be enough to maintain workers and their families; otherwise, workers could not survive and bring up a family.[114] The wages paid depend on the availability and supply of labor and size of fund (or capital stock) available for its purchase.[115] The availability of labor is connected to several factors such as scarcity of workers, difficulty in learning the trade, permanence of employment, degree of trust involved, season of the year, or agreeableness of the work. In some conditions, workers can have an advantage to bargain for higher wages. However, those demands cannot be superior to the available wage fund, which is part of the circulating capital owned by capitalists.[116] Wage fund increases would be dependent upon capital accumulation.

According to Smith, when a larger wage fund is used to increase wages, the end result can be an increase in the population. This idea relating means of subsistence, human reproduction and depletion of resources would later be popularized by Thomas Malthus (1766–1834). However, it can already be found in Smith, who observes that while poverty does not prevent generation, it is extremely unfavorable to rearing of children.[117] These phenomena would be especially important for working-class women, whom Smith sees as much more willing to bear children than wealthier women.[118] Still, Smith argues that humans, as other animal species, multiply in proportion to their means of subsistence and cannot multiply beyond it.[119] The increase in the numbers of what Smith calls *"the inferior ranks of people"*[120] will increase the availability of workers, therefore reducing wages to be paid. Likewise, if the subsistence wage declines, the number of births will decline and therefore the availability of workers in the long run, hence the proposed logic underlying a long-run equilibrium whereby wage levels tend to subsistence levels.

Similarly, Smith sees equilibrium in profits tending to the interest rate level in the long run, as wages to workers and their families' subsistence levels. Profits are seen as a form of surplus flowing to capitalists after rents and wages have been paid: *"The increase of stock, which raises wages, tends to lower profit."*[121] The capitalists would capture the surplus in order to face the trouble and risks incurred in combining the different factors of production:[122] The interest rate should be enough to compensate for the occasional losses to which every employment of stock is exposed.[123]

The declining rate of profit (another key theme in Marxism) would be a natural consequence of *prosperity*. Success brings other producers and merchants to offer competitive products, therefore diminishing prices.[124] When there is a similar increase in all different trades of the same society, then one should expect a similar effect.[125] Smith actually considers that profits ought to be lower in rich countries and higher in poor countries.[126]

As for rents, Smith see them as revenues originating on private property of the land. They can also be derived from mines or houses: "*As soon as land becomes private property, the landlord demands a share of almost all the produce which the labourer can either raise or collect from it.*"[127] However, the variation in rent value is not considered identical to that of wages and profits. Rent would be akin to a monopoly.[128] It depends on scarcity and productivity of land but also on the improvement of circumstances in society.[129] Increases in profits and wages tend to increase rents. Indeed, according to Smith: "*Rent . . . is naturally the highest which the tenant can adopt to pay in the actual circumstances of the land*" (except for rare liberality or more common ignorance of the landlord).[130] Rent would enter in the price of commodities in a different manner from wages and profits, which may increase prices. To Smith, high rents are the consequence of high prices.

7.5 Smith as a non-supporter of a self-regulating market (laissez-faire)

As noted by many mainstream economists, in *Theory of Moral Sentiments* and *Wealth of Nations*, Smith has identified a human desire for bettering our condition, which comes from the womb and will be with us until the grave. However, he also explains the capacity of bettering one's condition through frugality, which allows saving resources for forming capital to be used in production and trade.[131] Not selfishness, unabashed luxuries and riches. Through his explanation of national and individual wealth, Smith makes an indirect attack to Mandeville's theory of societal equilibrium based on human vices.[132] To Smith: "*every prodigal man appears to be a public enemy, and every frugal man a public benefactor.*"[133]

In fact, Smith criticizes employing revenues over activities or elements that do not increase exchangeable value from the annual produce of land and labor, for instance, the employment of a large battalion of what he calls nonproductive workers such as menial servants or expenses such opulent employment of nonproductive labor and the acquisition of frivolous objects such as "*little ornaments of dress and furniture, jewels, trinkets, gewgaws,*" which indicate "*not only a trifling, but a base and selfish disposition.*"[134] For Smith, self-interest and bettering one's condition is not selfishness. At his time, Smith did not know how to systematize a conception on a minority of the human population, the psychopaths and sociopaths, their incapability of feeling empathy and damage they can do unto others.[135] However, we can observe how Smith was quite far from the selfishness and greediness we observe in the mainstream *homo economics* concept.

Moreover, Smith could not be the creator of the expression "*laissez faire (et laissez passer),*"[136] a French expression credited to Vincent Gournay (1712–1759) and popularized by the Physiocrats.[137] The term *laissez-faire* can indeed be connected to the self-regulating market myth we have seen in Parts 1 and 2. On the other hand, market operations require investors. However, Smith was rather suspicious of investor motives. In many cases, their interests could be against the interest of the public: "*It comes from an order of men whose interest is never exactly the same with that of the public, who have generally an interest in deceiving the public and even to oppress the public.*"[138] From this viewpoint, Smith is against mercantilist policies that would protect some of investors against the interests of the public.

An example is imposing tariffs on foreign goods that would increase prices in the land or policies that could favor the formation of monopolies or oligopolies, where one producer/set of producers take hold of a market while imposing abusive conditions. For Smith, competition is the mechanism making transaction prices tend to natural prices. This process occurs for both profits and wages. Economic freedom would operate as follows. When a merchant has high profits with a certain commodity, other investors can move their resources to that industry. Smith criticizes mercantilist protectionist policies because they create monopolies and prevent transaction prices to adjust in the direction of his conception of natural prices, often benefiting investors against the public.[139] Smith's concept of competition is quite distinct from the contemporary mathematical mainstream concept in which there is a fictitious infinite and continuous number of buyers and sellers.

Clearly, Smith is not in favor of the allegory of a self-regulating market addressing all human needs. In *The Wealth of Nations* Book 5, he describes several areas where the state or sovereign must have an active role. These areas include the system of justice, the armed forces and activities of public interest where profit could not repay investments such as education, or transportation systems as bridges, roads or channels.[140] In the *Theory of Moral Sentiments*, Smith explain that public education should not only aim at knowledge but wisdom and moral sentiments.[141] Furthermore, Smith is well aware that the private property systems that allow markets to operate in mercantile/manufacturing societies are guaranteed by the state.[142] When criticizing state intervention, generally, Smith has in mind interventions that sideline with large investors' manufacturing and commercial interest against those interests of common people.[143]

7.6 Economic system's difficulty of capturing production beyond money

For Smith, work relevance is explained in relation to monetary flows. Work that generates revenues is defined as productive. Work that does not and may generate expenses is deemed as nonproductive. Work not reflected in monetary flows is neglected or ignored. However, nonproductive or neglected work includes very important human contributions to economic and societal production such as services, art, science and work at home essential for human survival and existence, let alone the perpetuation of the species.

Smith intends to explain wealth in terms of land produce and labor. However, these elements are to be measured in money, the perfectly tradable commodity. Hence, Smith, as most economists after him, became mystified with money as the measure for the tangible and intangible. They all confuse the tangibility of a monetary flow occurring in a precise point in space and time with the intangibility of monetary value. As a result, instead of considering monetary flows as phenomena to be explained, economists have taken them for granted. They observe money that the butcher, the brewer or the baker may receive, but not intangible flows necessary to get to that point or what happens with the food and drinks afterwards.

In Smith's time, tobacco and confections involving sugar were popular among wealthy classes. Cotton was used in innovative textile industries.[144] These products could be seen trading by monetary flows, as if under the market framework. However, a closer look must note that to large extent before reaching British mercantile societies, tobacco, sugar and cotton were produced by slave labor in the colonies. Through centuries, millions of people in deplorable conditions had been necessary for those products to be traded by monetary flows. Smith was aware of the existence of slavery in the colonies[145] or even in the coal mines of his homeland of Scotland.[146] In fact, Locke, who formulated a property theory of labor that founds Smith's work[147] and who wrote about the natural liberty of man from slavery,[148] was himself an investor at the Royal Africa Company (the prominent British slave-trading business).[149] Moreover, from 1673 to 1675 Locke was the Secretary of the Council of Trade and Plantations, a slave-related council.[150]

One can observe that Smith has made comments against slavery. However, he did not believe slavery could ever be abolished. Hence, hardly could he be a very effective campaigner against slavery. His comments can be divided along two themes: the moral dimension and economic efficiency of slavery.[151] The moral dimension regarding the suffering of slaves is addressed in the *Theory of Moral Sentiments* and in *Lectures on Jurisprudence* (published only in 1978). Smith acknowledges the miserable life of slaves for their property being at mercy of others.[152] Smith criticizes arbitrariness of punishment (LJ 181); absence of family rights (LJ 178) or the neglect of their children (LJ 193).[153] As for economic efficiency, Smith repeats several times the same argument in *The Wealth of Nations*. He claims that a wage earner is more productive and costs less than a slave.[154] A slave has no incentive to innovate.

> [W]ork done by slaves . . . is in the end the dearest [most expensive] of any. A person who can acquire no property, can have no other interest but to eat as much, and to labour as little as possible.[155]

Some authors have argued that this formulation was part of a strategy by Smith to promote abolition by means of the economic efficiency argument.[156] However, this argument is far from demonstrated.

In fact, contrary to others at the same time making important campaigns exposing the misery of slaves,[157] Smith did not believe that commercial/manufacturing societies would abandon slavery: "*It is indeed almost impossible that it should ever be totally or generally abolished.*"[158] If, as mentioned earlier, Aristoteles had a theory of the *natural slave*, Smith has a theory of the natural slave master: "*slavery takes place in all societies at their beginning, and proceeds from that tyrannic disposition which may almost be said to be natural to mankind.*"[159] Smith attempts to explain how in different societies slavery has been common such as in monarchies or ancient Rome. In a mercantile society, free owners, with their love of dominance, would not want to end their power over slaves.[160] Smith describes also that slaves have form of property capable of generating future income to slave owners and thus could be considered both capital and commodity. Abolition would deprive slaveholders from their property.[161]

Could a free mercantile society at least improve the conditions of slavery? On the contrary, according to Smith, it can even make them worse.[162] A poor and barbarous country may treat slaves better than a rich country. Smith offer two possible explanations. First, the rich country had more resources to acquire more slaves; hence, free men will be in lower numbers and need to be more aggressive and harsh to contain slaves' dissatisfaction and revolts. Second, the sentiment of sympathy toward others occurs with those who we consider as similar to us. In rich and successful countries, rich people tend to evermore look down on slaves and therefore worsen the conditions of the slaves. Furthermore, as seen earlier, workers' conditions in mercantile society would not be that wonderful as well. As shown earlier, for Smith, in equilibrium, workers are kept at subsistence level.[163]

Smith's system is fundamentally a human commodity framework. In the last two centuries, one can observe a drastic reduction in slavery, though not a total abolishment worldwide. He/she can also observe debates, advances, and setbacks in improving human life conditions. Yet, economics and other interrelated social sciences are still founded on this sad human commodity framework.

7.7 Conclusion

Smith has tried explaining how to address human necessities in a harmonious society. Throughout his works, he pays attention to several needs for human survival and existence such as food, clothing, shelter or raising a family. As observed by him, in a monetary society (termed by him as mercantile society) a wage laborer (and eventual family) must survive through his/her wage. Likewise, Smith has identified that for the greater part of rich people: "*the chief enjoyment of riches consists in the parade of riches . . . never so complete as when they appear to possess those decisive marks of opulence which nobody can possess but themselves.*"[164] Contrary to what could be inferred from mainstream economics and its *homo economicus* model, Smith displays contempt for greed, selfishness and prodigality. For Smith, self-interest can only contribute for general welfare when constrained by specific institutional arrangements.[165] Thus, he is far from defending the mythology of a self-regulating market capable of addressing all human requirements for life and existence.

Smith has systematized many ideas that were dispersed at the second half of the 18th century. He has reformulated concepts that still have great impact in economics and other social sciences. For him, human contributions to economic and societal production are both capital and commodities. Therefore, Smith's framework cannot be aligned to intangible flow theory. Although criticizing some policies of his time for being focused on bullion and money instead of the annual produce of land and labor, Smith has set economic analysis in terms of a commodity theory of money (even paper money should preferably be expressed in silver or gold).

Smith's system has many common elements to the system presented by the remarkable ancient philosopher Aristoteles. To Smith and Aristoteles, money is akin to a perfectly tradable commodity, the unit commodity that could be employed to measure both tangible and intangible elements. In view of that, labor values, natural values or commodity usefulness would be measurable in monetary terms. Although mainstream economics (and some Marxists) would later abandon the labor value theory presented by Smith (and previously formulated by others), mainstream economics and Marxism would continue to treat human contributions to economic and societal production as commodities if somehow related to monetary flows.

Smith has missed the complex evolution of money involving commodity money, coin money, banks, promissory notes, checks, paper money and, after his life, credit cards, digital money and cryptic money. Yet, by adopting the analogy of money as a commodity, Smith's synthesis has become mystified by money. This mystification would later provide the foundation for conceptions of human commodity, asset, capital or resource, which sway in economics. Human work and other human contributions not reflected in monetary flows would be neglected.

The idea that money would be a commodity brings about a theory explaining the occurrence of monetary flows. As many subsequent economists, Smith obsesses with monetary flow occurrences. Money is a commodity, and monetary flows happen to trade the money commodity by another commodity. In these pseudo-phenomena explanations, elements connected to monetary flows would automatically become commodities. These elements would include us human beings, work flows and other intangible flows. Thus, most economists thereafter become mystified with the micro moment of the market framework where a monetary flow might occur. However, they mostly neglect flows happening before, during and after that moment, without which economic and societal production would not be possible.

Furthermore, Smith's modification of the meaning of capital has had an enormous impact on economics and interconnected social sciences. For Smith, capital is no longer the concept of money investable or invested in business, which is still used in business circles. After Smith, capital implies elements involved in a production process that can be used to increase the wealth of countries or persons. Under this tautological explanation, every element with some connection to wealth creation becomes capital and can be treated as a commodity, for instance, we human beings and our intangible contributions to economic and societal production along with machines, buildings, robots, planes, boats, land and timber. The tautology is that capital generates wealth because capital is what generates wealth. From this modification, countless unsustainable tautological capital constructions have resulted such as social capital, human capital, intangible capital, brand capital, health capital and cultural capital.

Notes

1 System builder is an expression that can be found in Ekelund and Hébert (1997).
2 See, for instance, Bharat-Ram (2017); Dupont (2017), Ekelund and Hébert (1997); Norman (2018); Robbins (1998); Screpanti and Zamagni (2005).
3 Backhouse (2002), Dupont (2017), Rothbard (2006).
4 Idem.
5 The full title is *An Inquiry into the Nature and Causes of the Wealth of Nations.*
6 Backhouse (2002), Brue (2000), Dupont (2017), Ekelund and Hébert (1997), Robbins (1998), Screpanti and Zamagni (2005), Skinner (1999, 2003).
7 Idem.
8 Schumpeter (1954), Ortmann, Walraevens, and Baranowski (2019).
9 Rothbard (2006, pp. 435–436), Salim (1998, p. 3): "What is true in *The Wealth of Nations* is not original, and what is original is not true."
10 Backhouse (2002), Brue (2000), Dupont (2017), Friedman (1982), Ekelund and Hébert (1997), Greenspan (2007). Robbins (1998), Screpanti and Zamagni (2005), Skinner (1999, 2003).
11 For example, a group of French thinkers known as the Physiocrats, who presented a system that has identified capital but was centered on the land, or Richard Cantillon (1680–1734), who anticipated Smith's labor theory of value and production. Cantillon had proposed that although in the short run market prices might be determined by supply and demand, in the long run they should tend to their intrinsic value, which would be based upon land and labor necessary for production (Cantillon, 1755, 2015; Backhouse, 2002; Brue, 2000; Gailbraith, 1991; Dupont, 2017; Ekelund and Hébert, 1997; Screpanti and Zamagni, 2005; Skinner, 1999).
12 Backhouse (2002).
13 Backhouse (2002), Brue (2000), Ekelund and Hébert (1997), Robbins (1998), Screpanti and Zamagni (2005), Skinner (1999, 2003).
14 Who also taught rhetoric. Idem.
15 Backhouse (2002), Skinner (1999, 2003), Taylor (1965).
16 Although Smith was far from endorsing his friend's Skepticism, which could be traced back to the ideas of ancient Sophists and Skeptics, whom Hume commended.
17 Who is also considered a founder of liberalism and enlightenment. See Backhouse (2002), Skinner (1999, 2003), Taylor (1965).
18 Backhouse (2002), Brue (2000), Ekelund and Hébert (1997), Robbins (1998), Screpanti and Zamagni (2005), Skinner (1999, 2003), Taylor (1965).
19 Backhouse (2002), Machiavelli (1532, 1985), Screpanti and Zamagni (2005), Skinner (1999).
20 Idem.
21 Chapter XIII in Hobbes (1668, 2011), Backhouse (2002), Screpanti and Zamagni (2005), Skinner (1999), Robbins (1998).

22 Chapter XIII in Hobbes (1668, 2011), Backhouse (2002), Screpanti and Zamagni (2005), Skinner (1999), Robbins (1998).
23 Mandeville (1732, 1924) Backhouse (2002), Philipson (2012, pp. 79–88), Screpanti and Zamagni (2005), Skinner (1999), Robbins (1998).
24 *"Fraud, luxury and Pride must live, /While we the Benefits receive."* Mandeville (1732, 1924).
25 See Backhouse (2002), Brue (2000), Dupont (2017), Ekelund and Hébert (1997), Robbins (1998), Screpanti and Zamagni (2005), Skinner (1999, 2003). Indeed, this is a simplistic manner to divide human history complexity into unrefined stages, which is not uncommon among other social science writers, including Karl Marx, Emile Durkheim and Max Weber. Well afterwards, by the end of the 20th century, relativist poststructuralist writer Michel Focault (1977) was still trying to divide the history of punishment in human societies into three ad-hoc stages. Later, he would try to identify ad-hoc stages in the history of human sexuality (Foucault, 1976–1984).
26 See Backhouse (2002), Brue (2000), Dupont (2017), Ekelund and Hébert (1997), Robbins (1998), Screpanti and Zamagni (2005), Skinner (1999, 2003).
27 Idem.
28 Backhouse (2002), Brue (2000), Levy and Peart (2004), Khalil (2015), Screpanti and Zamagni (2005), Skinner (1999).
29 Drummond (2012), Levy and Peart (2004), Khalil (2015).
30 Backhouse (2002), Brue (2000), Levy and Peart (2004), Khalil (2015), Screpanti and Zamagni (2005), Skinner (1999).
31 Idem.
32 Idem.
33 Screpanti and Zamagni (2005).
34 Davies (2016), Ferguson (2009), Martin (2013), Weatherford (1997), Williams (1997).
35 Smith's contact with ancient Greece may have been driven by Hutcheson's lectures. Hutcheson was connected to other thinkers who have developed texts inspired in ancient Greece, such as Gershom Carmichael (1672–1729) and Samuel Pufendorf (1632–1694). Explanation suggested by Backhouse (2002, p. 112).
36 Gereffi, Humphrey, and Sturgeon (2005), Sturgeon, Van Biesebroeck, and Gereffi (2008).
37 Aristoteles (350 BC), Dupont (2017), Rothbard (2006).
38 Although objects with resemblance to proto-coins from around 600 BC have been found in the area of Black Sea and in China. You may see Davies (2016), Ferguson (2009), Martin (2013), Weatherford (1997), Williams (1997).
39 You may see Davies (2016), Ferguson (2009), Martin (2013), Weatherford (1997), Williams (1997).
40 Idem.
41 Although sovereigns sometimes implemented debasements, a process through which they would remove coins from circulation as to replace precious metals by metals of less worth, to later put coins in circulation back again. At times, these debasements would produce discontentment (Davies, 2016; Ferguson, 2009; Martin, 2013; Reinhart and Rogoff, 2009; Rogoff, 2016; Weatherford, 1997; Williams, 1997).
42 The other key functions of money for economists are reserve of value and means of payment. You may see Davies (2016), Ferguson (2009), Martin (2013), Weatherford (1997), Williams (1997).
43 Davies (2016), Ferguson (2009), Martin (2013), Weatherford (1997), Williams (1997).
44 Dupont (2017), Backhouse (2002), Rothbard (2006), Smith (1776a, 1999, pp. 393–429).
45 Especially so after the Bretton Woods agreement was dissolved between 1968 and 1973 (Davies, 2016; Ferguson, 2009; Martin, 2013; Michie, 2006; Reinhart and Rogoff, 2009; Weatherford, 1997; Williams, 1997).
46 Smith (1776a, 1999, pp. 389–427).
47 The Bank of Scotland was established by act of parliament in 1965. The Royal Bank was established by royal charter in 1727.

48 Smith (1776a, 1999, p. 397).
49 Smith was poorly impressed with two recent experiences we have no space to explore here but are referred to in *The Wealth of Nations*. One of those was led by another Scot named John Law, however, with poor reputation as a gambler and criminal. Law had been refused to create a system based on fiat money in Scotland, but went to create such a system in France. In the process, and along with other speculative ventures, he bankrupted the French Kingdom (Smith, 1776a, 1999, pp. 416–420). The other experience was the use of paper money in the then British colonies in North America, soon to be the US (Smith, 1776a, 1999, pp. 426–429). However, the use of fiduciary money would play a critical role in the independence of the US, as colonies with sparse resources found a monetary technology to assist the war effort. Still, it resulted in rampant inflation and money devaluation at the time.
50 Williams (1997), Martin (2013).
51 Polanyi (1944, 2001), Williams (1997), Martin (2013).
52 Ambrosi (2017).
53 Dupont (2017), Backhouse (2002), Rothbard (2006), Smith (1776a, 1999).
54 Later the distinction between use value and exchange value will also be of uttermost importance to Karl Marx.
55 Smith (1776a, 1999, p. 131).
56 Smith (1776a, 1999, p. 132).
57 Gailbraith (1991), Finley (1999), Pack and Dimand (1996).
58 Idem.
59 Idem.
60 Brue (2000, p. 140), Dupont (2017).
61 Smith did not share Aristoteles's disdain for loans charging interest. Times were different. However, Smith makes a distinction between the natural price and exchange price and tries to explain why they would diverge.
62 Philipson (2012).
63 Smith (1776a, 1999, pp. 457–458).
64 Drescher, Engerman, and Paquette (2009, p. 2).
65 Aristoteles (350 BC), Politics, Book 1.
66 Gailbraith (1991), Locke (1764, 1823), Backhouse (2002), Hume (1752), Locke (1690, 2017, Chapter V: Of Property), Screpanti and Zamagni (2005).
67 Hume (1752), Backhouse (2002) Screpanti and Zamagni (2005).
68 Smith (1776a, 1999, p. 439).
69 Smith (1776a, 1999, p. 348).
70 Smith (1776a, 1999, p. 346).
71 Idem.
72 Smith (1776a, 1999a, p. 136).
73 Smith (1776a, 1999, p. 133).
74 Smith (1776a, 1999, pp. 133–135). Before Smith, William Petty (1623–1687) and scholastic writers had already proposed a labor theory of value (Backhouse, 2002; Screpanti and Zamagni, 2005).
75 Smith, 1776a, 1999, p. 133.
76 Smith, 1776a, 1999, p. 135.
77 Smith (1776a, 1999, p. 133).
78 Skinner (1999).
79 Skinner (1999).
80 Hill (2001), Viner (1927).
81 Gailbraith (1991), Backhouse (2002), Dupont (2017), Robbins (1998), Screpanti and Zamagni (2005), Steiner (2003).
82 Gailbraith (1991).
83 Cantillon (1755, 2015), Backhouse (2002), Brue (2000), Gailbraith (1991), Dupont (2017), Ekelund and Hébert (1997), Screpanti and Zamagni (2005), Skinner (1999).

84 Idem.

85 Effective demand refers to those who can actually buy the commodity in opposition to those who may wish to have the commodity but have no financial means to ever obtain it.

86 Backhouse (2002), Brue (2000), Dupont (2017), Ekelund and Hébert (1997), Pack and Schliesser (2017), Robbins (1998), Screpanti and Zamagni (2005), Skinner (1999, 2003).

87 Smith, 1776a, 1999, p. 153. Note also that Smith consider that profits arise from another form of labor, namely, *"labor of inspection and direction"*. (Smith, 1776a, 1999, p. 151).

88 Not exactly for the same motives as Marx.

89 Cannan (1921), Hodgson (2014).

90 Schumpeter (1954).

91 Cannan (1921).

92 Cannan (1921, p. 480).

93 Smith (1776a, 1999a, p. 375.)

94 Smith (1776a, 1999, pp. 375–379).

95 Smith (1776a, 1999, p. 378).

96 Smith (1776a, 1999, p. 385).

97 Smith (1776a, 1999, p. 383).

98 Smith (1776a, 1999, pp. 430–431).

99 Smith (1776a, 1999, pp. 430–434).

100 Hodgson (2014) for more details.

101 For example, in Harrell and Klick (1980), Yin and Shanley (2008).

102 For instance, Stewart and Brown (2019) or Wright and McMahan (2011).

103 Hodgson (2014).

104 As suggested by Hodgson (2014).

105 Smith (1776a, 1999, p. 119).

106 See, for instance, Ekelund and Hébert (1997), Henderson (1954), Robbins (1998), Screpanti and Zamagni (2005).

107 Smith (1776a, 1999, p. 136).

108 Smith (1776a, 1999, pp. 118–120).

109 For instance, Aristoteles (350 BC, cited by Dupont, 2017, p. 52) while commenting on advantages he foresees about private property states: "How immeasurable greater is the pleasure, when a man feels a thing to be his own, for surely the love of self is implanted by nature and not given in vain, although selfishness is rightly censured."

110 Smith (1776a, 1999, p. 119).

111 Smith (1776a, 1999, p. 158).

112 Smith (1776a, 1999, p. 158).

113 Smith (1776a, 1999, pp. 158–159).

114 Smith (1776a, 1999, p. 170).

115 Skinner (1999).

116 Smith (1776a, 1999, p. 171).

117 Smith (1776a, 1999, pp. 182–183).

118 "A half-starved Highland woman frequently bears more than twenty children, while a pampered fine lady is often incapable of bearing any, and is generally exhausted by two or three. . . . Luxury in the fair sex, while it inflames perhaps the passion for enjoyment, seems always to weaken, and frequently to destroy altogether, the powers of generation" (Smith, 1776a, 1999, pp. 182–183).

119 Smith (1776a, 1999, pp. 182–183).

120 Smith (1776a, 1999, pp. 182–183).

121 Smith (1776a, 1999, p. 190).

122 Smith (1776a, 1999, pp. 199–200).

123 Smith (1776a, 1999, pp. 198–199).

124 "When the stocks of many rich merchants are turned into the same trade their mutual competition naturally tends to lower profits" (Smith, 1776a, 1999, p. 194).
125 Smith (1776a, 1999, p. 190).
126 Smith (1776a, 1999, p. 358).
127 Smith (1776a, 1999, p. 168).
128 Skinner (1999).
129 Smith (1776a, 1999, pp. 355–357).
130 Smith (1776a, 1999, p. 247).
131 Smith (1776a, 1999, pp. 429–450).
132 Mandeville (1732, 1924) Backhouse (2002), Screpanti and Zamagni (2005), Skinner (1999), Robbins (1998).
133 Smith (1776a, 1999, p. 441).
134 Smith (1776a, 1999, p. 449).
135 Adams (2016).
136 Let it do, let it pass.
137 Brue (2000, p. 39), Gailbraith (1991), Backhouse (2002), Dupont (2017), Robbins (1998), Screpanti and Zamagni (2005), Steiner (2003). Please note that Physiocratswere not addressing modern states.
138 Smith (1776a, 1999, pp. 357–359).
139 Smith (1776b, 1999, Book 4).
140 Smith (1776b, 1999, Book 5); Backhouse (2002), Thomas (2017), Viner (1927).
141 Idem.
142 Viner (1927).
143 Lindeman (1983, p. 32).
144 Brown (2010), Farr (2008).
145 Smith (1776a, 1999, Book 1 in the section on wages), Smith (1776b, 1999, Book IV both in the section on colonies and chapter on Physiocrats). See also Pack and Dimand (1996).
146 Smith (1978, p. 192). See also Pack and Dimand (1996).
147 Locke has also inspired United States' Declaration of Independence.
148 Locke (1690, 2017, Chapter IV: Of Slavery).
149 Brown (2010), Farr (2008).
150 Brown (2010), Farr (2008).
151 Brown (2010), Pack and Dimand (1996), Weingast (2015), Wells (2010).
152 Smith (1978, p. 178). See also Pack and Dimand (1996).
153 Brown (2010), Pack and Dimand (1996), Weingast (2015), Wells (2010).
154 Smith (1776a, 1999, Book 1 in the section on wages), Smith (1776b, 1999, Book IV both in the section on colonies and chapter on Physiocrats). See also Pack and Dimand (1996).
155 Smith (1776a, 1999, p. 490).
156 Pack and Dimand (1996), Wells (2010).
157 Brown (2010), Pack and Dimand (1996), Weingast (2015), Wells (2010).
158 Smith (1978, p. 181). See also Pack and Dimand (1996).
159 Smith (1978, p. 452). See also Pack and Dimand (1996).
160 Brown (2010), Pack and Dimand (1996), Weingast (2015).
161 Brown (2010), Pack and Dimand (1996), Weingast (2015), Wells (2010).
162 "this love of domination and tyrannizing, I say, will make it impossible for the slaves in a free country ever to recover their liberty" (Smith, 1978, p. 186). See also Brown (2010), Pack and Dimand (1996).
163 There is a debate about what subsistence level means to Smith. However, it should not be a level of excessive comfort for workers and their families.
164 Smith (1776a, 1999, p. 277).
165 Backhouse (2002), Blaug (1978, p. 63), Brue (2000), Vine (1927).

References

Adams, T. (2016). *The Psychopath Factory – How Capitalism Organises Empathy*. London: Repeater Books.

Ambrosi, G. (2017). Aristotle's geometrical accounting. *Cambridge Journal of Economics*, 42(2), 543–576.

Aristoteles (350 BC). *Politics*. Translated by Benjamin Jowett. Online at: http://classics.mit.edu/Aristotle/politics.html

Backhouse, R. (2002). *The Penguin History of Economics*. London: Penguin.

Bharat-Ram, V. (2017). *Evolution of Economic Ideas: Smith to Sen and Beyond*. New Delhi, India: Oxford University Press.

Blaug, M. (1978). *Economic Theory in Retrospect*. New York: Cambridge University Press.

Bourdieu, P. (1977). *Outline of a Theory of Practice*. Cambridge: Cambridge University Press.

Bourdieu, P. (1986). The forms of capital. In Richardson, J. (Ed.) *Handbook of Theory and Research for the Sociology of Education*. New York: Greenwood, 241–258.

Brown, M. (2010). Free enterprise and the economics of slavery. *Real-World Economics Review*, 52, 28–39.

Brue, S. (2000). *The Evolution of Economic Thought*. Mason, OH: Thomson/South Western.

Cannan, E. (1921). Early history of the term capital. *Quarterly Journal of Economics*, 35(3), 469–481.

Cantillon, R. (1755, 2015). *Essay on the Nature of Trade in General*. Indianapolis: Liberty Fund.

Davies, G. (2016). *A History of Money*. Cardiff, Walles: University of Wales Press.

Drescher, S., Engerman, S. and Paquette, R. (2009). Introduction. In Engerman, S., Drescher, S. and Paquette, R. (Eds.) *Slavery. Oxford Readers*. Oxford: Oxford University Press.

Drummond, J. J. (2012). Imagination and a presentation, sympathy and empathy. In Fricke, C. and Føllesdal, D. (Eds.) *Intersubjectivity and Objectivity in Adam Smith and Edmund Husserl: A Collection of Essays*. Volume 8. Boston: De Gruyter, 117.

Dupont, B. (2017). *The History of Economic Ideas: Economic Thought in Contemporary Context*. Oxon: Routledge.

Ekelund, R. and Hébert, R. (1997). *A History of Economic Theory and Method*. 4th Edition. New York: McGraw-Hill Companies.

Farr, J. (2008). Locke, natural law, and new world slavery. *Political Theory*, 36(4), 495–522.

Ferguson, N. (2009). *The Ascent of Money*. London: Penguin.

Finley, M. (1999). *The Ancient Economy*. Los Angeles, CA: University of California Press.

Friedman, M. (1982). *Capitalism and Freedom*. Chicago: The University of Chicago Press.

Gailbraith, J. (1991). *A History of Economics: The Past as the Present*. New York: Penguin.

Gereffi, G., Humphrey, J. and Sturgeon, T. (2005). The governance of global value chains. *Review of International Political Economy*, 12(1), 78–104.

Greenspan, A. (2007). *The Age of Turbulence: Adventures in a New World*. New York: Penguin.

Hanifan, L. (1916). The rural school community center. *Annals of the American Academy of Political and Social Science*, 67, 130–138.

Harrell, A. and Klick, H. (1980). Comparing the impact of monetary and nonmonetary human asset measures on executive decision making. *Accounting, Organizations and Society*, 5(4), 393–400.

Henderson, J. (1954). The macro and micro aspects of the wealth of nations. *Southern Economic Journal*, 25–35.

Hill, L. (2001). The hidden theology of Adam Smith. *The European Journal of the History of Economic Thought*, 8(1), 1–29.

Hobbes, T. (1668, 2011). *Leviathan or the Matter, Forme and Power of a Common-Wealth Ecclesiasticall and Civil*. San Francisco. CA: CreateSpace Independent Publishing Platform.

Hodgson, G. (2014). What is capital? Economists and sociologists have changed its meaning: Should it be changed back? *Cambridge Journal of Economics*, 38(5), 1063–1086.

Hume, D. (1752). *Political Discourses*. Edinburgh: Printed by R. Fleming, for A. Kincaid and A. Donaldson.

Khalil, E. L. (2015). The Fellow-Feeling Paradox: Hume, Smith and the Moral Order. *Philosophy*, 90(4), 653–678.

Levy, D. and Peart, S. J. (2004). Sympathy and approbation in Hume and Smith: A solution to the other rational species problem. *Economics & Philosophy*, 20(2), 331–349.

Lindeman, A. (1983). *A History of European Socialism*. New Haven: Yale University Press.

Locke, J. (1690, 2017). *Second Treatise of Government*. Online at: www.earlymoderntexts.com/assets/pdfs/locke1689a.pdf.

Locke, J. (1764, 1823). *The Works of John Locke*. Glasgow, UK: R Griffin and Co.

Machiavelli, N. (1532, 1985). *The Prince*. Chicago, IL: University of Chicago Press.

Mandeville, B. (1732, 1924). *The Fable of the Bees: Or, Private Vices, Public Benefits*. Oxford: Oxford University Press.

Martin, F. (2013). *Money: The Unauthorized Biography – From Coinage to Cryptocurrencies*. London: Vintage.

Michie, R. (2006). *The Global Securities Markets: A History*. London: Oxford University Press.

Norman, J. (2018). *Adam Smith: Father of Economics*. Boston: Basic Books.

Ortmann, A., Walraevens, B. and Baranowski, D. (2019). Schumpeter's assessment of Adam Smith and the wealth of nations: Why he got it wrong. *Journal of the History of Economic Thought*, 41(4), 531–551.

Pack, S. J. and Dimand, R. (1996). Slavery, Adam Smith's economic vision and the invisible hand. *History of Economic Ideas*, 4(1/2), 253–269.

Pack, S. J. and Schliesser, E. (2017). Adam Smith, natural movement and physics. *Cambridge Journal of Economics*, 42(2), 505–521.

Philipson, N. (2012). *Adam Smith: Uma Vida Iluminada*. Lisbon: Texto Editora.

Polanyi, K. (1944, 2001). *The Great Transformation*. Boston: Beacon Press.

Reinhart, C. and Rogoff, K. (2009). *This Time is Different: Eight Years of Financial Folly*. Princeton, NJ: Princeton University Press.

Robbins, L. (1998). *A History of Economic Thought*. Princeton, NJ: Princeton University Press.

Rogoff, K. (2016). *The Curse of Cash*. Princeton, NJ: Princeton University Press.

Rothbard, M. (2006). *Economic Thought Before Adam Smith*. Cheltenham, UK: Edward Elgar.

Salim, R. (1998). *The Myth of Adam Smith*. Cheltenham, UK: Edward Elgar.

Schumpeter, J. (1954). *A History of Economic Analysis*. London: Oxford University Press.

Screpanti, E. and Zamagni, S. (2005). *An Outline of the History of Economic Thought*. 2nd Edition. Oxford: Oxford University Press.

Skinner, A. (1999, 1776). Analytical introduction. In Smith, A. (Ed.) *The Wealth of Nations (Books I-III)*. London: Penguin.

Skinner, A. (2003). Adam Smith (1723–1790) theories of political economy. In Samuels, W., Biddle, J. and Davis, J. (Eds.) *A Companion to the History of Economic Thought*. Oxford: Basil-Blackwell.

Smith, A. (1759, 2000). *The Theory of Moral Sentiments*. London: Penguin.

Smith, A. (1776a, 1999). *An Inquiry into the Nature and Causes of the Wealth of Nations (The Wealth of Nations) (Books I-III)*. London: Penguin.

Smith, A. (1776b, 1999). *An Inquiry into the Nature and Causes of the Wealth of Nations (The Wealth of Nations) (Books IV-V)*. London: Penguin.

Smith, A. (1978). *Lectures on Jurisprudence*. Edited by Meek, R. L., Raphael, D. D. and Stein, P. G. Oxford: Oxford University Press.

Steiner, P. (2003). Physiocracy and French pre-classical political economy. In Samuels, W., Biddle, J. and Davis, J. (Eds.) *A Companion to the History of Economic Thought*. Oxford: Basil-Blackwell.

Stewart, G. and Brown, K. (2019). *Human Resource Management*. Hoboken, NJ: John Wiley and Sons.

Sturgeon, T., Van Biesebroeck, J. and Gereffi, G. (2008). Value chains, networks and clusters: Reframing the global automotive industry. *Journal of Economic Geography*, 8(3), 297–321.

Taylor, W. (1965). *Francis Hutcheson and David Hume as Predecessors of Adam Smith*. Durham, NC: Duke University Press.

Thomas, A. (2017). Adam Smith on the philosophy and provision of education. *Journal of Interdisciplinary Economics*, 30(1), 1–12.

Viner, J. (1927). Adam Smith and laissez faire. *Journal of Political Economy*, 35(2), 198–232.

Weatherford, J. (1997). *The History of Money*. New York: Random House/ Three Rivers Press.

Weingast, B. R. (2015). *Adam Smith's Theory of the Persistence of Slavery and Its Abolition in Western Europe*. Researchgate.net. Online at: https://www.researchgate.net/profile/Barry_Weingast/publication/280555359_Adam_Smith's_Theory_of_the_Persistence_of_Slavery_And_its_Abolition_in_Western_Europe/links/55b8d6b608ae092e965a7ee0/Adam-Smiths-Theory-of-the-Persistence-of-Slavery-And-its-Abolition-in-Western-Europe.pdf.

Wells, T. (2010). Adam Smith's real views on slavery: A reply to Marvin Brown. *Real-World Economics Review*, 53, 156–160.

Williams, J. (1997). *Money: A History*. London: British Museum Press.

Wright, P. and McMahan, G. (2011). Exploring human capital: Putting 'human' back into strategic human resource management. *Human Resource Management Journal*, 21(2), 93–104.

Yin, X. and Shanley, M. (2008). Industry determinants of the "merger versus alliance" decision. *Academy of Management Review*, 33(2), 473–491.

8 Theory of the human in mainstream economics

Utilitarianism as hedonism allegedly measurable in money

8.1 Introduction to the human being theory in economics

The theory of the human in mainstream economics is based upon Jeremy Bentham's (1748–1832) utilitarian philosophy,[1] which relaunches the olden philosophy of hedonism. It claims that the purpose of individuals is to seek pleasure and avoid pain.[2] Utilitarianism in economics has had several developments, which we will address in this book. In this chapter, we observe Bentham's hedonism, which conceived money as a quantitative measure for pleasure and pain. Furthermore, we will describe John Stuart Mill's (1806–1873) qualitative hedonism, formulated as a defense against strong criticism levelled toward hedonist utilitarianism in the 19th century. Mainstream economists would later abandon Mill's qualitative hedonism and simply ignore the criticism that Mill was trying to tackle. Furthermore, as we will see later, Mill, himself, would mostly follow quantitative hedonism to address economic affairs.

As described earlier, Smith has reformulated Aristoteles's distinction between use and exchange value. Both definitions attempt to measure intangible dimensions, a paradox (aporia) according to intangible flow theory. Nonetheless, to Smith the meaning of utility is connected to an element's use value. As in Aristoteles, an element's utility is akin to usefulness. Salt is useful to temper food, while food is useful to address hunger and so forth. To Bentham, the meaning of utility is modified to align with his hedonism.[3] It would become a guide to action and means for moral evaluation.[4] The collective utility of people, say a country, a family or an organization, could be found by adding their members' individual utilities, a sum allegedly quantifiable in terms of pleasure and pain units.

Bentham's hedonism is especially narcissistic and self-centered, if not (borderline) psychopathic. It is obsessed with his own pleasure/pain and has little empathy for others' fortunes. Society would be a fiction beyond the sum of each member's utility.[5] Individuals would act to maximize their utility, that is, to increase pleasure and diminish pain as much as possible. All this would eventually be measurable in money.[6] To the perfectly tradable commodity, Bentham attributes a new feature, namely, being the instrument of hedonist calculus. In many ways, Bentham has diverged from Smith and Aristoteles, who have based their theories on virtue (non-hedonist) moral theories. Although mainstream economics no longer measures utility affairs, as suggested by Bentham, it is still fundamentally founded on his hedonist philosophy.[7] While several of Bentham's proposals have been abandoned, mainstream economic theory of humanity, morality and action remain generally based upon Bentham's view that selfishly acting individuals would create general welfare,[8] which after more than two centuries is far from demonstrated.

Actually, hedonism as a general philosophy was never that popular. It had many opponents even in the ancient world. In seeking pleasure, one can seriously harm him-/herself and others around him/her as a gambling addict or a substance abuser may do. Seeking pleasure does not automatically results in benefiting society.[9] Moreover, rather than being a collective philosophy, hedonism tends to be centered on the individual and, thus, individualistic.[10] However, Bentham has promoted hedonism into a system of governing human existence, allegedly providing a pathway towards happiness for the many, that is, a hedonism that purportedly was for the common good.

In contemporary economics, the human appears undersocialized:[11] an atomized agent, motivated exclusively by his/her self-interest, deciding in isolation, selfish and detached from others and societal institutions. This description is commonly referred to as *homo economicus* because promoted by the discipline of (mainstream) economics. Similarly, the purpose of the human organization is described as to increase their owners/investors/shareholders' wealth. Wealth is seen as a manifestation of actual or potential hedonist pleasure and avoidance of pain. This perspective has impact upon other social disciplines further beyond economics.[12]

Both humans and organizations would be disconnected from social institutions, states, governments, communities, regulations and other organizations. In the self-regulating market myth, a crucial assumption is that participants, either individuals or organizations, could reach an equilibrium of sorts by merely matching their self-interests. The hedonist utility function is at the core of this description. In effect, hedonist utility is a mathematical expression of utilitarian/hedonist philosophy. This function appears in numerous microeconomics and macroeconomic textbooks and countless books and research papers. Several studies awarded Nobel prizes in economics worked on alleged variations and applications for this function. Though mathematics might be more sophisticated, when one looks carefully, he/she will generally find hedonist function assumptions in economics.

Currently, the manner to quantify utility affairs is different to the one proposed by Bentham in the 18th century.[13] However, it is still computed in money, which Bentham has suggested could be the instrument for hedonist calculus. Furthermore, the assumed goal of maximizing utility translates into presupposing that humans and organizations would act according to this peculiar hedonist utilitarian theory of action and morality.[14] A large portion of behavior economic research, which some hope could build a potential alternative to the mainstream, to a large extent, affiliates with utilitarian hedonism.[15]

8.2 Bentham hedonist utilitarianism

8.2.1 *Bentham relaunches a cruder version of hedonism supposedly for general well-being*

Part of Bentham's writings appear at a time where Europe was in turmoil with the French Revolution (1789), ensuing England-France war (1793–1815), Industrial Revolution, colonial insubordinations, and explorations of several parts of the globe yet unknown to Europeans. Furthermore, Bentham has observed crises in international trade, currency, production and employment. Back then, it may have seemed egalitarian to claim that the pleasure and pain of a king or an aristocrat would be equivalent to that of a common man. While using false equivalents, Bentham would avoid discussing how abundance experienced by kings and wealthy persons reflects a different existence to that of a beggar strained to daily find food. Bentham's egalitarianism was not very determined. Not even he fully believed in it.[16] Moreover, he was prompt to sacrifice egalitarianism for economic development.[17]

As insisted, times were very different. Britain and the recently independent US had chambers of representatives that would be models for other nations in the 19th century. However, most of the British and American population could not vote and was not represented by those chambers. The French Revolution would overthrow the monarchy under the guise of equality, but in the immediate years it would create an age of terror and later an emperor who wished to conquer Europe. In most areas where democratic polls were available, as for instance Britain, the vote was only attributed to wealthy citizens.

Bentham was made honorary citizen of France a few years after the revolution (in 1792). However, he would have contradictory feelings regarding the post-revolution.[18] Yet, in that period several persons who were involved in investing in commerce and manufacturing activities questioned privileges associated with aristocratic landowning.[19] To some extent, Bentham's arguments may have assisted those who could wish to challenge landowners' privileges resulting from traditional aristocracy. Moreover, Bentham has advocated other causes such as universal suffrage or prison reform. Still, his arguments are derived from his hedonism, which makes him contend against governmental or collective intervention and thus in favor of *laissez-faire*, forming initial versions of the self-regulating market myth.

Bentham was an eccentric and polemicist, who wrote many books and pamphlets. He studied law in Oxford. Although many of his texts criticize legal affairs and advocate juridical reformation, he himself never practiced the legal profession.[20] Despite his prolific writings, several of his texts were published only after his death. At some point in 1799, he received a heritage, which would assure him financial stability.[21] During his life, perhaps he could have been more influential in France than in his native Britain.[22] Yet, he gathered around him a group of associates and followers who would carry on his ideas. There were several vehicles to promote utilitarian ideas, such as the Radicals in Parliament, a group loosely revolving around utilitarian positions.[23] Further-more, there were newspapers such as the *Westminster Review* or the *Back Dwarf* and utilitarian venues where members could gather and socialize.

Some of most well-known economists of the 19th century were directly connected to Bentham. For example, Bentham claimed to be the spiritual father of James Mill (1773–1836), who would be the spiritual father of David Ricardo (1772–1823). Hence, according to Bentham, he could be the spiritual grandfather of Ricardo.[24] On the other hand, James Mill was the real father of John Stuart Mill (1806–1873), whom he tried to educate under a strict utilitar-ian philosophy.[25] In his own words, Bentham claimed to have deeply planted the *"tree of utility"* and to have spread it widely.[26] Indeed, he had followers who preached utilitarianism further beyond Britain in other countries as France, Prussia or the US. His hedonist utility formulation is indeed deeply ingrained in contemporary mainstream economics.

The key document for utilitarian philosophy might be *Introduction to the Principles of Moral Legislation* (1789), in which Bentham presents his principle of utility. It would provide a definition of *"right and wrong"*[27] and a manner of approving or disapproving *"every action"* both from individuals and govern-mental measures.[28] Bentham claims that *"Nature has placed mankind under the governance of two sovereign masters, pain and pleasure."*[29] His utilitarian system sug-gests putting humans and communities under the guises of pleasure and pain, while aiming at providing happiness for the greatest number of people. Utility is defined as

> that property in any object, whereby it tends to produce benefit, advan-tage, pleasure, good, or happiness (all of this in the present case comes to the same thing), or (what comes again to the same thing) to prevent the happening of mischief, pain, evil or unhappiness to the party whose interest is considered: if that party be the community in general, then the happiness of the community: if a particular individual, then the happiness of that individual.[30]

Thus, utility is described in terms of hedonism[31] and as a manner of governing human existence. This definition of utility differs from the definition as useful-ness in Smith, Hume[32] and Aristoteles.

According to Halévy (1928), Bentham's moral and political philosophy is based upon three major pillars. First is the greatest happiness principle, explained through hedonism via his utility definition. Second is universal egoism, as all humans are conceived as being obsessed with improving their own hedonism. Self-interest is considered as predominant over all other interests put together.[33] Third is an artificial identification of one's interest with those of others. As noted before, it is far from demonstrated that an obsessive search for one's pleasure contributes to the common good or even one's own good.

8.2.2 Utilitarianism as a theory of human action besides a moral theory

Besides changing the meaning of utility and happiness, Bentham's prolific texts seem to have created several new terms that would later provide standards of political, economic and social debates such as *"international," "maximize," "minimize"* and *"codification.".*[34] Along a moral theory (ethical hedonism),[35] utilitarianism conveys a theory of human action (psychological/motivational hedonism).[36] It is this moral and action theory that is currently reflected upon the *homo economicus* model in mainstream economics. The *homo economicus* is after all trying to maximize the hedonist utility, bounded by eventual constraints. A similar definition can be found in Bentham:

> My notion of man is, that, successfully or unsuccessfully, he aims at happiness, and so will continue to aim as long as he continues to be man, in every thing he does . . . self-regarding interest is predominant over all other interests put together.[37]

Through utilitarian hedonism, the human being is understood as the source of value and has the supreme value.[38] Accordingly, each individual would be the best judge of his/her own interests.[39]

In the chapter explaining *"human action in general"* in *An Introduction*, Bentham claims that the *"The business of government is to promote the happiness of the society, by punishing and rewarding."* The aim is to achieve the greatest happiness for the greatest number. Happiness is defined as before, namely, *"enjoyment of pleasures, security from pains."*[40] This formula is not entirely original though. The idea of maximum happiness for the greatest number had appeared before in Claude Adrien Helvetius (1715–1771) and in Cesare Beccaria (1738–1794).[41]

For Bentham, community (or society) is seen as *"a fictitious body."*[42] A community is no more than the sum of interests of all members who compose it. Interests are defined by total sum of pleasures minus the sum of all pains.[43] Thus, he contests the idea of a societal harmony out of a potential conflict among different groups of investors, landowners and workers we can find in Smith. Indeed, Bentham sees himself as enemy of the conception of natural law from where a natural harmony could arise. He was against the formulation that humans would adhere to an unwritten code of law and morals: *"Natural right is simple nonsense: natural and imprescriptible rights, rhetorical nonsense,- nonsense upon stilts."*[44] Several elements justified by natural law would be mere fictions, such as relations, rights, power or an unwritten social contract explaining how humans should behave.[45]

Not even a natural harmony from self-interest is acceptable by Bentham, which is an idea some scholars incorrectly claim to have extracted from Smith's invisible hand metaphor.[46] Although Bentham claims that individuals are mostly self-interested, for him there cannot be a natural harmony based upon egoism.[47] The existence of crime would provide a demonstration that natural harmony does not exist. What exists is an artificial identity of interests, where the interest of each individual must be identified with the general interest.[48] To achieve the artificial identity of interests, obligations and punishments should be designed in such a manner that the incentive to cause public harm through private action or enterprise was removed or at least reduced.[49]

8.3 The human and the paradox of measuring the intangible in utilitarianism

8.3.1 Freedom of contract fallacy and its application to the case of usury

While regularly ingratiating Adam Smith, Bentham diverges with him in many important ways. For instance, while Smith praised frugality, Bentham disparages asceticism: "*The ascetics are the mortal enemies of pleasures.*"[50] While Smith praises the sentiments of sympathy and benevolence towards others, Bentham claims that sympathy makes humans err on the side of leniency or severity. Allegedly, hedonist utility would provide an allegedly objective basis for decision making.[51]

In his *A Manual of Political Economy* (1800), Bentham states that on

> the genesis of the matter of wealth – the causes and mode of its production under its several modifications – reference may for the present be made to Adam Smith, who has not left much to do, except in the way of method and precision.

However, the divergence is certainly much broader than that about method and precision. Bentham assumes a laissez-faire (thus a preliminary self-regulating market) position based upon his utilitarian view that the individual would be the best judge of his/her own interest and society a mere sum of individual pleasure and pain. The government's role would be to "*be quiet.*"[52] This "*quietism*"[53] should exist because government intervention could either be needless or pernicious to the end in view.[54]

Bentham's perspective is indeed very distinct to Smith. The latter's hypothetical harmony among different groups in society is deemed as a fiction by the former. Smith's concern regarding moral sentiments are also not attended by Bentham. For instance, Bentham was in favor of usury, and for so he had previously argued against Smith, who was in favor of a maximum interest rate defined by the government for preventing abuses in the concession of loans.[55] Bentham, however, argued that setting a maximum interest rate would violate freedom of contract among individuals. He argued that neither the government nor any authority have the role of preventing usury and prodigality or repressing the temerity of projectors or protecting simplicity against imposition and indigence against extortion.[56] Furthermore, Bentham has alluded that speculators could generate economic growth.[57]

Later in mainstream economics, Bentham's "*freedom of contract*" argument would be made a recurrent as a defense against any possible moral argument.

Allegedly, if two or more contractual parties have accepted an interest rate, no one can say that the contract would not be fair. After all, individuals would be the best judges of their own interests. Protective measures issued by governments would interfere with individual liberties. This line of reasoning is inbuilt in the myth of a self-regulating market: It presupposes that when there are no government interventions, market transaction would be fair. Allegedly, explicit or implicit contracts for buying and selling would be established freely among two or more parties. Thus, market transactions (and respective prices) would be fair because of *freedom of contract*. Although Bentham may have not have used this argument to describe market equilibrium, future economists will heavily employ this line of reasoning. They will argue that if market transactions exist, they must be fair. Therefore, markets would be fair mechanisms.

Obviously, when entering into negotiation/bargaining, two or more parties may be rather unequal, which affects possible contractual outcome.[58] As explained by Kant, we humans are not entirely free from biological necessities and social constraints.[59] Furthermore, transactions are established in the context of existing social institutions.[60] The desperate mother may need to accept miserable salaries at her two jobs for the sake of her family. A dominant firm may impose conditions that his customers must have to face. The desperate man may enter into a loan, not out of fondness for contract, but for urgent family welfare needs. The loan shark may strike a deal with the naïve person who does not understand the established agreement. A dominant country may impose sanctions on another country, which has no power to impose sanctions back. Examples would go forth. Existence of a contract does not tautologically demonstrate that such contract is free and/or fair. Likewise, the micro moment of the market where a monetary flow occurs does not serve as enough evidence that markets would always be a perfect mechanism for handling economic and societal production, as inscribed in the self-regulating market myth. However, Bentham has proposed a freedom of contract under rational choice repetitious allegory, which lives on in mainstream economics.

8.3.2 Quantitative hedonism eventually measurable in money

Bentham's utilitarianism can be described as quantitative hedonism.[61] Apparently, one would be able to measure human pleasure and pain through a natural phenomenon perspective. Following the spirit of empiricism, Bentham aims employing mathematical operations analogous to Newtonian physics to measure hedonist utility.[62] While he is aware that he cannot formally demonstrate utility as a correct principle, he says such demonstration is needless, as every human creature[63] would defer to such principle in many if not most occasions of his/her life.[64]

He (1789, Chapter 4) would come up with a quantitative utilitarian method to inquire whether an action would be adequate. Although Bentham did not attribute a specific name to this method, it is frequently referred to as hedonic calculus, hedonist calculus, felicific calculus or utilitarian calculus in texts describing hedonism or Bentham's contributions to economics. This framework represents a consequentialist ethic theory because actions are evaluated by their consequences. Hedonist calculus would operate by units of pleasure and pain,[65] which are evidently intangible and not disconnected from many other complex phenomena. Paying little attention to all this, Bentham has suggested several dimensions to measure eventual units of pleasure and pain. These dimensions would be (i) intensity (of pleasure or pain), (ii) duration, (iii) certainty, (iv) propinquity/remoteness (how far in time the pleasure or pain will occur), (v) fecundity (probability that the action will be followed by similar sensations) and (vi) purity (probability that pleasure or pain will not be followed by opposite sensations), and (vii) extent of the people affected.[66]

Naturally, quantitative hedonism cannot solve some quite difficult objections to hedonism we will further observe in the next chapter. Moreover, one can observe that pleasure and pain may be intangible, as are dimensions used by Bentham to describe them. Moreover, they are highly subjective because different persons may make and feel different considerations about them. Interpersonal comparisons of utility would thus be quite subjective as well. Furthermore, Bentham's hedonisms undermine human relations as fictions beyond pleasure and pain. What is more, even if pleasure and pain could be measured with precision, it would be far from demonstrated they could fully explain humans, human action and morality. Furthermore, pleasures are treated as undistinguishable. The pleasure of reading a book would be equivalent to that of eating a sugar-strong pie, the affection of friendship to the decadence of drunkenness, and so forth.

Yet, in contemporary mainstream economics, quantitative hedonism has survived as the theory to explain humans, morality, action and our human societies. As we will observe in other works, at the end of the 19th and beginning of the 20th century, some key figures in economic thought such as William Stanley Jevons (1835–1882), Henry Sidgwick (1838–1900), Vilfredo Pareto (1848–1923), Francis Edgeworth (1845–1926) and Alfred Marshall (1842–1924) rescued quantitative utilitarianism. The later revival of utilitarianism is not unrelated to political clashes among different groups in society. The division of society proposed by Smith among landowners, investors and workers put a much larger set of humanity in the third group. Each group would have their advocates fighting fiercely for their interests. Artificially, however, inherent conflicts among these groups supposedly disappear in the utilitarian description of economic and societal production.

Yet, some arguments used to rescue quantitative hedonism at the end of the 19th century have been anticipated by Bentham himself. Although these arguments do not solve systematic problems in hedonist philosophies, they disguise quantitative hedonism in a pretense of scientificism. Let us observe two of the arguments anticipated by Bentham. The first was to measure utility variations (margins) instead of absolute utilities, which would allegedly solve the problem of subjectivity among interpersonal utility comparisons. The second was to make money the measure for pleasure and pain and thus for quantifying hedonist utility.

Faced with a mountain of criticisms regarding interpersonal comparisons of utility, utilitarian economists would later come up with the rhetorical solution of measuring variations in utility (marginal utility) instead of absolute utility. As we will see later, it is evident that major problems in hedonist calculus and philosophy remain unresolved. However, as they are camouflaged in economic utilitarianism, attention might be temporarily deflected. Bentham has himself referred to this contention in which he claims that the surplus of water, *"wine, grain and everything else"* loses value as it loses utility.[67] Or when Bentham observes that while wealth brings happiness, *"the quantity of happiness produced by a particle of wealth (each particle being of the same magnitude) will be less at every particle."*[68] Besides utility theory, Bentham has anticipated the marginal utility concept that mainstream economics still relies upon.

Another key rhetorical defense forestalled by Bentham was to transform money into the measure of pleasure and pain and therefore into a measure for quantitative hedonism/utilitarianism. He is very clear about considering money[69] as *"the most accurate measure of the quantity of pain or pleasure a man can be made to receive."*[70] In his solution, money would measure pleasure and pain, as the *"thermometer"* measures the temperature and the *"barometer"* the pressure of air.[71] Those who are not satisfied with the accuracy of this instrument ought to find a better one; otherwise, politics and morals would not be possible.[72] As is obvious, Bentham is defining that politics and morals are either defined in terms of his hedonism or they cannot be possible, which is a manner of biasing political and moral discussions towards his own views. This procedure suits well contemporary mainstream economic practices. To the view of money as a perfectly tradable commodity in Aristoteles and Smith, Bentham added a new feature: that of being able to measure quantitative hedonism. The self-interested *homo economicus* trying to maximize his/her monetary flows/wealth is after all trying to maximize his/her hedonism.

8.3.3 Human work (and other intangible contributions to production) as disutility

Quantitative hedonism provides the theory of human contributions to economic and societal production that is still dominant in economics. This view sees work as disutility and, thus, pain and sufferings. Humans would work exclusively for gratification, mostly in monetary form. Money would be both the perfectly tradable commodity and measure of pleasure and pain. Individuals would operate as atoms detached from social relations and institutions.

Although the disutility view of work was very much criticized in the 19th century, strangely, it seems fully accepted in contemporary mainstream economics.[73] Nonetheless, this hedonist description of human work undermines our integration in Earth's biosphere. It ignores our struggle of thousands of years to obtain resources that could assure our survival and existence as a species. Furthermore, it neglects our impact upon nature. Likewise, it can be used to undermine many human-related flows that are not reflected on monetary flows, such as fundamental household work, work necessary to the perpetuation of our species or protecting the environment, or creative/scientific work not generating cash flows. For quantitative hedonism, human activity becomes relevant as long as reflected in monetary flows (the measure of pleasure and pain).

At *Table of the Springs of Action*, Bentham tries to describe specific pleasures and pains regarding their positive (*eulogistic*), neutral and negative (*dyslogistic*) components. Labor is regarded as pain, leading to toil and fatigue. Bentham could not point out any positive element to it, only neutral or negative elements such as indolence or procrastination.[74] Note that Bentham can find positive elements even to death and bodily pains such as prudence, circumspection and cautiousness.[75] He sees work as necessary for acquisition of wealth and even for "*the preservation of existence*."[76] However, work is merely the means to the end of receiving a gratification.[77] Bentham does not believe people may generally desire or appreciate to work:

> the desire of it – of labour simply – desire of labour for the sake of labour, – of labour considered in the character of an end, without any view to any thing else, is a sort of desire that seems scarcely to have place in the human breast.[78]

There is no doubt that monetary resources are necessary for survival in contemporary societies. However, by reducing work to its gratification stance, Bentham evidently fails to appreciate production of our human societies, survival and existence.

When describing work as a commodity, economists see work-related activities as disutility, which exists to be compensated by pleasure derived from the gratification to be received. Gratification is generally expressed in monetary terms. As we will see throughout this book, these quantitative hedonist definitions are deeply foundational to mainstream economics and the human commodity framework. To mainstream economic judgement, the development of education, health, human skills or community integration are considered relevant only if reflected on future monetary flows.[79] Nonetheless, the mainstream economic stance that everyone has a similar negative attitude towards work is not at empirically substantiated. Findings seem to demonstrate that different human beings have different attitudes towards work. For example, humans who are high in neuroticism tend have much lower job satisfaction that those who are high in agreeableness and conscientiousness.[80]

8.4 J.S. Mill's qualitative utilitarianism as a defense and attempt to reformulate this philosophy

Throughout the 19th century, utilitarianism was widely contested. John Stuart Mill's (1863) *Utilitarianism* is a defense and attempt to reformulate this hedonist philosophy. Many years have passed since Bentham's (1789) seminal text had been launched. As we will see later, J.S. Mill was quite relevant for the evolution of economic ideas. His *Principles of Political Economy with Some of Their Applications to Social Philosophy* published in 1848[81] and, with several editions afterwards, was the key reference in the field until Marshal's *Principle of Economics* (1890). Mill felt the need for a defense of utilitarianism due to the many attacks against both utilitarianism and the discipline of political economy (as economics was referred back then).

For instance, Thomas Carlyle (1795–1881) had described utilitarianism as a *"pig philosophy."*[82] In his satirical writings, he claims that if *"swine and oxen could communicate to us on paper what their thoughts of the Universe"* would be, they would come with a philosophy resembling utilitarianism.[83] This philosophy would be akin to a religion for making notions of the universe, interests and duties, whereby human (or pig) would have no further purpose than the pursuit of desires and avoidance of pain.[84] Furthermore, Carlyle has described economics as a *"dismal science,"*[85] which would promise to find the *"secrets of the universe"*[86] in supply and demand. Moreover, it *"reduces the duty of human governors to that of letting men alone."*[87] From a not very distinct standpoint, John Ruskin (1819–1900) had announced three major criticisms against political economy and utilitarianism: (i) Political economy is scornful of religion and Christian morality. (ii) It professes to be a science of human relations; however, it abstracts from man all human characteristics and leaves only brutish ones. (iii) Even on its own basis, that of a commercial science, orthodox political economy is a false science.[88]

From our contemporary perspective, Carlyle and Ruskin have criticized utilitarianism and political economy from unstainable viewpoints. While praising work, they have made a defense of traditional systems such as feudalism and slavery as a solution against indigence and hunger, for instance, as a response to the great famine that affected Ireland between 1845 and 1849, which caused many deaths, diseases and mass immigration. Evidence we currently have about slavery and feudalism is in any manner compatible to Carlyle and Ruskin's utopian views about those traditional systems.[89] Nonetheless, if one is able to separate these writers' arguments from their fundamental perspective, the identification of utilitarianism as some sort of religion is indeed appropriate. Furthermore, the link between utilitarianism and the alleged science of economics is quite sensible. On one hand, and as noted earlier, some of the most famous political economists of the time were associated to Bentham. On the other hand, many ideas developed in economics were directly linked to utilitarianism, such as employing money as some sort of hedonist measure. Clearly, Mill felt the need to refute these criticisms in 1863, that is, 15 years after the first edition of his leading political economy book.[90]

Mill was educated by his father as a utilitarian. Some economic historians question whether he was always a utilitarian during his life or could have had moments of doubt. However, there is certainty that when writing *Principles* and *Utilitarianism* he holds a utilitarian position. He defines his utilitarianism as follows:

> Utility, or the Greatest Happiness Principle, holds that actions are right in proportion as they tend to promote happiness, wrong as they tend to produce the reverse of happiness. By happiness is intended pleasure, and the absence of pain; by unhappiness, pain, and the privation of pleasure.[91]

Nevertheless, he acknowledges that followers of this philosophy *"from Epicurus to Bentham"*[92] have been accused of holding the philosophy of a pig since the time of Epicurus in ancient Greece. Likewise, *"modern holders of the doctrine are occasionally made the subject of equally polite comparisons by its German, French, and English assailants."*[93]

Nonetheless, Mill does not grasp such criticism as entirely without merit. In his famous sentence, Mill notes:

> It is better to be a human being dissatisfied than a pig satisfied; better to be Socrates dissatisfied than a fool satisfied. And if the fool, or the pig, are a different opinion, it is because they only know their own side of the question. The other party to the comparison knows both sides.[94]

To address these apparent contradictions, Mill has suggested a clarification that he claims had originated in Epicurus (but was apparently ignored by Bentham and his followers): establishing a separation between higher and lower pleasures.[95] That is, Mill proposes what has been defined as *qualitative hedonism* through which different types of pleasures and pains would be qualitatively qualified. Higher pleasures would include pleasures of intellect, of feelings and imagination, and of moral sentiments.[96] Lower pleasures would include sensory pleasures, some of which we humans may share with pigs and other animals.[97]

With this qualitative hedonist framework, Mill would then try to incorporate in utilitarianism some thought currents that stand in direct opposition to hedonism, philosophies such as Stoicism[98] or Christianity[99] (also a religion), which praise asceticism and warn about the illusory nature of many earthly pleasures. Instead of arguing why utilitarianism would be a superior philosophy to those other philosophies, Mill has tried instead to incorporate opponent philosophies in utilitarianism without conceding theoretical ground to them.[100] Furthermore, Mill did not solve systemic problems in hedonism to which we will return later.

Thus, utilitarianism may indeed operate as some sort of religion. Indeed, Mill has reinforced the idea in Bentham that money could be a measure for hedonism, an important idea founding mainstream economics:

> the love of money is not only one of the strongest moving forces of human life, but money is, in many cases, desired in and for itself; the desire to possess it is often stronger than the desire to use it. . . . It may, then, be said

truly, that money is desired not for the sake of an end, but as part of the end. From being a means to happiness, it has come to be itself a principal ingredient of the individual's conception of happiness.

Utilitarianism claims to be a philosophy based upon happiness, and money could be used to infer such a happiness. However, such a feature would attribute metaphysical powers to money, which would operate as a religious entity.

What is worse, Mill's qualitative hedonism is a deviation from the course that economics would take.[101] As we will see later, quantitative hedonism directly derived from Bentham would be restored by authors such as Sidgwick (1874, 1907; 1877, 2000), Jevons (1874, 1890), Edgeworth (1881, 2003) and Marshall (1884, 1975).[102] Although claiming to admire Mill, they would support the idea that hedonism must be quantitative. Different forms of pleasure and pain would be equivalent.[103] Quantitative hedonism, they would later argue, could be addressed mathematically and quantitatively through money. Therefore, they have dismissed Mill's concerns along very relevant criticism levelled against utilitarianism, as if they had been settled. Obviously, they have not been settled. Furthermore, as we will see later, Mill himself fundamentally adopts quantitative hedonism when addressing economic matters.

8.5 Conclusion

Every year without admitting it (or in some cases being aware of it), economics professors lecture the moral philosophy of hedonism to thousands of talented young persons who will later become top executives, public servants, researchers, politicians or community leaders or who will perform other prominent societal roles.[104] Following Bentham's advice, pleasure and pain are deduced from money, which requires no further mention. To the explanation of money as perfectly tradable commodity in Smith, Bentham has added a new feature, namely, to be the instrument for hedonist calculus. Even the expression utilitarianism needs no longer be invoked by economics. Utility measurement is no longer conducted in the same manner proposed by Bentham. However, by focusing economics on studying utility functions, it is thereby assumed that humans and organizations behave according to quantitative hedonism. Some economists may not even be aware that the ubiquitous utility function, which also pervades behavioral economic research, is the mathematical translation of utilitarianism. In the 19th century, however, this theory has been accused of being a religion rather than a theory, which would aim to explain the purpose of human existence and the mysteries of the universe with its hedonist self-interest models along hedonist supply and demand frameworks.

It would not be correct to restrict utilitarian theory to economic affairs. It is, instead, an overreaching doctrine about human existence, a theory of humanity, morality and human action. Its framework treats human work and other intangible flows necessary for economic and societal production as disutility. These intangible flows would only be praised when generating gratification, mostly in the form of monetary flows allegedly consubstantiating hedonist calculus. Otherwise, they are to be undermined. This description puts the human individual's pleasures and pains at the center of the universe. Thus, it promotes narcissism and contributes to conceptually disconnect humanity from the biosphere, which is indispensable for human survival and existence. Furthermore, it sabotages the existence of human communities, which are deemed as a fiction beyond the sum of members' pleasure and pain.

Notes

1 Backhouse (2002), Brue (2000), Commons (1936), Hurtado (2008), Mitchell (1918), Moore (2013), Riley (2016), Screpanti and Zamagni (2005) Van Daal (1996).
2 Brue (2000), Feldman (2001), Moore (2013), Weijers (2019).
3 Brue (2000), Backhouse (2002), Screpanti and Zamagni (2005), Stigler (1950a, 1950b), Sweet (2019), Witztum and Young (2013).
4 Witztum and Young (2013).
5 The same conception we find in many contemporary economic studies.
6 Brue (2000), Backhouse (2002), Commons (1936), Dolfsma and Negru (2019), Mitchell (1918), Screpanti and Zamagni (2005), Stigler (1950a, 1950b), Sweet (2019), Warke (2000).
7 Idem.
8 Idem.
9 Even though the hedonist in Bentham can wait for greater pleasures in the future beyond the popular view of hedonism regarding immediate pleasures (Brue, 2000; Sweet, 2019).
10 Sweet (2019), Moore (2013).
11 Giddens (1976, 1979), Granovetter (1985).
12 For instance, Becker (1976, 1981, 2013), Coleman (1990, 1973) and Downs (1957) try to use the rational homo economics model to explain humans for tackling sociological and political research questions.
13 Brue (2000), Backhouse (2002), Screpanti and Zamagni (2005), Stigler (1950a, 1950b), Sweet (2019), Warke (2000).
14 Brue (2000), Backhouse (2002), Screpanti and Zamagni (2005), Stigler (1950a, 1950b), Sweet (2019), Warke (2000).
15 See next chapter on this topic.
16 As Bentham explains: "By equality is here meant, not the utmost conceivable equality, but only practicable equality. The utmost conceivable equality has place only in the field of physics; it applies only to weight, measure, time, and thence to motion."(Bentham, 1954, 2005, p. 310).
17 Dupont (2017, p. 64), Bentham (1843, p. 312).
18 See, for instance, Bentham (1795, 2003) or Bentham (1830b).
19 The bourgeoisie in Marxism.
20 Brue (2000), Backhouse (2002), Screpanti and Zamagni (2005), Sweet (2019), Warke (2000).
21 Brue (2000), Backhouse (2002), Screpanti and Zamagni (2005).
22 Brue (2000), Backhouse (2002), Screpanti and Zamagni (2005).
23 The term radical may offer us a glance about how his ideas were perceived back then.
24 Cited by Brue (2000, p. 135).
25 Brue (2000), Backhouse (2002), Screpanti and Zamagni (2005), Stigler (1950a, 1950b), Sweet (2019), Witztum and Young (2013).
26 Cited by Brue (2000, p. 142) and Stigler (1950a, p. 307).
27 Bentham (1789, Chapter 1).
28 Bentham (1789, Chapter 1, II).

29 Bentham (1789, Chapter 1, II).
30 Bentham (1789, Chapter 1, II).
31 From the earlier definition, it results that pleasure would be equivalent to benefit, advantage, good or happiness. On the other hand, pain would be equivalent to mischief, evil or unhappiness. See also Bentham (1789b, 1838–1843)
32 Although Hume is sometimes credited to have found utilitarianism (Dupont, 2017, p. 37), when Hume refers to an agent's useful consequences, he uses the term utility as synonymous to usefulness in *Enquiry Concerning the Principles of Morals* (Fieser, 2019).
33 Screpanti and Zamagni (2005).
34 Sweet (2019). See for instance Bentham (1830a).
35 Moore (2013).
36 Moore (2013), Weijers (2019).
37 Bentham (1954, 2005, p. 293).
38 Sweet (2019).
39 Sweet (2019).
40 Bentham (1789, Chapter 7, I).
41 "*la massima felicità divisa nel maggior numero.*" You may also see Screpanti and Zamagni (2005, pp. 83–85). The Declaration of Independence of the US (1776) also mentions "Life, Liberty and the pursuit of Happiness" as undeniable rights. Happiness is a term used by other writers such as Thomas Jefferson or Thomas Paine or contemporary writers do. However, they do not necessarily entail the hedonist meaning of happiness as in Bentham.
42 Bentham (1789, Chapter 1, II). One must be careful in employing the argument that economic and societal elements are fictitious, as used by Polanyi (1944, 2001), because Bentham has himself used the same line of reasoning for different purposes.
43 Bentham (1789, Chapter 1, II).
44 Bentham (1795, 2003, p. 207). See also Moore (2013).
45 Moore (2013).
46 See previous Chapter, Hill (2001), Viner (1972).
47 Ekelund and Hébert (1997).
48 Ekelund and Hébert (1997). In many respects, Bentham tries to break from Smith.
49 Ekelund and Hébert (1997, pp. 209–210).
50 Bentham (1789, Chapter 2).
51 Bentham (1789, Chapter 2).
52 Bentham (1800, Chapter 1).
53 Bentham (1800, Chapter 1).
54 Bentham (1800, Chapter 1).
55 Smith (1776, 1999, pp. 456–458), Hollander (1999).
56 Bentham (1787, 1818).
57 Bentham (1787, 1818).
58 See point 8.5.3.2. Rawls (1971).
59 See next chapter.
60 See next chapter. Rawls (1971).
61 Feldman (2001), Moore (2013), Van Daal (1996), Weijers (2019).
62 Ekelund and Robert (1997).
63 "however stupid or perverse" Bentham (1789, Chapter 1).
64 Bentham (1789, Chapter 1).
65 In describing hedonism, these units are often referred to as hedons and dolors.
66 Bentham (1789, Chapter 4), Feldman (2001), Moore (2013), Van Daal (1996), Weijers (2019).
67 Bentham (1801, 1954, 2005, p. 56). Recall that Bentham associated use value with his reformulated concept of utility.
68 Bentham (1952, 2005, p. 113) see also Bentham (1954, 2005, p. 313).
69 Money understood as the ratio of a given sum of money to the total sum of a man's capital (Bentham, 1954, 2005, p. 306; Bentham, 1830c, p. 254).

70 Bentham repeats this definition at least twice in Bentham (1954, 2005, p. 306) and Bentham (1830c, p. 254).
71 Bentham (1952, 2005, p. 117).
72 Bentham (1952, 2005, p. 117).
73 See Chapter 10 and Spencer (2009).
74 Bentham (1838–1843, No XII).
75 Bentham (1838–1843, No XIII).
76 Bentham (1954, 2005, p. 298).
77 Bentham (1954, 2005, p. 298).
78 Bentham (1954, 2005, p. 298).
79 Becker (1976, 1981, 2013), Hurtado (2008), Posner (1993).
80 See, for instance, Judge, Heller, and Mount (2002).
81 Mill (1848, 1820, 1871a, 1871b).
82 Carlyle (1850, 1898, pp. 319–323).
83 Carlyle (1850, 1898, pp. 319–323). Note that if pig and oxen could indeed write their thoughts, it is not certain they could not be offended to be described as utilitarian/hedonist thinkers.
84 Carlyle (1850, 1898, p. 348).
85 Carlyle (1849, 1888, vol. 7, pp. 83–84), Groenewegen (2001).
86 Carlyle (1849 1888, vol. 7, pp. 83–84), Groenewegen (2001).
87 Carlyle (1849 1888, vol. 7, pp. 83–84), Groenewegen (2001).
88 These three points summarizing Ruskin's criticism were identified by Fain (1943); see also Henderson (2000).
89 Groenewegen (2001), Fain (1943), Henderson (2000), Spencer (2009).
90 Carlyle is referred to in Mill (1863, 2001, p. 15).
91 Mill (1863, 2001, p. 10).
92 Mill (1863, 2001, p. 9). Here, Mill makes a reference to the ancient Greek philosopher Epicurus (341–271 BC), founder of Epicureanism, a form of normative hedonism (Weijers, 2019; Tsouna, 2017). Bentham himself refers to Epicurus in his major work as an inspiration to his utilitarianism: "Epicurus, it is true, is the only one among the ancients who has the merit of having known the true source of morality"(Bentham, 1789, Objections to the Principle Of Utility Answered). However, contrary to Bentham, Epicurus distinguished among different types of pleasures and pains and advised his followers to avoid towns, and especially marketplaces, in order to limit the resulting desires for unnecessary things (Weijers, 2019; Tsouna, 2017). As explained earlier, hedonism was never a very popular philosophy, even in the ancient world where it faced may rival philosophies.
93 Mill (1863, 2001, p. 10).
94 Mill (1863, 2001, p. 13).
95 Moore (2013), Bhardwaj (2010), Heydt (2019), Weijers (2019).
96 Mill (1863, 2001, Chapter 2), Bhardwaj (2010), Heydt (2019).
97 Mill (1863, 2001, Chapter 2), Bhardwaj (2010), Heydt (2019). Note, however, that as explained in Chapter 3, contrary to what was once thought, other animals may have consciousness and what appear as moral feelings (for instance, of fairness).
98 Mill (1863, 2001, pp. 15, 22).
99 Mill (1863, 2001, pp. 19, 23, 25, 28): "In the golden rule of Jesus of Nazareth, we read the complete spirit of the ethics of utility. To do as you would be done by, and to love your neighbour as yourself, constitute the ideal perfection of utilitarian morality."
100 Skelton (2005). On page 55, Mill (1863, 2001) also argues in relation to Judaism.
101 Sotiropoulos (2009).
102 See also Riley (2016) and Sotiropoulos (2009).
103 Brue (2000), Backhouse (2002), Screpanti and Zamagni (2005), Stigler (1950a, 1950b), Sweet (2019), Riley (2016) and Sotiropoulos (2009).

104 Jung (2014), Fourcade and Khurana (2013), Maclean, Harvey, and Chia (2012), Maclean, Harvey, and Kling (2014), Mizruchi (2013); Navarro (2008), Reed (2012); Thomas (1984); Zald and Lounsbury (2010).

References

Backhouse, R. (2002). *The Penguin History of Economics*. London: Penguin.

Becker, G. (1976, 2013). *The Economic Approach to Human Behaviour*. Chicago: Chicago University Press.

Becker, G. (1981). *A Treatise on the Family*. Cambridge, MA: Harvard University Press.

Bentham, J. (1787, 1818). Defence of usury. In Bentham, J. (Ed.) *Defence of Usury; Shewing the Impolicy of the Present Legal Restraints on the Terms of Pecuniary Bargains; in Letters to a Friend. To Which Is Added a Letter to Adam Smith, Esq. LL.D. on the Discouragements Opposed by the Above Restraints to the Progress of Inventive Industry; and to Which Is Also Added, a Protest Against Law-Taxes*. London: Payne and Foss.

Bentham, J. (1789a, 1838–1843). An introduction to the principles of morals and legislation. In Bowring, J. (Ed.) *The Works of Jeremy Bentham, 11 vols*. Volume 1. Edinburgh: William Tait. Online at: https://oll.libertyfund.org/titles/bentham-works-of-jeremy-bentham-11-vols.

Bentham, J. (1789b, 1838–1843). Objections to the principle of utility answered. In Bowring, J. (Ed.) *The Works of Jeremy Bentham, 11 vols*. Volume 1. Edinburgh: William Tait. Online at: https://oll.libertyfund.org/titles/bentham-works-of-jeremy-bentham-11-vols.

Bentham, J. (1795, 2003). Anarchical fallacies. In Medema, S. and Samuels, W. (Eds.) *The History of Economic Thought: A Reader*. London: Routledge.

Bentham, J. (1800, 1838–1843). A manual of political economy. In Bowring, J. (Ed.) *The Works of Jeremy Bentham*, 11 vols. Volume 3. Edinburgh: William Tait. Online at: https://oll.libertyfund.org/titles/bentham-works-of-jeremy-bentham-11-vols.

Bentham, J. (1801, 1954, 2005). The true alarm. In Stark, W. (Ed.) *Jeremy Bentham's Economic Writings*. Volume III. London: Routledge.

Bentham, J. (1830a, 1838–1843). Official aptitude maximized; Expense minimized: As shown in the several papers comprised in this volume. In Bowring, J. (Ed.) *The Works of Jeremy Bentham*, 11 vols. Volume 11. Edinburgh: William Tait. Online at: https://oll.libertyfund.org/titles/bentham-works-of-jeremy-bentham-11-vols.

Bentham, J. (1830b, 1838–1843). A table of the springs of action. In Bowring, J. (Ed.) *The Works of Jeremy Bentham*, 11 vols. Volume 1. Edinburgh: William Tait. Online at: https://oll.libertyfund.org/titles/bentham-works-of-jeremy-bentham-11-vols.

Bentham, J. (1830c). *The Rational for Punishment*. London: R. Heward.

Bentham, J. (1830d, 1838–1843). Jeremy Bentham to his fellow-citizens of France, on houses of peers and senates. In Bowring, J. (Ed.) *The Works of Jeremy Bentham*, 11 vols. Volume 4. Edinburgh: William Tait. Online at: https://oll.libertyfund.org/titles/bentham-works-of-jeremy-bentham-11-vols.

Bentham, J. (1952, 2005). The philosophy of economic science. In Stark, W. (Ed.) *Jeremy Bentham's Economic Writings*. Volume I. London: Routledge.

Bentham, J. (1954, 2005). The psychology of economic man. In Stark, W. (Ed.) *Jeremy Bentham's Economic Writings*. Volume III. London: Routledge.

Bhardwaj, K. (2010). Higher and lower pleasures and our moral psychology. *Res Cogitans*, 1(1), 16.

Carlyle, T. (1849, 1888). The nigger question. In *Miscellaneous Essays*. Volume 7. London: Chapman and Hall, 79–110.

Carlyle, T. (1850, 1898). *Latter-Day Pamphlets*. London: Chapman and Hall.

Coleman, J. (1973). *The Mathematics of Collective Action*. London: Heinemann.

Coleman, J. (1990). *Foundations of Social Theory*. Cambridge: Belknap Press.

Commons, J. (1936). Institutional economics. *The American Economic Review*, 26(1), 237–249.

Dolfsma, W. and Negru, I. (2019). Introduction. In Dolfsma, W. and Negru, I. (Eds.) *The Ethical Formation of Economists*. Oxon: Routledge.

Downs, A. (1957). *An Economic Theory of Democracy*. New York: Harper and Brothers.

Dupont, B. (2017). *The History of Economic Ideas: Economic Thought in Contemporary Context*. Oxon: Routledge.

Edgeworth, F. Y. (1881, 2003). *Mathematical Psychics: An Essay on the Application of Mathematics to the Moral Sciences*. London: Kegan Paul/ Newman.

Ekelund, R. and Hébert, R. (1997). *A History of Economic Theory and Method*. 4th Edition. New York: McGraw-Hill Companies.

Fain, J. T. (1943). Ruskin and the orthodox political economists. *Southern Economic Journal*, 1–13.

Feldman, F. (2001). Hedonism. In Becker, L. C. and Becker, C. B. (Eds.) *Encyclopedia of Ethics*. London: Routledge.

Fieser, J. (2019). David Hume (1711–1776). In *The Internet Encyclopedia of Philosophy: A Peer Reviewed Resource*. Online at: www.iep.utm.edu/hume/.

Fourcade, M. and Khurana, R. (2013). From social control to financial economics: The linked ecologies of economics and business in twentieth century America. *Theory and Society*, 42(2), 121–159.

Giddens, A. (1976). *New Rules of Sociological Method*. London: Hutchinson.

Giddens, A. (1979). *Central Problems in Social Theory*. London: Macmillan.

Granovetter, M. (1985). Economic action and social structure: The problem of embeddedness. *American Journal of Sociology*, 91(3), 481–510.

Groenewegen, P. (2001). Thomas Carlyle, 'the dismal science', and the contemporary political economy of slavery. *History of Economics Review*, 34(1), 74–94.

Halévy, E. (1928). *The Growth of Philosophic Radicalism*. London: Faber & Faber.

Henderson, W. (2000). *John Ruskin's Political Economy*. London: Routledge.

Heydt, C. (2019). John Stuart Mill (1806–1873). *The Internet Encyclopedia of Philosophy: A Peer Reviewed Resource*. Online at: www.iep.utm.edu/milljs/.

Hill, L. (2001). The hidden theology of Adam Smith. *The European Journal of the History of Economic Thought*, 8(1), 1–29.

Hollander, S. (1999). Jeremy Bentham and Adam Smith on the usury laws: A 'Smithian' reply to Bentham and a new problem. *The European Journal of the History of Economic Thought*, 6(4), 523–551.

Hurtado, J. (2008). Jeremy Bentham and Gary Becker: Utilitarianism and economic imperialism. *Journal of the History of Economic Thought*, 30(3), 335–357.

Jevons, W. S. (1874, 1890). Utilitarianism. In Adamson, R. and Jevons, H. A. (Eds.) *Pure Logic and Other Minor Works of W.S. Jevons*. London: Macmillan.

Judge, T. A., Heller, D. and Mount, M. K. (2002). Five-factor model of personality and job satisfaction: A meta-analysis. *Journal of Applied Psychology*, 87(3), 530–541.

Jung, J. (2014). Political contestation at the top: Politics of outsider succession at U.S. corporations. *Organization Studies*, 35, 727–764.

Maclean, M., Harvey, C. and Chia, R. (2012). Reflexive practice and the making of elite business careers. *Management Learning*, 43(4), 385–404.

Maclean, M., Harvey, C. and Kling, G. (2014). Pathways to power: Class, hyper-agency and the French corporate elite. *Organization Studies*, 35, 825–855.

Marshall, A. (1884, 1975). On utilitarianism: A summum bonum. In Whitaker, J. K. (Ed.) *The Early Economic Writings of Alfred Marshall, 1867–1890*. Volume 2. New York: Free Press.

Mill, J. S. (1848, 1820). *Principles of Political Economy with Some of Their Applications to Social Philosophy*. London: Longmans and Green and Co. Online. Mill, J. S. (1848). *Principles of Political Economy with some of their Applications to Social Philosophy*. London: Longmans and Green and Co.

Mill, J. S. (1863, 2001). *Utilitarianism*. Kitchener, ON: Batoche Books.

Mill, J. S. (1871a). *Principles of Political Economy with Some of Their Applications to Social Philosophy*. Volume 1. 7th Edition. London: Longmans and Green, Reader and Dyer.

Mill, J. S. (1871b). *Principles of Political Economy with Some of Their Applications to Social Philosophy*. Volume 2. 7th Edition. London: Longmans, Green, Reader and Dyer.

Mitchell, W. (1918). Bentham's felicific calculus. *Political Science Quarterly,* 33(2), 161–183.

Mizruchi, M. (2013). *The Fracturing of the American Corporate Elite*. Cambridge, MA: Harvard University Press.

Moore, A. (2013). Hedonism. In *Stanford Encyclopedia of Philosophy*. Online at: https://plato.stanford.edu/entries/hedonism/.

Navarro, P. (2008). The MBA core curricula of top ranked U.S. Business schools: A study in failure? *Academy of Management Learning and Education,* 71, 108–123.

Polanyi, K. (1944, 2001). *The Great Transformation: The Political and Economic Origins of Our Time*. Boston: Beacon Press.

Posner, R. A. (1993). Gary Becker's contributions to law and economics. *The Journal of Legal Studies,* 22(2), 211–215.

Rawls, J. (1971). *A Theory of Justice*. Cambridge, MA: Harvard University Press.

Reed, M. (2012). Masters of the universe: Power and elites in organization studies. *Organization Studies,* 33, 203–221.

Riley, J. (2016). Utilitarianism and economic theory. *The New Palgrave Dictionary of Economics,* 1–15.

Screpanti, E. and Zamagni, S. (2005). *An Outline of the History of Economic Thought*. 2nd Edition. Oxford: Oxford University Press.

Sidgwick, H. (1874, 1907). *The Methods of Ethics*. 7th Edition. London: Macmillan.

Sidgwick, H. (1877, 2000). Bentham and Benthamism in politics and ethics. In Singer, M. G. (Ed.) *Essays on Ethics and Method: Henry Sidgwick*. Oxford: Clarendon Press.

Skelton, A. (2005). Review of Bart Schultz and Georgios Varouxakis (Eds.), utilitarianism and empire. *Notre Dame Philosophical Reviews: An Electronic Journal*. Online at: https://ndpr.nd.edu/news/utilitarianism-and-empire/.

Smith, A. (1776a, 1999). *An Inquiry into the Nature and Causes of the Wealth of Nations (The Wealth of Nations) (Books I-III)*. London: Penguin.

Sotiropoulos, D. (2009). Why John Stuart Mill should not be enlisted among neoclassical economists. *The European Journal of the History of Economic Thought,* 16(3), 455–473.

Spencer, D. (2009). Work in utopia: Pro-work sentiments in the writings of four critics of classical economics. *The European Journal of the History of Economic Thought,* 16(1), 97–122.

Stigler, G. J. (1950a). The development of utility theory. I. *Journal of Political Economy,* 58(4), 307–327.

Stigler, G. J. (1950b). The development of utility theory. II. *Journal of Political Economy,* 58(5), 373–396.

Sweet, W. (2019). Jeremy Bentham (1748–1832). In *The Internet Encyclopedia of Philosophy: A Peer Reviewed Resource*. Online at: www.iep.utm.edu/bentham/.

Thomas, A. (1984). The value of MBA's? The fitting role of business schools. *Management Learning,* 15(3), 201–208.

Tsouna, V. (2017). Epicureanism and hedonism. In Golob, S. and Timmermann, J. (Eds.) *The Cambridge History of Moral Philosophy*. Cambridge: Cambridge University Press, 57–74.

Van Daal, J. (1996). From utilitarianism to hedonism: Gossen, Jevons and Walras. *Journal of the History of Economic Thought*, 18(2), 271–286.

Viner, J. (1972). *The Role of Providence in the Social Order*. Philadelphia: American Philosophical Society.

Warke, T. (2000). Mathematical fitness in the evolution of the utility concept from Bentham to Jevons to Marshall. *Journal of the History of Economic Thought*, 22(1), 5–27.

Weijers, D. (2019). Hedonism. In *The Internet Encyclopedia of Philosophy: A Peer Reviewed Resource*. Online at: www.iep.utm.edu/bentham/.

Witztum, A. and Young, J. (2013). Utilitarianism and the role of utility in Adam Smith. *The European Journal of the History of Economic Thought*, 20(4), 572–602.

Zald, M. and Lounsbury, M. (2010). The wizards of Oz: Towards an institutional approach to elites, expertise and command posts. *Organization Studies*, 31, 963–996.

9 Intangible flow theory is not aligned with quantitative or qualitative utilitarianism

9.1 Introduction to the divergence between intangible flow theory and hedonism

Parts 1 and 2 show that intangible flow theory cannot be compatible with quantitative hedonism. The latter tries to measure the intangible, which is a paradox according to the new theory. Furthermore, many flows of concern for quantitative hedonism are consummated by intangible flows that are demonstrable but cannot be measured with precision. Likewise, there is no evidence that money could be an adequate measure for hedonist calculus. Money does not necessarily represent consequences of moral decisions. In some cases, money can be used to implement non-hedonist moral decision, for example, to contribute to moral causes, the community or family.[1] Moreover, there are indeed many things money cannot buy[2] or measure.

However, given that J.S. Mill has presented a qualitative form of hedonism, a question could be raised on whether qualitative hedonism would be compatible with intangible flow theory. It does not suffice for a theory to be qualitative in order to be congruent with the new theory. In fact, intangible flow theory praises quantitative research methodologies to address phenomena that can be measured or quasi-measured with precision. Furthermore, the definition of human in intangible flow theory is much broader than in hedonism's definition. For the new theory, a human is defined as a *homo sapiens*, which allows incorporating knowledge from many scientific disciplines that study humans, either individually or collectively. Instead, hedonism tries to impose the theory that pleasure and pain are the main drivers of human morality and behavior, without presenting supportive evidence. For this motive, utilitarian hedonism has been accused of behaving as a creed or religion by some of J.S. Mill's contemporaries.

This chapter introduces (non-extensively) several reasons that intangible flow theory is not aligned with either quantitative or qualitative hedonist utilitarianism. First, hedonist theory has several important systematic weaknesses. Second, J.S. Mill is far from being the only thinker presenting a moral theory who tries to address intangible dimensions. Indeed, to contrapose hedonism lectured in economic classes, mainstream economists could very well lecture other moral theories to students and anyone still seeking their opinions. We will briefly mention as examples two non-hedonist moral theories, which also address intangible dimensions. Third, although most behavioral economic research pays reference to the utility function, and therefore to hedonism, psychological and neurological studies could instead challenge the hedonist framework.

9.2 Systematic flaws in hedonism shared by mainstream economics

The previous chapter focused upon Bentham's hedonist utilitarianism. It did not cover other forms of hedonism with less bearing on mainstream economics, which include several contemporary varieties. Nonetheless, different forms of hedonism tend to share systematic problems, which help explain why hedonism has never been a massively popular philosophy (apart from economics when disguised as utilitarianism, it seems).[3] Three of those weaknesses are that (i) pleasure and avoidance of pain are not the only sources of intrinsic value, (ii) some forms of pleasure and pain avoidance are not valuable and can even be harmful to oneself and others around him/her, and (iii) hedonism promotes pleasure as the supreme value without having any coherent and unifying definition of pleasure.[4]

Moreover, the use of money as a measure for hedonist calculus in mainstream economics was never accompanied by any demonstration that money could be used for such purpose. Thus, money is described as having metaphysical properties, as some form of contemporary divine and mystical instrument. Neither quantitative nor qualitative utilitarianism can cope with these systematic problems.

9.3 Examples of other ethical schools that could be studied by economics

9.3.1 Introduction

Utilitarianism is often defined as a consequentialist moral theory because it evaluates rightness of actions/decisions according to their potential outcomes (consequences). This classification distinguishes it from non-consequentialist theories or virtue theories, which look out for different criteria to evaluate actions/decisions. There are several non-consequentialist and virtue theories. We will briefly observe a non-consequentialist and a virtue moral theory, which could also be studied by economics. Several other important philosophies with provisions against hedonism are not described here, for instance, Stoicism, Platonism or Confucianism in the ancient world or more than a few contemporary non-hedonist philosophies. Furthermore, we are not including in this debate important human religions. However, mainstream economics must care to address how its latent hedonism conflicts with them.

The purpose of this subsection is not to make a comprehensive evaluation of alternative moral theories, but to demonstrate the oddness of camouflaging a hedonist moral theory in the mathematical framework of mainstream economics. Furthermore, this subsection aims to show that besides J.S. Mill's qualitative utilitarianism, there are other moral theories addressing intangible dimensions.

9.3.2 Kant's categorical imperatives

Immanuel Kant's (1724–1804) non-consequentialist moral theory is often considered the main rival to consequentialist utilitarianism.[5] In Prussia, Kant developed his deontological moral theory roughly at the same time as Bentham.[6] However, they seem not to have engaged or made any direct comment about each other's moral theory.[7] Nevertheless, they wish to address common questions such as what the superior moral principle is to guide human action or what is freedom.[8] The answers provided are nonetheless quite different.

Kant's accept that humans feel pleasure and pain, which constrain their (our) behavior. However, pleasure and pain cannot be the basis for an ethical/moral system, which should instead be derived from the capacity of reasoning. A system based on pleasure and pain could better be replaced by instinct. To further understand Kant's moral system, we need to understand how his concept of freedom is different from the utilitarianism's. According to Kant, one is only free when he/she can act freely from dictates of nature or social pressure. Thus, when we do what our appetites tell us to avoid pain, we are not really acting freely. For example, one can choose among different supermarkets or restaurants to buy food. However, he/she is constrained by his/her need for food. One is not free to live without food or water or shelter. Likewise, one is constrained by social norms regarding how to behave. According to Kant, we are only free when we have autonomy to decide. Non-autonomy implies non-freedom.

Besides this distinctive freedom concept, Kant's system is founded on two further pillars. The first is intention; that is, an ethical act is performed out of a deliberated intent. The other is reason, which should be more important than sentiments in reaching ethical decisions. With these three pillars, Kant distinguishes hypothetical imperatives from categorical imperatives. The former tells us what we should do in order to achieve some objective as in the consequences sourced out by hedonist utilitarianism. Instead, the categorically imperative comprehends actions that are objectively necessary regardless of their relation to further ends. Their necessity arises from freedom, intent and reason,

Sandel (2012) presents an example to help distinguish between hypothetical and categorical imperatives. Suppose that a young child enters a shop with a 20 euro (or dollar or pound) bill to buy an ice cream that costs, say, 2 euros. Why should the shopkeeper return 18 euros in exchange to the child who does not know how money works? If the shopkeeper is concerned with the consequences, for instance, the kid might tell his parents who will damage the shopkeeper's reputation in the neighborhood, consequently making him loose good business in the future, his decision is based upon a hypothetical imperative (as in utilitarianism). If the shopkeeper returns the right amount because that is the correct behavior derived from freedom, reason and intent, such a decision is based upon a categorical imperative. Likewise, if a firm is reducing its pollution levels because of reputational concerns and with the aim of capturing business from ecologically conscious consumers, it would be acting according to a hypothetical imperative. On the other hand, if the firm decides to limit pollution damages to the environment for reasons beyond economic or other consequences, it might be acting according to a categorical imperative.

Concurring to Kant, we may have imperfect duties resulting from sentiments such as kindness or benevolence. However, perfect duties are those that result from categorical imperatives. An ethical act is one that is based upon intention, freedom and reason. These three pillars conduct Kant to three formulas to evaluate duties. Those three formulas cannot be accepted by Bentham and his hedonist followers: the formula of acting as if under a universal law, the formula of treating people as ends and not means to ends, and the formula of acting as if there is universal acceptability for the action/decision we may take/ make. Kant's system may face some difficulties, for example, in demonstrating that morality always comes from reason or in distinguishing hypothetical from categorical imperatives or in presupposing that all humans are aware of a natural law or in coping with instinct. Nevertheless, it offers a congruent alternative to hedonist utilitarianism, which is generally ignored by mainstream economics.

9.3.3 Aristoteles's virtue ethics

Aristoteles, from whom Adam Smith has adapted part of his economic framework, based his economic framework also on a broader moral theory. Perhaps a great deal of misunderstanding could be addressed by contrasting the Aristotelean framework to the mainstream economic utilitarian view. Aristoteles was a towering figure in the ancient world. Many of his ideas would provide foundations for Western thinking during many centuries to come.[9] He was a Macedonian from Stagira, who would found the Lyceum in Athens and tutor among others Alexander the Great (365–323 BC).

Aristoteles perceived the human as a social animal. Nature would not do things in vain. It has given humans the ability of speaking. Aristoteles was not entirely correct in assuming that the human was the only living being capable of communicating, but he was working with the information of his time. It is from the faculty of language that we often define concepts such as right, wrong, good/evil or justice. Aristoteles based his moral theory among three key interrelated concepts, namely, the community (polis), virtue and human flourishing on a good life.

As a social animal, the human requires to live in social groups/communities that become towns and cities (polis). The isolated human, who is not capable of association or the benefit of sharing, he/she who is self-sufficient, is not part of the polis. He/she may well be a beast (an irrational animal) or a divinity.

However, he/she would be of little use to the community. Virtue theory differs from consequentialist and non-consequentialist moral theories because it focuses on character instead of actions. It encourages the question about what type of person we need to be in order to be ethical. What personal qualities must we have to be ethical?

Aristoteles is not always clear about what he means by virtue. However, he suggests that virtue is generally at the middle of two vices, which are extremes. For instance, courage is a virtue that is at the middle of the vices of cowardice and rashness. Likewise, good temper is a virtue that is at the middle between irascibility and inirascibility (too little anger). Modesty is at the middle of shamelessness (too little shame) and bashfulness (too much shame). Furthermore, virtue is a matter of practice. A brave person is not someone who claims to be brave, but someone who acts with courage. A wise person is not someone who says to be knowledgeable, but someone who acts with wisdom. A fair person is not someone who says to be fair, but someone who acts with fairness. Aristoteles believed that there cannot be human flourishing and a good life without virtue, which must be defined in relation to the polis. Hence, virtue must be defined in terms of a good human good life and the polis.

However, can one not obtain gratification such as money and rewards (that would be defined as pleasure or avoidance of pain in hedonist calculus at hedonist utilitarianism) by not being virtuous, for instance, by cheating, lying or stealing? Aristoteles says that non-virtuous behavior may in the short term lead to external advancements, which generate external fruition, for instance, gratification in the form of money or status. However, non-virtuous behavior cannot lead to internal fruition such as satisfaction, exhilaration, or personal development. Someone obtaining advantage for being non-virtuous could not obtain internal fruition because he/she would be suffering from personal feelings such as regret, shame or guilt. As Adam Smith, Aristoteles generally does not consider a small group of human beings who cannot be constrained by these feelings as malignant narcissists, psychopaths and Machiavellians.[10] Nonetheless, Aristoteles's distinction between natural and nonnatural use of money, which has inspired Adam Smith (and latter Ricardo and Karl Marx) comes from this moral theory. The natural use of money is made to enhance virtue, human development and flourishing at the polis. The nonnatural use of money, for example, to enrich oneself through usury and interests over loans, can only lead to external fruition. To enable virtue and human flourishing, a polis must develop an excellence of frameworks to keep external fruition in its proper place.

Numerous important contemporary frameworks can be connected to Aristoteles's virtue ethics, for instance, the idea that the management of human organizations and organizations themselves can be virtuous or not.[11] Another idea is the concept of communities of practice, which explains that much further beyond their economic activities, human organizations are embedded along domains and human communities.[12] Another contemporary ramification of Aristoteles's moral theory is the stakeholder view of the human organization,[13] which argues that several persons and groups (the stakeholders) have interest in an organization beyond making money for shareholders/owners. Besides being created by humans, organizations may interact with many other humans as in the community expressed by the polis. We can also identify hints of Aristoteles's ideas when Sen (1992) argues that humans require capabilities/skills in order to be able to enjoy a good life.

Aristoteles lived in a slave-based society of a very distant era, much distinct from ours. Back then, although a small fraction of the population could have some access to a quite limited form of Athenian democracy, slaves made up a substantial part of economic and societal production. Technology was quite underdeveloped when compared to our time. As explained before, Aristoteles had a view of the *natural slave*, which is unacceptable to our contemporary standards. Nonetheless, he was able formulate a moral theory based upon the three pillars of virtue, polis and human flourishing on a good human life, which still informs important contemporary debates, that is, debates that are conduced mostly outside mainstream economics.

9.4 That psychological and behavioral studies could challenge hedonism/utilitarianism

Behavioral economic research asserts to increase the explanatory power of economics by providing it with more "*realistic*" psychological foundations.[14] Cognitive bias is incorporated in models, for example, wishful thinking, overconfidence, false consensus effects, magical beliefs, self-serving bias and confirmation bias.[15] Mental accounting processes are considered, for instance, the different uses/purposes attributed to distinct income sources and accounts (e.g., one may spend an amount gained on a lottery ticket differently from income saved out of wages over the years).[16] Humans cannot be fully rational, as we have imperfect information and a bounded capacity to process all available information.[17] Decision making under risk and uncertainty is also addressed.[18] Other examples of economic phenomena studied by behavioral economics can be why people save less than they plan, have unbearable credit card bills, or hold on to poorly performing investments instead of selling them.[19]

Certainly, insights from psychology and other behavioral sciences are hardly needed. However, in most behavioral economic research, the major explanation for humans, morality and action is still utilitarianism.[20] Countless studies attempt to improve utility functions used in mainstream economics with insights from psychology.[21] Thus, without assuming it (or in many cases being aware of it), they adopt psychological versions of quantitative hedonism already recommended in Bentham's work.[22] Often, behavioral economics tries to paradoxically quantify what Mill qualitative hedonism would define as higher pleasure forms, such as friendship or integrity. Therefore, those studies hardly could be a threat to mainstream economics' status.[23] To large extent, they are another application of utilitarian philosophy. Frequently, they bring excuse sets for why humans do not maximize their hedonism, as predicted in the main-stream model.

Mainstream economics offers the *homo economicus* model, derived from the utility function, to generally explain both individual and organizational behavior. Behavioral economics tries to add further components to such a model. Nevertheless, there are many insights from psychology and behavioral sciences of great interest for the social sciences, which can be used to challenge hedonist economic explanations. However, these event opportunities would represent ruptures to mainstream behavioral research.

Rather than for the aim of publishing in high-ranked publications and status, it is difficult to understand why behavioral economic research is trying to accommodate hedonist utility functions. For human behavior, the *homo economicus* model is rather inferior to descriptions already existing in psychological research. While in economics there is a one-model-would-fit-everybody explanation of human behavior, in psychology there is a much richer and nuanced understanding. For instance, a concept generally lacking in economics is that of personality, whereas personality psychology tries to understand patterns underlying human behavior.[24] That is, why do humans with different personalities tend to behave differently?[25] It studies behavior typologies, cognition typologies and emotional patterns that evolve from biological and environmental/situational factors.[26] A well-known model tries to classify human personalities according to five different dimensions (the big-five personality factors), namely, openness to experience, conscientiousness, extraversion, agreeableness and neuroticism.[27] Likewise, relevant studies address social relations and human interactions. Why then should researchers with an advanced understanding of human behavior accept the non-empirically validated and flawed *homo economicus* model?

There should be no doubt that pleasure and pain are relevant to humans. However, human behavior can hardly be limited to motivations based upon pleasure and pain. Human beings have distinct personalities and motivations and participate in complex societies and different social groups. What is worse, a small subgroup of human beings seem to have what is called the dark triad of personality, for they are at the same time psychopaths, narcissists and Machiavellian.[28] When describing individuals or human organizations,[29] to what extent is the *homo economicus* model related with this small group of humans who cannot feel empathy towards the fortunes of other or shame or guilt or respect for norms?

Likewise, psychology and behavioral sciences may help further demonstrate that several forms of pleasure and pain avoidance are not valuable. They may cause great harm to oneself or to others. Furthermore, instead of considering money as neutral measure of pleasure and pain, psychology and behavioral sciences can help better understand what money is and what it means for human beings[30] or whether money, in some cases, may actually change human behavior.[31] It has not yet been demonstrated that after a certain level of income/wealth, more money could automatically increase happiness.[32]

Behavioral economics can help build the alternative to mainstream economics, which has recurrently promised but has not yet delivered. It needs, nonetheless, to stop uncritically accepting the hedonist framework. Behavioral economics cannot be a serious alternative to the mainstream until it breaks free from utilitarian explanations.

9.5 Conclusion

J.S. Mill understood the seriousness of the criticism levelled towards utilitarianism and the utilitarian discipline of economics, which were being described as *pig philosophy*.[33] Furthermore, it was being described as a religion-creed declaring to designate humankind's purpose and solve the universe's mysteries. Thus, Mill tried to present a defense, which could eventually reformulate utilitarianism. His qualitative hedonism tried to incorporate opponent moral theories without conceding defeat to them, a questionable intellectual procedure. For instance, non-consequentialist or virtue moral theories stand in opposition to consequentialist utilitarianism. They cannot be compatible to hedonism.

Furthermore, Mill did not solve systematic problems in hedonism, such as that pleasure and pain are not necessarily intrinsically valuable or that some pleasure and pain avoidance types can be harmful to oneself and others or the lack of a coherent and unifying pleasure definition. Moreover, Mill accepted the idea that money could be an adequate measure for hedonic calculus, without any sort of empirical evidence, thus as a creed. Because Mill's qualitative hedonism may involve intangible elements, it does not make it necessarily compatible with intangible flow theory. Several other non-consequentialist or virtue moral theories address intangible dimensions.

Furthermore, although mainstream behavioral economic research has to a great extent been aligned with the utility function (thus, utilitarianism), it can be used to produce contradictory findings regarding hedonist explanations. Intangible flow theory has a broader definition of the human being than does hedonist utilitarianism. While the latter tries to define humans, morality and action in terms of pleasure and pain, the new theory defines human beings as homo sapiens, which allows integrating many scientific disciplines studying human beings.

Notes

1 Bandelj, Wherry, and Zelizer (2017), Bandelj et al. (2017), Zelizer (1997).
2 Sandel (2012).
3 Moore (2013), Bhardwaj (2010), Feldman (2001), Tsouna (2017), Weijers (2019).
4 This section benefited very much from Weijers (2019), Feldman (2001) and Moore (2013).
5 Fryer (2015), Mackinnon and Fiala (2017), Sandel (2012), Timmermann (2014).
6 Kant's key texts describing his moral theory are as follows: *Groundwork of the Metaphysics of Morals* (1785), *Critique of Practical Reason* (1788), *and Metaphysics of Morals* (1797). This subsection provides a summary that greatly benefited from Fryer (2015), Jankowiack (2019), Mackinnon and Fiala (2017), Sandel (2012) and Timmermann (2014).
7 Timmermann (2014).

8 As explained by Timmermann (2014), it is not uncontroversial that there is a supreme principle of moral.
9 The summary of Aristoteles's moral theory in this subsection greatly benefited from Fryer (2015), Sandel (2012), Mackinnon and Fiala (2017), Sachs (2019), as well as Aristoteles (1999, 2019).
10 See, for instance, Furnham, Richards, and Paulhus (2013), Paulhus and Williams (2002).
11 See, for instance, Intezari and Pauleen (2014), Gavin and Mason (2004) Manz et al. (2008).
12 Cox (2005), Roberts (2006), Wenger (1999), Wenger and Snyder (2000).
13 See, for instance, Laplume, Sonpar, and Litz (2008), Freeman, Wicks, and Parmar (2004), or Gibson (2000).
14 Berg and Gigerenzer (2010), Camerer (1999), Camerer and George (2003), Kahneman (2003), Sent (2004), Thaler (2000, 2016, 2017), Wilkinson and Klaes (2017).
15 Berg and Gigerenzer (2010), Camerer (1999), Camerer and George (2003), Kahneman (2003), Sent (2004), Thaler (2000, 2016, 2017), Wilkinson and Klaes (2017).
16 Berg and Gigerenzer (2010), Camerer (1999), Camerer and George (2003), Kahneman (2003), Sent (2004), Thaler (2000, 2016, 2017), Wilkinson and Klaes (2017).
17 Berg and Gigerenzer (2010), Camerer (1999), Camerer and George (2003), Kahneman (2003), Sent (2004), Thaler (2000, 2016, 2017), Wilkinson and Klaes (2017).
18 Berg and Gigerenzer (2010), Camerer (1999), Camerer and George (2003), Kahneman (2003), Sent (2004), Thaler (2000, 2016, 2017), Wilkinson and Klaes (2017).
19 Morduch (2017), Tversky and Kahneman (1974), Thaler (2016), Thaler and Sunstein (2008).
20 Berg and Gigerenzer (2010), Camerer (1999), Camerer and George (2003), Kahneman (2003), Nagatsu (2015), Read (2007), Sent (2004), Spiegler (2019), Thaler (2000, 2016, 2017), Wilkinson and Klaes (2017).
21 Berg and Gigerenzer (2010), Camerer (1999), Camerer and George (2003), Kahneman (2003), Nagatsu (2015), Read (2007), Sent (2004), Spiegler (2019), Souleles (2019), Thaler (2000, 2016, 2017), Wilkinson and Klaes (2017).
22 Hédoin (2015).
23 Berg and Gigerenzer (2010), Nagatsu (2015), Sent (2004), Hédoin (2015).
24 Corr and Matthews (2009), Fonagy and Higgitt (1984), Eysenck (2017), Hampson (2019).
25 Corr and Matthews (2009), Fonagy and Higgitt (1984), Eysenck (2017), Hampson (2019).
26 Corr and Matthews (2009), Fonagy and Higgitt (1984), Eysenck (2017), Hampson (2019).
27 Digman (1990), Judge, Heller, and Mount (2002), Wiggins (1996).
28 See, for instance, Furnham, Richards, and Paulhus (2013), Paulhus and Williams (2002).
29 Duchon and Drake (2009).
30 See, for instance, Furnham and Argyle (1998), Furnham (2014), Mitchell and Mickel (1999).
31 See, for instance, Furnham and Argyle (1998), Furnham (2014), Mitchell and Mickel (1999).
32 On the Easterlin paradox see, for instance, Easterlin et al. (2010), Economist (2019), Graham (2012).
33 As noted before, if pigs could express their thought to us on paper, perhaps they could be offended by the comparison.

References

Aristoteles. (1999). *The Metaphysics*. London: Penguin.
Aristoteles. (2019). *The Nicomachean Ethics*. Oxford: Oxford University Press.
Bandelj, N., Boston, T., Elyachar, J., Kim, J., McBride, M., Tufail, Z. and Weatherall, J. (2017). Morals and emotions of money. In Bandelj, N., Wherry, F. F. and Zelizer, V. A.

(Eds.) *Money Talks: Explaining How Money Really Works*. Princeton, NJ: Princeton University Press.

Bandelj, N., Wherry, F. F. and Zelizer, V. A. (2017). Advancing money talks. In Bandelj, N., Wherry, F. F. and Zelizer, V. A. (Eds.) *Money Talks: Explaining How Money Really Works*. Princeton, NJ: Princeton University Press.

Berg, N. and Gigerenzer, G. (2010). As-if behavioral economics: Neoclassical economics in disguise? *History of Economic Ideas*, 133–165.

Bhardwaj, K. (2010). Higher and lower pleasures and our moral psychology. *Res Cogitans*, 1(1), 16.

Camerer, C. (1999). Behavioral economics: Reunifying psychology and economics. *Proceedings of the National Academy of Sciences*, 96(19), 10575–10577.

Camerer, C. and George, L. (2003). Behavioral economics: Past, Present, Future. In *Advances in Behavioral Economics*. Roundtable series in behavioral economics. Princeton, NJ: Princeton University Press, 1–61.

Corr, P. and Matthews, G. (2009). *The Cambridge handbook of Personality Psychology*. Cambridge: Cambridge University Press. ISBN 978-0-521-86218-9.

Cox, A. (2005). What are communities of practice? A comparative review of four seminal works. *Journal of Information Science*, 31(6), 527–540.

Duchon, D. and Drake, B. (2009). Organizational narcissism and virtuous behavior. *Journal of Business Ethics*, 85(3), 301–308.

Digman, J. M. (1990). Personality structure: Emergence of the five-factor model. *Annual review of psychology*, 41(1), 417–440.

Easterlin, R., McVey, L., Switek, M., Sawangfa, O. and Zweig, J. (2010). The happiness – Income paradox revisited. *Proceedings of the National Academy of Sciences*, 107(52), 22463–22468.

Economist (2019). Economic growth does not guarantee rising happiness. *The Economist*, March 21, 77. Online at: https://www.economist.com/graphic-detail/2019/03/21/economic-growth-does-not-guarantee-rising-happiness

Eysenck, H. (2017). *The Biological Basis of Personality*. London: Routledge.

Feldman, F. (2001). Hedonism. In Becker, L. C. and Becker, C. B. (Eds.) *Encyclopedia of Ethics*. London: Routledge.

Fonagy, P. and Higgitt, A. (1984). *Personality Theory and Clinical Practice*. New York: Routledge.

Freeman, R., Wicks, A. and Parmar, B. (2004). Stakeholder theory and "the corporate objective revisited". *Organization Science*, 15(3), 364–369.

Fryer, M. (2015). *Ethics Theory and Business Practice*. Los Angeles: Sage.

Furnham, A. (2014). *The New Psychology of Money*. London: Routledge.

Furnham, A. and Argyle, M. (1998). *The Psychology of Money*. Hove: Psychology Press.

Furnham, A., Richards, S. and Paulhus, D. (2013). The Dark Triad of personality: A 10 year review. *Social and Personality Psychology Compass*, 7(3), 199–216.

Gavin, J. and Mason, R. (2004). The virtuous organization: The value of happiness in the workplace. *Organizational Dynamics*, 33(4), 379–392.

Gibson, K. (2000). The moral basis of stakeholder theory. *Journal of Business Ethics*, 26(3), 245–257.

Graham, C. (2012). *Happiness Around the World: The Paradox of Happy Peasants and Miserable Millionaires*. Oxford: Oxford University Press.

Hampson, S. E. (2019). *The Construction of Personality: An Introduction*. New York. Routledge.

Hédoin, C. (2015). From utilitarianism to paternalism: When behavioral economics meets moral philosophy. *Revue de philosophie économique*, 16(2), 73–106.

Intezari, A. and Pauleen, D. (2014). Management wisdom in perspective: Are you virtuous enough to succeed in volatile times? *Journal of business ethics*, 120(3), 393–404.

Jankowiack, T. (2019). *Immanuel Kant. The Internet Encyclopedia of Philosophy: A Peer Reviewed Resource*. Online at: www.iep.utm.edu/kantview/.

Judge, T. A., Heller, D. and Mount, M. K. (2002). Five-factor model of personality and job satisfaction: A meta-analysis. *Journal of Applied Psychology*, 87(3), 530–541.

Kahneman, D. (2003). Maps of bounded rationality: Psychology for behavioral economics. *American Economic Review*, 93(5), 1449–1475.

Laplume, A., Sonpar, K. and Litz, R. (2008). Stakeholder theory: Reviewing a theory that moves Us. *Journal of Management*, 34(6), 1152–1189.

Mackinnon, B. and Fiala, A. (2017). *Ethics: Theory and Contemporary Issues*. New York: Cengage Learning.

Manz, C. C., Cameron, K. S., Manz, K. P. and Marx, R. D. (2008). The virtuous organization: An introduction. In Manz, C. C., Cameron, K. S., Manz, K. P. and Marx, R. D. (Eds.) *The Virtuous Organization: Insights from Some of the World's Leading Management Thinkers*. London: World Scientific Publishing, 1–16.

Mitchell, T. and Mickel, A. (1999). The meaning of money: An individual-difference perspective. *Academy of Management Review*, 24(3), 568–578.

Moore, A. (2013). Hedonism. In *Stanford Encyclopedia of Philosophy*. Online at: https://plato.stanford.edu/entries/hedonism/.

Morduch, J. (2017). Economics and the social meaning of money. In Bandelj, N., Werry, F. and Zelizer, V. (Eds.) *Money Talks: Explaining How Money Really Work*. Princeton, NJ: Princeton University Press.

Nagatsu, M. (2015). Behavioral economics, history of. In Wright, J. (Ed.) *International Encyclopedia of the Social and Behavioral Sciences*. 2nd Edition. Amsterdam: Elsevier.

Paulhus, D. and Williams, K. (2002). The dark triad of personality: Narcissism, Machiavellianism, and psychopathy. *Journal of Research in Personality*, 36(6), 556–563.

Read, D. (2007). Experienced utility: Utility theory from Jeremy Bentham to Daniel Kahneman. *Thinking and Reasoning*, 13(1), 45–61.

Roberts, J. (2006). Limits to communities of practice. *Journal of Management Studies*, 43(3), 623–639.

Sachs, J. (2019). Aristotle: Ethics. In *The Internet Encyclopedia of Philosophy: A Peer Reviewed Resource*. Online at: www.iep.utm.edu/aris-eth/.

Sandel, M. J. (2012). *What Money Can't Buy: The Moral Limits of Markets*. London: Macmillan.

Sen, A. (1992). *Inequality Re-Examined*. Oxford: Clarendon Press.

Sent, E. M. (2004). Behavioral economics: How psychology made its (limited) way back into economics. *History of Political Economy*, 36(4), 735–760.

Spiegler, R. (2019). Behavioral economics and the atheoretical style. *American Economic Journal: Microeconomics*, 11(2), 173–194.

Souleles, D. (2019). The distribution of ignorance on financial markets. *Economy and Society*, 48(4), 510–531.

Thaler, R. H. (2000). From homo economicus to homo sapiens. *Journal of Economic Perspectives*, 14(1), 133–141.

Thaler, R. H. (2016). Behavioral economics: Past, Present, and Future. *American Economic Review*, 106(7), 1577–1600.

Thaler, R. H. (2017). Behavioral economics. *Journal of Political Economy*, 125(6), 1799–1805.

Thaler, R. and Sunstein, R. (2008). *Nudge: Improving Decisions About Health, Wealth, and Happiness*. New Haven, CT: Yale University Press.

Timmermann, J. (2014). Kantian ethics and utilitarianism. In Eggleston, B. and Miller, D. (Eds.) *The Cambridge Companion to Utilitarianism*. Cambridge: Cambridge University Press.

Tsouna, V. (2017). Epicureanism and hedonism. In Golob, S. and Timmermann, J. (Eds.) *The Cambridge History of Moral Philosophy*. Cambridge: Cambridge University Press, 57–74.

Tversky, A. and Kahneman, D. (1974). Judgment under uncertainty: Heuristics and biases. *Science*, 185(4157), 1124–1131.

Weijers, D. (2019). Hedonism. In *The Internet Encyclopedia of Philosophy: A Peer Reviewed Resource*. Online at: www.iep.utm.edu/bentham/.

Wenger, E. (1999). *Communities of Practice: Learning, Meaning, and Identity*. Cambridge: Cambridge University Press.

Wenger, E. and Snyder, W. (2000). Communities of practice: The organizational frontier. *Harvard Business Review*, 78(1), 139–146.

Wiggins, J. S. (Ed.) (1996). *The Five-Factor Model of Personality: Theoretical Perspectives*. New York: Guilford Press.

Wilkinson, N. and Klaes, M. (2017). *An Introduction to Behavioral Economics*. London: Macmillan.

Zelizer, V. A. R. (1997). *The Social Meaning of Money*. Princeton, NJ: Princeton University Press.

10 Ricardo, Malthus and the human commodity framework into context

10.1 Introduction: A very diverse group grasping with Smith's system

"Classical economists" is a term recurrently attributed to a diverse group of writers who were apparently inspired by Adam Smith's *Wealth of Nations* (1776a, 1776b).[1] Their writings would be published up until the second half of the 19th century, a relatively short period. They shared perhaps Smith's and Aristoteles's system based upon money as a perfectly tradable commodity and Smith's description of three productive factors (work, capital and land) and respective forms of income (wages, profits and rents). However, among them they could have and frequently had substantial divergences regarding details, implications and conclusions.

The Industrial Revolution intensified in the 19th century's first half, first in Britain and later in future German states and France. By the end of the century, most European countries were industrialized. During this century, Europe was the most technologically advanced region of the world.[2] She would also develop the economic theories that would rule the 20th century.[3] Coal-based and later electricity-based technologies would have a prominent role in propelling innovative manufacturing and transport machines. The telegraph, and later the telephone, would revolutionize human communication. Real-time communication would become possible despite large geographical distances. Likewise, trains and railways would transform human transportation. By 1850 there were already 23,036 km of railways built in Europe, 14,624 km in North America, and a railway mania.[4] The population, however, was still mostly agrarian. Roughly in this period in several European countries, many humans started having their livelihood depend upon factories, which are themselves highly reliant upon human work. Various cities would grow around factory production, where numerous human beings would settle in precarious lodgings. In the most industrialized countries, some historians claim a new class was born or formed (the proletariat, or waged worker class) because it did not exist in previous periods.[5] These humans could frequently work 12 hours a day or more, up to seven days a week. At first, there were little if any limitations for child work, which would not be uncommon.[6] These new, large factories would distinguish themselves from traditional artifice shops, which had only few workers, generally in close relationship to the shop owner. Investors in large manufacturing would now require substantial funds that must be owned or loaned, which further separate them from workers.

After a turbulent French Revolution, Napoleon and his allies got a hold on power. Napoleonic wars have ravaged Europe (1804–1815), causing great economic and social convulsion. The years just after Napoleon's defeat in 1815 are often known as the Restoration Era.[7] Over Europe, aristocratic forces, whose legitimacy arises mostly from tradition, would aim to restore rights and privileges lost through the revolution's impacts and sequels. The Vienna Congress (1814–1815) was a representation of this movement. Yet, the political map of Europe would only partially be restored. Amsterdam, for instance, never recovered the status it had before the war as main financial center of Europe.[8] Many institutions and reforms created after the revolution subsisted in France and in other countries, for instance, numerous law codes or public servant forces/organisms that could assist governments. On the other hand, investors in factories and bankers advanced their claims and gained political influence throughout the most industrialized countries.

This period's economists were a very diverse group, which included a retired stock broker, David Ricardo (1772–1823); an ex-cleric and scholar, Thomas Malthus (1766–1834); a banker, Henry Thornton (1760–1815); the first chair of the discipline of political economy in Oxford, Nassau Senior (1790–1864); a retired colonel and newspaper owner, Robert Torrens (1780–1864); a newspaper editor and academic professor of political economy, John McCulloch (1789–1864); an aristocratic Earl of Lauderdale, member of the House of Lords and lawyer, James Maitland (1759–1839); members of the East India Company, James Mill (1773–1836) and his son John Stuart Mill (1806–1873); a British judge who served in India, Edward West (1782–1828); and a public servant, Edwin Chadwick (1800–1890).[9] Generally, they were politically engaged, and some of them served or contributed with reports to Parliament. Many of their discussions had policy making in sight.[10] The group was not limited to British persons. For instance, Jean-Baptiste Say (1767–1832) was a French businessman that for a short spell collaborated with Napoleon's government until he retired to the business world, and Jean Sismondi (1773–1842) was a Swiss historian and essayist. We also have, for instance, Karl Heinrich Rau (1792–1870), a German scholar who created an encyclopedia of economic knowledge greatly inspired by Adam Smith (1826–1837).[11]

These writers had substantial disagreements among them. Senior (1836, 1965, p. 88) is representative of these debates:

> According to the usual language of Political Economists, Labour, Capital, and Land are the three Instruments of Production; Labourers, Capitalists, and Landlords are the three classes of Producers; and the whole Produce is divided into Wages, Profit, and Rent: the first designating the Labourer's share, the second that of the Capitalist, and the third that of the Landlord.

We approve, on the whole, of the principles on which this classification is founded, but we have been forced, much against our will, to make considerable alterations in the language in which it has been usually expressed; to add some new terms, and to enlarge or contract the signification of some others.

Correspondingly, Senior proposes that both land and landlords were too restrictive definitions, which should be replaced by natural agents and proprietors of natural agents. Natural agents would not be the creation of humankind as wages and profits would. In France, Say had also used the expression natural agents, where he had included, for instance, gravitation or magnetism (Say, 1803–1817, p. 29 and p. 53). Ricardo (1821, 1888, p. 39), however, defined rent as "*that portion of the produce of earth, which is paid to the landlord for the use of the original and indestructible powers of the soil,*" a concept that could also be applied to the rent of mines (p. 51–53). As we can observe in this example, although linked to Smith's system, these economists would frequently disagree.[12]

10.2 Population as commodities regulated by monetary wages

10.2.1 Population-commodity theory

A population-wage-commodity doctrine is commonly attributed to Malthus.[13] However, Chapter 7 displays that Smith had already related population rise to his component of capital said to pay wages (circulating capital). He had noticed that while poverty does not prevent having children, it is quite adverse for human reproduction.[14] This phenomenon would specially concern working-class women who are much more willing to have children in comparison to women from higher "*ranks of people.*"[15] In the various editions of his book about principles of the population, Malthus recurrently cites Smith, with whom he disagrees, however, in supposing that an increase of a country's wealth, or combined stock and revenue (capital accumulation), necessarily improves the condition of the working poor.[16] Nonetheless, Malthus has reinforced the population theory presented by Smith: "*Little or no doubt can exist, that the comforts of the labouring poor depend upon the increase of the funds destined for the maintenance of labour; and will be very exactly in proportion to the rapidity of this increase.*"[17] In fact, at the second edition's preface, Malthus acknowledges "*Hume, Wallace, Adam Smith, and Dr. Price,*"[18] after whom he has developed his population principle.

The first edition was anonymously published in 1798, as a reaction to ideas connected to the French Revolution.[19] The full essay title was "An Essay on the Principle of Population, as it affects the future Improvement of Society, with Remarks on the Speculations of Mr. Godwin, M. Condorcet, and Other Writers." Therefore, it was a direct attack on William Goodwin (1756–1836) and the Marquis du Condorcet (1743–1794), who believed in the perfectibility of humanity through education, knowledge cultivation and virtue.[20] Moreover, they believed in equality of individuals and of nations. Furthermore, they contested the fatality of private property, whereby idle and nonproductive persons would be supported by working poor. Population growth would not be a problem because when the limit could be achieved, humanity would refuse to propagate further.[21]

Malthus could not disagree more.[22] He emphasizes that Condorcet has died out of pressures from his fellows French revolutionaries with whom he had fallen from grace.[23] To Malthus, inequality would be the natural state of affairs, resulting from the requirement of private property.[24] He was skeptical about the possibility of improving humankind.[25] Although in subsequent editions, Godwin and Condorcet are no longer referred to in the title, they are still discussed within the essay.[26] Accordingly, an unchecked population growth would be problematic because it would deplete food resources. When unconstrained, population has a geometric growth, which would be much faster than food resources' arithmetic growth.[27] Malthus, of course, is essentially concerned with the population growth of the poor. Population growth would be constrained by both birth and death rate factors. Affecting the birth rate are moral restraint, of which Malthus approves, and vices such as birth control, laziness or prostitution, of which he does not approve.[28] Factors increasing the death rate are, for instance, famine, misery, plague, wars or natural phenomena.[29] At the time, there was not a strong public opinion requiring state/public authority to address these phenomena. Public services were yet very rudimental when compared to the 21st century. Nonetheless, Malthus clearly saw death rates as necessary to contain population growth.[30]

Following Smith, Malthus describes work and workers as commodities defined by money. As workers receive monetary flows for working, they would also be commodities. The only means to improve the working poor's conditions would be reducing their reproduction numbers:

> the mode of essentially and permanently bettering the condition of the poor, we must explain to them the true nature of their situation, and shew them, that the withholding of the supplies of labour is the only possible way of really raising its price, and that they themselves, being the possessors of this commodity, have alone the power to do this.[31]

If workers received low wages and were poor, that would be their own fault for they would be reproducing too much.[32] In Malthus's logic, low wages along with natural disasters, diseases and wars could be means to solve the *problem*.

Certainly, a species' survival is related to the resources available for its livelihood and existence. Darwin (1859) might have been partially inspired by Malthus (thus, Smith and others) in forming his theory of the evolution of the species.[33] Moreover, the human population is indeed interfering in Earth's biosphere in dramatic manners. After the Industrial Revolution in the 19th century, we may have reached what has been called the Anthropocene epoch, where we humans are causing drastic changes to the planet Earth, our current home.[34] Human populations have triggered extinctions of many species, high pollution levels, depletion of natural resources and dramatic changes in landscapes.

Modern Malthusian theory evolved to entail the concept of Earth's carrying capacity, which is an estimation of the number of people and/or food supply that a region (or the planet itself) can support.[35] During many decades, several attempts have been made, which are however difficult to estimate.[36] Still, the impact of humankind on Earth's biosphere is real and observable. On the other hand, without ignoring human effects on Earth's biosphere, one must notice that if we humans move on to inhabit the vast universe, indeed great numbers of us are necessary. We are currently making efforts to put some of us on Mars. Hopefully, we will be able to reach other planets and solar systems in the future.

However, Malthus's debate was mostly conducted in terms of population as a set of commodities, money and food supply. His later editions contain (apparent) case studies of population checks, from the ancient world to different countries of his time.[37] However, there is no manner to disregard that most of his predictions failed completely.[38] The food resources for the human population accompanied population growth. In 1800 in Europe, perhaps only London and Paris could have more than 500,000 habitants,[39] which currently would represent a medium or small city in most industrialized countries. Population has grown from the 1 billion people estimated in 1804 to 7.7 billion people in 2019.[40] Malthus failed to predict technological innovations and improved use of natural resources, which would allow food quantity expansion, along with improving its nutrition and ingredients. Moreover, he failed to understand how technological development and better practices would decrease child mortality and expand human life (quality and longevity). Likewise, it was proven wrong that when we humans receive larger monetary incomes, we automatically reproduce more. Likewise, Malthus failed to predict technologies used to limit human reproduction and modifications in human behavior.[41] As a matter of fact, many of his contemporaries refused to accept Malthus's conclusions. They claimed that Malthus was trying to blame the poor for their misery and undermining the human spirit.[42] Nonetheless, the population–commodity formulation was highly influential to that period's political economists.

10.2.2. Workers as commodities at subsistence level

As we have seen before, Smith considers as the natural condition of workers to receive wages that would allow them and their families to be at subsistence level. If wages were above the hypothetical natural level, the theory would declare that workers would reproduce more rapidly, which in the end, would result in a greater supply of workers. Accordingly, wages would return to the so-called natural level because constraints would occur in the means to hire more workers and food and necessaries to maintain their families. The opposite would occur if wages were below the alleged natural level.[43] Malthus's population–commodity doctrine is fundamentally aligned to this view. Sismondi (1819) has recovered the term proletariat from Latin to expose this view. Workers without property were as the lowest class in ancient Rome, whose major function would be to provide *"offspring"* (proles) then to the empire and in the 19th century for the factories.[44]

Ricardo is also a follower of Smith, from whom he has derived his distinction between exchange and use value. For instance, Ricardo (1821, 1888) notes the paradox of water's high usefulness in comparison to the much higher exchange value of gold. This comparison is a mere variation of the water-diamond paradox in Smith (that was derived from Aristoteles).[45] Thus, although Bentham claimed that Ricardo would be his spiritual grandson, Ricardo is still using the conception of utility as usefulness instead of Bentham's hedonist version.

As Smith, Ricardo does not deny that in the short run, pressures and accidents may temporarily affect exchange prices, wages, rents and profits. As Smith, Ricardo considers that temporary pressures and accidents cannot disturb the general tendency of prices, wages and profits to tend to their so-called natural value.[46] The exchange price of work should be related to the population and money available to hire workers. Likewise, Ricardo aims at finding what he calls laws that would explain natural values of prices, wages and profits.[47] Both Smith and Ricardo believe that a natural value would exist for commodities, which for them would include workers and work (and other human-related intangible flows). Moreover, they both believe that such natural values could be measured by money, the perfectly tradable commodity.

Still, Smith made a distinction between workers who are paid from capital, described as productive workers, and those other workers called nonproductive, who are paid from revenues, such as menial servants, maids, opera singers and entertainers. Such a distinction no longer appears in Ricardo, where workers are generally paid by circulating capital. However, workers could find other means of subsistence or even organize themselves. Perhaps, if one could have raised this problem to Ricardo, he may have considered it, which he generally did not.[48] However, their description reinforces the idea of workers being utterly dependent on capitalists to survive and reproduce. That is, that they would be the *proles* described by Sismondi.

Ricardo treats labor as a regular commodity:

> Labour, like all other things which are purchased and sold, and which may be increased or diminished in quantity, has its natural and its market price. The natural price of labour is that price which is necessary to enable the labourers, one with another, to subsist and to perpetuate their race, without either increase or diminution.[49]

In effect, Ricardo does not restrict the subsistence level associated to work *"natural"* value to means of food, as Malthus population doctrine implies: " *The natural price of labour, therefore, depends on the price of the food, necessaries, and conveniences required for the support of the labourer and his family.*"[50] It is not necessarily fixed for depending on *"habits and customs of the people,"* which may change through time.[51] However, in many cases Ricardo has food in his mind[52] and follows Smith-Malthus population doctrine: "*labour is dear when it is scarce, and cheap when it is plentiful. However much the market price of labour may deviate from its natural price, it has, like commodities, a tendency to conform to it.*"[53]

To Ricardo, the natural price of labor cannot be seen merely in monetary terms. It must be seen in relation to the relative prices of food, necessities and conveniences required by workers and their families. Thus, a surge in wages, which is inferior to a surge in the prices of foods and for instance clothing, would make workers worse off.[54] And vice versa. Nonetheless, Ricardo puts the worker at the center of production. He adapts Smith's reformulated definition of capital in relation to work: "*Capital is that part of the wealth of a country which is employed in production, and consists of food, clothing, tools, raw materials, machinery, etc., necessary to give effect to labour.*"[55] As Smith, Ricardo refers to circulating capital as the component of capital from where funds are used to support labor.[56]

Some of Ricardo's followers such as Torrens (1821), Fawcet (1863) and McCulloch (1825) would contend that there could be a fixed and non-variable fund (wage fund) from circulating capital to maintain workers and their families.[57] Eventually, they may have not anticipated all possible consequences of such a position.[58] Indeed, a fixed and non-changeable wage fund would conflict with the interest of a nascent movement of labor unions and workers representatives trying to improve their constituents' conditions. Ricardo does not necessarily claim that the amount of capital used to maintain workers and their families would be fixed and non-variable.[59] However, Ricardo reinforced Smith's system in treating human beings who receive wages as commodities, whose long-run perspective would be the subsistence level. Ricardo and several of his followers reified this view as a natural law of things.

10.2.3 Resultant position in relation to the Poor Law

As displayed on the second part, Polanyi considers the Poor Law Amendment Act (1834), as the key moment when economists contributed to transform work, land and money into fictitious commodities.[60] This act substantially modified the previous model of assistance to the poor. Nonetheless, we also have seen that Polanyi struggled to explain why work, land and money would not be commodities. He defines commodities in terms of monetary flows, thus incorporating the economists' framework. Intangible flow theory presents an alternative explanation whereby monetary flows do not necessarily make or define the commodity.

The first Poor Law Act in England goes back at least to the 16th century, hence, much before Malthus and Ricardo. Furthermore, there was previous legislation to deal with vagrants and beggars.[61] More recently to Malthus and Ricardo, the Spenhamland Act (1795) intensified the assistance to the poor in several regions of England and Wales. Its model was perhaps not that distant to the contemporary idea of a basic income guaranteed to the poor.[62] There were actual abuses of the Poor Law,[63] but generally the poor were indeed having a difficult time as a result of higher food prices ensuing from Napoleonic wars and a few bad harvests.[64] Therefore, the cost of assistance to the poor had dramatically increased.[65] Later, the full conversion of money into gold would make assistance to the poor even more expensive. Moreover, there were cases where some farmers could also abuse the law through paying lower wages to their workers because they had a minimum income guaranteed by the law.[66]

For around at least three centuries, poor laws had operated as a *"welfare state in miniature"*[67] assisting elderly persons, widows, children, sick persons, disabled persons and the unemployed and underemployed.[68] At the period, however, we can see several economists arguing for the removal or abolition of several parts of the act, in the belief that markets would solve most problems, including those of the poor. Although the arguments were not identical, several economists shared a common system of beliefs. Malthus raised the issue that that parish assistance to the poor would increase population growth without a corresponding increase in the food sources (in part because the poor would allegedly refuse to work). Therefore, a Poor Law would cause surplus in the "commodity" of labor, promoting idleness.[69]

Ricardo had a similar perspective, where he would use Bentham's freedom of contract argument[70]:

> Like all other contracts, wages should be left to the fair and free competition of the market, and should never be controlled by the interference of the legislature. The clear and direct tendency of the poor laws is in direct opposition to these obvious principles: it is not, as the legislature benevolently intended, to amend the condition of the poor, but to deteriorate the condition of both poor and rich; instead of making the poor rich, they are calculated to make the rich poor.[71]

He worries that assistance to the poor could increase so dramatically until it would consume all revenue of the country, given that the poor would not wish to work to produce food and would show no restraint in increasing their numbers, as allegedly demonstrated by Malthus.[72] Thus, here Ricardo also adopts Bentham's disutility of work perspective: well-fed people would have no concern or wish to work and produce. Ricardo claims that *"every friend to the poor must ardently wish for their abolition* [Poor Law]."[73] Market competition, it was alleged, would solve the poverty problem.[74]

After the swing riots by many agricultural workers in 1830 protesting low wages and worsening conditions, agricultural machines were destroyed. Including among others Senior and Chadwick, a commission was appointed by the Parliament to study poor laws. Chadwick had previously been Bentham's personal secretary, besides his disciple. Senior was also moved by hedonist ideas, as we will see later. Their report has been described as a major victory for Bentham's utilitarianism.[75] It aligns to the wages–population growth doctrine concerning food sources, indolence of the poor and lack of freedom of contract. Furthermore, it supports Bentham's idea that the pauper could only receive assistance out of a working house, where they must work to pay for the respective expense, besides adhering to harsh discipline and other means. Bentham had proposed that *"maintenance at the expense of others should not be made more desirable than self-maintenance."*[76] Similarly, the report suggested that working houses ought to be disinviting places.

Though inspired by the report, not all ideas in it were incorporated in the Poor Law Amendment Act (1834). A central authority was created to manage assistance previously conducted at the parish level. The requirements for receiving assistance were made much harsher. The recommendation regarding full elimination of outdoor relief was not adopted. However, most of the relief would be related to working houses. As suggested by Bentham and noted by Polanyi, these working house were so uncomfortable and disinviting and had such negative social stigma that several poor persons preferred indigence instead of attending them. Families requiring assistance could and would be separated among different working houses.[77] Working houses generated many protests and quite a few scandals. They were an object of popular literature denouncing their operation by Charles Dickens, Jack London and Frances Trollope. Later, these working houses would be abandoned.[78]

Importantly, however, although in some moments assistance to the poor may have been diminished,[79] human populations tended to continue caring for their poor. Poor laws would later be replaced by several reforms that would evolve into the contemporary welfare models. Hence, the poor in industrialized countries would not be completely abandoned to the monetary flows of a self-regulating market, as proposed by several economists. Polanyi is not completely right in defining the Poor Law Amendment Act (1834) as such a landmark of the interference of economists in society, which in any case would refer to a law in a specific Western country. A wage payment does not transform a human being into a commodity. An error in his analysis is to endorse the same definition used by the economists whereby a monetary flow would make and/or define a commodity, which are pseudo-phenomena. Yet, Polanyi is rather correct in noticing how several economists would entirely abandon humankind to the self-regulating market myth.

10.3 Ricardo's (embodied) labor theory of value and quest for an invariable measure of value

Ricardo starts his *Principles* explaining that:

> The value of a commodity, or the quantity of any other commodity for which it will exchange, depends on the relative quantity of labour which is necessary for its production, and not on the greater or less compensation which is paid for that labour.[80]

As Smith, Ricardo puts the work *"commodity"* at the center of production and distribution, relating use and exchange value. In later editions, Ricardo felt the need to clarify the difference between value and riches:

> "A Man is rich or poor," says Adam Smith, "according to the degree in which he can afford to enjoy the necessaries, conveniences, and amusements of human life." Value, then, essentially differs from riches, for value depends not on abundance, but on the difficulty or facility of production.[81]

> The labour of a million of men in manufactures will always produce the same value, but will not always produce the same riches.[82]

Ricardo tries to distinguish himself from others who according to him would wrongly confuse concepts of value and riches, such as Say (or Malthus). Nonetheless, Ricardo is referring to a conception of riches with some proximity to virtue ethics, which can be found in Smith and Aristoteles, that is, to an appeal for a good human life. Hence, once again, we have Ricardo not entirely aligned with Bentham's hedonist utilitarianism.

Exchange value could temporarily diverge from purported natural value, as a result of pressures or accidents. According to Ricardo (and Smith), both would tend to converge in the long run.[83] It is difficult to identify how long that long run would be. It could be at least 15 years.[84] To Ricardo, though a commodity must have utility (usefulness) to have exchange value, utility does not explain value: *"Possessing utility, commodities derive their exchangeable value from two sources: from their scarcity, and from the quantity of labour required to obtain them."*[85] Indeed, scarcity alone commands the value of rare commodities, which are dependent from *"the varying wealth and inclinations of those who are desirous to possess them."*[86] Those commodities' value would not depended on the labor quantity necessary to produce them. Ricardo is thinking in goods such as *"rare statues and pictures, scarce books, coins, wines of a peculiar quality."*[87] Ricardo further admits other cases where a pure labor theory of value would not apply such as goods produced under a monopoly, paper money or goods entering international trade.[88] However, these would be rare cases. Thus, a labor theory of value would generally apply.[89] Likewise, Ricardo has acknowledged several difficulties in applying his theory, such as differences in workers' labor quality, distinct capital-labor ratios among different industries, and high variability of incomes along workers, capitalists and landowners. However, Ricardo has dismissed these problems as minor, not seriously troubling his labor value theory.[90]

Ricardo's position is not entirely identical to Smith's on the fine detail. Ricardo pays more attention to relative prices among elements. For instance, if all prices were to vary in the same proportion, no change in value would occur.[91] Moreover, Ricardo claims that the basis of value is the work quantity necessary to produce a commodity (embodied labor). Yet, Smith had established a difference between primitive and more sophisticated societies. In primitive societies, the basis of value would be embodied labor. In more sophisticated societies, with monetary complications and relations among capitalists, landowners and workers, the basis of value would become labor commanded (that could be bought), instead of embodied labor necessary for production.[92] Ricardo disagrees. He sees the difference between primitive and advanced economies as artificial.[93]

Nonetheless, Ricardo has adapted Smith's reformulated concept of capital in relation to labor. To Ricardo, capital is the wealth component employed in production and *"necessary to give effect to labour."*[94] Thus, it is defined in terms of labor and time.[95] The exchange and natural value of capital goods should also revolve around embodied labor necessary for their production. Ricardo gives several examples of his idea. For instance, when canoes are necessary for fishing, canoes would be considered capital. However, they have been produced by labor.[96] Hence, Ricardo submits that embodied labor would determine canoes' natural value.[97]

Perhaps Ricardo's followers such as James Mill or McCulloch were more extreme than Ricardo himself in holding a pure labor value view, given that Ricardo had introduced some qualifications in applying his theory of labor value.[98] Ricardo may have dreamt of finding an invariable measure of value, which would compare to relative variations of value among commodities.[99] Through this comparison, one would be able to infer whether an actual change in value had indeed occurred.[100] Or Ricardo may not have taken such invariable value measure very seriously.[101] In any case, he was aware of the difficulty in finding such a measure. No single commodity could realistically possess the requisite properties for invariance of value.[102] Hence, he has settled with embodied labor instead, for which he attributed the limitations described earlier.

10.4 Rent, profits, landlords, capitalists and how to feed the human commodities

10.4.1 Corn Laws and theory of rent

After 1815, British Corn Laws imposed tariffs and restrictions to imports of cereal grains and other foods. During Napoleonic wars, Britain's international trade was very disturbed by war and Napoleonic blockage. When the war was soon to be ended, British landowners, many of them descendants from traditional aristocracy, feared that food imports could endanger their affairs. As food prices could become much cheaper, the use of British lands for farming could become unnecessary. Thus, less food would be produced/sold and less rent collected. Therefore, representatives of landowners managed to have government and Parliament approving Corn Laws. Legislative initiatives in favor of traditional aristocratic interests were in accordance with the restoration spirit reigning all over Europe. There were protests and tumults at the time, for the population had realized that such laws would increase food prices.[103]

We can find Ricardo and Malthus on opposite sides regarding Corn Laws. Nevertheless, they both agreed on the basics concerning rent and land productivity theory. In fact, several elements had already been mentioned by the Physiocrats, Smith, Torrens and West.[104] This theory is summarized as follows. For the same land, as a farmer keeps adding labor and capital, productivity decreases. The most fertile lands are cultivated first. Lands of secondary quality are cultivated only when the most fertile lands are no longer available. However, as those less fertile lands are cultivated only when they are needed, landowners will charge as much or more rent as for the most fertile lands already in use. As these less fertile lands can produce less food with the same labor, capital, and rent, there is negative marginal productivity. This much, Ricardo and Malthus generally accepted. However, it is not necessarily correct. Marginal productivity of agriculture may increase with further cultivation. This theory ignores technological innovations and developments improving productivity or human adaptation,[105] that is, advances that also have rendered the population–food resources doctrine wrong.

However, it was clear that Corn Laws did increase food prices and rents paid to landowners. The divergences of Malthus and Ricardo were essentially about political assessment. Malthus generally sided with aristocratic landowners' interests, whereas Ricardo was for repealing Corn Laws. The effective repeal would only happen in 1849, after three years of gradual reduction. Around 1845, after some bad harvests, great famines in Ireland (still part of Great Britain) would expose dangerously high food prices along food shortages. During more than 30 years all over Britain, petitions, a league, publications, and social movements attempted to repeal Corn Laws to no avail. These laws' longevity demonstrates how Ricardo's ideas were far from widely accepted.

10.4.2 Role of landlords

Indeed, aristocratic landlords would benefit from the Corn Laws. Some manufacturing investors could also have used profit revenues to invest in lands and agriculture. Malthus sees inequality as the general state of affairs: "*The great mass of society will be divided chiefly into two classes, the rich and the poor, one of which will be in a state of abject dependence upon the other.*"[106] Accordingly, a class of wealthy landlords would be essential to employ numerous humans through personal services, a term Malthus uses to replace nonproductive labor in Smith.[107] Bestowing to Malthus, personal services would be less appreciated by those who live from profits of stock (capitalists).[108] Furthermore, wealthy landowners would have developed a refined taste for acquiring fine products, which would be out of reach by the poor.[109] This conception in Malthus may have anticipated the idea of a leisure class in Veblen, a class of individuals who do not contribute to economic and material production, but conspicuously enjoy its outcome with impact upon economic activity.[110] Furthermore, although defending inequality, Malthus is aware of the social relations of production much before Marx.

Ricardo agrees that Corn Laws contribute to increase landowners' revenues. That is why he wants to repeal those laws. It is often misconstrued that Ricardo considers that only capital and work would contribute to value, whereas rents could not contribute to it. Indeed, Ricardo agrees that rents contribute to price values of goods and thus to their exchange values. Rents are incorporated in the price paid by the consumer, who will bear them.[111] Taxes are also incorporated in prices paid by consumers. What Ricardo disagrees with is that rents (and landowners in that regard) could contribute to the creation of riches/wealth. Rents would be *"a value purely nominal, forming no addition to the national wealth, but merely as a transfer of value, advantageous only to the landlords, and proportionally injurious to the consumer."*[112] A rise in the price of food would contribute to a rise in rents, which further increases the price of food. An increase in the price of food increases the natural price of labor and, thus, requires higher wages. The capitalist, constrained by higher wages and higher rents, would have less profits. Thus, the accumulation of capital would be reduced or eliminated. Ricardo follows Smith in describing the accumulation of capital as the key mechanism for creation of wealth. Malthus does not entirely agree.

10.4.3 Supply creating monetary means to generate demand or market gluts?

As a close follower of Smith, Ricardo adopts the view that the supply of commodities creates also monetary means to generate further demand. This perspective has been erroneously attributed to Say by Keynes (1936). It would become known as the *Say law*, which Keynes wished to dispute. Keynes provides high praise to Malthus as his precursor as the first Cambridge economist, while neglecting negative views that many of Malthus's contemporaries had of his ideas.[113] Although yet circumstantial, this evidence will later help us build the case in future works that Keynesianism is not an actual rupture to mainstream economics because it generally aligns with key mainstream postulates.

Say's contemporaries did not use the expression *Say law* or attribute this idea to him.[114] Furthermore, there is still a dispute about what Say meant, because he was of the view that, far from being neutral, monetary affairs could interfere with the economy.[115] Moreover, it is clear that Smith and James Mill also referred to a related formulation.[116] Possibly, Keynes may have not completely grasped the conception in Smith, Mill and Ricardo,[117] who see money as means of exchange, not an end in itself. As described by Say: *"for money, as money, has no other use than to buy with it."*[118] Through generating revenues, sold commodities generate means to purchase more commodities. Those moneys would be spent elsewhere, creating demand there. Proponents of this view had a belief that markets can adjust by moving capital and work to where it would be more profitable.

Thus, according to this view, there could not be general gluts or unemployment. Capital and work would just need to move to more productive activities. For instance, if the repeal of Corn Laws made the production of food lose money, capital and work would just move to manufacturing industries that could be more profitable:

> It is then the desire, which every capitalist has, of diverting his funds from a less to a more profitable employment, that prevents the market price of commodities from continuing for any length of time either much above, or much below their natural price.[119]

Thereby, the accumulation of capital is increased. Ricardo is rather unclear about how this adjustment process would work. He admits that some industries can be kept temporarily out of pace by a temporary or accidental cause. However, according to Ricardo, sooner or later, capital and work would move to other industries as in a natural law,[120] in the indefinite long run at least.

Malthus disagrees.[121] According to him, lack of buyers for products could generate an overabundance of products, economic contractions and lack of employment. An argument he once again uses to defend privileged classes of landlords:

> There must therefore be a considerable class of persons who have both the will and power to consume more material wealth than they produce, or the mercantile classes could not continue profitably to produce so much more than they consume. In this class the landlords no doubt stand preeminent; but if they were not assisted by the great mass of individuals engaged in personal services, whom they maintain, their own consumption would of itself be insufficient to keep up and increase the value of the produce, and enable the increase of its quantity more than to counterbalance the fall of its price.[122]

Thus, to Malthus, there could be excess of supply if no purchasers exist to buy products being offered. Privileged landlord classes would be of great assistance to capitalists, while workers were the previously described commodities (as to Ricardo). To Malthus, capitalists would suffer for lack of taste and disposition to enjoy in great consumption levels necessary to buy commodities on sale.

10.4.4 The role of capitalists

The argument that supply provided monetary means to generate further demand was also an indirect manner to attack traditional aristocratic interests.[123] This position is summarized by Ricardo in the following two formulas: "(1) *the interest of the landlord is always opposed to that of the consumer and manufacturer . . . (2) the interest of the landlord is always opposed to the interest of every other class in the community.*"[124] As Smith, Ricardo sees capital accumulation as the mechanism to increase wealth (riches).[125] Capitalists would therefore have leading roles in creating wealth to society. That high monetary flows to capitalists would be the purpose of society is a claim that quite obviously supports the interests of large monetary investors in factories, banks and other ventures. In France, Say, for instance, already addressed the concept of entrepreneur as someone who organizes commodity production.[126] He also distinguishes a scientific discovery from its application to generate revenues, anticipating Frank Knight and Joseph Schumpeter by more than a century.[127]

Nevertheless, Ricardo's and Smith's labor theories of value might lead to a theory of profits as a surplus captured by capitalists out of workers. Given that work (embodied in Ricardo or commanded in Smith) would produce natural value, profits result from value created by work. In later writings, Ricardo also notes that an improvement in machine technologies that could replace human jobs may improve the situation of capitalists and worsen that of the working classes.[128] However, apparently Ricardo did not clearly express a concern for the exploitation of workers, as other writers would have.[129] In fact, he was accused of providing arguments for keeping the status quo while damaging the interests of workers,[130] who would be put at subsistence levels in the long run. Nevertheless, Ricardo-Smith labor theories of production, value and existence would generate great debates, conflicts and polemics in the 19th century.

10.4.5 The stationary state

Having three conflicting classes of capitalists, landowners and workers, similarly leads Ricardo to the conclusion that in the long run the system would reach a stationary state. As profits could no longer be accumulated, no growth of riches could occur. In Smith's theory, profits do not tend to zero in the long run but to the market interest rate. Ricardo adapted the theory as an attack on the Corn Laws. The premises of his conclusions are based on previously described theories of population and rent. With an increase in profits, capital accumulation may rise. Thus, funds available to pay workers (circulating capital) also increase. Hence, the demand for labor may rise, resulting into higher wages. With an increase in wages above the subsistence level, the population would grow, as workers (that is, human commodities) would reproduce more. Thus, more food would be needed. Given the Corn Laws preventing food imports, less productive land would be further cultivated at higher rents to be paid to landlords. Thus, profits would diminish or disappear altogether through higher rents and higher wages. Hence, capital accumulation and growth would cease to be possible.[131]

Stationary state is a term used by other economists of the period, such as Malthus, James Mill, West or John Stuart Mill.[132] It refers only to an eventual distant future. The reasoning would not be dissimilar, however, that the system they were describing would be somehow the end of human history. It is not very distinct from the manner in which contemporary mainstream economics describes human societies.

10.5 Conclusion

Besides being artificial, the division of human beings into workers, capitalists and landowners is time-specific. A human can be a member of none or of two or more of these categories. Furthermore, monetary technologies had allowed landowners to receive rents through monetary means, while centuries earlier they would be compensated, for instance, in vegetables, foods, artifacts or services. Monetary rents in the 19th century could be compared to other monetary flows deriving from investment such as profits or interest payments. On the other hand, landowners' monetary activities would have similarities to those of manufacturing investors. Landowners could use their rent proceedings to invest in manufacturing organizations or banks. Likewise, factory and bank investors could apply profits to buy land or even hereditary aristocratic titles. In 1818, Ricardo did just that when he bought Lord Portarlington's seat in Parliament.[133] With Parliament membership, Ricardo gained public notoriety, which would not be available for the poor who could not attend to even their basic needs.

Malthus was openly in favor of inequality. To him, the existence of a privileged group of people consuming more than they produce would be an essential component of economic harmony. As others at the time, he has taken on board a sort of new group division in society besides the three classes identified by Smith. Instead, Malthus has proposed a division between the rich and the poor who totally depend on the rich.[134] However, he also starts abandoning the focus on the division of labor, which was quite important in Smith's analysis.

This period's debates were generally linked to policy making purposes.[135] Malthus was mostly concerned with the aristocratic landlords' interests, whereas Ricardo would oppose them. Yet, both Malthus and Ricardo agree on common features of rents, wage-population doctrines, and opposing assistance to the poor, whom they saw as commodities that would reproduce according to wages levels. To large extent, these positions underlie these economists' discussions. Still, most predictions in their population-commodity and rent doctrines have failed. They have ignored how technology, organization or human adaptability could impact production and human existence. Some of Malthus's and Ricardo's predictions have disappointed quite a few of their contemporaries, who argued that Malthus, Ricardo and other economists defended the status quo, blamed the poor for their misery and undermined the human spirit.[136] Nonetheless, although part of Smith's system would later be abandoned, many of its components would remain uncontested until the 21st century such as the human commodity framework, not just in mainstream economics, but in other social sciences as well.

In mainstream economics, the failure of population and rent doctrines can be implied as a pretense alibi to discard non-monetary inquiries about human integration within the biosphere, that is, it inquires beyond market/monetary analysis, as if the market allegory that treats human beings as commodities would have solved every problem faced by humans. As if the micro moment of the market, where a monetary flow occurs, would be an adequate mechanism to entirely cope with humankind survival and existence. Yet, economic and societal production cannot be explained merely in monetary flow terms. Population and industry growth have an actual impact upon the planet Earth, our present home, which we must address.[137] Furthermore, our human life and existence is utterly dependent upon Earth's biosphere. However, if we humans move on to explore the vast universe, we will need indeed great population numbers.

Notes

1 Brue (2000), Backhouse (2002), Ekelund and Hébert (1997), Dupont (2017), Landreth and Collander (2001), Screpanti and Zamagni (2005).
2 Remond (2014b), Reynaert (2017), Hirst (2019).
3 Idem.
4 Michie (2006).
5 The term proletariat was adapted by an ancient roman term (*ad prolem generandam*) by Sismondi to describe the condition of working classes of his time (Sismondi, 1819, p. 7, p. 240; Lutz, 2006, pp. 91–93; Brue, 2000, p. 176). See also Remond (2014a, 2014b).
6 Remond (2014b), Brue (2000).
7 Remond (2014a, 2014b), Screpanti and Zamagni (2005).
8 Michie (2006).
9 Brue (2000), Backhouse (2002), Ekelund and Hébert (1997), Dupont (2017), Harris (1964), Landreth and Collander (2001), Screpanti and Zamagni (2005) Ekelund and Hébert (1997).
10 Idem.
11 Lehrbuch der politischen Ökonomie (1826–37). As explained before, we have no space in these volumes to address all economists. Our purpose it to relate the new theory to key landmarks in economics.
12 Malthus (1836, p. 31) provides a list of several examples where economists diverge: "The definitions of wealth and of productive labour – The nature and measures of value – The nature and extent of the principles of demand and supply – The origin and progress of rent – The causes which determine the wages of labour and the profits of stock – The causes which practically retard and limit the progress of wealth – The level of the precious metals in different countries – The principles of taxation, &c. On all these points, and many others among the numerous subjects which belong to political economy, differences have prevailed among persons whose opinions are entitled to attention."
13 Brue (2000), Backhouse (2002), Ekelund and Hébert (1997), Dupont (2017), Landreth and Collander (2001), Screpanti and Zamagni (2005).
14 Smith (1776a, 1999, pp. 182–183), see also Chapter 8.
15 Smith (1776a, 1999, pp. 182–183).
16 Malthus (1798, pp. 82–85), Taussig (1896).
17 Malthus (1798, p. 82).
18 Malthus (1826a, p. 7). To explore these connections here would be out of the scope of these books.
19 Brue (2000), Ekelund and Hébert (1997)
20 See, for instance, Godwin (1793) or Condorcet (1793).
21 See, for instance, Godwin (1820).
22 Malthus (1798, 1826a, 1826b).
23 Malthus (1798, p. 44). "Mr. Condorcet's Esquisse d'un tableau historique des progrès de l'esprit humain was written, it is said, under the pressure of that cruel proscription

which terminated in his death." Although Condorcet has died in prison, the circumstances are not yet entirely clear. Nonetheless, Malthus is right in noticing that Condorcet had been captured, arrested and possibly tortured by fellow supporters of the same revolution.

24 Malthus (1826a, p. 44).
25 Malthus (1798, 1826a, 1826b).
26 Malthus (1826a, 1826b).
27 Malthus (1798, 1826a, 1826b), Brue (2000), Backhouse (2002), Ekelund and Hébert (1997), Dupont (2017), Harris (1964), Landreth and Collander (2001), Screpanti and Zamagni (2005), Ekelund and Hébert (1997).
28 Idem.
29 Idem.
30 Idem.
31 Malthus (1826b, p. 121).
32 Beaty (1969), Brue (2000), Screpanti and Zamagni (2005).
33 Vorzimmer (1969), Herbert (1971), Remoff (2016).
34 See, for instance, Lewis and Maslin (2015) or Steffen et al. (2011).
35 Dupont (2017, pp. 231–233).
36 See, for instance, Dupont (2017, pp. 231–233), Ehrlich (1968), Simon (1981).
37 Malthus (1826a, 1826b).
38 Brue (2000), Backhouse (2002), Ekelund and Hébert (1997), Dupont (2017), Landreth and Collander (2001), Screpanti and Zamagni (2005), Ekelund and Hébert (1997).
39 Remond (2014a, 2014b).
40 www.worldometers.info/world-population/world-population-by-year/
41 In some cases, government policies can directly interfere in human reproduction, as in China's one-child policy.
42 See, for instance, Beaty (1969), Lowenthal (1911), Ravenstone (1821, 1966), Sismondi (1819), Thompson (1824, 1963), Hodgskin (1827, 1966).
43 Brue (2000), Backhouse (2002), Ekelund and Hébert (1997), Dupont (2017), Landreth and Collander (2001), Screpanti and Zamagni (2005), Ekelund and Hébert (1997).
44 Sismondi (1819), Stewart (1984, p. 231). See also Lutz (2006) and Remond (2014a, 2014b).
45 Ricardo (1821, 1888, pp. 22–23).
46 Ricardo (1821, 1888, p. 54).
47 Ricardo (1821, 1888, p. 54). As we will observe later, Ricardo does not include rents to have natural values. That is, rents could contribute to form exchange value, but not natural value. Ricardo considers taxes in the same sense.
48 Brue (2000), Backhouse (2002), Ekelund and Hébert (1997), Dupont (2017), Landreth and Collander (2001), Screpanti and Zamagni (2005), Taussig (1896).
49 Ricardo (1821, 1888, p. 56).
50 Ricardo (1821, 1888, p. 56).
51 Ricardo (1821, 1888, p. 58).
52 Taussig (1896).
53 Ricardo (1821, 1888, p. 56).
54 Ricardo (1821, 1888, p. 57/58).
55 Ricardo (1821, 1888, p. 56).
56 See, for instance, Ricardo (1821, 1888, pp. 146–147).
57 Brue (2000), Backhouse (2002), Ekelund and Hébert (1997), Dupont (2017), Landreth and Collander (2001), Screpanti and Zamagni (2005), Taussig (1896).
58 J.S. Mill also seems to have held a limited wage fund perspective for some time, but when criticized by William Thornton (1869, 1969), he may have changed his position to be more accommodating. There is still debate ongoing on this issue (see, for instance, Brue, 2000; Ekelund and Hébert, 1997, pp. 188–189).

59 Taussig (1896), Hollander (1991).
60 Polanyi (1944, 2001).
61 Boyer (2002), Slack (1988).
62 Boyer (1990), Blaug (1963, 1964).
63 Hutzel (1969).
64 Boyer (1990), Blaug (1963, 1964).
65 Boyer (1990), Blaug (1963, 1964), Hutzel (1969).
66 Boyer (1990), Brundage (1978), Backhouse (2002).
67 Blaug (1963, 1964).
68 Blaug (1963, 1964).
69 Hutzel (1969).
70 See previous chapter.
71 Ricardo (1821, 1888, pp. 62–63).
72 Ricardo (1821, 1888, pp. 62–63).
73 Ricardo (1821, 1888, pp. 62–63).
74 Undoubtedly, Ricardo has an idealized view of the monetary payments to wage work-ers: "By gradually contracting the sphere of the poor laws; by impressing on the poor the value of independence, by teaching them that they must look not to systematic or casual charity, but to their own exertions for support, that prudence and fore-thought are neither unnecessary nor unprofitable virtues, we shall by degrees approach a sounder and more healthful state" (Ricardo, 1821, 1888, p. 63).
75 Edsall (1971, p. 1), Halevy (1961, p. 210).
76 Bentham (1838–1843).
77 Edsall (1971).
78 Edsall (1971), Halevy (1961).
79 MacKinnon (1987).
80 Ricardo (1821, 1888, p. 22).
81 Ricardo (1821, 1888, p. 151).
82 Ricardo (1821, 1888, p. 151).
83 Ricardo (1821, 1888, p. 54).
84 Landreth and Collander (2001, p. 169).
85 As noted earlier, Ricardo's concept of utility is still related to the usefulness of an ele-ment, not the hedonist version of the concept. See Ricardo (1821, 1888, p. 22).
86 Ricardo (1821, 1888, p. 23).
87 Ricardo (1821, 1888, p. 23).
88 Dupont (2017, p. 89).
89 Brue (2000), Backhouse (2002), Ekelund and Hébert (1997), Dupont (2017), Landreth and Collander (2001), Screpanti and Zamagni (2005), Ekelund and Hébert (1997).
90 Brue (2000, pp. 119–120).
91 See, for instance, Ricardo (1821, 1888, pp. 166–167), or: "By improvements in machin-ery and agriculture, the whole produce may be doubled; but if wages, rent, and profit be also doubled, these three will bear the same proportions to one another as before, and neither could be said to have relatively varied. But if wages partook not of the whole of this increase; if they, instead of being doubled, were only increased one-half; if rent, instead of being doubled, were only increased three-fourths, and the remaining increase went to profit, it would, I apprehend, be correct for me to say, that rent and wages had fallen while profits had risen;" Ricardo (1821, 1888, p. 31).
92 Brue (2000), Backhouse (2002), Ekelund and Hébert (1997), Dupont (2017), Landreth and Collander (2001), Screpanti and Zamagni (2005), Ekelund and Hébert (1997).
93 Idem.
94 Ricardo (1821, 1888, p. 56).
95 Brue (2000), Ekelund and Hébert (1997).
96 Ricardo (1821, 1888, pp. 28–31).

97 Stigler (1991; see also Konus, 1991) claimed that Ricardo held not an analytical labor theory of value, but merely an empirical theory. As Ricardo concedes that other factors affect prices, according to Stigler, it would be at most a 93% theory of labor value. However, Ricardo describes natural values in terms of wages and profits, given that Ricardo does not includes rents as Smith does. Stigler disregards that Ricardo also defines capital to where profits flow in terms of accumulated labor through time.

98 Ekelund and Hébert (1997), De Vivo (2017).

99 Ricardo (1821, 1888, pp. 38–45), Brue (2000), Ekelund and Hébert (1997), Hollander (1991), Johnson (1984), Roberts (2009), Sraffa (1960).

100 Ricardo (1821, 1888, pp. 38–45), Brue (2000), Ekelund and Hébert (1997), Hollander (1991), Johnson (1984), Roberts (2009), Sraffa (1960).

101 Hollander (1979)

102 Roberts (2009, p. 589), Hollander (1979).

103 www.bbc.com/news/uk-england-cambridgeshire-36276197

104 Brue (2000), Backhouse (2002), Ekelund and Hébert (1997), Dupont (2017), Landreth and Collander (2001), Screpanti and Zamagni (2005).

105 See for instance, Beaty (1969), Lowenthal (1911), Ravenstone (1821, 1966), Sismondi (1819), Thompson (1824, 1963), Hodgskin (1827, 1966).

106 Malthus (1836, p. 53).

107 Malthus does not appreciate the classification nonproductive workers. He gives the example of education, which develops skills necessary for production. Furthermore, he considers that persons who do not directly contribute to generate capital may also save and consume (Malthus, 1836, pp. 44–55).

108 Malthus (1836, p. 53).

109 Malthus (1836, pp. 44–55).

110 Veblen (1994, 1899).

111 An opinion Ricardo (1821, 1888, p. 219) shares with Sismondi and Buchanan.

112 Ricardo (1821, 1888, p. 219).

113 Baumol (1999, 1977), Brue (2000), Jonsson (1995), Thweatt (1979).

114 Baumol (1999, 1977), Brue (2000), Jonsson (1995), Thweatt (1979).

115 Jacoud (2017), Baumol (1977), Kates (2003), Béraud (2003).

116 Baumol (1999, 1977), Brue (2000), Mill (1808a, 1808b), Thweatt (1979).

117 Baumol (1999, 1977), Brue (2000), Jonsson (1995), Thweatt (1979).

118 Say (1803, 1880).

119 Ricardo (1821, 1888, pp. 54–55).

120 Idem.

121 Sismondi (1819) also disagrees.

122 Malthus (1836, p. 53), see also Brue (2000).

123 Baumol (1977).

124 Ricardo (1821, 1888, pp. 181, 336).

125 We have seen before that this explanation is tautological.

126 A concept previously addressed by Cantillon. See Say (1803, 1817), Elkjaer (1991), Fontaine (1999), Steiner (1997).

127 Say (1803, 1817), Elkjaer (1991), Fontaine (1999), Steiner (1997).

128 Ricardo (1821, 1888, p. 181, Chapter XXXI), Ramirez (2019).

129 Ricardo (1821, 1888), Brue (2000), Backhouse (2002), Ekelund and Hébert (1997), Dupont (2017), Landreth and Collander (2001), Screpanti and Zamagni (2005), Ekelund and Hébert (1997).

130 Taussig (1896), Lowenthal (1911).

131 Ricardo (1821, 1888), Brue (2000), Backhouse (2002), Ekelund and Hébert (1997), Dupont (2017), Landreth and Collander (2001), Screpanti and Zamagni (2005), Ekelund and Hébert (1997).

132 Schumpeter (1954), Kolb (1994).

133 For £4,000, as part of the terms of a loan of £25,000 (Brue, 2000; Thorne, 1986).
134 Malthus (1836, p. 53). The division of society between the rich and the poor had been previously identified by Sismondi and McCulloch among others (Clément, 2005).
135 As still happens today, although perhaps more disguised in mathematical/quantitative argurments.
136 See, for instance, Beaty (1969), Hodgskin (1827, 1966), Lowenthal (1911), Ravenstone (1821, 1966), Sismondi (1919), Thompson (1824, 1963).
137 Anthropocene era.

References

Backhouse, R. (2002). *The Penguin History of Economics*. London: Penguin.

Baumol, W. J. (1999). Retrospectives: Say's law. *Journal of Economic Perspectives*, 13(1), 195–204.

Baumol, W. (1977). Say's (at least) eight laws, or what say may really have meant. *Economica*, 44, 145–162.

Beaty, F. (1969). Byron on Malthus and the population problem. *Keats-Shelley Journal*, 18, 17–26.

Bentham, J. (1838–1843). Tracts on poor law and pauper management. In Bowring, J. (Ed.) *The Works of Jeremy Bentham*, 11 vols. Volume 8. Edinburgh: William Tait. Online at: https://oll.libertyfund.org/titles/bentham-works-of-jeremy-bentham-11-vols.

Béraud, A. (2003). Jean-Baptiste Say et la théorie quantitative de la monnaie. In Potier, J.-P. and Tiran, A. (Eds.) *Jean-Baptiste Say. Nouveaux Regards Sur Son Oeuvre*. Paris: Economica.

Blaug, M. (1963). Myth of the old poor law and the making of the new. *Journal of Economic History*, 23(2), 151–184.

Blaug, M. (1964). The poor law report reexamined. *Journal of Economic History*, 24(2), 229–245.

Boyer, G. (1990). *An Economic History of the English Poor Law, 1750–1850*. Cambridge: Cambridge University Press.

Boyer, G. (2002). *English Poor Laws. EH.Net Encyclopedia*. Edited by Whaples, Robert. Online at: http://eh.net/encyclopedia/article/boyer.poor.laws.england.

Brundage, A. (1978). *The Making of the New Poor Law*. New Brunswick, NJ: Rutgers University Press.

Brue, S. (2000). *The Evolution of Economic Thought*. Mason, OH: Thomson/South Western.

Clément, A. (2005). Changing perceptions of the poor in classical economic thought. *Cahiers D'économie Politique/Papers in Political Economy*, 2, 65–86.

Condorcet, M. (1793). *Sketch of an Historical Picture of the Progress of the Human Spirit*. Paris: Chez Agasse.

Darwin, C. (1859). *On the Origin of Species by Means of Natural Selection, or Preservation of Favoured Races in the Struggle for Life*. London: John Murray.

De Vivo, G. (2017). Whatever happened to Ricardo's theory of value? Mill, Mcculloch, and the case of 'oak-trees' and 'wine'. *Contributions to Political Economy*, 36(1), 25–42.

Dupont, B. (2017). *The History of Economic Ideas: Economic Thought in Contemporary Context*. Oxon: Routledge.

Edsall, N. (1971). *The Anti Poor Law Movement – 1834–1844*. Manchester: Manchester University Press.

Ehrlich, P. (1968). *The Population Bomb*. San Francisco: Sierra Club Books.

Ekelund, R. and Hébert, R. (1997). *A History of Economic Theory and Method*. 4th Edition. New York: McGraw-Hill Companies.

Elkjaer, J. R. (1991). The Enterpreneur in economic theory. An example of the development and influence of a concept. *History of European Ideas*, 13(6), 805–815.

Fawcet, H. (1863). *Manual of Political Economy*. London/ Cambridge: Macmillan.

Fontaine, P. (1999). Classical political economy between two fires: Jean-Baptiste Say and Frank H Knight on the enterprise economy. *History of Political Economy*, 31(1), 1.

Godwin, W. (1793). *Enquiry Concerning Political Justice*. 1st Edition. London, England: G.G.J. and J. Robinson.

Godwin, W. (1820). *Of Population. An Enquiry Concerning the Power of Increase in the Numbers of Mankind*. London: Longman, Hurst, Rees, Orne and Brown.

Halevy, E. (1961). *A History of the English People in the Nineteenth Century*. New York: Ernest Benn.

Harris, A. L. (1964). John Stuart Mill: Servant of the East India Company. *Canadian Journal of Economics and Political Science/Revue canadienne de economiques et science politique*, 30(2), 185–202.

Herbert, S. (1971). Darwin, Malthus, and selection. *Journal of the History of Biology*, 4(1), 209–217.

Hirst, J. (2019). *Breve Historia da Europa*. Lisboa: Dom Quixote.

Hodgskin, T. (1827, 1966). *Popular Political Economy*. New York: A. M. Kelley.

Hollander, J. H. (1991). The development of Ricardo's theory of value. In Wood, D. (Ed.) *David Ricardo: Critical Assessments*. Volume 2. London: Routledge.

Hollander, S. (1979). *The Economics of David Ricardo*. Toronto: University of Toronto Press.

Hutzel, J. (1969). Malthus, the poor law, and population in early nineteenth-century England. *Economic History Review*, 22(3), 430–452.

Jacoud, G. (2017). Why is money important in Jean-Baptiste Say's analysis? *The European Journal of the History of Economic Thought*, 24(1), 58–79.

Johnson, L. E. (1984). Ricardo's labor theory of the determinant of value. *Atlantic Economic Journal*, 12(1), 50–59.

Jonsson, P. (1995). On the economics of Say and Keynes' interpretation of say's law. *Eastern Economic Journal*, 21(2), 147–155.

Kates, S. (2003). *Two Hundred Years of Say's Law*. Cheltenham: Edward Elgar.

Keynes, J. (1936). *The General Theory of Employment Interest and Money*. London: Macmillan St Martin's Press.

Kolb, F. R. (1994). The stationary state of Ricardo and Malthus: Neither pessimistic nor prophetic. In Wood, J. (Ed.) *Thomas R Malthus: Critical Assessement*. Volume 3. London: Routledge.

Konus, A. A. (1991). The empirical assumptions of Ricardo's 93% labour theory of value: A comment. In Wood, D. (Ed.) *David Ricardo: Critical Assessments*. Volume 2. London: Routledge.

Landreth, H. and Collander, D. (2001). *History of Economic Thought*. 4th Edition. Boston: Cengage Learning.

Lewis, S. and Maslin, M. (2015). Defining the Anthropocene. *Nature*, 519(7542), 171.

Lowenthal, E. (1911). *The Ricardian Socialists*. New York: Columbia University Press.

Lutz, M. (2006). Humanistic economics: History and basic principles. In Ekins, P. and Max-Neef, M. (Eds.) *Real Life Economics*. London: Routledge, 91–93.

Malthus, R. (1798). *An Essay on the Principle of Population, as it Affects the Future Improvement of Society, with Remarks on the Speculations of Mr. Godwin, M. Condorcet, and Other Writers*. London: J. Johnson.

Malthus, R. (1826a). *An Essay on the Principle of Population, or a View of its Past and Present Effects on Human Happiness; with an Inquiry into our Prospects respecting the Future Removal or Mitigation of the Evils which it Occasions – Volume 1*. 6th Edition. London: John Murray.

Malthus, R. (1826b). *An Essay on the Principle of Population, or a View of its Past and Present Effects on Human Happiness; with an Inquiry into our Prospects Respecting the Future Removal or Mitigation of the Evils which it Occasions – Volume 1*. 6th Edition. London: John Murray.

Malthus, R. (1836). *Principles of Political Economy*. London: W. Pickering.

MacKinnon, M. (1987). English poor law policy and the crusade against outrelief. *The Journal of Economic History*, 47(3), 603–625.

McCulloch, J. (1825). *Principles of Political Economy: With a Sketch of the Rise and Progress of the Science*. Edinburgh: William Tait.

Michie, R. (2006). *The Global Securities Markets: A History*. Oxford: Oxford University Press.

Mill, J. S. (1808a). *Commerce Defended*. London: C. and B. Baldwin.

Mill, J. S. (1808b). Mill's commerce defended. *Eclectic Review*, 4, 554–559.

Polanyi, K. (1944, 2001). *The Great Transformation: The Political and Economic Origins of Our Time*. Boston: Beacon Press.

Ramirez, M. (2019). Marx and Ricardo on machinery: A critical note. *The European Journal of the History of Economic Thought*, 26(1), 81–100.

Ravenstone, P. (1821, 1966). *A Few Doubts as to the Correctness of Some Opinions Generally Entertained on the Subjects of Population and Political Economy*. New York: A. M. Kelley.

Remoff, H. (2016). Malthus, Darwin, and the descent of economics. *American Journal of Economics and Sociology*, 75(4), 862–903.

Remond, R. (2014a). *L'Ancien Regime et la Révolution 1750–1815: Introduction à l'histoire de notre temps*. Paris: Points.

Remond, R. (2014b). *Le XIX Siécle 1815–1914: Introduction à l'histoire de notre temps*. Paris: Points.

Reynaert, F. (2017). *A grande historia do mundo*. Lisboa: Clube de Autor.

Ricardo, D. (1821, 1888). Principles of political economy and taxation. In McCulloch, J. (Ed.) *The Works of David Ricardo. With a Notice of the Life and Writings of the Author*. 3rd Edition. London: John Murray.

Roberts, B. (2009). Ricardo: Standard commodity: Marx: ?   . *Review of Political Economy*, 21(4), 589–619.

Say, J.-B. (1803a, 1817). *Traite d'economie politique*. 3rd Edition. Paris: Déterville.

Say, J.-B. (1803b, 1880). *A Treatise on Political Economy*. Philadelphia: Claxton, Remsen and Haffelfinger.

Schumpeter, J. (1954). *History of Economic Analysis*. Edited from the manuscript by Schumpeter, Elizabeth Boody. New York: Oxford University Press.

Screpanti, E. and Zamagni, S. (2005). *An Outline of the History of Economic Thought*. 2nd Edition. Oxford: Oxford University Press.

Senior, N. (1836, 1965). *An Outline of the Science of Political Economy*. New York: Sentry Press.

Simon, J. (1981). *The Ultimate Resource*. Princeton, NJ: Princeton University Press.

Sismondi, J. (1819). *Nouveaux príncipes D'economie politique, Ou De la richesse dans ses Rapports avec la population*. Paris: Delaunay.

Slack, P. (1988). *Poverty and Policy in Tudor and Stuart England*. London: Longmans.

Smith, A. (1776a, 1999). *An Inquiry into the Nature and Causes of the Wealth of Nations (The Wealth of Nations) (Books I-III)*. London: Penguin.

Smith, A. (1776b, 1999). *An Inquiry into the Nature and Causes of the Wealth of Nations (The Wealth of Nations) (Books IV-V)*. London: Penguin.

Sraffra, P. (1960). *Production of Commodities by Means of Commodities*. Cambridge: Cambridge University Press.

Steffen, W., Grinevald, J., Crutzen, P. and McNeill, J. (2011). The Anthropocene: Conceptual and historical perspectives. *Philosophical Transactions of the Royal Society A: Mathematical, Physical and Engineering Sciences*, 369(1938), 842–867.

Steiner, P. (1997). La théorie de l'entrepreneur chez Jean-Baptiste Say et la tradition Cantillon-Knight. *Actualité Économique*, 73, 611–628.

Stewart, R. (1984). Sismondi's forgotten ethical critique of early capitalism. *Journal of Business Ethics*, 3, 227–234.

Stigler, G. J. (1991). Ricardo and the 93% labor theory of value. In Wood, D. (Ed.) *David Ricardo: Critical Assessments*. Volume 2. London: Routledge.

Taussig, F. (1896). *Wages and Capital, an Examination of the Wages Fund Doctrine*. New York: Appleton & Co.

Thompson, W. (1824, 1963). *An Inquiry into the Principles of the Distribution of Wealth Most Conducive to Human Happiness*. New York: A. M. Kelley.

Thorne, R. (1986). Ricardo, David (1772–1823), of Gatcombe Park, Glos. In Thorne, R. (Ed.) *The History of Parliament: The House of Commons 1790–1820*. Online at: www.historyofparliamentonline.org/volume/1790-1820/member/ricardo-david-1772-1823.

Thornton, W. (1869, 1969). *On Labour: Its Wrongful Claims and Rightful Dues, Its Actual Present and Possible Future*. Rom: Edizioni Bizzarri.

Thweatt, W. (1979). Early formulators of "say's" law of markets. *Quarterly Review of Economics and Business*, 19, 79–96.

Torrens, R. (1821). *An Essay on the Production of Wealth*. London: London, Longman, Hurst, Rees, Orme, and Brown.

Veblen, T. (1994, 1899). *The Theory of the Leisure Class: An Economic Study of Institutions: Penguin Twentieth-Century Classics*. New York: Penguin.

Vorzimmer, P. (1969). Darwin, Malthus, and the theory of natural selection. *Journal of the History of Ideas*, 30(4), 527–542.

11 Prototypes of hedonist arguments

11.1 Introduction

The political economists' theses were quite disputed in the decades after Smith's *Wealth of Nations*. Conflict of ideas could be linked to social tensions and unrest in European countries (besides conflicts and uprisings at European colonies). Moreover, several writers were engaged in attempting alternative theories and social systems. Many workers and their families faced dire living conditions, working 12 hours or more a day, in many cases seven days a week in factories. Moreover, they may have been installed with precarious means within dodgy, insalubrious and dirty lodgings. Through the Industrial Revolution and decades before Marx, many writers have identified groups of humans surviving in difficult conditions out of wages. As noted earlier, wage laborers were compared to slaves. Before Karl Marx, several writers had made proposals to improve the existence and livelihood of the working poor. Some of them anticipated several Marxist ideas (which was not always acknowledged by Marx). Others had advanced alternative theories. For reasons of space, we must address these social relations of production and existence writers in another book. There, we will also observe that Marxism represents a return to work-based theories derivable from Smith's system. Hence, it is hardly a major alternative.

Indeed, Smith and Ricardo had proposed work-based formulations. Yet, somehow during the 19th century in the political economy discipline, Ricardo would become the representative of work-based theories before Marx. Important writers who have addressed social relations regarding means of production and existence would simply be neglected or ignored, as if an attack to Ricardo and Smith would suffice to settle dismissive arguments towards work theories of production, value and existence. The rival hedonist economic theory after Bentham will be introduced in the following chapters. It was developed by a few economists who, while contemporaries of David Ricardo, have actively engaged in contesting work-based theories. Their writings precede Marx. Among others, we will pay closer attention to five already mentioned writers: Thomas Malthus (1766–1834), Jean-Baptiste Say (1767–1832), James Maitland (1759–1839),[1] Nassau Senior (1790–1864) and John Stuart Mill (1806–1873). They created a few arguments that, while still unrefined, would contribute towards the hedonist outline that sustains mainstream economics and its human commodity framework.

It has been suggested that attacks on Ricardo's writings were motivated by concerns with social relations writers we will address in another book, especially with their case that privileged classes would be idle and nonproductive, mere opportunists exploiting the dynamic classes of working poor. Thus, an attack on Ricardo's ideas would be an indirect attack on social relations writers.[2] Regrettably, such a hypothesis cannot be straightforwardly demonstrated.[3] Ricardo's own followers were concerned with the social relations writers. For instance, James Mill was quite prolific in penning his apprehension to Francis Place and Lord Brougham.[4] In 1832, in a letter to the latter, James Mill said:

> The nonsense of which your Lordship alludes about the rights of the labourer to the whole produce of the country, wages, profits, rent, all included. . . . These opinions, if they were to spread, would be the subversion of civilized society; worse than the overwhelming deluge of Huns and Tartars.[5]

Moreover, many of the social relations of production writers were themselves against Ricardo's and Smith's methods and conclusions.[6] A possible aversion that Ricardo's and Smith's ideas could cause would need to be plainly distinguished from a reaction against the social relations writers.

Nonetheless, the hostility was manifest. There seems to be no doubt that Malthus, Say and Senior have openly contested Ricardian economics.[7] Maitland, who is less noticed than the others, contested some future Ricardian ideas such as a universal measure of value even before Ricardo's writings. He did this through criticizing Smith.[8] In substance, whether directly or indirectly, these writers have helped promote a hedonist agenda that can be linked to Bentham's. Furthermore, J.S. Mill is generally described as a key economist, appearing at the end of that (classical) period, who would make a synthesis among Ricardian ideas and those of his critics.[9] However, although using a language that could appear as Ricardian, J.S. Mill made several statements that Smith, Ricardo and the social relations writers could hardly support.[10]

11.2 Justifying unrealistic and flawed hedonist economics

11.2.1 The alleged neutrality of (positive) hedonist utilitarians

In the 20th century, a well-known defense of economics' blatant failure to describe economy and society was presented, among others,[11] by Paul Samuelson (1915–2009) and Milton Freedman (1912–2006). Both would hold Nobel prizes in economics. Building upon the John Neville Keynes's (1852–1949)[12] distinction between normative and positive science, they have claimed that economics would be positive, for it would describe how things are, instead of normative, that is, attempting to describe how things ought to be. In view of that, economics must avoid proposals about how economy and society could be improved. Allegedly, economics would be somewhat neutral.

However, Samuelson, Freedman and J.N. Keynes assume, without evidence, that people and organizations ought to behave according to a hedonist utilitarian model, which is obviously a description of how things ought to be according to utilitarian philosophy. Thus, concurring to their own definition, these writers hold normative stances. Samuelson uses mathematical methods to presuppose (without evidence) that people and organizations attempt to maximize their utility, which in the case of the latter can also be approximately termed as expected returns or profits.[13] Utility would be measurable in money, as advised by Bentham. From this prescribed behavior, an equilibrium in economic systems would allegedly ensue.[14] Friedman (1953, 2008), in his highly influential essay "The Methodology of Positive Economics," accepts that mainstream economics' assumptions can be and often are rather unrealistic.[15] However, he tries to present the case that false and/or wrong assumptions would not be an issue.

A positive science would be about predicting phenomena that have not yet occurred, not all phenomena, but only those which could interest economists. That is, instead of aiming to general predictive adequacy, economics should aim only at narrow predictive success.[16] As a result, mainstream economics would not need to eliminate assumptions contradicted by observed facts, as often is the case.[17] Obviously, such reasoning would allow Friedman to move economics away from phenomena that could explicitly confirm its lack of empirical support, let alone scientific inadequacy. Instead of assuming defeat, Friedman argues somewhat as a lawyer who, when presented with undeniable evidence against his/her client, tries to undermine the evidence's relevance. Still, economics is quite far from achieving empirical corroboration.[18] Failing to admit that mainstream economics suffers from dangerous predicaments, Friedman blames instead those who try to expose its fragile foundations.

The "*positive*" argument, in fact, defends normative assumptions of utilitarianism in humans and organizations. During many decades to come, abiding by this argument, perhaps millions of mainstream economists around the world would have a rhetorical toolbox to entrench themselves in the moral philosophy of hedonism, many of them perhaps without even noticing it. Quite appropriately, such a position was frequently criticized and even described as nonscientific.[19] Yet, although recent empirical studies have attempted to test key assumptions, for example, with experiments and replications, this "positive" reasoning remains generally undisputed in mainstream economics.

Perhaps as part of the hedonist argumentative strategy, the "*positive*" case had previously been formulated in the 19th century by Senior and J.S Mill. J.N. Keynes (1899, 1999, p. 12) recognizes his predecessors: "*Senior and J. S. Mill were the earlier English economists who definitely formulated principles of economic method.*" When advocating the pseudo-neutrality of political economy, Senior and Mill were also defending the discipline against a barrage of criticism, for instance, towards their utilitarian assumptions or lack of sound empirical evidence to support master tenets.[20]

11.2.2 *Senior case for utilitarian and positive economics*

At first sight, Senior may not seem a hedonist who follows Bentham's philosophy. For instance, he restricts the political economy's purpose as "*to the Nature, Production, and Distribution of Wealth*"[21] and criticizes those who could present other drivers for its study, such as human welfare or happiness.[22] Thus, Senior's position could appear to contradict Bentham's hedonist principle of maximum hedonist happiness to the maximum of people.[23] However, this eventual contradiction would be deceptive. As a major principle of political economy, Senior states: "*that every man desires to obtain additional wealth with as little sacrifice as possible.*"[24] Hence, hereby he summarizes a hedonist perspective, where wealth would be akin to pleasure. Work and other human means to obtain wealth (or even survive) would be akin to sacrifice/pain (disutility of work). Furthermore, Senior defines Wealth as "*those things and those things only that have Value.*"[25] Nevertheless, as we will see with more detail later, Senior, along with Say, Maitland, Malthus and J.S. Mill, drafted a utilitarian theory of value (in exchange). Moreover, Senior employs the hedonist definition of utility, instead of the previous definition as usefulness in Smith and Ricardo. For Senior, utility "*denotes no intrinsic quality in the things we call useful, it merely expresses their relation to the pains and pleasures of mankind.*"[26] Thus, he had a hedonist agenda.

Interestingly, Senior also provided an initial draft to the "*positive*" argument. Senior assumes that humans and organizations act according to normative hedonism. However, he would proclaim that economists would not be authorized to provide advice about how things ought to be:

> But his conclusions, whatever be their generality and their truth, do not authorize him in adding a single syllable of advice. That privilege belongs to the writer or the statesman who has considered all the causes which may promote or impede the general welfare of those whom he addresses, not to the theorist who has considered only one, though among the most important, of those causes. The business of a Political Economist is neither to recommend nor to dissuade, but to state general principles. . . . To decide in each case how far those conclusions are to be acted upon, belongs to the art of government, an art to which Political Economy is only one of many subservient Sciences.[27]

Senior recommends that political economists should focus their study on matters of wealth and altogether "*disregards all consideration of Happiness or Virtue.*"[28] However, he defines wealth in relation to hedonist utility. Moreover, he presupposes that humans and organizations generally act according to the moral theory of utilitarianism. As pointed out by Brue (2000, p. 148), Senior did not follow his own prescription as to not offer advice regarding political affairs. In his long career, he made many policy matter suggestions without clearly explaining corroborating evidence or compatibility with his economic framework. Generally, his position would be against the position of those who claimed to represent the working poor. For instance, we saw earlier that Senior co-wrote the report to Parliament advising measures to reformulate or remove poor laws. Moreover, he was against the possibility of workers creating their representative organizations, actively campaigning for the law not to author-ize the existence of labor unions. Furthermore, although Senior could accept regulating child labor, he was against reducing daily working hours for adult workers. At a time when workers had to endure in many factories 12 hours of work or more daily, there were popular movements in support of a 10-hour maximum workday. Senior was against such reduction because according to him investors' profits (and capital accumulation) would be derived from work-ers' last hours of work.[29]

11.2.3 J.S. Mill's argument

J.S. Mill was a utilitarian, trained in this moral philosophy by his father James Mill, who was also Bentham's friend and associate.[30] We have seen before that, to some extent, J.S. Mill's qualitative hedonism diverges to Bentham's quanti-tative version. In qualitative utilitarianism, Mill tried (and failed) to integrate arguments from opponents to utilitarianism, without conceding that they could dangerously contradict utilitarian philosophy. Curiously, he employed a similar approach in his *Principles of Political Economy* (1848), the reference book with many editions, which has trained so many economists before Marshal's *Principle of Economics* (1890). Several ideas, concepts and themes from enemies to politi-cal economy were included in Mill's book. Among them are contributions from the social relations of production and existence writers. For instance, Mill discusses workers' organizations such as cooperative production,[31] taxation over inheritances and legacies,[32] social distribution of income,[33] or the acceptance of several forms of government intervention.[34] Furthermore, Mill manifested concern for the wage workers, their problems and difficult conditions, as some opponents of the discipline would also.[35] Moreover, Mill directly discussed some ideas from social relation writers.[36] Although, here and there he makes some minor conceptions, he scarcely accepts that adversaries to the discipline of political economy (and hedonist utilitarianism) could cause any serious dam-age to the discipline. Moreover, while in his qualitative hedonism J.S. Mill attempted a differentiation between higher and lower pleasures, in addressing political economy Mill mostly follows a quantitative hedonist approach.

Intriguingly likewise, Mill's assumptions closely resemble those advocated by contemporary mainstream economics. Likewise, Mill assumes that people and organizations behave according to normative hedonism. Concurring with Mill, political economy

> predicts only such of the phenomena of the social state as take place in consequence of the pursuit of wealth. It makes entire abstraction of every other human passion or motive; except those which may be regarded as perpetually antagonizing principles to the desire of wealth, namely,

aversion to labour [disutility of work], and desire of the present enjoyment of costly indulgences.[37]

Rendering to him, "*Political Economy considers mankind as occupied solely in acquiring and consuming wealth*,"[38] which would be limited by the mentioned two counter-motives, namely, the disutility of work and present enjoyment of expensive pleasures.

In "*On the Definition of Political Economy and the Method of Investigation Proper to It*," J.S. Mill (1836, 2008) similarly anticipates many arguments later advocated by J.N. Keynes, Samuelson and Friedman. Mill concedes that political economy's complex phenomena are influenced by many factors. Therefore, the discipline cannot study them through direct experience (*a posteriori*), for it could not disentangle the many relationships involved. Political economy needs to use an indirect "*mixed method of induction and ratiocination*" (*a priori*), which would be based upon assumptions.[39] As Senior, J.S. Mill restricts political economy to the study of the pursuit of wealth:

> It does not treat of the whole of man's nature as modified by the social state, nor of the whole conduct of man in society. It is concerned with him solely as a being who desires to possess wealth, and who is capable of judging of the comparative efficacy of means for obtaining that end.[40]

As Friedman, Mill did not go so far as to say that empirical evidence contradicting economics' predictions must be discarded. Contradictory empirical evidence may cause "*frictions*" and "*disturbances*" in a few cases.[41] Hence, Mill is akin to contemporary mainstream economists who refuse to admit that contradictory evidence could ever refute economics. It would be impossible to evaluate the multitude of influencing circumstances, and there would be limited capacity of varying the experiments.[42] Political economy would be an abstract science that is true in the abstract. Henceforth, inconsistent evidence would only apply to a restricted number of situations, not the entire discipline.

While Friedman has used a well-known metaphor with an expert billiard player, who may excel at play without knowing mathematical formulas describing his performance,[43] J.S. Mill uses a metaphor involving geometry.

> Political Economy, therefore, reasons from assumed premises – from premises which might be totally without foundation in fact, and which are not pretended to be universally in accordance with it. The conclusions of Political Economy, consequently, like those of geometry, are only true, as the common phrase is, in the abstract; that is, they are only true under certain suppositions, in which none but general causes – causes common to the whole class of cases under consideration – are taken into the account. This ought not to be denied by the political economist.[44]

A separation between theory and practice should not be an issue,[45] which is the standard economics' attitude.

11.3 Changing the meaning of utility and shifting attention to consumption

11.3.1 Jean-Baptiste Say and James Maitland contest labor theories of production, value and existence

After the start of the Napoleonic wars, Maitland (1804) tactfully contested Smith's work-based theory for not taking into consideration economic elements' scarcity, which could make supply and demand the determinants of value. He doubted that commodities could have *"real, intrinsic, or invariable value."*[46] Although circumspect to some extent, Maitland exhibited that it would be possible to contest Smith's system. Jean-Baptiste Say was more openly conflictual. Among other divergences to Adam Smith's system, Say explicitly contested Smith's work-based theory from the second edition onwards of his *A Treatise on Political Economy* (1814).[47] By contesting Smith's legitimacy, Say has likewise demonstrated that different theories of production, value and existence would be possible.

Nonetheless, Say did not subscribe to the methodological position recommended by Senior and J.S. Mill (and thus Samuelsson, Friedman and countless mainstream economists). Instead, Say's position could be described as realist and anti-deductivist,[48] which differs from the position held by many previous and subsequent political economists.[49] Indeed, Say was against separating theory and practice. To Say, theory must be confirmed and supported by facts:

> What is theory, if it be not a knowledge of the laws which connect effects with their causes, or facts with facts? And who can be better acquainted with facts than the theorist who surveys them under all their aspects, and comprehends their relation to each other?[50]

Eventually shocking to contemporary economists, Say was of the view that mathematical abstractions were dangerous and had no place in the study of political economy.[51] It is a curious enough irony that a writer with such an aversion to mathematical economics has contributed so much to the hedonist foundations underlying mainstream economics.

In contesting Smith and Ricardo, Say could not simply be reacting to social relations writers. Apart from earlier writers such as Condorcet, Goodwin or others related to the French Revolution, Say put pen to paper before many of the social relation writers we will address in another book. Nonetheless, Say witnessed the turbulence of the French Revolution and how radical Jacobins led by Maximilien de Robespierre (1758–1794) assumed power for a short spell, forming what later would be called the age of terror, or simply the terror

(1793–1794). Jacobin leaders (many of whom would themselves be executed) claimed to be defenders of the people of France. Yet, summary executions were conducted against alleged enemies of the revolution (a blurred and murderous definition), some of whom belonged to rival political factions that also had supported the revolution (for instance, the Girondins). A program of radical economic measures was implemented during the terror, involving, for instance, large expropriations, fixing prices and salaries, or issuing larger quantities of a new paper money (the *assignat*), which was not convertible into precious metals.[52] An economic crisis ensued, with an impact on production, inflationary prices and scarcity of goods necessary to attend human necessities. After the fall of the Jacobins, Say would contribute to the Tribunat under Napoleon's government, a post he would occupy for four years.[53] Nevertheless, although the Jacobins had fallen, during many years later, writings would still appear to defend them.[54]

Moreover, in France there were several economic writers before Smith who had tried to present other economic systems, for instance, Anne-Robert Jacques Turgot (1727–1781), Richard Cantillon (1680–1734) or the Physiocrats. These writers, who had also influenced Smith, exhibit that there might be alternative explanatory systems. Moreover, Say was involved in business affairs. He owned and managed at least a factory with hundreds of workers, namely, a cotton spinning mill. Thus, he had actual insight on manufacturing production.[55] Eventually, he could wish to downplay a potential conflict between businesspersons such as himself and workers. On the other hand, Say could simply fail to appreciate Smith's system in its entirety. Without a doubt, it would be difficult to disentangle all reasons that Say contested the work-based theories of Smith and Ricardo.

Curiously, Say published the second edition of his compendium when Napoleon was about to be defeated and the Restoration Era in Europe about to begin. While his framework was influenced by Smith, Say would dispute several elements in Smith's system from the onset. One of those *"imperfections"* was to consider labor as the source of value:

> To the labour of man alone he [Smith] ascribes the power of producing values. This is an error. A more exact analysis demonstrates, as will be seen in the course of this work, that all values are derived from the operation of labour, or rather from the industry of man, combined with the operation of those agents which nature and capital furnish him. Dr. Smith did not, therefore, obtain a thorough knowledge of the most important phenomenon in production; this has led him into some erroneous conclusions, such, for instance, as attributing a gigantic influence to the division of labour, or rather to the separation of employment.[56]

In undermining the relevance of work to value, Say is also undermining the relevance of work and the division of labor for production, which had uttermost importance at Smith's system.

11.3.2 *Constructing a hedonist utility*

On 23 November 1823, a shocked David Ricardo wrote to John Ramsay McCulloch complaining about Say's writings:

> I have looked over carefully all the new matter in his fourth edition without discovering anything to induce me to alter the opinion which I have given of the confusion of his ideas respecting value. Utility, riches, value, according to him are all the same thing.[57]

As described before, Ricardo has added an additional chapter to his *Principles* to contest the use of these terms as equivalent. To his associates and correspondents, Ricardo raised the possibility that Say did not understand his economic framework.[58] This hypothesis can still be found in contemporary writers.[59]

It is possible. Say has written several letters to Ricardo praising him and recurrently promising to incorporate Ricardo's criticisms in his own work. However, Say systematically failed to do so.[60] Yet, Say could have instead acted out of politeness as to avoid contesting Ricardo, whom he deemed *"a recommendable man, who honoured me* [Say] *with his friendship."*[61] Eventually, some degree of hypocrisy may have been involved. Say might have concealed a deep-seated negative attitude towards work-based theories. After Ricardo's death, Say became much more outspoken, overtly attacking, contesting and diminishing Ricardo's economics.[62] Say excused himself for not having publicly expressed his true feelings, while claiming that he did directly expressed those feelings to Ricardo:[63]

Ricardo, nonetheless, was persuaded that Say was using the term utility as he and Smith were, namely, as usefulness. In a letter to Say in 1815, Ricardo told: *"A commodity must be useful to have value but the difficulty of its production is the true measure of its value. For this reason, Iron though more useful is of less value than gold."*[64] Likewise, in a later edition of his *Principles*, Ricardo disparaged Say's theory of utility value, which Ricardo misperceived as a theory of use value:

> If two sacks be of the value that one was of before, he evidently obtains the same value and no more, – he gets, indeed, double the quantity of riches – double the quantity of utility – double the quantity of what Adam Smith calls value in use, but not double the quantity of value, and therefore M. Say cannot be right in considering value, riches, and utility to be synonymous.[65]

Although in some instances, Say did use the term of utility as usefulness, he often encompassed a much more hedonistic definition, where usefulness becomes linked to the satisfaction of human wants:

> It is universally true, that, when men attribute value to anything, it is in consideration of its useful properties; what is good for nothing they set no

price upon. To this inherent fitness or capability of certain things to satisfy the various wants of mankind, I shall take leave to affix the name of utility. And I will go on to say, that, to create objects which have any kind of utility, is to create wealth; for the utility of things is the ground-work of their value, and their value constitutes wealth.[66]

In *Catéchisme d'Économie Politique* (1815, 1826, p. 11–13), Say further explained that utility, according to him, is related to attend human desires. Because of our desires, humans would sacrifice things to obtain the (hedonist) utility of elements:

Because the utility that it has makes it desirable, and brings men to make a sacrifice for to possess it. We give nothing to have what is good for nothing; but we give some quantity of things we own (a certain amount of silver coins, for example) to get the thing you need. That's what makes it worth it.

Thus, this idea of connecting utility to human desire and sacrifice clearly resembles Bentham's pleasure and pain and recalls Senior's and Mill's hedonist utility earlier. Likewise, Maitland defined wealth as *"all that man desires as useful and delightfull to him"*[67] or, alternatively, that a commodity to have value requires to be *"useful or delightful to man, should be an object of his desire."*[68] It may be unclear how Bentham could have inspired Say's writings for he barely refers Bentham.[69] Nonetheless, both men knew each other and spent substantial time together.[70] These writers significantly advanced the hedonist agenda.

Here, Senior describes the inventive alteration in meaning:

utility, which comes nearest to it, being generally used to express the quality of preventing pain or of indirectly producing pleasure, as a means. We shall venture to extend the signification of that word, and consider it as also including all those things which produce pleasure directly. We must admit that this is a considerable innovation in English language. It is, however, sanctioned by Mr. Malthus, (Definitions, p. 234,) and has been ventured by M. Say in French, a language less patient of innovation than our own. . . . Utility, thus explained, is a necessary constituent of value.[71]

As we will see later, value to hedonist economic theory must also be considered primarily in exchange. It would apply to the elements that *"in other words, [are] to be lent or sold, hired or purchased."*[72] Indeed, Malthus considers use value as a metaphorical rather than a literal conception, which should have little application for political economy: *"We do not often hear of the value of air and water, although they are bodies in the highest degree useful, and indeed essentially necessary to the life and happiness of human beings."*[73] Value should imply exchange value, unless it is to *"be marked by the addition in use."*[74]

To Mill, the word value in political economy means value in exchange, unless an associated word is put to it.[75] Furthermore, to Mill exchange value would be connected to a hedonist utility. Hence, Mill too contributed to disavow Smith's, Ricardo's and Aristoteles's use-exchange value distinction. To Mill, in political economy even the word use would not be related to usefulness but generating hedonist utility: "*The use of a thing in political Economy means its capacity to satisfy a desire, or serve a purpose*."[76] To exemplify, Mill addresses the water-diamond paradox in Smith, where diamonds, contrary to water, would have little usefulness and high exchange value. According to Mill, diamonds' high exchange value would be explained by their high utility, that is, capacity to satisfy desires or serve purposes.[77] To Mill, therefore, Smith's failure would be to not have adopted hedonist philosophy. Senior also addresses the diamond value paradox, arriving at a similar viewpoint.[78]

None of these hedonist writers addressed in this chapter claim that prices automatically measure hedonist utility values, for supply, demand, money and other intermediate factors could also impact prices. However, these writers argue that prices are fundamentally related to hedonist utility. Still, while Senior recognized that the change in meaning to the word utility would be somehow innovative, J.S. Mill would proclaim that hedonism defines utility in political economy. Combining with his argument for positive economics, he would set the pace for many rhetoric constructions still employed in mainstream economics.

11.3.3 Production and work would be about creating hedonist utility via consumption

Along the meaning modification to the term utility, another important hedonist argument has been brought further: The purpose of production and/or human work would not be mere generation of outputs with distinct aims (e.g., tangible commodities, intangible flows, products, hybrid products). Instead, their purpose would be generation of hedonist utility. In this sense, consumption (paid for through monetary flows) would come to the fore because final consumption would be necessary to generate hedonist utility. Thus, to some extent, consumption would become blurred in actual production. For utility to be produced, consumers would be required. Consumers, however, would need to have monetary means to consume. This detail is not without relevance. It legitimizes the interests of those who hold larger sums of money.

In this context, we can understand Say's extraordinary claim that the purpose of production would be producing hedonist utility. It still has great bearing in contemporary economics: "*Production is the creation, not of matter, but of utility. It is not to be estimated by the length, the bulk, or the weight of the product, but by the utility it presents*."[79] Say went further by claiming that the consumer would be the producer.[80] The other writers follow along these lines, with only minor divergences. Senior defines consumption primarily as making use of a thing[81] and notes how Malthus describes consumption as the greatest purpose and end of all production.[82] Likewise, J.S. Mill alleges the universality of consumption: "*All members of the community are not labourers, but all are consumers.*"[83]

Moreover, these hedonist writers contested Smith's distinction amid productive and unproductive work. These hedonist writers would come up with another distinction: productive and unproductive consumption.[84] Indeed, Say asserted that Smith had erred in not having discriminated between these two types of consumption.[85] Productive consumption would generate utility incorporated in further means of production/capital, whereas unproductive consumption would be related to the final consumer's utility, which does not generate further means of production/capital. Similarly, human work would be about producing either final or intermediate utility. Thus, the aim of work would merely depend on the paying consumer's inclinations. Furthermore, as Mill noticed, a labor theory would have the most difficult time in identifying what actual work would have contributed to a specific product. Besides the direct work eventually observable, there would be several forms of indirect work with relevance for production, such as labor in producing the subsistence of workers (for instance, finding and preparing their food), labor of producing materials and tools and machines (implements) of production, labor of invention and discovery or even labor that has to do with raising, nurturing and educating children who later might become workers, which might have been necessary for the direct work of production to be possible.[86] Furthermore, forms deemed by Smith as unproductive labor might actually be required for production.

Still, hedonist writers generally claim that they would be able to solve these actual difficulties through their quantitative hedonism: The purpose of work could instead be understood as generating hedonism to paying consumers payable in hedonist calculus (hence money). According to Mill, human work could produce three forms of hedonist utility, namely (i) utilities fixed and embodied in outward objects, (ii) utilities fixed and embodied in human beings, for instance, the work of educators and governments that aim at the improvement of people or physicians that save lives, and (iii) utilities not fixed or embodied in any object, but consisting in a mere service rendered, a pleasure given, an inconvenience or a pain averted, during a longer or a shorter time, but without leaving a permanent acquisition in the improved qualities of any person or thing, for instance, the work of a musician but also that of the army or that of a judge who keeps the law and tranquility in a society.[87]

Say described that final consumption satisfies human wants and destroys utility, thus wealth.[88] This destruction of utility could be faster (as in a theater play) or slower (as in living in a house).[89] On the other hand, productive consumption would transfer utility to means of further production and consumption/capital. However, as a first proponent of this hedonist formulation, Say would later be rectified in the details by Malthus, Senior and Mill. Perhaps to attend his fellow critics, Say would come up with a distinction between natural and social wealth. The latter would be wealth that could be exchanged (by money).[90] The former would include elements

> such as air, water, or solar light. These may be denominated natural wealth, because they are the spontaneous offering of nature; and, as such, mankind is not called upon to earn them by any sacrifice or exertion whatever; for which reason, they are never possessed of exchangeable value.[91]

Say went further and claimed that only social wealth could be the object of "*scientific research.*"[92] Curiously, as demonstrated in Appendix 5.A, Say identified several properties of human-related intangible flows. However, he assumed that intangible flows associated with monetary flows would be akin to commodities. Other intangible flows could not be the object of scientific research as they could not be exchanged.[93] In this regard, immaterial products or values consumed when produced would be akin to commodities as in mainstream economics and affiliated disciplines.[94]

Malthus considered that it would be too vague defining that wealth could be anything capable of addressing human wants, as in Say or Maitland.[95] He would exclude from wealth elements such as "*leisure, agreeable conversation, cultivated tastes, and general information.*"[96] Moreover, Malthus cynically argued how impractical it would be to contemplate virtue as wealth in political economy.[97] He advocates against completely abandoning matter in defining wealth.[98] Yet, by defining value as value in exchange, Malthus implied that the transaction of a monetary flow would transform intangible objects/flows as services into material objects, which the material flow has not power to do. As described earlier, Malthus was of the view that a functioning society must support the existence of unproductive wealthy classes who would consume more than they produce. Likewise, Senior distinguishes between commodities and services and yet reaches the same equivalence between services and commodities as Malthus. By considering them in relation to hedonist production and market parable, in practice Senior treats services as akin to commodities having their purpose and value established through hedonism.[99]

Senior disagreed with Say that consumption would necessarily imply destruction of utility. There would be products that keep their utility despite of being used such as land, a house, or a statue in a gallery.[100] Likewise, a product could lose its utility despite not being consumed, for instance, through an accident or a natural disaster.[101] Interestingly, Senior makes a distinction among things being purchased. His typology distinguishes commodities and services, as also implied in Malthus:

> we are ready to admit the convenience of the distinction between services and commodities themselves, and to apply the term service to the act of occasioning an alteration in the existing state of things, the term commodity to the thing as altered; the term product including both commodities and services.[102]

Nonetheless, Senior uses the term value in terms of monetary exchange and thus market purchases: "*The principal circumstance, however, is the mode in which the payment is made.*"[103] Thus, Senior further implies that monetary transactions would transform services into objects akin to commodities.

Mill starts by declaring himself as approving of Say (and McCulloch) when they disparage Smith's "*productive work*" expression. Human beings, as Say had noticed, would not be capable of producing particles of matter.[104] Instead, Mill explains, "*we produce, or desire to produce, is always, as M. Say rightly terms it, an utility. Labour is not creative of objects, but of utilities.*" Providing evidence of the eclecticism he was sometimes pejoratively attributed,[105] Mill would a few paragraphs later claim to aim at restoring the traditional use of the term productive labor as labor that creates utility in material objects.[106] One needs to observe that created wealth is not described by Mill as the object, but the hedonist utility in the object, a stance that Smith and Ricardo's writings did not envisage. Furthermore, Mill describes how difficult it would be to identify what human work could have contributed to the utility of a material object, which is a manner to dispute Smith and Ricardo's classification. For example, the object may have benefited from indirect work necessary for production, the security provided by the Navy and the Army, the laws of a legislator, or the merchant who moves commodities from one place to another.[107] Furthermore, Mill mentions, for instance: "*The skill, and the energy and perseverance, of the artisans of a country, are reckoned part of its wealth, no less than their tools and machinery.*"[108] Hence, although in appearance Mill could be seen as defending Smith's typology of productive and unproductive work, Mill attempted to reformulate it to make it align with hedonist utilitarianism.

11.4 Money: A mystical commodity for calculating hedonistic utility

Say, Maitland, Senior, Malthus and J.S. Mill treat money as the commodity that creates/defines other commodities, along a barter theory of money. This much already appeared in Smith's system. Furthermore, their position can be approximated to a quantitative theory of money, where quantity in circulation would affect prices of (other) commodities.[109] However, they are far from having a simplistic description whereby an increase/decrease in the mass of money in circulation would automatically increase/decrease prices in the same proportion.[110] Only recently has the complexity of these authors' monetary theories been further researched.[111] Say,[112] Maitland,[113] Senior,[114] Malthus[115] and J.S. Mill[116] mention the phenomenon of money circulation velocity (or "*rapidity*") as a mediating effect of the quantity of money on prices. Furthermore, they generally do not consider money as neutral to the economic activity, that is, as only interfering with prices. At least in the short run, the quantity of money (and credit) may increase/decrease production and employment.[117]

However, money needs to be neutral for hedonist calculus to be achievable; otherwise, money's non-neutrality could interfere in calculations.[118] Moreover, these five writers relate monetary transactions to (hedonist) utility of traded elements and money itself. These features were not traditional components in quantitative theories of money. Smith's and Ricardo's perspective was that value would be measured in human work/toil, though it may be expressed in monetary terms. Instead, hedonist writers recommended that money should become the standard measure to hedonist calculus. Accordingly, prices and monetary flows would somehow be connected to pleasure and pain. When a monetary transaction occurs (the market in economics), it would be related to hedonist utility. As described by Say: "*In fact, when one man sells any product to another, he sells him the utility vested in that product; the buyer buys it only for the sake of its utility, of the use he can make of it.*"[119] Money was no longer to be considered as mere means of circulations to products of man and nature. Money, as the tool for hedonist calculus, was to become measure for value/wealth.

According to these hedonist writers, a monetary transaction may not necessarily define an element's utilitarian value. There might be interfering factors in supply and demand such as the quantity and velocity of money in circulation, the scarcity and difficulty of attainment of elements, government interventions and regulations, taxes, number of producers and monopolies. However, prices would be linked to hedonist utility. A wage would be a price expressing the hedonist utility that human work (commodity) would generate to the final consumer or be incorporated in intermediate products.

Thus, money becomes a mystical token to hedonism, a symbol for pleasure and pain, underlying the formulation of the market parable with its hedonist supply and demand propositions. Supposedly, without the multitude of factors and phenomena interfering in monetary transactions, money could measure hedonist utility, which becomes the major explanation for the occurrence of tangible flows of physical goods and money. Money becomes a transcendent commodity that could at once demonstrate hedonist philosophy. Money was turned into a sacred idol of a hedonist creed.

11.5 Conclusion

The hedonist utilitarian theory of production, value and existence underlying mainstream economics cannot be considered a mere reaction to Marxism because it precedes Marx's writings. However, no full clarity exists as to what extent this hedonist theory could have been a reaction to social relations writers who will be addressed in another book. Furthermore, we will see that anti-Marxist economists, who are often deemed as marginalist or neoclassical,[120] have employed several ideas formulated by earlier hedonist writers. While retaining key features of Smith's system, Say, Maitland, Senior, Malthus and J.S. Mill have presented a profoundly different theory of production, value and existence. This theory has great implications for the description of human participation in economic and societal production.

The hedonist writers followed more closely in this chapter were contemporaries of Ricardo. However, they would develop a economic theory derived from Bentham's hedonism. They can be distinguished, for instance, from Torrens (1821) or McCulloch (1864) who, despite adopting definitions of wealth connected to utilitarianism, still adopt theories of value and production that can be linked to Smith's system.[121] Likewise, they can be distinguished from Bailey (1825) who, although a Benthamite hedonist,[122] tried to counterpoint the logical inconsistencies of Ricardo's labor theory of value (and absolute measure of value), with attempts to form a cost theory of value involving other costs besides labor.[123] Instead, the writers followed more closely here[124] have presented a hedonist theory based on money as the instrument for hedonist calculus, which would blur consumption and production.

Beside the pseudo–neutrality of the normative hedonist, a crucial argument was the alteration of the meaning of utility. To Smith and Ricardo, utility implied usefulness, as in water has more utility than a diamond because water can be used to drink, cook, clean, produce goods and raw materials, produce energy, form oceans and rivers, rain on vegetables and forests, integrate living beings and so forth. However, a diamond would have much less usefulness based mostly on human status, aesthetical purposes, and a few industrial uses. On the other hand, hedonist writers use the word utility to imply an association with pleasure and pain. Alternative words may intermediate, such as wants, desires, sacrifices or burdens. However, hedonist philosophy is their end, as in a diamond has more utility than water because the former could produce more pleasure in attending human wants and desires (this claim could hardly be empirically demonstrated).

Extraordinarily, the aim of production and/or human work would no longer be the generation of outputs such as commodities, intangible flows, products that combine characteristics of tangibility and intangibility, or hybrid products (according to intangible flow theory). Instead, the purpose would be generation of (poorly defined) hedonist utility. Hence, paying consumers' pleasure and avoidance of pain would become the intent of production. Clearly, in conjoining production to consumption, two or more complex phenomena are described as being just a simple phenomenon. Yet, each of the former phenomena is less explained and comprehensible than before. When production becomes blurred to consumption, the desires of moneyed individuals are primarily attended to in economics. The purpose of human work would be defined as to produce hedonist utility for the (moneyed) final consumers or intermediate means/capital that would be capable of producing further utility.

As the previous part explained, delivery of products/outputs to members of society can require quite complex tangible and intangible flows. Frequently, productive resources need to be obtained directly from the biosphere. Furthermore, production and delivery can entail organization, coordination and cooperation of countless human beings. By shifting the attention from production to consumption, Say, Maitland, Senior, Malthus and J.S. Mill moved the focus to a much more individualistic stance. Humans in monetary societies generally can consume either alone or in the privacy of families or small groups. In the extreme, consumption can be narcissistic and selfish. Instead, many human connections are still necessary for production to occur and flows of products to be delivered.[125] Several contemporary global production chains involve the cooperation of millions of humans spread around the planet.

Even Mill, elsewhere self-defined as a qualitative hedonist, is to a large extent a quantitative hedonist in political economy. Smith's system already defined money as some sort of mystical commodity that could create/define commodities. A monetary transaction would imply the transaction of a commodity. However, Smith or Ricardo did not consider money as a measure of value, even though labor or natural value were to be quantified in money. Otherwise, hedonist writers start connecting monetary transactions to hedonist value and implying money could somehow measure pleasure and pain.[126]

There is no doubt that one can buy a product that gives him/her pleasure or prevents his/her pain. However, these effects can merely be temporary. For instance, immediate gratification can result in further pain in the future. How then do we deal with the passage of time and unstoppable decay and suffering of human bodies?[127] How do we deal with the suffering arising from expectations and delusions in human relations? Moreover, it has not been demonstrated that pain and pleasure could be the exclusive motivations of human activity. Empirical evidence does not exist to demonstrate that a monetary transaction could adequately measure pleasure and avoidance of pain caused upon a consumer or contained in an intermediate product/material. Besides falling upon the paradox (aporia) of trying to measure intangibility, these extraordinary hedonist assumptions cannot explain the complex tangible and intangible flows involved in the delivery of products/ outputs to members of society. Importantly, when human- or nonhuman-related flows that are indispensable for economic and societal production are not reflected upon monetary flows, they are mostly deserted by hedonist economics.

Appendix A

That Say has identified some human-related intangible flows but treats them as akin to commodities when reflected on monetary flows.

Say has realized that some outputs of the production process are intangible, for instance, the services of a physician who visits a sick patient and saves his life or those of a musician or an actor, which "*yields a product of the same kind.*"[128] Indeed, Say has identified some attributes that contemporary studies use to distinguish physical goods from services, which were previously reviewed in Part 2, for example, that intangible products are perishable,[129] are immaterial,[130] must be consumed when produced[131] or are very difficult to be stored ("*accumulated*").[132] Nevertheless, Say wishes to contest Smith's typology of productive and unproductive work, where the former would be related mostly to the production of material flows and the latter to services that do not generate material flows of physical goods and money. To demonstrate that immaterial products could be productive, Say applies the standard of hedonist utility, in that those intangible products could be productive because, for example, they would generate pleasure and amusement or could avoid pain.[133] All outputs, either material and immaterial, would be evaluated according to hedonist utility. When someone pays to obtain such immaterial flows, he/she would be demonstrating that those products would have (hedonist) utility; otherwise, no money would be transferred. Thus, Say defines immaterial flows as equivalent to physical commodities, for the monetary flow would imply the commodity. Hence, although identifying intangible flows to some extent, Say treats them as equivalent to commodities when reflected upon monetary flows. On the other hand, if intangible flows are not reflected on monetary flows, according to Say they could not be object of scientific economic research.

Thus, Say's theoretical proposal suffers from several inaccuracies demonstrated by intangible flow theory, which could already be found in Smith's system and are maintained in contemporary mainstream economics, for instance, the pseudo-phenomenon that the monetary flow creates/defines the commodity or that money could measure intangibility. Several of these pseudo-phenomena are necessary hold together a hedonist utilitarian theory of us humans and our societies. Following this moral philosophy, Say and countless mainstream economists afterwards neglect human-related intangible flows not reflect upon monetary flows but that however are vital for our survival and existence.

Notes

1 Earl of Lauderdale, and also referred to in writings as Lord Lauderdale or Lauderdale.
2 Backhouse (2002), Screpanti and Zamagni (2005), Hollander (1980), Lowenthal (1911), Meek (1967).
3 Hollander (1980).
4 Foxwell (1899).
5 Mill (1832, cited by Foxwell, 1899, p. lxxvi).
6 See previous chapter, Burkitt (1984, Chapter 3), King (1983), Lowenthal (1911), Ryan (1980) and Menger (1899).
7 Brue (2000), Backhouse (2002), Ekelund and Hébert (1997), Dupont (2017), Landreth and Collander (2001), Screpanti and Zamagni (2005).
8 Maitland (1804, p. 12).
9 Brue (2000), Backhouse (2002), Ekelund and Hébert (1997), Dupont (2017), Landreth and Collander (2001), Screpanti and Zamagni (2005).
10 Brue (2000), Screpanti and Zamagni (2005).
11 You may see, for instance, Robins (1932).
12 Father to the famous economist John Maynard Keynes. See Keynes (1899, 1999).
13 Samuelson (1947, 1983).
14 Idem.
15 As described by Brunner (1969) and Hausman (2018), Friedman's essay employ different meanings for the term "unrealistic."
16 Hausman (2018, 2008).
17 Leontief (1971), de Marchi (1970).
18 As several serious crises and collapses of countries, organizations, social groups and systems would demonstrate. Empirical evidence quite frequently rails against economic theories and assumptions (Hausman, 2018; de Marchi, 1970).
19 Backhouse (2010), Blaug (1980), Hausman (2018), Cross (1982), Popper (1967), Machlup (1969), Mongin (2006), de Marchi (1970).
20 de Marchi (1970), Blaug (1956).
21 Senior (1836, 1965, pp. 2–3).
22 Idem.
23 As explained earlier, Bentham was not this principle's first proponent.

24 Senior (1836, 1965, p. 26).
25 Idem.
26 Senior (1836, 1965, p. 7).
27 Senior (1836, 1965, pp. 3–4), see also Brue (2000, pp. 145–146) and Depoortère (2013).
28 Senior (1836, 1965, p. 3).
29 Blaug (1958), Brue (2000, pp. 145–146), Johnson (1969), Walker (1941). Maitland was also a bitter opponent of reducing working hours because according to him it would breach the principle that labor "ought to be free" (Walker, 1941, p. 173).
30 Brue (2000), Backhouse (2002), Ekelund and Hébert (1997), Dupont (2017), Landreth and Collander (2001), Screpanti and Zamagni (2005).
31 See, for instance, Mill (1848, 1920, p. 169, 1871a, p. 259).
32 See, for instance, Mill (1848, 1920, p. 176–185, 532, 1971a, p. 273).
33 For example, in his famous reasoning, Mill (1848, 1920, p. 164) claims that "The laws and conditions of the Production of Wealth partake of the character of physical truths. There is nothing optional or arbitrary in them. It is not so with the Distribution of Wealth. That is a matter of human institution solely. The things once there, mankind, individually or collectively, can do with them as they like. They can place them at the disposal of whomsoever they please, and on whatever terms. The Distribution of Wealth depends on the laws and customs of society." This is a theme to which we will return.
34 See, for instance, Mill (1848, 1920, 1871b, Book V).
35 Mill (1848, 1920, Book IV).
36 See, for instance, Mill (1848, 1920, pp. 170–176, 1871a, pp. 263–269).
37 Mill (1836, 2008, pp. 41–42).
38 Idem.
39 Mill (1836, 2008, p. 54).
40 Mill (1836, 2008).
41 Mill (1836, 2008, pp. 48–50).
42 Mill (1836, 2008, pp. 50–51): "the difficulty (not to say impossibility) of our being assured "a priori that we have taken into account all the material circumstances." J.S. Mill (1836, 2008, p. 57): "But this can seldom be done in the moral sciences, owing to the immense multitude of the influencing circumstances, and our very scanty means of varying the experiment."
43 Friedman (1953, 2008, p. 158).
44 Mill (1836, 2008, p. 46).
45 Mill (1836, 2008, p. 53).
46 Maitland (1804, p. 12).
47 Gehrke and Kurz (2001, pp. 449–450).
48 A position Say held also as a criticism to the methods employed by Ricardo. See Gehrke and Kurz (2001, p. 472) and Whatmore (1998).
49 Idem.
50 Say (1821, 1971, p. xxi).
51 Gehrke and Kurz (2001, p. 453) and Whatmore (1998).
52 See Say (1821, p. 285). To face the Napoleonic war against France, Britain also ceased the convertibility of money into precious metals. A matter that brought Ricardo along with Thornton to prominence in Britain was the defense of the return to full convertibility (Brue, 2000; Backhouse, 2002; Ekelund and Hébert, 1997; Dupont, 2017; Landreth and Collander, 2001; Screpanti and Zamagni, 2005).
53 Schoorl (2012), Jacoud (2017).
54 Menger (1899), Lindeman (1983).
55 Schoorl (2012).
56 Say (1821, p. xi).
57 Ricardo (1951–73) vol. VIII: 298–299, cited by Gehrke and Kurz (2001, p. 458). In Ricardo (1821, 1888, p. 154), a similar doubt is expressed: "M. Say, notwithstanding the corrections he has made in the fourth and last edition of his work, 'Traité d'Economie

Politique,' appears to me to have been singularly unfortunate in his definition of riches and value. He considers these two terms as synonymous, and that a man is rich in proportion as he increases the value of his possessions, and is enabled to command an abundance of commodities."

58 Idem and also letter to Malthus on 24 November 1820 (Ricardo, 1951–73, VIII: 301–2; cited by Gehrke and Kurz, 2001, p. 459).
59 For instance Gehrke and Kurz (2001, p. 467).
60 Gehrke and Kurz (2001, p. 476).
61 Say (1825, pp. 718–719), Gehrke and Kurz (2001, p. 476).
62 "David Ricardo in the third edition of his book, appears to be disenchanted that I did not adopt what he considers an important doctrine. It is precisely because I do not consider it important that I have not said anything about it. I only consider important what is useful and applicable" Say (1828–1829, 1852, V. II, p. 68). See also Gehrke and Kurz (2001, pp. 476–477).
63 "nonetheless privately fought some battles with him in the interest of truth" (Say, 1825, pp. 718–719).
64 Ricardo (1951–73, vol. VI: 247–248), cited by Gehrke and Kurz (2001, p. 452).
65 Ricardo (1821, 1888, p. 154).
66 Say (1821, p. 62).
67 See Maitland (1804, p. 56), Whately (1836, 1965, p. 229). Through this definition, Maitland tries to point a difference that he claims has escaped to Smith, namely, between public wealth and private wealth, where the latter is scarce to the individual.
68 Besides being scarce (Maitland, 1804, p. 12).
69 For instance, in Say (1821), Bentham is only mentioned in a general acknowledgment directed also to several others and a footnote involving taxes on p. 156.
70 Schoorl (2012).
71 Senior (1836, 1965, p. 6). Malthus may not have been as enthusiastic about the new meaning of utility as implied by Senior (Hollander, 1997, pp. 263–271).
72 Senior (1836, 1965, p. 13).
73 Malthus (1836, p. 58).
74 Idem.
75 "the word value used without adjunct" (Mill, 1848, 1920, p. 315).
76 Mill (1848, 1920, p. 314, see also p. 318).
77 Idem.
78 Senior (1836, 1965, pp. 13–14), White (1992).
79 Say (1821, p. 62).
80 Say (1821, p. 390). It reminds us of the famous postmodernist claim that the reader would be the writer.
81 Senior (1836, 1965, p. 54). As described bellow in the text, Senior is concerned with the idea in Say that consumption would be the destruction of utility, whereas for instance someone can live in a house without destroying its utility.
82 Senior (1836, 1965, pp. 53–54). To be more precise, Malthus described that population as the greatest source of consumption. An increase in population leads therefore to an increase in demand for an increase of produce. This increase in demand would lead to an increase in supply (Malthus, 1836, p. 216).
83 Mill (1871a, p. 66).
84 Say (1821, Book III), Senior (1836, 1965, pp. 53–56), Malthus (1836, p. 217), Mill (1871a, pp. 64–68). This distinction is not clear in Maitland.
85 "although the phenomena of the consumption of wealth are but the counterpart of its production, and although Dr. Smith's doctrine leads to its correct examination, he did not himself developed it; which precluded him from establishing numerous important truths. Thus, by not characterizing the two different kinds of consumption, namely, unproductive and reproductive, he does not satisfactorily demonstrate, that the consumption of values saved and accumulated in order to form capital, is as perfect as the consumption of values which are dissipated" Say (1821, pp. xIII–xllll).

86 Mill (1871a, pp. 37–53).
87 Mill (1871a, pp. 55–56).
88 Say (1821, pp. 392–393). Say was followed by McCullough in this definition (Senior, 1836, 1965, p. 54).
89 Say (1821, pp. 387–388). To Say, when an item is bought there is not loss of wealth, which occurs only when the item is consumed (Say, 1821, p. 393).
90 Say (1821, pp. 286–287), Gehrke and Kurz (2001), Whately (1836, 1965, p. 229).
91 Say (1821, p. 286).
92 Idem.
93 Idem.
94 Say (1821, pp. 119–123).
95 A similar definition also criticized by Malthus in Torrens (1821) and McCulloch (1864). See also Hollander (1997, pp. 263–271).
96 Malthus (1836, p. 47), Hollander (1997, pp. 263–271).
97 Idem.
98 "I should define wealth to be the material objects, necessary, useful, or agreeable to man, which are voluntarily appropriated by individuals, or nations" (Malthus, 1836, p. 48).
99 Senior (1836, 1965, pp. 51–53).
100 Idem.
101 Idem.
102 Idem.
103 Idem.
104 Mill was not entirely correct, as we humans have been able to add new elements to the periodic table.
105 Screpanti and Zamagni (2005).
106 Mill (1871a, pp. 58–60).
107 Idem.
108 Idem.
109 Brue (2000), Backhouse (2002), Bowley (2013), Ekelund and Hébert (1997), Dupont (2017), Gehrke and Kurz (2001), Hollander (1997, 2005), Jacoud (2017), Landreth and Collander (2001), Screpanti and Zamagni (2005). The theory of money is an instance where Say has praised David Ricardo (Gehrke and Kurz, 2001).
110 As often described by mainstream economists. See, for instance, Papademos and Modigliani (1990), Hoover (1988) or Humphrey (1991).
111 See two endnotes earlier.
112 Say (1821, p. 142), Jacoud (2017).
113 Maitland (1804, p. 264).
114 Senior (1840, p. 8). See also Senior (1830) and Bowley (2013).
115 Hollander (1997, pp. 558, 561).
116 Mill (1871b, pp. 17–19).
117 Humphrey (1991), Mill (1871b, pp. 36–72), Maitland (1829).
118 Say (1821, Book 2 Chapter 3), Senior (1836, pp. 11–14), Malthus (1836, pp. 58–61).
119 Say (1821, p. 65).
120 Or Austrian economists.
121 Torrens's capital theory of value is still derived from Smith's system tree factors of production. You may also see de Vivo (1996).
122 Once called the "*Bentham de Hallamshire*" (Elliott, 1876, p. 127).
123 de Vivo (2014).
124 It is possible that further research will demonstrate that this hedonist economic theory may have benefited from contributions from other writers. These writers were however part of the process in creating it.
125 Idea adapted from Menger (1899).
126 As explained in this chapter's introduction, although in moral philosophy J.S. Mill tried to present a version of qualitative hedonism (see Chapters 9 and 10), when addressing

political economy he has to large extent a quantitative hedonist approach, which is inspired in Bentham's writings.

127 Jackson (1991, 1998).
128 Say (1821, p. 119). To Say, land, for instance, of a park or a garden, can also produce an immaterial product (Say1821, p. 125).
129 Say (1821, p. 119, footnote).
130 As synonymous to intangible (Say, 1821, pp. 119, 123).
131 Idem.
132 Say (1821, pp. 119–127).
133 Idem.

References

Backhouse, R. (2002). *The Penguin History of Economics*. London: Penguin.

Backhouse, R. (2010). *The Puzzle of Modern Economics*. Cambridge: Cambridge University Press.

Bailey, S. (1825). *A Critical Dissertation on the Nature, Measures and Causes of Value, Chiefly in Reference to the Writings of Mr. Ricardo and His Followers*. London: R. Hunter.

Blaug, M. (1956). The empirical content of Ricardian economics. *Journal of Political Economy*, 64, 41–58.

Blaug, M. (1958). The classical economists and the factory acts – A re-examination. *The Quarterly Journal of Economics*, 72(2), 211–226.

Blaug, M. (1980, 1992). *The Methodology of Economics: Or How Economists Explain*. 2nd Edition. Cambridge: Cambridge University Press.

Bowley, M. (2013). *Nassau Senior and Classical Economics*. London: Routledge.

Brue, S. (2000). *The Evolution of Economic Thought*. Mason, OH: Thomson/South Western.

Brunner, K. (1969). 'Assumptions' and the cognitive quality of theories. *Synthese*, 20, 501–525.

Burkitt, B. (1984). *Radical Political Economy*. New York: New York University Press.

Cross, R. (1982). The Duhem-Quine Thesis, Lakatos and the appraisal of theories in macroeconomics. *Economic Journal*, 92, 320–340.

de Marchi, N. (1970). The empirical content and longevity of Ricardian economics. *Economica*, 37, 257–276.

Depoortère, C. (2013). William Nassau Senior and David Ricardo on the method of political economy. *Journal of the History of Economic Thought*, 35(1), 19–42.

de Vivo, G. (1996). Ricardo, Torrens, and Sraffa: A summing up. *Cambridge Journal of Economics*, 20(3), 387–391.

de Vivo, G. (2014). Samuel Bailey and the subversion of the classical theory of value: A note. *Contributions to Political Economy*, 33(1), 55–60.

Dupont, B. (2017). *The History of Economic Ideas: Economic Thought in Contemporary Context*. Oxon: Routledge.

Ekelund, R. and Hébert, R. (1997). *A History of Economic Theory and Method*. 4th Edition. New York: McGraw-Hill Companies.

Elliott, E. (1876). *The Poetical Works of Ebenezer Elliott*. Londres: King and Co.

Foxwell, H. (1899). Introduction and bibliography. In Menger, A. (Ed.) *The Right to the Whole Produce of Labour. The Origin and Development of the Theory of Labour's Claim to the Whole Product of Industry*. New York: Macmillan.

Friedman, M. (1953, 2008). The methodology of positive economics. In Hausman, D. (Ed.) *The Philosophy of Economics: An Anthology*. Cambridge: Cambridge University Press.

Gehrke, C. and Kurz, H. (2001). Say and Ricardo on value and distribution. *The European Journal of the History of Economic Thought*, 8(4), 449–486.

Hausman, D. (2008). Why look under the hood. In Hausman, D. (Ed.) *The Philosophy of Economics: An Anthology*. Cambridge: Cambridge University Press.

Hausman, D. (2018). Philosophy of economics. In Zalta, E. N. (Ed.) *The Stanford Encyclopedia of Philosophy*, Fall. Online at: https://plato.stanford.edu/archives/fall2018/entries/economics/.

Hollander, S. (1980). The post-Ricardian dissension: A case-study in economics and ideology. *Oxford Economic Papers*, 32(3), 370–410.

Hollander, S. (1997). *The Economics of Thomas Robert Malthus*. Toronto: University of Toronto Press.

Hollander, S. (2005). *Jean-Baptiste Say and the Classical Canon in Economics: The British Connection in French Classicism*. New York: Routledge.

Hoover, K. (1988). Money, prices and finance in the new monetary economics. *Oxford Economic Papers*, 40(1), 150–167.

Humphrey, T. M. (1991). Nonneutrality of money in classical monetary thought. *FRB Richmond Economic Review*, 77(2), 3–15.

Jacoud, G. (2017). Why is money important in Jean-Baptiste Say's analysis? *The European Journal of the History of Economic Thought*, 24(1), 58–79.

Jackson, W. (1991). On the treatment of population ageing in economic theory. *Ageing and Society*, 11(1), 59–61.

Jackson, W. (1998). *The Political Economy of Population Ageing*. Cheltenham: Edward Elgar.

Johnson, O. (1969). The "last hour" of senior and Marx. *History of Political Economy*, 1(2), 359–369.

Keynes, J. N. (1899, 1999). *The Scope and Method of Political Economy*. London: Batoche Books.

King, J. E. (1983). Utopian or scientific? A reconsideration of the Ricardian socialists. *History of Political Economy*, 15(3), 345–373.

Landreth, H. and Collander, D. (2001). *History of Economic Thought*. 4th Edition. Boston: Cengage Learning.

Leontief, W. (1971). Theoretical assumptions and non observed facts. *American Economic Review*, 61(1), 1–7.

Lindeman, A. (1983). *A History of European Socialism*. London: Yale University Press.

Lowenthal, E. (1911). *The Ricardian Socialists*. New York: Columbia University Press.

Machlup, F. (1969, 1978). Positive and normative economics. In Machlup, F. (Ed.) *Methodology of Economics and Other Social Sciences*. New York: Academic Press.

Maitland, J. [Earl of Lauderdale] (1804). *An Inquiry into the Nature and Origin of Public Wealth: And into the Means and Causes of its Increase*. Edinburgh: Archibald Constable and Co.

Maitland, J. [Earl of Lauderdale] (1829). *Three Letters to the Duke of Wellington on the Fourth Report of the Select Committee of the House of Commons, Appointed in 1828 to Enquire into the Public Income and Expenditure of the United Kingdom: In Which the Nature and Tendency of a Sinking Fund Is Investigated and the Fallacy of the Reasoning by Which it Has Been Recommended to Public Favour Is Explained.*

Malthus, R. (1836). *Principles of Political Economy*. London: W. Pickering.

Marshall, A. (1890). *Principles of Economics*. London: MacMilllan.

McCulloch, J. (1864). *The Principles of Political Economy, with Some Inquiries Respecting Their Application*. 5th Edition. Edinburgh: Adam and Charles Black.

Meek, R. (1967). *Economics and Ideology and Other Essays: Studies in the Development of Economic Thought*. London: Chapman and Hall.

Menger, A. (1899). *The Right to the Whole Produce of Labour. The Origin and Development of the Theory of Labour's Claim to the Whole Product of Industry*. New York: Macmillan.

Mill, J. S. (1836, 2008). On the definition and method of political economy. In Hausman, D. (Ed.) *The Philosophy of Economics: An Anthology*. Cambridge: Cambridge University Press.

Mill, J. S. (1848, 1920). *Principles of Political Economy with Some of Their Applications to Social Philosophy*. London: Longmans and Green and Co. Online. Mill, J. S. (1848). *Principles of Political Economy with Some of Their Applications to Social Philosophy*. London: Longmans and Green and Co.

Mill, J. S. (1871a). *Principles of Political Economy with Some of Their Applications to Social Philosophy*. Volume 1. 7th Edition. London: Longmans and Green, Reader and Dyer.

Mill, J. S. (1871b). *Principles of Political Economy with Some of Their Applications to Social Philosophy*. Volume 2. 7th Edition. London: Longmans, Green, Reader and Dyer.

Mongin, P. (2006). Value judgments and value neutrality in economics. *Economica*, 73(290), 257–286.

Papademos, L. and Modigliani, F. (1990). The supply of money and the control of nominal income. In Friedman, B. and Hahn, F. (Eds.) *Handbook of Monetary Economics*. Volume 1. Amsterdam: North-Holland/Elsevier.

Popper, K. (1967). La Rationalité et le Statut du Principe de Rationalité. In Classen, E. (Ed.) *Les Fondements Philosophiques des Systèmes Économiques*. Paris: Paypot, 142–150.

Ricardo, D. (1821, 1888). Principles of political economy and taxation. In McCulloch, J. (Ed.) *The Works of David Ricardo. With a Notice of the Life and Writings of the Author*. 3rd Edition. London: John Murray.

Ricardo, D. (1951–73). *The Works and Correspondence of David Ricardo*. Edited by P. Sraffa with the collaboration of M. H. Dobb, 11 vols. Cambridge: Cambridge University Press.

Robins, L. (1932). *An Essay on the Nature and Significance of Economic Science*. London: Macmillan.

Ryan, C. C. (1980). Socialist justice and the right to the labor product. *Political Theory*, 8(4), 503–524.

Samuelson, P. (1947, 1983). *Foundations of Economic Analysis*. Boston: Harvard University Press.

Say, J.-B. (1815, 1826). Catéchisme d'Économie Politique. In Say, J.-B. (Ed.) *OEuvres de Jean-Baptiste Say*. Volume 4. 3rd Edition. Paris: Publiée du vivant de l'auteur.

Say, J.-B. (1821, 1971). *A Treatise on Political Economy or The Production, Distribution and Consumption of Wealth*. New York: Augustus M. Kelley Publishers.

Say, J.-B. (1825). Examen critique du discours de M. MacCulloch sur l'économie politique, review of J.R. McCulloch: Discourse on the rise, progress, peculiar objects and importance of Political Economy. *Revue Encyclopédique*, 27, 694–719. Reprinted in Say (1848), 261–279.

Say, J.-B. (1828–1829, 1852). *Cours complet d'économie politique pratique*. 3rd Edition. Paris: Guillaumin.

Schoorl, E. (2012). *Jean-Baptiste Say: Revolutionary, Entrepreneur, Economist*. London. Routledge.

Screpanti, E. and Zamagni, S. (2005). *An Outline of the History of Economic Thought*. 2nd Edition. Oxford: Oxford University Press.

Senior, N. (1830). *Three Lectures on the Cost of Obtaining Money*. London: William Clowes.

Senior, N. (1836, 1965). *An Outline of the Science of Political Economy*. New York: Sentry Press.

Senior, N. (1840). *Three Lectures on the Value of Money*. Oxford: B. Fellowes.

Torrens, R. (1821). *An Essay on the Production of Wealth*. London: Longman, Hurst, Rees, Orme, and Brown.

Walker, K. (1941). The classical economists and the factory acts. *The Journal of Economic History*, 1(2), 168–177.

Whately, R. (1836, 1965). On certain terms which are peculiarly liable to be used ambiguously in Political Economy. Appendix in Senior, N. (Ed.) *An Outline of the Science of Political Economy*. New York: Sentry Press.

Whatmore, R. (1998). Everybody's business: Jean-Baptiste say's" general fact" conception of political economy. *History of Political Economy*, 30(3), 451.

White, M. V. (1992). Diamonds are forever(?): Nassau senior and utility theory. *The Manchester School*, 60: 64–78.

12 Hedonist theory of value, production and existence emerges

12.1 Introduction

Despite being originated in the 17th and 18th century in Europe, hedonist economic theory still endures in mainstream economics in the 21st century. The market in economics is a theoretical description that casts off devotion to quantitative hedonism. Obviously, there are many instances where products (outputs of production as defined by intangible flow theory) are exchanged by monetary flows. However, a relation between prices and quantities traded had been described much before Bentham's hedonist writings.[1]

In monetary societies, generally, lower prices imply that more humans may wish to buy and fewer to sell the priced products. Vice versa for higher prices. These relations are not applicable to all products. As Veblen[2] observed, a few luxury and status goods (e.g., sport cars, watches) bought by moneyed individuals increase trading with an increase in price. Other products, however, remain at similar trading levels despite small changes in prices (e.g., bread, water, basic products). Still, it is fair to say that most products observe a negative price-traded quantity relation.[3] Furthermore, we have seen that writers before Smith already noticed that an increase in the quantity of money in circulation could increase prices. For thousands of years when money was involved, such a price–quantity relation must have been known to persons who regularly participated in commodity trading[4] and who have profited from them.[5] Such relations must have been present in the ancient monetary societies of Athens or Rome.

Therefore, hedonist theory did not discover the relation between prices and quantities offered or demanded for trading. Nor is hedonist economic theory fundamentally concerned with how humans make monetary and product flows, from or to where. Hedonist economic theory's focus is placed upon the micro moment in which monetary flows establish trade, which hedonists claim also establishes hedonism (and the market parable). Smith's system already displayed the pseudo-phenomena that money would create/define other commodities. Through quantitative hedonism, money acquires a new attribute: to be the instrument for hedonist calculus. Actual production beyond monetary micro moments would be obscured as phenomena generally unworthy of investigation.

When studying the concept of market in economics in comparison to other social sciences, Jackson (2019) reviews important observations that are common at institutional,[6] geographic[7] and economic-sociology[8] research: Economics lacks basic understanding about institutional, spatial and social arrangements necessary for monetary transactions to function at a given society. For instance, governments, laws and judicial systems, money management procedures, organizations, territories, families, culture, and so on are omitted or treated as secondary. As Polanyi had discerned, the description of the market in economics appears (artificially) disembedded from the rest of society.[9] Moreover, mainstream economics pays scarce attention to how human life and existence are fundamentally dependent upon the biosphere.

Mainstream economists mostly ignore basic features that characterize/distinguish specific markets, such as location, participation, accessibility, pricing systems, information channels, transport and delivery systems, regulatory context or arbitration of conflicts among participants.[10] Likewise, social relationships beyond monetary flows are mostly discarded. In the few instances when any of these characteristics appear, generally they do as mere supplements that may interfere with supply and demand constructions. This lack of concern for contexts and characteristics is a manifestation of the allegory that the market represents to quantitative hedonism: to be the social mechanism of hedonist calculus. In hedonist markets, when someone buys products, he/she/they would be buying hedonist utility contained somewhere in the products. Any undue interference with markets (or money) would be an interference with the social mechanism of hedonism.

Hedonist theory presents the case for market self-regulation (*laissez-faire*), which should replace any other form of production, for instance, from governments but also from not-for-profit organizations or human communities. Work-based theories of production, value and existence do not present a similar defense of the self-regulating myth. Indeed, in labor theories, human work as well as nature and money are treated as a commodity. Yet, in hedonist theory, a commodity's purpose is specifically defined as generating pleasure and avoiding pain to final consumers or integrating hedonist utility into intermediate products and materials. The focus is once again at the micro moment when a monetary flow is traded by an element, but with an added quantitative hedonist emphasis.

Allegedly, markets would be self-regulated because they could compute hedonist calculus by themselves. Any intervention in monetary affairs and/ or beyond market operations would intrude a mystical hedonist equilibrium. As defining features, supply, representing production of hedonist utility, and demand, representing potential consumers with monetary means to buy hedonist utility, would match around hedonist calculus expressed in money. This theory is presented along with other hedonist theories, which serve as scapegoats when markets flagrantly fail, causing societal havoc, hunger, despair, social conflicts, diseases or even wars.

12.2 Drafting the hedonist theory of production, value and existence

12.2.1 Mystical hedonist supply and demand constructions

Mainstream economics' contemporary market representation is derived from hedonist supply and demand constructions in the market parable. Yet, the ambition of several heterodox economic critics is at most to add further components to that description, for instance, institutions, moral aspects or human behavioral phenomena. Nonetheless, the mainstream market representation entails a tautological explanation: Prices would explain values because prices are the value in so-called competitive markets. Supply and demand would match at the price, because the price would be the value. Hence, supply and demand would be some sort of mystical elements that both define and explain hedonist production, value and human existence. Money keeps being referred to as a measure for the intangible and definer of commodities, such as in work theories. As suggested by Bentham, nonetheless, a hedonist emphasis was added to make money the instrument for hedonist calculus.

Hedonist theory would have eliminated the separation between use and exchange value in Aristoteles and Smith.[11] Unless stated otherwise, the term value would apply to what could be exchanged. As explained by Senior, to things that can be *"lent or sold, hired or purchased."*[12] From this inner logic would result that human flows would be akin to commodities when somehow peripherally connected to monetary flows. Say did imply that there were elements with value for humans that could not be object of exchange (*"natural values"*). However, after some criticism from others, he would focus his *"scientific"* study of political economy on those elements that could be object of exchange (*"social values"*). Likewise, although Senior and Malthus admit a separation between commodities and services, in practical terms they treat the latter as akin to commodities in hedonist market contexts.

These writers' explanations are not exactly coincidental on the details but move alongside. To Maitland (1804), value would depend on commodities' (hedonist) utility and scarcity.[13] He introduced a version of the theoretical relation stating that the value of things would depend on the proportion between quantity and demand for them. However, hedonist utility would be the key element.[14] Yet, the price–quantity relation had already been known much before. Maitland cites Gregory King (1648–1712) as an authority aware of the price–quantity relation many years before him.[15] Likewise, Maitland exemplified individuals who had taken actions (long before his book) to benefit from this relation, for example, when Dutch merchants destroyed spiceries[16] or Virginia planters refrained from planting tobacco[17] to make it scarcer and thus increase prices and profits. Maitland's eventual contribution would be to add a hedonist explanation to a known price–quantity traded empirical relation.

Senior's formulations move along these lines. To him, value depends on three factors: hedonist utility, limitations in supply and transferableness.[18] The previous chapter described his definition of utility. Limitation in supply is a concept resembling scarcity in Maitland, for an element with unlimited supply would be rendered valueless for political economy.[19] Economists may also discuss where limitations in supply arise from.[20] By transferableness, Senior means: *"to express that all or some portion of its powers of giving pleasure, or preventing pain, are capable of being transferred, either absolutely, or for a period."*[21] He gives examples of what he considers utility that could only be partially transferred. One of those would be our personal qualities.[22] Another would be objects associated to *"peculiar mental associations, or adapted to the peculiar wants, of individuals,"*[23] for instance, a family's mansion one can put on the market without attaching the sentimental value of the generations of the same family who could have lived there.[24] Transferableness could be associated with property, as property can be transferred. In the same manner, Say associates the right of revenue with the right of property.[25]

As value was linked to monetary exchange, that is, by money, only hedonist utility that could be transferred (at least temporarily) would have (exchange) value. Thus, we are tautologically conducted to hedonist supply and demand as explainers of both value and prices. Demand cannot only represent consumption, for it must also comprehend (monetary) capacity to consume. Senior cites Mill to define demand: *"'A Demand,' says Mr. Mill, Political Economy, p. 23, 3d edition, 'means the will to purchase and the power of purchasing.'"*[26] On the other hand, on supply: *"In ordinary language, as well as in the writings of Political Economists, it is used to signify the quantity of a commodity actually brought to market."*[27] Willingness to bring commodities to market would outline limitations in supply. Similarly to Malthus:

> by the introduction of a medium of exchange and measure of value, a distinction has been made between buyers and sellers, the demand for any sort of commodities may be defined to be, the will of persons to purchase them, combined with their general means of purchasing; and supply, the quantity of the commodities for sale, combined with the desire to sell them.[28]

Following hedonist conceptions, Malthus refers to the buyer's monetary flow as a *"sacrifice"*[29] (as in hedonist pain) and demand as the will to make such a sacrifice.[30] Price would not be defined by supply alone or demand alone, but from the interactions between the two.

As explained by Malthus, Senior and Say,[31] costs are still considered as constraints when someone contemplates selling commodities. Higher costs than selling prices may make producers decide it would be better not to trade or produce those products. Likewise, as a consumer's sacrifice, prices higher than the expected hedonist utility would represent constraints. Potential consumers, who are restrained by monetary means, may prefer not to buy the commodities. Senior appears to hint at what later would be called the principle of marginal utility. He declares that utility diminishes with the quantity of a commodity consumers obtain: "*Not only are there limits to the pleasure which commodities of any given class can afford, but the pleasure diminishes in a rapidly increasing ratio long before those limits are reached.*"[32] This insight might have been shared by the others. For instance, Mill refers to a law of diminished returns from production from the soil on the application of labor and capital.[33] Similarly, these authors have clarified that an increase in costs or competition may reduce profitability and, thus, supply.

As explained by Say:

> The demand for all objects of pleasure, or utility, would be unlimited, did not the difficulty of attainment, or price, limit and circumscribe the supply. On the other hand, the supply would be infinite, were it not restricted by the same circumstance, the price, or difficulty of attainment: for there can be no doubt, that whatever is producible would then be produced in unlimited quantity, so long as it could find purchasers at any price at all. Demand and supply are the opposite extremes of the beam, whence depend the scales of dearness and cheapness; the price is the point of equilibrium, where the momentum of the one ceases, and that of the other begins. This is the meaning of the assertion, that, at a given time and place, the price of a commodity rises in proportion to the increase of the demand and the decrease of the supply, and vice versa; or in other words, that the rise of price is in direct ratio to the demand, and inverse ratio to the supply.[34]

Say further suggests forming aggregate supplies and demand to represent the entire national activity regarding wealth.[35] These aggregate hedonist supplies and demand can contemporarily be found in mainstream economics, as describing entire societies. Without demonstrating that we humans act according to hedonist theory, hedonist demand and supply constructions represent therefore mystical explanations intruding among previous known relations between prices and quantities traded.

12.2.2 Hedonist market constructions combined with a hedonist theory of money

The hedonist market parable is paired with a hedonist quantitative theory of money, introduced in the previous chapter. To attain hedonist equilibrium in hedonist calculus, money would need to be a neutral commodity (vis-à-vis quantity and velocity) in establishing exchange value,[36] which would be a relation between two values. Price would generally be the value in money (or precious metals).[37] Indeed, the pairing of these two theories offer hedonist writers an escape route. When hedonist calculus flagrantly fails (generating, for instance, chaos, crises, misery, diseases and even wars), hedonists can blame it on the intervention of governments, banks or other institutions for jeopardizing the neutrality of money required for hedonist calculus.[38] This rhetorical strategy is used with other excuses to justify flagrant market failures, for instance, monopolies which would be deemed as mere departures from hedonist equilibrium instead of arising from possible structural circumstances in production of certain products. As constructed, however, these paired hedonist theory of value and production and theory of money offer no avenues to be either confirmed or refuted, which could perhaps help explaining their longevity.

To these writers, these joint theories are clear-cut. Say explains that current prices in commercial dealings are understood as *"money valuations."*[39] However, he distinguishes two different price variations. Real variations would involve no equivalent variation in the object of exchange (that is, money or precious metals). For instance, they can result from competition out of producers or invention of a new machine for production that reduces production costs.[40] Relative variations arise from an alteration of the ratio of value of one particular commodity to other commodities and, in particular, the commodity used as object of exchange (money or precious metals).[41] Senior distinguishes between intrinsic and extrinsic causes of value. The former include *"The causes which give utility to a commodity and limit it in supply."*[42] On the latter: those that *"limit the supply and occasion the utility of the commodities for which it is to be exchanged* (generally money or precious metals), *may be called the extrinsic causes of its value.* Malthus adopts Senior's distinction between intrinsic and extrinsic causes of value[43] and suggests further characterizing intrinsic value. He distinguishes value in use as the intrinsic hedonist utility of the object. Nominal value in exchange would be the price. Intrinsic value in exchange would be the value that is not affected by extrinsic causes. The latter are described by Senior in relation to the means of exchange (money or precious metals): *"The estimation that any commodity is held at any place and time, determined in all cases by the state of the supply compared with the demand, and ordinarily by costs of production."*[44] This hedonist theory of money functions as an excuse set for any failings of the mystical hedonist supply and demand constructions in computing the pseudo-phenomena of hedonist calculus.

12.3 Mill addresses criticisms and heads hedonist theory to current mainstream economics

12.3.1 Mill (allegedly) dismisses criticisms against hedonist theory

As supply and demand constructions in the market parable would explain production, value and existence, what could prevent hedonist theory to turn political economy into a *science* of (hedonist) exchange? Indeed, that was the direction openly taken by two followers of Senior as Chair of Political Economy in Oxford. Richard Whately (1787–1863), who had been Senior's tutor and was his friend, suggested that economics should be denominated as *"catal-lactics"* or a science of exchange.[45] As Senior, he would approximately formulate what later would be called the difference between absolute and marginal utility (varying with quantity).[46] Whately later become Archbishop of Dublin. There, he found fellow writers to defend catallactics such as Samuel Longfield (1802–1884), who studied hedonist supply and demand intensity on prices.[47] Meanwhile, William Foster Lloyd (1795–1852) replaced Whately as Chair in Oxford and went further in defending economics as a science of exchange. He further formalized a principle of marginal utility.[48]

However, treatment of political economy as a science of exchange would leave the discipline feeble to many attacks. This modification would represent a substantial overhaul to the work-based systems advocated by Smith and Ricardo. No longer there would be a substantial concern with production and division of labor. Commodities would appear magically materialized in supply and demand constructions. What about the humans who do the hard work for production to occur and yet can live miserable lives? What about the poor? Mill (1848) would come to try and rescue political economy from its many critics. He employed a similar rhetorical strategy to the one he would employ later to defend the moral philosophy of hedonist utilitarianism from its many opponents: Here and there he accepts minor criticisms and pretends to engage with the critics. However, he refuses to admit that the discipline could ever be challenged. Allegedly, he could only find minor annoyances that could not divert hedonists from their formidable political economic theory.

Thereby, Mill accepts that those who had treated political economy as catal-latics, or a science of exchange, or those others who have treated it as a science of values may have gone too far.[49] The *"laws of production"* would be the same as they are if the arrangements of society did not depend on or admit exchange.[50] The laws of production would depend on labor and nature, which would provide not only materials but also powers such as *"air, heat, electricity, chemical agencies, and the other powers of nature employed by manufacturers."*[51] Indeed, Mill discussed models of society proposed by social relations writers. He calls them *"assailants of the principle of individual property,"*[52] even though some of them accepted individual property. He divides them into two groups termed as communists and socialists. The communism group would include those *"whose scheme implies absolute equality in the distribution of the physical means of life and enjoyment."*[53] Members would be Robert Owen and his followers, Louis Blanc and Etienne Cabet. The socialist group would include those *"who admit inequality, but grounded on some principle, or supposed principle, of justice or general expediency, and not, like so many of the existing social inequalities, dependent on accident alone."*[54] The second group did not defend complete abolition of private property, but that land and the instruments (means) of production should be the property, not of individuals, but of communities, of associations or of the government.[55] This second group was to include Saint-Simon and Charles Fourier.[56] Here we take Mill division at prima facie. We are just describing how he demises critics while pretending to engage with them.

Mill declares himself against the first type of scheme where private property would be completely abolished. Out of his conception of disutility of work, workers would not be motivated to work and would certainly evade their obligations.[57] However, Mill admits that the second scheme could be given "*opportunity of trial. They are all capable of being tried on a moderate scale, and at no risk, either personal or pecuniary, to any except those who try them.*"[58] Yet, he reinforces that these trials would be mere experiments:

> that the political economist, for a considerable time to come, will be chiefly concerned with the conditions of existence and progress belonging to a society founded on private property and individual competition; and that the object to be principally aimed at, in the present stage of human improvement, is not the subversion of the system of individual property, but the improvement of it, and the full participation of every member of the community in its benefits.[59]

Thus, while giving the impression to make small concessions to Saint-Simon, Fourier and their followers, Mill is advocating hedonist theory.

A similar strategy is used in defense of private property. Mill defines property as follows:

> when limited to its essential elements, [property] consists in the recognition, in each person, of a right to the exclusive disposal of what he or she have produced by their own exertions, or received either by gift or by fair agreement, without force or fraud, from those who produced it. The foundation of the whole is the right of producers to what they themselves have produced.[60]

Mill admits that customs and laws of society in defense of property can cause inequality.[61] An important part of his definition is that property cannot be transferred by force or fraud. However, he claims that property is related to production by own exertion. Yet, moneyed individuals can transfer their property to their sons, daughters and other family members or associates, without the latter having produced anything according to work theories of value. Aligning with other hedonist writers, as will see in the next chapter, part of Mill's argument is to use hedonism to claim that mere ownership of capital and land (means of production) are active parts of hedonist utility production. The other part of the argument is to do an elegant speech displaying sympathy for limiting heritage transfers among families, without however many concrete details.[62] In Book 4, Mill argues that the progress of the system of private property will tend to eliminate inequality and benefit the working poor.[63] That is, although apparently aligning with Smith and Ricardo in a concern that a monetary system would lead to a stationary state, Mill then claims that such a stationary state will greatly benefit the working poor somewhere in a distant future.[64] As shown, while appearing to criticize hedonist writers' excesses, J.S.

Mill actually provided a rhetorical defense for hedonist theory.[65] Notwithstanding the possibility of Mill praising elsewhere some partial support (or dilettantism) for alternative forms of economic production, Mill's quantitative hedonist approach underlies the many editions of his *Principles of Political Economy*.[66]

12.3.2 Mill presents hedonist supply and demand relation as that of an equation (contemporary mainstream economic form)

Mill headed hedonist theory into a format anticipating contemporary mainstream economics and its hyper mathematization. He clarified how hedonist supply and demand constructions would mathematically operate. As mentioned earlier, supply would be constrained by costs. Mill claims these costs would be what Smith and Ricardo would define as "*Natural Value (or its Natural Price)*."[67] Accordingly, competition among suppliers would lead prices of commodities to equate their costs. Hence, Mill insinuates that Smith and Ricardo were defending a hedonist theory of production, value and existence, which, of course, they never did.

On the other hand, demand, Mill argues, would also be constrained by the price–utility relation:

> As was pointed out in the last chapter, the utility of a thing in the estimation of the purchaser is the extreme limit of its exchange value: higher the value cannot ascend; peculiar circumstances are required to raise it so high.[68]

Thus, from here one could deduct that prices at marginal sales[69] could be equal to the alleged hedonist utility of consumers. When the price would be higher than such consumers' utility, no further business would be conducted. Resulting from competition, costs and utility would match in hedonist supply and demand. Furthermore, Mill made another important contribution to hedonist theory. As we have seen earlier, Maitland and Say among others proposed that the relation between supply and demand would be that of ratios. Instead, Mill would claim that the supply–demand relation would be that of an equation relating prices and quantities: "*the proper mathematical analogy is that of an equation*."[70]

Moreover, Mill suggested schedules of prices and quantities for these equations.[71] Thus, he roughly presented the same hedonist theory of production, value and existence we find in contemporary mainstream economics. However, apparently, he did not exhibit the famous diagrams representing supply and demand in markets, so popular in economics. Those diagrams would be presented at the turn of the century by Alfred Marshall, Francis Edgeworth and other neoclassical economists, who were described as also reacting to the excesses of marginalist economists of their day.[72] Indeed, perhaps with a certain exaggeration, Scott (2006, p. 85) claims that "*Marshall's key advance* (to social theory) *being the analysis of demand and supply through intersecting curves on a graph*."

12.4 Hedonist theory, *laissez-faire* and the self-regulating market myth

Although Maitland and Malthus helped developing prototypes of hedonist arguments and economic theory, they cannot be fully classified as earlier proponents to the self-regulating market myth. Maitland supposed that there could be underconsumption in markets, which would require government interventions.[73] Similarly, Malthus was unsure about leaving hedonist market constructions to their own devices. As we have seen earlier, Malthus was still in favor of some market regulations, especially if they could favor wealthy individuals whom he deemed as the center of economic activities, for instance, as in the Corn Laws. Malthus did not believe supply could create its own demand, as Say did. Malthus thought that in times of economic crises, government interventions could assist in settling things out and encouraging production. For his positions, sensibly a century later, Malthus would be praised by J.M. Keynes,[74] who also accepted several tenets from hedonist economic theory. Keynes's divergences have more to do with the conclusions that with the postulates.[75] However, Say, Senior and Mill can be identified as earlier proponents of the self-regulating market myth, which they derive from the hedonist market parable. This identification does not claim to be definitive and exhaustive. Further research might identify other earlier proponents of this myth.

As explained by Mill, "*laws of value and price*" to be generated out of the hedonist economic theory are those "*in which values and prices are determined by competition alone.*"[76] Mill admits exceptional cases.[77] However, competition would be the general rule: competition among sellers for trade and profits (for sellers would obtain hedonist utility through money generated) but also competition among buyers. Therefore, one could infer that only markets let alone to their devices could correctly attain *laws* of value and price. Mill summarizes this strange belief based on the market parable: "*value always adjusts itself in such a manner, that the demand is equal to the supply.*"[78]

Through this manner, hedonist theory recommends against market interventions. For instance, it recommends against government production, taxation, regulations, not-for-profit production, communal production outside markets, and any other form of intervention that could challenge the hedonist utopia. As noted earlier, this theory comes along with provisions for shifting blame elsewhere when it is empirically contradicted. For example, the price should identify (hedonist exchange) value in so-called competitive markets, but when prices do not, one could blame it on money in circulation or lack of competition, for instance, in the form of monopolies.[79] The value of money would also be associated with both the (hedonist) utility of the traded elements and to its own (hedonist) utility, which at that time was not a traditional claim in the quantitative theory of money. However, hedonist theory is generally little concerned with production of actual products. It deals with abstract buyers and sellers in the form of mathematical equations. Somehow, commodities magically materialize in hedonist market constructions.

With incidental discrepancies, we can find Say, Senior and Mill (and later their many followers) promoting the self-regulating market myth. As an accomplished advocate, let us observe Say's writings. He may have been inspired by previous French writers such as Vincent Gournay and the Physiocrats, who invoking different arguments had presented a case for nonintervention of governments in markets (and seem to have created the *laissez-faire* expression). Nonetheless, Say devised a complete rhetorical toolbox to be followed by future mainstream economists. Say understands that hedonist utility appraisal must be subjective:

> It would be out of place here to examine, whether or not the value man-
> kind attach to a thing be always proportionate to its actual utility. The
> accuracy of the estimate must depend upon the comparative judgment,
> intelligence, habits, and prejudices of those who make it.[80]

To the political economist, however, monetary prices could operate as estimative for the actual utility attributed to elements. Supposedly, unconstrained and unregulated markets would trade products by monetary flows near their hedonist utility value.

Say argues that:

> Although price is the measure of the value of things, and their value the
> measure of their utility, it would be absurd to draw the inference, that, by
> forcibly raising their price, their utility can be augmented. Exchangeable
> value, or price, is an index of the recognized utility of a thing, so long
> only as human dealings are exempt from every influence but that of the
> identical utility: in like manner as a barometer denotes the weight of the
> atmosphere, only while the mercury is submitted to the exclusive action
> of atmospheric gravity.[81]

Here we have a direct application of Bentham's advice regarding having money to measure pleasure and pain (hedonist calculus).[82] Say exemplifies phenomena that could raise prices without raising utility such as an "*authority grants to a particular class of merchants the exclusive privilege of carrying on a certain branch of trade*" or "*the value of the tax* [placed on a commodity] *that the government thinks fit to exact, for permitting its manufacture, transport, or consumption.*"[83] Likewise, Senior and Mill declare that monopolies affect the hedonist equilibrium that could be found in competitive markets, shifting the blame for obvious instances in which no hedonist equilibrium could be foreseen.[84]

Capturing the spirit of hedonist theory, Say declares that "*there is no actual production of wealth, without a creation or augmentation of* (hedonist) *utility.*"[85] Furthermore, "*current prices approximate to the real value of things, in proportion to the liberty of production and mutual dealing.*"[86] The utilitarian writers are far from having a simplistic view of money, in which a monetary price would imply utility appraisal. Research has started to identify the complexity and relevance of the monetary theories of Say, Senior and Mill, neglected for a long period.[87]

For instance, Say's position has been approximated to a quantitative theory of money, a rare instance in which he has praised David Ricardo.[88] Say treats money as a commodity[89] and to some extent as means of circulation.[90] He was concerned with monetary overissuance, the means used as money, or paper money used as symbol of values.[91] Moreover, he discussed the role of credit in production and prices, which in some cases could be beneficial.[92] Nonetheless, Say's quantitative theory of money was primarily hedonist.

These hedonist writers had no doubt in treating human work as a commodity. However, they were against considering work as the absolute measure of value, as argued by Smith and Ricardo.[93] Nonetheless, these hedonist writers did not intend that money could be considered an absolute measure of value,[94] but a *"relative measure of value"*:

> The utmost, therefore, that can be done is, merely to estimate or reckon the relative value of commodities; in other words, to declare, that at a given time and place, one commodity is worth more or less than another. . . . If this be all that is meant by the term, measure of value, admit that money is such a measure; but so, it should be observed, is every other divisible commodity, though not employed in the character of money.[95]

An advantage of money (and precious metals) would be because *"its value is more generally known, than that of other commodities."*[96] As suggested by Bentham, money would compute hedonistic calculus. Money was no longer to be considered as mere means of circulations to the real product and wealth of humans and nature. Money, as the tool for hedonist calculus, was to become the approximate measure of value and wealth.

Hedonist theory led Senior to suggest that one key *"cause of the productiveness of Labour"* was to be *"the absence of Government interference"* that could allow *"the degree of freedom with which he* [the worker] *is allowed to direct his industry."*[97] Senior can only understand the intervention of government in industry in the context of it being a *"necessary evil."*[98] Although Senior, Say and Mill can accept government intervention on the grounds of increasing hedonist utility through, for instance, education of the population or producing great infrastructures as bridges and dams unavailable through hedonist markets, they are generally against government interventions in production and exchange. Such interventions would undermine alleged equilibriums out of hedonist calculus and market constructions.[99] For instance, Mill declares himself in favor of *laissez-faire* (hence the self-regulating market myth), which he claims should be the general practice: *"every departure from it, unless required by some great good, is a certain evil."*[100] Mill admits exceptions to the general rule, but those tend to involve only government interventions (and to exclude, therefore, other forms of production such as not-for-profit production, communal production outside market contexts, or production not related to monetary flows). Moreover, those exceptions could only serve to confirm the general rule and his support for *laissez-faire*.[101]

To Mill, exceptions to *laissez-faire* where he could favorably view governmental interventions would include the following: cases in which the consumer is an incompetent judge of the commodity; education of the population; cases of persons exercising power over others as to protect, for instance, children and young persons or lower animals; cases of contracts in perpetuity; cases of delegated management; cases in which public intervention may be necessary to give effect to the wishes of the persons interested; cases of acts done for the benefit of others than the persons concerned, or colonization.[102] Indeed, Mill admits that government intervention may be necessary by default when private agency is not available even when private agency would be more suitable. However, according to him, were private enterprising to start being available, it must replace government interventions. Generally, unconstrained hedonist markets would address issues at stake better than any government (or form of production) could.[103] We have found, therefore, significant hedonist utilitarian writings supporting the self-regulating market myth, which can still be found in mainstream economics.

12.5 Hedonist supply and demand as occult science solving mysteries of the universe

As previously seen, some contemporaries to these hedonist writers understood that political economy was being transformed into an application of the moral philosophy of hedonist utilitarianism. Carlyle and his disciple Ruskin compared hedonist economics to a new religion and a fake science. For many observers at the time, political economy was becoming repulsive.[104] Among them, we could find romantic poets such as Samuel Taylor Coleridge, Robert Southey or William Wordsworth, who manifested their hostility towards hedonist economic theory.[105]

These specific writers can be connected to a broader movement that was occurring not just in Britain but throughout Europe, namely, Romanticism. While writers concerned with social relations of production and existence did often discuss potential new models for human society, some Romantics tended to be nostalgic of the past and support the restoration movement.[106] The traditional monarchic order over Europe was severely disturbed after the French Revolution. Quite a few Romantic writings were inclined to defend a return to old ways, bringing back traditional aristocratic privileges and an eventual reinstatement of feudalistic and slave-based systems. Carlyle, supported by Ruskin and others,[107] deemed economics a *"dismal science"* in a direct defense to slavery and feudalism.[108]

Romanticism was far from limited to economic affairs. It also involved the arts, philosophy and other scientific disciplines, which found support among aristocrats and religious bodies.[109] Some members of this movement would consider themselves as *"counter-revolutionaries"*[110] as in their antagonism to disruptive changes happening in Europe, for instance, with French Revolution effects, aimed equality of rights or new industries being formed. Nonetheless,

Romanticist movements would be connected to several nationalistic movements that would cause many tensions, conflicts and battlegrounds anticipating the next century Great Wars.[111]

Romantics have generally been described as against the new. Several of them tried to argue against reason, even defending that philosophers and scientists should reach conclusions through intuition and divine revelation.[112] As we have seen in Part 2, although this position could be anti-reason, it would not necessarily contradict several contemporary relativist positions that also campaign against science based on reason and logic. Accordingly, Romanticism would be just another paradigm, episteme or system of truth appealing to the adequate interpretative community. Still, one must be careful in using standards of our own time to compare past epochs. It has been suggested that in defending slavery and feudalism, Romantics were following Rousseau, who saw human beings as naturally good, only corrupted, wicked and miserable by civilization and ways of society.[113] From here, one could eventually infer that without the damage caused by civilization and society, naturally good humans would convey naturally good feudal and slave-based systems. However, it would be quite difficult to demonstrate that every Romantic writer held such view. Furthermore, our contemporary evidence demonstrates that many Romantic writers suggested benign views of slavery and feudalism that are empirically unsustainable.[114] However, lack of empirical support for the romantic view is not support for hedonist theory. Indeed, several Romantics have raised difficulties that have not yet been solved by mainstream economic theory, simply discarded or ignored, for instance, Carlyle's ironic proposition that as part of a religion, hedonist supply and demand could solve the mysteries of the universe.

Another important misgiving identified by Romantic writers was the fragility of the mystical hedonist money-commodity theory. Contrary to mainstream economists' claims, money could hardly function by itself without supporting institutions and societal structures. In the spirit of Romanticism, Adam Muller's (1779–1829) and Johann Gottlieb Fichte's (1762–1814) theories of money were undeniably nationalistic, for they aimed at enhancing German nationhood through the community-building power of monetary symbols.[115] However, those monetary theories referred to cultural, ethical and societal elements of money and to the dependence of money on states to function. Muller and Fichte were attentive to the importance of the non-neutral role of credit. They have even proposed the formalization of a central agency (termed as central banks) to supervise monetary affairs.[116] Because they were concerned with actual phenomena, it would be incorrect to dismiss Muller's and Fichte's monetary theories as simply metaphysical and/or empirically averse.[117] Curiously, we can find some of these themes in Polanyi[118] or in contemporary heterodox economic theories of money,[119] which are likewise ignored by mainstream economics.

In Marxism, a similar problem occurs regarding social relations of production writers. Marx and Engels would claim to have the one true scientific socialism. Hence, they advocate discarding previous social relations of productions as mere romantics or utopians. However, several writers have anticipated many concepts in Marx and Engels. Moreover, they addressed important issues that were ignored both by Marxism and mainstream economics. For instance, Sismondi, who displayed perils of the factory systems, would later be dismissed as a Romantic socialist by Marx's followers.[120] Indeed, Sismondi suggested the agriculturally based economy as a good model for the industrial sector to follow.[121] However, Sismondi was concerned with the human condition and the difficult effects industrialization was having on the working poor.[122] He travelled over Europe and directly testified to many a factory worker's miserable livelihood and how easily they could be replaced by machinery.[123]

Furthermore, Sismondi understood part of the transformation being implanted in political economy.[124] He understood that the focus on chrematistics being advocated by hedonists, and later disguised by Mill, was a reorientation of political economy's focus from humankind to wealth.[125] Sismondi actually identified the term chrematistics (Chrématistique) in Aristoteles to represent the nonnatural use of money (for one's enrichment and self-fruition), hence, to represent an abandonment of the focus in human toil and existence in work-based theories.[126] Thus, Sismondi warned that political economy was being transformed into an "*occult science*," losing contact with facts for the purpose of better calculation of chrematistic theories.[127]

Sismondi also understood that production involves transfers over time lags.[128] Therefore, production could not be represented solely by chrematistics hedonist markets (parable), which as noted before are micro moments where monetary flows occur. As did Polanyi, Sismondi advocated that markets and competition if abandoned to themselves would cause societal havoc. An interventionist state would be recommended to protect the working poor in old age or in sickness or to assure education for the population. These proposals have anticipated governmental functions that would be recurrent in many countries in the following century. Moreover, Sismondi advocated innovative schemes at the time, such as having workers participating in profits, minimum wage or restricting the maximum daily working hours.[129]

Yet, Sismondi fell upon a similar error as the Romantics. Undeniably, he noted that hedonist writers supported the factory system and mass production. Logically, thus, the monetary benefits flowing to means of production owners: "*chrematistic school utters cheering cries of admiration*" when a factory can massify production, "*but what a strange forgetfulness of humankind never to enquire what becomes of the man which the great factory has displaced.*"[130] However, It would be just a short misstep to allow considering that because hedonist writers supported means of production owners, factory systems and mass production, the hedonist writers could understand them or that they could understood the Industrial Revolution going along. Unfortunately, this error persists until today, namely, to suppose that because mainstream economics supports monetary societies, and moneyed individuals, it could somehow understand and thus adequately explain them. That is, mainstream economics could understand production, value, existence or money. Hedonist economic theory can explain none of that.

Notes

1 Evans (1967) suggests that Gregory King or Charles Davenant arrived first at this definition by the end of the 16th century.
2 Veblen (1899), Bagwell and Bernheim (1996), Trigg (2001).
3 Which does not mean that sellers automatically reduce prices when fewer people buy from them.
4 For instance, Ricardo himself a stock trader, had in view the effects of tariffs on prices when discussing Corn Laws.
5 These phenomena, Aristoteles would call a nonnatural use of money to the aim of getting richer.
6 See, for instance, Chavance (2008), Commons (1936), Hodgson (2000), Rutherford (2001).
7 See, for instance, Clark et al. (2018), Peck, Sheppard, and Tickell (2004).
8 See, for instance, Smelser and Swedberg (2010).
9 Polanyi (1944, 2001). See Book 1.
10 Jackson (2019, pp. 6–11).
11 Later, Karl Marx will again allude to the difference between use and exchange value.
12 Senior (1836, 1965, p. 13).
13 Maitland (1804, p. 12).
14 Maitland (1804, p. 13).
15 Maitland (1804, p. 51) cites: "Gregory King's Calculation, published by Davenant." See also Evans (1967, p. 485).
16 Maitland (1804, p. 54).
17 Maitland (1804, p. 55).
18 Senior (1836, 1965, pp. 6–8).
19 For instance: "The water in a river is in general more than sufficient for all the domestic purposes for which it can be required; nobody pays therefore for permission to take a bucketfull: but it is seldom sufficient for all those who may wish to turn their mills with it; they pay, therefore for that privilege" Senior (1836, 1965, p. 7).
20 Senior (1836, 1965, pp. 6–8).
21 Senior (1836, 1965, p. 8).
22 Senior (1836, 1965, p. 9).
23 Idem.
24 Evidently, not everyone has grown up in a mansion.
25 Say (1821, pp. 292–294).
26 Senior (1836, 1965, p. 15). Smith also considered will and the means to buy to be effectual demand.
27 Idem.
28 Malthus (1836, p. 65).
29 Malthus (1836, p. 68).
30 Malthus (1836, p. 69) explains why Ricardo had a different concept of demand, while in specific cases such as monopolies or temporary prices could accept Maitland's understanding.
31 Say (1821, Book 2, Chapter 1), Senior (1836, 1965, pp. 16–20), Malthus (1836, pp. 64–70).
32 Senior (1836, 1965, pp. 11–12), Screpanti and Zamagni (2005, p. 103). Likewise, Senior declares to be one of the four elementary propositions of the science of political economy the marginal productivity of labor in agriculture: "That, agricultural skill remaining the same, additional Labour employed on the land within a given district produces in general a less proportionate return, or, in other words, that though, with every increase of the labour bestowed, the aggregate return is increased, the increase of the return is not in proportion to the increase of the labour" Senior (1836, 1965, p. 26).
33 Mill (1871a, pp. 220–236).

34 Say (1821, p. 293).
35 Say (1821, pp. 304–305 footnote). In this claim, Say argues to be correcting Maitland, Malthus and Sismondi.
36 Idem.
37 These authors extraordinarily agree with Ricardo in recommending full convertibility of paper money in precious metals. See, for instance, Say (1821, Book 2 Chapter 3), Senior (1836, 1965, pp. 11–14), Malthus (1836, pp. 58–61). They fail, however, to explain where the value of precious metals comes about.
38 In reference to relativists Lakatos (1978) and Duhem (1951), Kukla (2000, p. 80) refers to *Duhemian manouvre* as a defense used by the proponents of a theory who when faced with contradictory evidence attempt to shift the blame to an auxiliary hypothesis and theories. Relativists, however, have no solution in sight.
39 Say (1821, p. 288).
40 Say (1821, pp. 301–304).
41 Say (1821, p. 307).
42 Senior (1836, 1965, p. 16).
43 Malthus (1836, p. 62).
44 Malthus (1836, p. 64).
45 Whately (1831), Levy and Peart (2010), Screpanti and Zamagni (2005, pp. 103–104).
46 Idem.
47 Longfield (1833), Levy and Peart (2010), Moss (1976), Screpanti and Zamagni (2005, pp. 103–104).
48 Lloyd (1834); Levy and Peart (2010), Screpanti and Zamagni (2005, pp. 103–104).
49 Mill (1848, p. 313).
50 Idem.
51 Mill (1848a, pp. 30–33).
52 Mill (1848, p. 188).
53 Idem.
54 Mill (1848, pp. 188–189).
55 Idem. The concept of the means of production was well known before Karl Marx. Likewise, Senior (1836, 1965, p. 26) states as an elemental principle of political economy: "That the Powers of Labour, and of the other Instruments which Produce Wealth, may be indefinitely increased by using their products as the means of further production."
56 Mill (1848, pp. 188–189). Note also that Mill's definitions of communism and socialism are far from consensual.
57 Mill (1848, Book 2, Chapter 1).
58 Mill (1848, p. 175).
59 Idem.
60 Idem.
61 Mill (1848, pp. 164–165).
62 Mill (1848, Book 2, Chapter 2, and Book 5, Chapter 9). Essentially, Mill contests the system of primogenity where the older son would have preference in receiving the heritage. Still, he does not seem to foresee a great change in heritage law in the immediate future: "The laws of inheritance, however, have probably several phases of improvement to go through, before ideas so far removed from present modes of thinking will be taken" Mill (1848, p. 623).
63 See Mill (1848, Book 4 and 5).
64 Idem.
65 "In the meantime we may, without attempting to limit the ultimate capabilities of human nature, affirm, that the political economist, for a considerable time to come, will be chiefly concerned with the conditions of existence and progress belonging to a society founded on private property and individual competition; and that the object to be principally aimed at, in the present stage of human improvement, is not the subversion of the system of individual property, but the improvement of it, and the full participation of every member of the community in its benefits." Mill (1848, p. 175).

66 Mill (1848, 1871a, 1871b).
67 Mill (1848, p. 325).
68 Mill (1848, p. 318).
69 That is, the minimal price that a sale of a product can be made at.
70 Mill (1848, p. 322). He may have been inspired by De Quincey (1844, 1859) in referring to the relation of supply and demand as that of an equation because Mill (1848, Book 3, Chapter 2) cites De Quincey's treatment of difficulty of attainment and utility as mathematical variables D and U. See, for instance, Groenewegen (2002).
71 Mill discussed two extreme cases where at one extreme would be goods that are absolutely limited in quantity (e.g., a work of art) and at the other things that could have unlimited supply without altering relative cost. However, most goods would be somewhere amid the middle of these two extremes. They would not be limited in quantity, but an increase in production could increase costs (Brue, 2000; Backhouse, 2002; Ekelund and Hébert, 1997; Dupont, 2017; Landreth and Collander, 2001; Mill, 1848, 1871a; Screpanti and Zamagni, 2005).
72 Idem.
73 Maitland (1804, 1819), Mann (1959).
74 Baumol (1999, 1977), Brue (2000), Jonsson (1995), Thweatt (1979).
75 Backhouse (2002), Brue (2000), Screpanti and Zamagni (2005), Togati (2019).
76 Mill (1871a, p. 542).
77 Mill admits special cases to the rule of competition setting prices, such as those that have absolute limitation in supply (for instance, ancient sculptures or pictures, Mill, 1871a, pp. 546–547) or commodities with potential infinite supply because they would be susceptible to multiplication without increase in costs (Mill, 1871a, p. 555) or a special case which is intermediate between the previous two: "There are commodities which can be multiplied to an indefinite extent by labour and expenditure, but not by a fixed amount of labour and expenditure. Only a limited quantity can be produced at a given cost" (Mill, 1871a, pp. 547–548). An example is agricultural produce that would require containing the population and paying the rent (idem). Or "all kinds of raw material extracted from the interior of the earth metal, coals, precious stones, etc., are obtained from mines differing considerably in fertility, that is, yielding very different quantities of the product to the same quantity of labour and capital" (Mill, 1871a, pp. 605–606). Or fisheries (Mill, 1871a, pp. 583–584). Or patents and exclusive privileges that would operate similarly to rents (Mill, 1981a, p. 586). Otherwise, for the common commodity, the rule of competition based upon hedonist supply and demand would apply.
78 Mill (1871a, p. 588).
79 See, for instance, Mill (1871a, pp. 539–541).
80 Say (1821, p. 65, footnote).
81 Say (1821, pp. 65–66).
82 Previously, we saw that Bentham recommended money to measure pleasure and pain, as the "thermometer" measures the temperature and the "barometer" the pressure of air.
83 Say (1821, pp. 65–66).
84 Senior (1836, 1965, pp. 103–114), Mill (1848, pp. 407–410). Furthermore, Mill (1848, Book 3, Chapter 16) observes other *"peculiar cases of value"* where exchange value might not match an hedonist equilibrium as the cases of joint produced commodities, articles that can be produced infinitely at the same costs, and articles that can be produced infinitely but not at the same costs. In the two latter cases, value would be determined by costs instead of hedonist equilibrium.
85 Say (1821, p. 66).
86 Say (1821, p. 66, footnote).
87 Bowley (2013), Forget (1999), Glasner (2000), Kates (2018), Jacoud (2017), Skaggs (1994), Tiran (2006).
88 Say (1815, 1826, 1821, 1828), Gehrke and Kurz (2001), Jacoud (2017), Tiran (2006).
89 Idem.
90 Idem.

91 Idem.

92 Idem.

93 "Labour, like commodities, may vary in the supply and demand; and its value, like value in general is determined by the mutual accord of the adverse interests of buyer and seller, and fluctuates accordingly" (Say, 1821, p. 245). He presents further reasons to not consider labor as an invariable measure of value, such as being "affected materially by its quality. The labour of a strong and intelligent person is worth much more than that of a weak and ignorant one. Again, labour is more valuable in a thriving community, where there is a lively demand for it, than in a country overloaded with population. . . . Labour is probably one of the most fluctuating of valuer, because at times it is in great request, and at others is offered with that distressing importunity occasionally witnessed in cities where industry is on the decline" (idem).

94 "There is, in fact, no such thing as a[an absolute] measure of value, because there is nothing possessed of the indispensable requisite, invariability of value" (Say (1821, p. 245).

95 Say (1821, p. 243).

96 Say (1821, p. 247).

97 Senior (1836, 1965, pp. 176–180).

98 Idem.

99 See, for instance, Mill (1848, Book 5) and Say (Book 3, Chapters 6 and 7).

100 Mill (1871b, pp. 572–573).

101 Mill (1871b, Book 5).

102 Mill (1871b, pp. 576–605).

103 Mill (1871b, pp. 606–610).

104 Bronk (2009), Fulford (2001), Lowy and Sayre (2002), Mann (1958), Waterman (1991, 2003).

105 Cook (2018), Connell (2005), Waterman (2003), Mann (1958). The novelist Charles Dickens might to some extent have been partially influenced by them (idem).

106 Connell (2005), Ferber (2010), Honour (1979), Mann (1958), Remond (2014).

107 Groenewegen (2001), Levy (2001), Waterman (2003).

108 In comparison to a "*gay science*" he would suggest. Evidently, the word gay has been used by Carlyle to have a different meaning than our contemporary use. He used the expression gay science to imply a joyful science in comparison to a dismal science represented by economics: "Not a 'gay science,' I should say, like some we have heard of; no, a dreary, desolate, and indeed quite abject and distressing one; what we might call, by way of eminence, the dismal science" (Carlyle, 1849, 1888, vol. 7, pp. 83–84).

109 Ferber (2010), Honour (1979), Mann (1958).

110 Mann (1958, p. 336).

111 Ferber (2010), Honour (1979), Mann (1958), Remond (2014).

112 Ferber (2010), Honour (1979), Mann (1958), Remond (2014), Waterman (2003).

113 Lovejoy (1941), Mann (1958, p. 337), Waterman (2003, p. 93).

114 Fain (1943), Groenewegen (2001), Henderson (2000), Spencer (2009).

115 Mann (1958), Gray (2003, 2018).

116 Idem.

117 Idem.

118 See Parts 1 and 2.

119 See, for instance, Ingham (2013), Lawson (2016), Peacock (2017), Skidelsky (2018).

120 Anikin (1975, p. 286), Lenin (1960, p. 220), Stewart (1984).

121 Lutz (2002), Sismondi (1819), Sowell (1972), Spiegel (1971), Stewart (1984).

122 Idem.

123 Idem.

124 Sismondi (1819), Sowell (1972), Stewart (1984).

125 Stewart (1984).

126 Sismondi (1819, pp. 8–9): "Aristote, dans le premier livre de son Traité de la République a consacré quatre ou cinq chapitres (VIII à XIII) à la science qui nous occupe; il

lui donne même un nom plus propre à la désigner que celui que nous avons adopté: (Chrématistique, gr χρηματιστικη), la Science des Richesses."
127 "humanity should be on guard against all generalization of ideas that causes us to lose sight of the facts. . . . There is perhaps no manner of reasoning that exposes itself to more errors than that which consists of constructing a hypothetical world entirely different from the real world for the purpose of applying one's calculations" (Sismondi, 1827, cited by Adams and Brock, 1994 p. 125).
128 Barucci (1975), Sismondi (1819), Sowell (1972), Stewart (1984).
129 Barucci (1975), Sismondi (1819), Sowell (1972), Spiegel (1971), Stewart (1984).
130 Sismondi (1847) cited by Stewart (1984, p. 231).

References

Adams, W. and Brock, J. (1994). Economic theory: Rhetoric, reality, rationalization. In Babe, R. (Ed.) *Information and Communication in Economics*. New York: Springer.

Anikin, A. (1975). *Science in Its Youth*. Moscow: Progress Publishers.

Backhouse, R. (2002). *The Penguin History of Economics*. London: Penguin.

Bagwell, L. and Bernheim, B. (1996). Veblen effects in a theory of conspicuous consumption. *American Economic Review*, 86(3), 349–373.

Barucci, P. (1975). Sismondi revisited. *Rivista internazionale di scienze economiche e commerciali*, 22(10), 977–992.

Baumol, W. J. (1977). Say's (at least) eight laws, or What Say may really have meant. *Economica*, 44, 145–162.

Baumol, W. J. (1999). Retrospectives: Say's law. *Journal of Economic Perspectives*, 13(1), 195–204.

Bowley, M. (2013). *Nassau Senior and Classical Economics*. Oxon: Routledge.

Bronk, R. (2009). *The Romantic Economist: Imagination in Economics*. Cambridge: Cambridge University Press.

Brue, S. (2000). *The Evolution of Economic Thought*. Mason, OH: Thomson/South Western.

Carlyle, T. (1849, 1888). The nigger question. In Carlyle, T. (Ed.) *Miscellaneous Essays*. Volume 7. London: Chapman and Hall.

Chavance, B. (2008). *Institutional Economics*. Oxon: Routledge.

Clark, G. L., Feldman, M. P., Gertler, M. S. and Wójcik, D. (Eds.) (2018). *The New Oxford Handbook of Economic Geography*. Oxford: Oxford University Press.

Cook, P. (2018). *The Romantic Legacy of Charles Dickens*. Cambridge: Macmillan.

Commons, J. (1936). Institutional economics. *The American Economic Review*, 26(1), 237–249.

Connell, P. (2005). *Romanticism, Economics and the Question of Culture*. Oxford: Oxford University Press.

De Quincey, T. (1844, 1859). The logic of political economy. In De Quincey, T. (Ed.) *The Logic of Political Economy and Other Papers*. Boston: Ticknor and Fields.

Duhem, P. (1951). *The Aim and Structure of Physical Theory*. Princeton, NJ: Princeton University Press.

Dupont, B. (2017). *The History of Economic Ideas: Economic Thought in Contemporary Context*. Oxon: Routledge.

Ekelund, R. and Hébert, R. (1997). *A History of Economic Theory and Method*. 4th Edition. New York. McGraw-Hill Companies.

Evans, G. (1967). The law of demand – The roles of Gregory King and Charles Davenant. *Quarterly Journal of Economics*, 81(3), 483–492.

Fain, J. T. (1943). Ruskin and the orthodox political economists. *Southern Economic Journal*, 1–13.

Ferber, M. (2010). *Romanticism: A Very Short Introduction*. Oxford: Oxford University Press.

Forget, E. (1999). *The Social Economics of Jean-Baptiste Say*. London: Routledge.

Fulford, T. (2001). Apocalyptic economics and prophetic politics: Radical and romantic responses to Malthus and burke. *Studies in Romanticism*, 40(3), 345–368.

Gehrke, C. and Kurz, H. (2001). Say and Ricardo on value and distribution. *European Journal of the History of Economic Thought*, 8(4), 449–486.

Glasner, D. (2000). Classical monetary theory and the quantity theory. *History of Political Economy*, 32(1), 39–59.

Gray, R. (2003). Economic romanticism: Monetary nationalism in Johann Gottlieb Fichte and Adam Müller. *Eighteenth-Century Studies*, 36(4), 535–557.

Gray, R. (2018). *Money Matters: Economics and the German Cultural Imagination, 1770–1850*. Washington, DC: University of Washington Press.

Groenewegen, P. (2001). Thomas Carlyle, 'the dismal science', and the contemporary political economy of slavery. *History of Economics Review*, 34(1), 74–94.

Groenewegen, P. (2002). Thomas De Quincey: 'Faithful disciple of Ricardo'? In Groenewegen, P. (Ed.) *Classics and Moderns in Economics*. Volume 1. Oxon: Routledge.

Henderson, W. (2000). *John Ruskin's Political Economy*. London: Routledge.

Hodgson, G. (2000). What is the essence of institutional economics? *Journal of Economic Issues*, 34(2), 317–329.

Honour, H. (1979). *Romanticism*. London: Allen Lane.

Ingham, G. (2013). *The Nature of Money*. Cambridge: Polity Press.

Jackson, W. (2019). *Markets: Perspectives from Economic and Social Theory*. Oxon: Routledge.

Jacoud, G. (2017). Why is money important in Jean-Baptiste Say's analysis? *European Journal of the History of Economic Thought*, 24(1), 58–79.

Jonsson, P. (1995). On the economics of Say and Keynes' interpretation of Say's law. *Eastern Economic Journal*, 21(2), 147–155.

Kates, S. (2018). Making sense of classical theory. *Journal of the History of Economic Thought*, 40(2), 279–283.

Kukla, A. (2000). *Social Constructivism and the Philosophy of Science*. Oxon: Routledge.

Lakatos, I. (1978). *The Methodology of Scientific Research Programmes*. Cambridge: Cambridge University Press.

Landreth, H. and Collander, D. (2001). *History of Economic Thought*. 4th Edition. Boston: Cengage Learning.

Lawson, T. (2016). Social positioning and the nature of money. *Cambridge Journal of Economics*, 40(4), 961–996.

Lenin, V. (1960). *Collected Works. Volume 2: 1895–1897*. London: Ed Conroy Bookseller.

Levy, D. (2001). How the dismal science got its name: Debating racial quackery. *Journal of the History of Economic Thought*, 23(1), 5–35.

Levy, D. and Peart, S. J. (2010). Richard Whately and the gospel of transparency. *American Journal of Economics and Sociology*, 69(1), 166–187.

Lloyd, W. F. (1834). *A Lecture on the Notion of Value: As Distinguishable not Only from Utility, but also from Value in Exchange: Delivered Before the University of Oxford, in Michaelmas Term 1833*. London: Roake and Varty.

Longfield, S. M. (1833). *Lectures on Political Economy Delivered in Trinity and Michaelmas Terms*. Dublin: Richard Milliken and Son.

Lovejoy, A. (1941). The meaning of romanticism in the history of ideas. *Journal of the History of Ideas*, 2(2), 257–278.

Lowy, M. and Sayre, R. (2002). *Romanticism Against the Tide of Modernity*. Durham: Duke University Press.

Lutz, M. (2002). *Economics for the Common Good: Two Centuries of Economic Thought in the Humanist Tradition*. Oxon: Routledge.

Mann, F. (1958). The romantic reaction. *Journal of Economics*, 18(3), 335–357.

Mann, M. (1959). Lord Lauderdale: Underconsumptionist and Keynesian Predecessor. *Social Science*, 34(3), 153–162.

Maitland, J. [Earl of Lauderdale] (1804). *An Inquiry into the Nature and Origin of Public Wealth: And into the Means and Causes of Its Increase*. Edinburgh: Archibald Constable and Co.

Maitland, J. [Earl of Lauderdale] (1819). *An Inquiry into the Nature and Origin of Public Wealth: And into the Means and Causes of Its Increase*. 2nd Edition. Edinburgh: Archibald Constable and Co.

Malthus, R. (1836). *Principles of Political Economy*. London: W. Pickering.

Mill, J. S. (1948a). *Essays on Some Unsettled Questions of Political Economy*. London: London School of Economics.

Mill, J. S. (1848b, 1820). *Principles of Political Economy with Some of Their Applications to Social Philosophy*. London: Longmans and Green and Co. Online. Mill, J. S. (1848). *Principles of Political Economy with Some of Their Applications to Social Philosophy*. London: Longmans and Green and Co.

Mill, J. S. (1871a). *Principles of Political Economy with Some of Their Applications to Social Philosophy*. Volume 1. 7th Edition. London: Longmans and Green, Reader and Dyer.

Mill, J. S. (1871b). *Principles of Political Economy with Some of Their Applications to Social Philosophy*. Volume 2. 7th Edition. London: Longmans, Green, Reader and Dyer.

Moss, L. (1976). *Mountifort Longfield: Ireland's First Professor of Political Economy*. Ottawa: Green Field.

Peacock, M. (2017). The ontology of money. *Cambridge Journal of Economics*, 41(5), 1471–1487.

Peck, J., Sheppard, E. and Tickell, A. (Eds.) (2004). *Reading Economic Geography*. Oxford: Basil-Blackwell.

Polanyi, K. (1944, 2001). *The Great Transformation: The Political and Economic Origins of Our Time*. Boston: Beacon Press.

Remond, R. (2014). *Le XIX Siécle 1815–1914: Introduction à l'histoire de notre temps*. Paris: Points.

Rutherford, M. (2001). Institutional economics: Then and now. *Journal of Economic Perspectives*, 15(3), 173–194.

Say, J.-B. (1815, 1826). Catéchisme d'Économie Politique. In Say, J.-B. (Ed.) *OEuvres de Jean-Baptiste Say*. Volume 4. 3rd Edition. Paris: Publiée du vivant de l'auteur.

Say, J.-B. (1821, 1971). *A Treatise on Political Economy or The Production, Distribution and Consumption of Wealth*. New York: Augustus M. Kelley Publishers.

Say, J.-B. (1828–1829, 1852). *Cours complet d'économie politique pratique*. 3rd Edition. Paris: Guillaumin.

Scott, J. (2006). *Social Theory: Central Issues in Sociology*. London: Sage.

Screpanti, E. and Zamagni, S. (2005). *An Outline of the History of Economic Thought*. 2nd Edition. Oxford: Oxford University Press.

Senior, N. (1836, 1965). *An Outline of the Science of Political Economy*. New York: Sentry Press.

Skaggs, N. (1994). The place of JS Mill in the development of British monetary orthodoxy. *History of Political Economy*, 26(4), 539–567.

Skidelsky, R. (2018). *Money and Government: A Challenge to Mainstream Economics*. Milton Keynes: Penguin.

Sismondi, J. (1819). *Nouveaux príncipes D'economie politique, Ou De la richesse dans ses Rapports avec la population*. Paris: Delaunay.

Smelser, N. and Swedberg, R. (Eds.) (2010). *The Handbook of Economic Sociology*. Princeton, NJ: Princeton University Press.

Sowell, T. (1972). Sismondi: A neglected pioneer. *History of Political Economy*, 4(1), 62–88.

Spencer, D. (2009). Work in utopia: Pro-work sentiments in the writings of four critics of classical economics. *The European Journal of the History of Economic Thought*, 16(1), 97–122.

Spiegel, H. (1971). *The Growth of Economic Thought*. Upper Saddle River, NJ: Prentice-Hall.

Stewart, R. E. (1984). Sismondi's forgotten ethical critique of early capitalism. *Journal of Business Ethics*, 3(3), 227–234.

Thweatt, W. (1979). Early formulators of "Say's" law of markets. *Quarterly Review of Economics and Business*, 19, 79–96.

Tiran, A. (2006). Jean-Baptiste Say: The project for a monetary reform in Ricardo's style. *History of Economics Ideas*, 14(3), 35–47.

Togati, T. (2019). How can we restore the generality of the General Theory? *Cambridge Journal of Economics*, 43(5), 1397–1415.

Trigg, A. (2001). Veblen, Bourdieu, and conspicuous consumption. *Journal of Economic Issues*, 35(1), 99–115.

Veblen, T. (1899, 1994). The theory of the leisure class. In *The Collected Works of Thorstein Veblen*. Volume 1. London: Routledge, 1–404.

Waterman, A. (1991). *Revolution, Economics and Religion: Christian Political Economy, 1798–1833*. Cambridge: Cambridge University Press.

Waterman, A. (2003). Romantic political economy: Donald Winch and David Levy on Victorian literature and economics. *Journal of the History of Economic Thought*, 25, 91–102.

Whately, R. (1831, 1832). *Introductory Lectures on Political Economy*. 2nd Edition. London: B. Fellowes.

13 Humans, human flows and Mother Nature integrated upon the hedonist market parable

13.1 Hedonist theory, means of production owners and other moneyed persons

Hedonist self-regulating market constructions provide a rhetorical defense for owners of the means of production and other moneyed persons. When hedonist economic theory was being developed, moneyed persons faced contentious claims that they would be forming lazy classes depending on and exploiting the toil of the working poor. Moneyed persons also faced other perilous claims, such as that they would not provide benefic contributions to production.[1] Several social relations writers raised these concerns. Social movements were creating serious distress. Related interpretations could be perhaps extracted from Smith's and Ricardo's writings. After all, Smith's system was based on a work theory of production, value and existence. Furthermore, Ricardo had accused landlords of not contributing to production, despite obtaining rents from it (and increasing commodity prices in the process). Labor-capital dichotomies could imply latent conflicts. The self-regulating market myth emergence must be understood on the context of these historical and theoretical circumstances.

We have seen that although Maitland and Malthus conclusively contributed to prototype hedonist arguments and economic theory, they did not reach a full-steam advocacy of the self-regulating market myth (or *laissez-faire*). To a large extent, their position anticipates that of J.M. Keynes and his many orthodox and heterodox followers, who although diverging with the conclusions tend to accept theoretical postulates.[2] On the other hand, Say, Senior, Mill and other hedonist writers made a collective effort (either conscious or not) to align shielding arguments advocating moneyed persons' status vis-à-vis the centrality of workers in work-based theories. The self-regulating market myth resulted from these efforts. Its skeleton argument is as follows: According to the hedonist market parable, production was no longer production of products, but that of hedonist utility. Hence, capital and nature (including land) would be productive agents required to produce such hedonist utility. Therefore, owners of means of production/productive agents would provide agency of capital and natural agents for hedonist production. Subjugated to the construction of hedonist utility to be enjoyed by moneyed consumers, the relevance of human-related flows would theoretically diminish. Henceforth, workflows and other human-related flows would be purposed to generate hedonist utility to the moneyed consumers, either final or intermediate consumers. As commodities, humans, nature and money would be explained through hedonist supply and demand constructions. Unless reflected in quantitative hedonism, human-related flows and Mother Nature were to be discarded or neglected as barely irrelevant. Money holders would command hedonist calculus.

13.2 A role for investors, interests and even usury

13.2.1 *Profits to capital would originate in superintendence and abstinence/sacrifice (from pleasure as in hedonism)*

Say, Senior and Mill have departed from Smith's three factors, namely, capital, land (nature) and work. However, hedonist theory would integrate them quite differently. In this sub-point, we observe the case of capital, which continues to be a tautological construction in hedonist theory and subsequent mainstream economic writings.[3] Smith had already suggested that part of the income from capital, namely profits, could be associated with actual work such as *"labor of inspection and direction."*[4] Indeed, Say, Senior and Mill had no issue with investors justifying part of profits with their work. For instance, Mill refers that a component of profits originates in *"remuneration for the labour and skill required for superintendence."*[5] Senior claims that it would be very difficult to characterize revenues for work performed by investors (e.g., superintendence) as either profits or wages: *"to be productive of profit, must be employed, and that the person who directs its employment must labour."* On the other hand, Say has inverted the proposition to sustain that workers would receive profits (here he tries to rename wages as profits) as the man of knowledge/science[6] and the *"entrepreneur"* of industry[7] receive profits for their active agency in industry. Nonetheless, social relations writers such as Owen or Saint-Simon also recognized the importance of work on what today we would call management and innovation regarding human organizations, for example, the relevance of directing other human beings on production methods or technologically innovating on products.

The real quarrelsome issue was how to explain other components of profits indicated by Smith's system, which, apparently, did not originate in any type of work done by investors (or landlords). Extensively, Smith alerted to the possibility of manufacturers, merchants and investors assuming abusive and exploitative positions. By removing landlords from production (but not from prices, as rent would affect prices), Ricardo created a work theory of value and production based upon the capital–labor (as a human commodity) dichotomy. It is just a short step to foresee potential conflicts and exploitive dimensions of such relations. Karl Marx and Friedrich Engels would later develop their writings out of these dialectic dichotomies already identifiable in many social relations of production writings. Nevertheless, Marx and Engels would also bring along a talent for agitation and political organization over requites of serious crises over the industrialized world. Marxism, nonetheless, is based upon a human commodity framework.

Before the advent of Marxism, however, the self-regulating market myth would rhetorically justify profits (and rents) generated out of apparently no work whatever. After claiming that wages to workers would be akin to profits, Say advocates that besides investors' agency at industry, mere employment of capital would generate agency of capital in producing (hedonist) utility. Thus, it must be monetarily rewarded. Allegedly, capital would provide services in producing hedonist utility:

> From all which it is impossible to avoid drawing this conclusion that the profit of capital, like that of land and the other natural sources, is the equivalent given for a productive service, which though distinct from that of human industry, is nevertheless its efficient ally in the production of wealth.[8]

Senior came up with the idea[9] that the instrument of production would not be capital per se, but the abstinence of investors who would provide capital rather than consuming it. Accordingly, there would be two primary instruments of production, namely, labor and natural agents (no longer merely land). To these two instruments, a third secondary instrument must be added, namely, abstinence of owners of capital (thus, means of production).[10] This formulation is undeniably hedonist, for it praises investors on the grounds that instead of investing they could be consuming, thereby having pleasure expressed in hedonist utility. For this pleasure withdrawal, investors would need to be monetarily compensated. Senior considers to have therefore found a manner to justify profits without any work involvement: the abstinence of consumption deferring hedonist enjoyment.[11]

> By the word Abstinence, we wish to express that agent, distinct from labour and the agency of nature, the concurrence of which is necessary to the existence of Capital, and which stands in the same relation to Profit as Labour does to Wages.[12]

Say might be close to Senior's idea of hedonist abstinence when he declared that revenues of capital would partially originate out of its owners' frugality, which would imply avoidance of hedonist enjoyment towards consumption.[13] Similarly, Mill adopts an abstinence-based explanation based upon the hedonist market parable: Investors must be compensated for delaying their hedonist pleasure in order to form implements of production (e.g., machines, raw materials) or assisting on the division of labor for instance with food and provisions for workers and their families[14]:

> As the wages of the labourer are the remuneration of labour, so the profits of the capitalist are properly, according to Mr. Senior's well-chosen

expression, the remuneration of abstinence. They are what he gains by forbearing to consume his capital for his own uses, and allowing it to be consumed by productive labourers for their uses. For this forbearance he requires a recompense.[15]

13.2.2. *The entrepreneur enters hedonist economic theory*

Say employed the term "*entrepreneur*" to justify that investors themselves could actively contribute to production and thus must be rewarded for it. He made his point in different texts.[16] Nevertheless, the idea underlying the term entrepreneur had been used for centuries before. In French, the word is derived from "*entreprendre*," which implies to do or to undertake.[17] French was preceded by Latin language. The entrepreneur term seems to come from the Latin "*imprisia*," employed in French as "*emprise – enterprise*," to imply something as being bold, firm and daring.[18] Without entirely coincidental meanings, these ideas have been around at least since the ancient world, having substantial use over the Middle Ages.[19]

Richard Cantillon and Turgot specifically used the idea of entrepreneur in context of production before but closer to Say.[20] Cantillon associated it with the problem of uncertainty,[21] for instance, when an investor might buy raw materials at known prices or use newly discovered methods of production but has yet unknown results. This notion would later be explored by Frank Night at the beginning of the 20th century.[22] Turgot also observed the relevance of reorganizing productive activities in relation to the requirements of production and physical constraints. Due to needs associated with the division of labor, independent producers could reorganize and innovate farming methods.[23] Similarly, he observed that due to manufacturing developments, artisans were being divided into different groups as "*entrepreneurs, capitalists and simple workers*." Entrepreneurs were gaining importance in organizing and innovating production.[24] Likewise, several writers among social relations writers had praised the relevance of innovation and management. What is more, some of them were involved in productive activities, for instance, Owen who held and managed the then famous New Lanark Cotton Spinning Mills in Scotland. Saint-Simon supported industrialists involved in production. Engels, close associate and financial backer to Marx, would for several years manage some of his family's factories. Hence, appreciation did exist for management and innovation. Entrepreneurs need not be linked to hedonist economic theory.

However, Say devised an integration of the entrepreneur into hedonist theory, which curiously remains in mainstream economics: The aim of the entrepreneur would become that of creating hedonist utility in order to maximize his/her own hedonist utility (through money, the hedonist calculus instrument). Schumpeter, who is frequently attributed this idea, openly admits that he adapted it from Say.[25] Schumpeter, nonetheless, would typify different forms through which opportunities for creating hedonist value could be obtained. These opportunities include launching new products, new methods of production, new markets, new sources of supply regarding raw materials or reorganization of industries.[26] Likewise, none of these innovations need to necessarily be connected to hedonist economic theory or quantitative hedonism.

Creative destruction and destructive creation ideas are remarkably ancient to humankind. When Schumpeter introduced these ideas, he may also have been influenced by Nietzsche[27] and the German economist Werner Sombart.[28] However, in ancient Egyptian and Greek myths, there was phoenix reborn from the ashes. In foundational Hinduism, Shiva the God of Destruction would also enable Creation.[29] Siddhārtha Gautama (the Buddha; 563/480–483/400 BC) explained the impermanence of things. The philosopher Heraclitus (535–475 BC) lectured on the permanent change he saw in the world, the flux and becoming, the permanent flow.[30] Jesus Christ wished to destroy merchants' and money changers' activities at the Temple to create a restored Temple. Despite ancient formulations, creative destruction and destructive creation remain very important to humankind.

Yet, in contemporary mainstream economics and affiliated disciplines, entrepreneurship's purpose has been described as that of generating hedonist utility. Largely, this purpose would be achieved through more money to flow to the owners of the means of production.[31] Thus, instead of discovering the entrepreneur, hedonist economic theory tries to domesticate him/her for the intent of pseudo-validating hedonist theory. As noted by critical studies, mainstream economics and affiliated disciplines can employ the entrepreneur notion for ideological purposes, for example, to justify monetary flows to moneyed individuals.[32] The entrepreneur appears as a mythical figure, who by his/her individual actions could effectuate change at an organization or social group.[33] He/she is presented as some sort of modern prince/princess.[34] In managing resources, this mythical figure is displayed as treating other humans as commodities (assets, capital or resources). However, such a description naturally ignores the social embeddedness of economic and societal production[35] and many human-related flows involved. Entrepreneurial agency is conducted on social[36] and biophysical settings. Indeed, the hedonist delimited entrepreneur view can be used to ideologically justify monetary flow appropriation by investors who, besides moving their financial resources to the organization sometime in the past, have made little or no contribution to production, management or innovation, for instance several contemporary hedge funds, daily traders at stock markets, investment funds and investment banks.[37]

However, mainstream economic theory and affiliated disciplines still follow Say's lead in relating a hedonist entrepreneur conception to a defense of moneyed persons and social groups' status. Yet, entrepreneurial activities need not be explained by hedonist theory. These activities entail a legitimate field of study that can be addressed by other disciplines: psychology, sociology, management and so forth.[38] We need to move past Say's attempt to domesticate the entrepreneur into hedonist theory. Indeed, ancient formulations of creative destruction and destructive creation remain quite relevant. They may be applicable to small and large organizations and for-profit, not-for-profit, communal or governmental organizations.[39] These ideas may apply to monetary and non-monetary societies. Likewise, they may impact upon many human-related flows not directly connected to monetary flows, but with great bearing upon economic and societal production.

13.2.3 Hedonist theory of profits and interest rates, which aligns with Bentham's defense of usury

Senior did not seem to entirely grasp the relevance that interest rates could have for his case. He still seems perplexed with potential conflicts among workers and investors arising in labor theories. Senior observes: "*Rent, then, being considered as something extrinsic, and Taxation a mode of expenditure, the only remaining deduction from Wages is Profit.*"[40] He might have been sidetracked by his own claim regarding the difficulty of distinguishing profits originating in investors' work to other forms of profit. Undeniably, still, he bought upon a resemblance between profits and interest rates. To him, profits could be defined simply in financial terms as comparison between monetary advancements made by the investor and his/her monetary returns.[41] As remuneration from hedonist abstinence ("*the act of deferring enjoyment*"[42]), profits would depend on two factors, namely, general rate of profit in the country on the advance of capital for a given period and a period that has elapsed.[43] Hence, one could deduce that profits would be an entitlement to investors out of their hedonist abstinence, which, as loans' interests, would grow with time.

On his part, Say mentions (hedonist) sacrifice of enjoyments to partially justify investors' profits.[44] Nonetheless, he seems to have addressed monetary matters with greater depth than Senior.[45] Moreover, Say has wished distinguishing revenues originating at entrepreneurial activities (addressed on the previous point) from those originating at capital "*services.*" Accordingly, mere allocation of capital would offer a service to hedonist production out of what Say names as "*productive agency of capital.*"[46] Capital owners were to be compensated for providing such services. After all, they would have sacrificed hedonist enjoyments.[47] Say has divided revenues to capital into two types, namely, interests from loans and profits of capital.

Interest rates from loans would arise from the price (or rent) of capital[48] added by the premium of insurance against the risk of its partial or total loss.[49] Though apparently not mentioning Bentham,[50] Say clearly sides with him in defense of usury, an expression he wants to be eliminated for having a negative connotation. Contrary to Adam Smith,[51] Say is against having governments imposing any maximum interest rate to protect debtors from lenders' abuses. If any legal limit was to exist, it would be a minimal interest rate for lenders to concede loans.[52] Interest rates should be defined merely out of hedonist supply and demand of available capital.[53] Profits to capital (excluding therefore those from agency/industry) would arise from so-called services of capital towards hedonist production. Hence, profits could be compared to interest rates from loans.[54] The most beneficial employment of capital to investors would be that investment that while having *"equal risk yields the largest profit."*[55] Consequently, there would be no big difference between profits from capital and interests from loans, excluding, of course, risks that might be involved. As many a contemporary mainstream economist, Say claims that while not all applications of capital would be beneficial to society, those applications that tend to be most beneficial would yield a higher rate of profit (hence, of interests).[56]

J.S. Mill follows Senior, Say and Bentham to present his profits-interests theory: Gross profit of capital could be divided into three parts, namely: (i) insurance that would arise as the premium for the risk incurred for potential losses and hazards (as Say had suggested), (ii) wages of superintendence that would arise from the work (and trouble) conducted by investors (as Say and Senior had suggested), and (iii) interest that would pay investors for their abstinence (of pleasure, as Senior had suggested and Say had implied).[57] Likewise, Mill advocates that interest rates should be formed through the hedonist market parable. He also admits that interest rates might be disturbed or connected to crises and other annoyances. Moreover, the interest rate might have a role in stimulating some production or in pricing several economic elements in the short run, given that credit can impact them. Overall, however, the hedonist market parable would be capable of allocating the fittest interest rate to lenders and debtors, investors and organizations. Mill claims that Bentham[58] corrected Adam Smith on matters regarding usury. As Bentham, Mill refers to the so-called freedom of contract and advocates that governments should not interfere on matters of hedonist markets. Governments ought to have no role in protecting borrowers from eventual abuses by lenders. Granted, loans could be used to speculate or gamble, or even bankrupt oneself, but they could also create hedonist utility. The profit-interests of capital component in hedonist theory is usually presented as if profits, interests and the hedonist market parable would generally be knowledgeable about what would be better for entire human societies. Indeed, this formulation recalls that of a mystical cult. In contemporary mainstream economics, to a great extent, we can find this very same hedonist theoretical explanation.

13.3 A role for owners of natural agents to contribute with the hedonist service of nature

The biosphere and biophysical world would also be integrated into the hedonist market parable. In the process, rents become akin to profits and landlords justified as investors (capitalists) for contributing to hedonist production. Nature's assessment would be delimited to hedonist production measurable by hedonist calculus (in money). On record, we can find Senior, Say and Mill claiming that nature and/or natural agents (hence, the biosphere and biophysical world) would provide some sort of productive agency to hedonist production. For this alleged service, owners of natural agents (a modification of the terminology previously attributed to landlords) ought to be monetarily (hedonistically) compensated. Furthermore, Say and Mill move in the direction of implying that Mother Nature would be akin to capital or commodities. Landlords who owned land to be rented could instead be considered as capitalists investing in land. The same would apply to mines, fisheries, houses, patents or privileges. Thus, as the biosphere and biophysical world become capital or commodities, owners of natural agents would have similar hedonist entitlements. As akin to capitalists, they would allegedly provide services of nature *"capital."* When an item is scarce, it would need to be owned, contrary to natural agents that are not scarce, for instance, air.

As describer earlier, Senior suggested reformulating the labor, land and capital typology into labor, natural agents and abstinence. Natural agents would be a reduced-word version of *"Agents offered to us by nature,"*[59] which were to include *"every productive agent so far as it does not derive its powers from the act of man."*[60] He gives several examples:

> The principal of these agents is the land, with its mines, its rivers, its natural forests with their wild inhabitants, and, in short, all its spontaneous productions. To these must be added the ocean, the atmosphere, light and heat, and even those physical laws, such as gravitation and electricity, by the knowledge of which we are able to vary the combinations of matter.[61]

Indeed, this explanation is contradictory because, as Senior himself notes, these elements can contribute to human production when humans have knowledge on how to use them and, in many instances, exert toil on them. Yet, Senior implies that natural agents by themselves, land chiefly among them, could mysteriously generate profits (that is, without association with human-related flows).[62]

Hence, the proposed change in nomenclature: proprietors of natural agents instead of landlords. However, Senior can accept the term rent to describe their income,[63] which would be justifiable in hedonist terms. Proprietors of natural agents would have enabled the *"gift"* of nature:

> The surplus is taken by the proprietor of the natural agent, and is his reward, not for having laboured or abstained, but simply for not having withheld what he was able to withhold; for having permitted the gifts of nature to be accepted.[64]

Ownership of natural agents could allow for hedonist utility to be computed; otherwise, it could not.[65] Investors in natural agents could be seen as akin to investors in capital. Senior asks rhetorically what difference it would make if the one who exploits, for instance, the soil were the landowner or the tenant.[66] He claims that it could be difficult distinguishing profits from rents, as earlier we saw that he argued that it would be difficult distinguishing profits from wages in many cases.[67] Thus, he seems keen to eliminate Smith's system distinctions among capital, natural agents and work.

Say likewise proposed the natural agent terminology to replace that of land, which would be a special case of natural agency. Say might have gone a little further in attempting to define natural agents' productive agency as akin to the productive agency of capital (and that of human agency/industry). Natural agents would be defined in

> a very extensive sense; comprising not merely inanimate bodies, whose agency operates to the creation of value, but likewise the laws of the physical world, as gravitation, which makes the weight of a clock descend; magnetism, which points the needle of the compass: the elasticity of steel; the gravity of the atmosphere; the property of heat to discharge itself by ignition, etc. etc.[68]

As for Senior, land would be a case of natural agency among others. To Say, it would be very difficult if not impossible distinguishing productive agency of natural agents from that of capital.[69] Both would be required for conducting human work. Therefore, in hedonist production we would find capital, natural agents and industry (agency) of workers and also industry of entrepreneurs (investors) and persons of knowledge/science.[70]

For generating pleasure and avoiding pain in hedonist production, labor would not be only that of humankind. It would include also labor of machinery and of nature.[71] These work forms would allegedly be similar. Hence, the correct term in most revenue forms generated by all these working agents should be profits. That is, profits would not only be revenue of capital. There should also be profits for human industry (agency) and for natural agency.[72] Say exemplifies this with the case of land. For him, land agency value should be assessed through hedonist supply and demand.[73] Profits generated by land may be similar when it is either the proprietor or a tenant entrepreneur who has leased it to explore the soil.[74] Thus, rents would be profits of the land.[75] Moreover, the landowner in many cases acts just as a capitalist when he/she invests on the land:

> When the proprietor himself expends a capital in the improvement of his land, in draining, irrigation, fences, buildings, houses, or other erections, the rent then includes, in addition to the profit of the land, the interest likewise of the capital so expended.[76]

Likewise, Mill declares that (hedonist) production requires appropriate natural objects[77] and land would be a productive agent.[78] He raises a sensitive point that human labor can have limited interference on nature, which would provide not only materials but also powers as that of the air wind, chemical agency or electricity[79]: "*Labour, then, in the physical world, is always and solely employed in putting objects in motion; the properties of matter, the laws of nature, do the rest.*"[80] Here, Mill seems to adopt a sensible realist stance upon that human agency could only have a limited impact and control upon the biophysical world. However, his stance is soon to be captured by his fervent hedonist position. A similar position occurs in Say, who observes that *"No human being has the faculty of originally creating matter which is more than nature itself can do."*[81] However, both Say and Mill align their explanations towards their feverous hedonist framework.

Mill asks too whether revenues compensating capital sunk in the soil, in productive agricultural improvements and related investments should be termed as rent or profit. As Say, Mill claims that in many cases it would be difficult to distinguish rents from profits[82]: This profit/rent would be determined through the hedonist market parable based upon supply and demand constructions.[83] Hence, from here the hedonist justification for (capitalists) investors to receive profits would apply likewise to individuals previously referred to as landlords who have invested in their properties. Although, as noted earlier, Mill displayed some reservations regarding inherited wealth, he also finds it difficult to see the differences between a capitalist who had invested in a factory and a landlord who had invested in natural agency. Mill can understand why Ricardo had suggested that rents would not contribute to costs of production, for the basic elements in production would be wages and profits. However, Mill argues that in many cases rents enter costs of production in the same manner that profits out of capital do.[84]

Therefore, the biosphere and the biophysical world would be constrained by the hedonist self-regulating market parable. Evidently, Senior, Say, Mill and their many followers cannot explain how nature could systematically generate monetary flows without association with human-related flows.[85] Yet, their relevance would be to mysteriously generate monetary flows entailing hedonist calculus pseudo-phenomena. Components of the biosphere not reflected on monetary flows would mostly be irrelevant or negligible. By equating nature or natural agents to capital, the hedonist economic theory further assigns to the biosphere and biophysical world the tautological features already present in Smith's system reformulation of the capital concept: Capital, nature and natural agents would create wealth, because they would be what creates wealth. Once again, we encounter a mystical explanation, which would integrate Mother Nature into the hedonist market parable.

13.4 Human workers as commodities and capital purposed to generate hedonism in self-regulating markets

Hedonist writers have also identified relevant work-related problems in work-based theories, which would need to identify the exact work involved in production processes. However, such identification is nearly impossible. To demonstrate this problem, Mill identified indirect forms of work required for commodities to come into being.[86] For instance, labor for the subsistence of the workforce such as gathering and preparing food, labor for production of implements and tools, labor for the security of the workforce and production, labor for transport and distribution of production, labor of invention and discovery, and even the work of having children (future workers, thus human commodities), raising and educating them.[87] Mill has gone so far as declaring that, in some cases, it might be difficult distinguishing work in agriculture, manufacturing and commerce. As we have seen before, hedonist writers contested separations between nonproductive and productive work, asserting that Smith's system had classified many activities necessary for production as nonproductive, for example, security, law production, legal services and education.

However, as for the relation of nature to production, value and existence, hedonist writers propose to solve work-related difficulties through their hedonist prejudices: By changing the purpose of production to that of producing hedonist utility, they could explain human participation.[88] Hardly their prejudices could be more manifest than when they adopt Bentham's concept of disutility of work. Work would represent merely pain, and workers would merely work to obtain gratification. For instance, Senior defines as an elementary proposition of the science of political economy: "*That every man desires to obtain additional Wealth with as little sacrifice as possible*,"[89] which is a summary of Bentham's concept of disutility of work. Senior further asserts that "*The word, employment is merely a concise form of designating toil, trouble, exposure, and fatigue*."[90] Workers would work in order to obtain "*food, clothing, shelter, and fuel-in short, the materials of subsistence and comfort, that the labouring classes require*,"[91] not to obtain employment per se. Mill expresses a negative view not only of work but of workers themselves, whom he sees as rude and uneducated.[92] Likewise, Say undermines the relevance of human work for production, value and existence. He defines work as "*continuous action, exerted to perform any one of the operations of industry, or a part only of one of those operations*."[93] Industry would not be only execution. It would require as well theory and application, thus, persons of knowledge and entrepreneurs as exhibited earlier.[94] However, human work would only be a form among productive services (to hedonism). There would also be work or productive service of nature and of capital (to hedonism).[95] Thereafter, "*profits*" of work would be equivalent to profits of nature and capital.

Thereafter, Say, Senior and Mill move on to further integrate humans and our related flows upon the hedonist market parable. An initial explanation was formed about how hedonist supply and demand could explain wages. The demand would be the capital that capitalists would have to hire workers, and supply would be the number of workers that could, however, be affected by workers' skills and characteristics. Out of the hedonist demand and supply of work, hedonist markets would form rates of wage. Senior take these claims to be self-evident.[96] Say asserts that the value of the productive services of capital, nature and industry like those of any other commodity, "*rises in direct ratio to the demand, and inverse ratio to the supply*."[97] Mill was perhaps more cautious, admitting that a few cases could exist where wages depend on law or custom when competition (broadly and ambiguously defined) could not be free.[98] However, he sustains that political economy should apply to situations of competition where according to him: "*Wages, then, depend mainly upon the demand and supply of labour; or as it is often expressed, on the proportion between population and capital.*"[99]

These initial constructions treating hedonist demand as amount of capital available to hire and sustain workers (and their families) will later be reformulated by subsequent hedonist writers, who will take issue with the claim that the amount of money to hire workers would be fixed. A newly hired worker can generate revenues with their work, and part of those revenues could be used to pay his/her salary. There is no doubt that Mill has adopted the fixed fund doctrine on the various editions of his *Principles*. Nonetheless, a polemic exists about why Mill in a book review would cast doubts about whether the amount of money to hire workers could be instead flexible and dependent upon revenues to be generated by workers' future work.[100] Undeniably, however, hedonist economic theory is fundamentally reliant on integrating humans and human flows in the hedonist market parable.

As for supply, the broad explanation was to consider it as the number of workers. Nonetheless, this provision would allow to blame workers for low wages and eventually their misery on the grounds that they would be reproducing (that is, having babies) too much. It would be their fault, for investors would only operate according to the hedonist market parable, and there could not be a conflict between profits and wages. Smith's and Ricardo's writings were made the targets. Say, Senior and Mill based their reasoning in what was known as Malthus's population doctrine.[101] Hence, Malthus, the proto hedonist and self-appointed enemy of equality, was once again invoked. Workers would be commodities reproducing according to hedonist supply and demand.[102] As seen earlier, Senior was a major proponent of the report to Parliament advising reformulation of poor laws, to constrain aiding the poor. Mill openly supports this reformulation.[103] Say discusses the possibility of limiting marriages among working poor, though is not entirely conclusive on the issue.[104] Mill brusquely faults the poor on the matter: "*Every one has a right to live. We will suppose this granted. But no one has a right to bring creatures into life, to be supported by other people.*"[105] Furthermore, Mill makes a defense of Malthus's principle of population against those who treated it as "*hard-hearted Malthusianism.*"[106] According to Mill, opponents who had demonstrated that Malthus was entirely wrong in sustaining that food sources grow arithmetically and populations geometrically had obtained only an easy victory. Allegedly, Malthus was only presenting an allegory.[107] Once again, Mill uses his recurrent rhetorical strategy of pretending to engage with critics while simply dismissing them as irrelevant.

Curiously, Mill suggested two solutions to address "*oversupply*" of "*human commodities*" (that is, poor people). Although neither of them is hedonist market-based, he fails to see contradictions. The first solution would be education. The poor should be educated to be more productive, have better manners and make fewer babies. This is summarized by Mill as an "*effective national education system.*"[108] However, this system would need to be partially or totally provided by the government and communities, hence, outside hedonist constructions that the market would solve most if not all human challenges. The second solution would be to send the oversupply of workers to the colonies of European empires, which he announces to be a *"golden opportunity"* that should not be wasted by rulers.[109] However, conquering and forming colonies go much further beyond any possible hedonist market construction. It may require governments, infrastructures, armies, financial means and eventually wars generating armed conflicts with local populations and other empires. Truly, during the 19th century, European powers went on prodigious armed conflicts to hoard non-European territories and establish colonies. Even Mill himself cannot maintain the hedonist market parable for very long.

Nonetheless, hedonist writers have likewise anticipated the contemporary mainstream concept of human capital, which is roughly defined in mainstream economics as the set of skills of the labor force (workers).[110] It involves, thus, a metaphor of capital embodied in people that would generate monetary flows.[111] Therefore, workers' skills and characteristics reflected on hedonist calculus. These writers could then summon Smith who had identified factors that impact wages such as scarcity of workers, difficulty in learning the trade, permanence of employment, degree of trust involved, season of the year, or agreeableness of the work.[112] However, Smith and Ricardo had a fundamentally different theory of production, value and existence. The hedonist writers claimed that these distinctive factors affected production of hedonism captured in hedonist calculus, which evidently Smith and Ricardo never did. Likewise, Smith and Ricardo may also have related population dynamics with the capital available to hire workers and number of workers. However, they never did consider the purpose of production to be the production of hedonism for the moneyed consumer. To a great extent, Smith's system and Ricardo's reformulation were a direct focus of contestation to hedonist economic theory.[113]

Perhaps the greatest modification conducted by hedonist theory, which enabled the emergence of the self-regulating market myth, was the description of profits as akin to costs (and vice versa),[114] that is, the blurring of the distinction between profits and costs. In labor theories derived from Aristoteles's and Smith's system, profits are revenues out of investments, which are computed after costs of production are deducted. Therefore, profits can be displayed as a surplus. Investors move along different industries when the profit rate is reduced. In hedonist theory, profits would be akin to costs that pay services of capital to hedonism (as in Say) or the abstinence of hedonist pleasure from investors (as in Senior, Mill and Malthus). Poor Mother Nature is itself conceptually transformed into capital. By treating everything as a cost, there can no longer exist coherent theories of costs or profits.[115] However, adequate management human organizations require cost and profit accounting to be adequately computed. Yet, in hedonist theory, commodities (including human commodities) would magically appear in the hedonist market. In the fortunate description from Sraffa, mainstream economic theory would describe a production of *"commodities by the way of commodities."*[116] As in labor theories, humans and our related flows would keep being described as commodities. However, capital and Mother Nature would also become commodities to produce hedonism;

otherwise, they would be irrelevant. Every element participating in production would be a commodity or capital (or asset or resource).

Owners of the means of production and moneyed persons would thereafter have an economic theory that would put them at the command of production, value and existence. According to economic hedonism, Adam Smith had errored in treating capital, Mother Nature and workers as distinct factors of production, which had led him to attribute an exaggerated importance to labor.[117] Furthermore, capitalists would generally be the most entitled party in receiving monetary flows from production:

> The usual practice is to consider one of the parties as entitled to the whole product, paying to the others a price for their co-operation. The person so entitled is uniformly the capitalist: the sums which he pays for wages and rent are the purchase-money for the services of the labourer, and for the use of the natural agent employed.[118]

Owners of the means of production and moneyed persons would no longer have complete responsibility on accumulating obnoxious profits[119] because they would be exposed to mystical forces of the hedonist market, which would operate as a sort of deity to be venerated.

13.5 The case of slavery

Regarding slavery, Mill has entered the infamous "*The Negro Question*" polemic with Carlyle, who as we have seen earlier was a defender of slavery.[120] In Mill's political economy book, though economic efficiency was not the only concern, part of his argument goes in this direction, namely, that waged work would be more efficient, as Smith had already had suggested.[121] Moreover, while defending abolition, Mill displays actual concern that end of slavery would imply slave owners' monetary losses.[122] In "*The Negro Question*," Mill sides more clearly with abolitionist movements and "*the great national revolt of the conscience of this country against slavery and the slave-trade.*"[123] Nevertheless, he once again promotes the hedonist agenda. He argues from the perspective of Bentham's disutility of work: "*Work, I imagine, is not a good in itself. There is nothing laudable in work for work's sake.*"[124] Mill's solution to abolish slavery would be to "*import negroes*" and subject them to the hedonist market parable, where human beings are treated as commodities.[125] Furthermore, as his father, Mill has spent his working career at East India Company[126] that had a traditional practice of relying and trading on slaves[127] (not to mention opium trade and wars[128]).

In the various editions of *Traité d'economie politique*, Say changed his position regarding slavery.[129] In the first edition, he, contrary to Smith, was convinced that slave work would be more productive and cheaper than waged work.[130] For this position, he was publicly accused of providing arguments in favor of slavery.[131] However, in later editions he displayed more concern over the misery, suffering and underdevelopment of slave populations. Moreover, he manifested against use of force and fear on slave workforces. Yet, he also had a hedonist disutility view of work, as Senior likewise did. Their hedonist market parable would make them oblivious that several factories they were commending were receiving raw materials out of slave work.

We must be cautious in applying standards of our own time to previous epochs. Nonetheless, hedonist theory is not needed to make the case against slavery. The 19th century heaped on movements and initiatives that fortunately have succeeded in abolishing servitude and slavery. The economic argument was certainly not the only one condemning traditional practices. However, some slavery forms would continue after abolition, especially in US and European colonies around the World.[132] Still, monetary technologies would allow compensating urban workers through wages that had not been available before.[133] Likewise, treatment of agriculture workers could be modified from that of servants, serfs or slaves because they could receive monetary wages for their work.[134] Nonetheless, given factory workers' conditions for existence at the time, some writers such as Sismondi, de Lamennais or Mackintosh[135] have argued that they could barely distinguish a wage earner from a slave: "*The difference between the system of trafficking in the bodies of African slaves, and the toil of European slaves* [waged workers] *is only nominal.*"[136]

13.6 Conclusion

Hedonist writers have identified actual problems regarding nature and work in labor theories of value, production and existence. However, Senior, Say and Mill would claim to solve those problems with quantitative hedonism, while appealing to no further evidence than their hedonist prejudices. Invoking pseudo-phenomena of hedonist calculus (in money) along mystical demand and supply constructions in the market parable, they would claim to have developed hedonist explanations for production, value and existence. Hedonist theory overemphasizes the micro moment of the monetary flow, which it suggests should replace the centrality of work in labor theories. Consequently, hedonist theory expands the tautological concept of capital onto Mother Nature, humans and our human-related flows. Unless reflected in quantitative hedonism (that is, money), they (we) would be treated as irrelevant or negligible. This theoretical position carries great levels of irresponsibility regarding humankind, our societies and our integration upon the biosphere and biophysical world.

Furthermore, hedonist theory denies that production could be fundamentally based upon human-related flows. Although hedonist theory also adopts a human commodity framework, it treats workflows and other human-related flows as commodities determined by hedonist supply and demand constructions. Supply and demand of workflows have been described by Senior, Say and Mill, yet in an introductory manner. Supply of human commodities would be the number of workers. Demand would be the capital available to hire workers (hence, Malthus's, Ricardo's and Smith's analyses over human commodity population growth were once again called for). Hedonist economic theory will later evolve. It will continue to treat workers as commodities (or assets, capital or resources) in the market parable. However, instead of considering a fixed monetary amount to hire workers, it will also integrate money generated from work after hiring workers. For instance, a shop that hires more workers might increase sales. A factory that hires more workers may increase production and thus sales. Added revenues might be used to pay wages, profits and other monetary flows.

Whether or not their proponents were conscious of the implications (which likely they were), the hedonist self-regulating market myth supports the status of means of production owners and other moneyed persons. When these constructions were being formed in recently industrialized societies, means of production owners and large money holders were under attack from social relations writers and ongoing social movements. Indisputably, moneyed persons are quite benefited by hedonist theory vis-à-vis work-based theories. As work and other human-related flows would have lost primary explanatory ground, owners of means of production could contribute, at least theoretically, with services or agency for the formation of hedonist production. Profits, rents and interests would be justifiable because investors had sacrificed their hedonist enjoyment through consumption in order to contribute to production. Moreover, as the purpose of production would be that of producing hedonist utility to the paying moneyed consumers, moneyed consumers could freely become narcissistic and entitled in their search for hedonist pleasure, which provides the foundation for the *homo economicus* model agent we contemporarily find in mainstream economics. This agent was formed out of hedonist utilitarian constructions. Markets would only need to operate by themselves, without interventions from governments, not-for-profit or communal production, or any other interference affecting mystical hedonist equilibrium. There could be a role for governments, for instance, in security, education and infrastructure production, only if it did not interfere with private agency and pseudo-phenomena of hedonist equilibrium.

Notes

1 For instance Saint-Simon referred to them as parasitic benefiting from the work of others while avoiding working themselves (Saint-Simon, 2016, pp. 194–198).
2 Backhouse (2002), Brue (2000), Screpanti and Zamagni (2005), Togati (2019).
3 And many relativist writings as well.
4 Smith (1776, 1999, p. 151).
5 Mill (1848, p. 293).
6 Say (1841, 2011 p. 230).
7 Say (1841, 2011 p. 231). In an English edition of the time, the term entrepreneur has been translated to: "*master agent or adventurer*" (Say, 1821, 1971, p. 329).
8 Say (1821, 1971, pp. 356–357).
9 Senior (1836, 1965, pp. 57–60).
10 Senior (1836, 1965, pp. 57–60): "a term by which we express the conduct of a person who either abstains from the unproductive use of what he can command, or designedly prefers the production of remote to that of immediate results."

11 Senior (1836, 1965, p. 185).
12 Senior (1836, 1965, p. 59). Senior continues to insist that some part of profits is still originated in investors' work (p. 60). Capital, notwithstanding, would result from "a combination of all the three great instruments of production – labour, abstinence, and the agency of nature" (idem).
13 Say (1821, 1971, pp. 292–293).
14 Senior (1836, 1965, pp. 60–80). Division of labor is described in generic terms.
15 Mill (1848, p. 292).
16 Say (1828–1829, 1815, 1826, 1821, 1971, 1829, 1852, p. 43).
17 Filion (2011, p. 42), Verin (1982).
18 Idem.
19 Filion (2011, p. 42), Schumpeter (1954), Verin (1982).
20 Boutillier and Uzunidis (2014), Cantillon (1755, 2011), Filion (2011), Jones and Spicer (2009), Ravix (2014), Schumpeter (1954), Steiner (1997).
21 Idem.
22 Boutillier and Uzunidis (2014), Cantillon (1755, 2011), Knight (1921), Steiner (1997).
23 Turgot (1766, pp. 568–570). See also Ravix (2014).
24 *"entrepreneurs, capitalistes et simples ouvriers"* Turgot (1766, p. 569). See also Ravix (2014).
25 To Schumpeter (1954, p. 529), Say was the first person "to assign to the entrepreneur – per se and as distinct from the capitalist – a definite position in the schema of the economic process." See also Filion (2011).
26 Schumpeter (1934, 66).
27 Harvey (1990, p. 17) and Reinert and Reinert (2006).
28 Reinert and Reinert (2006).
29 From Indian philosophy, the idea entered the German literary and philosophy tradition. Thus, the idea of creative destruction also precedes Nietzsche's conception of philosophical destruction by thousands of years (see Reinert and Reinert, 2006 for more details).
30 Note that an ever-changing reality is not the same as relativism of the truth.
31 See, for instance, Fayolle (2007), Filion (2011), Kao (1993), Jones and Spicer (2009), Long (1983), Parker (2018).
32 Jones and Murtola (2012) da Costa and Saraiva (2012).
33 Dodd and Anderson (2007), Jones and Spicer (2009), Levy and Scully (2007).
34 Levy and Scully (2007).
35 Dodd and Anderson (2007), Jones and Spicer (2009), Levy and Scully (2007).
36 Idem.
37 Dodd and Anderson (2007), Jones and Spicer (2009), Levy and Scully (2007).
38 Filion (2011), Jones and Spicer (2009), Nodoushani and Nodoushani (1999), Sánchez (2011).
39 Idem.
40 Idem.
41 Senior (1836, 1965, p. 185).
42 Idem.
43 Senior (1836, 1965, pp. 185–195).
44 For instance, Say (1815, 1826, pp. 97–98).
45 See, for instance, Say (1821, 1971, Book 1, Chapters XXI and XXII).
46 Say (1821, 1971, p. 73): "At present it is enough to have a distinct conception, that, without it, industry could produce nothing. Capital must work, as it were, in concert with industry; and this concurrence is what I call the productive agency of capital."
47 Say (1821, 1971, p. 343, 1815, 1826, pp. 97–98).
48 Say (1821, 1971, p. 343):

> The interest of capital lent, improperly called the interest of money, was formerly denominated usury, that is to say, rent for its use and enjoyment; which, indeed, was the correct term; for interest is nothing more than the price, or rent, paid for the

enjoyment of an object of value. But the word has acquired an odious meaning, and now presents to the mind the idea of illegal, exorbitant interest only, a milder but less expressive term having been substituted by common usage.

49 Say (1821, 1971, p. 354).
50 Bentham (1787, 1818). See previous chapters.
51 See Chapter 8 and, for instance, Paganelli (2003).
52 Say (1821, 1971, p. 352).
53 Say (1821, 1971, pp. 349–352). Say emphasizes that supply and demand of capital must not be confused with supply and demand of money. Later, J.S. Mill will also insist on this point, claiming that the interest rate dependents on the demand and supply of loans, not money (Mill, 1971b, pp. 191–206).
54 Say (1815, 1826, 1821, 1971, pp. 354–357, 1815, 1826, pp. 97–101).
55 Say (1821, 1971, p. 358): "It is very fortunate, that the natural course of things impels capital rather into those channels, which are the most beneficial to the community, than into those, which afford the largest ratio of profit."
56 Idem.
57 Mill (1848, p. 455, 1871a, p. 495). In a previous essay, Mill (1844, 1948) had addressed the issue.
58 Mill (1848, pp. 646–650, 1871b, pp. 542–548).
59 Senior (1836, 1965, p. 85).
60 Idem.
61 Idem.
62 Idem.
63 Senior (1836, 1965, pp. 93–95).
64 Idem.
65 Senior, 1836, pp. 89–90. Furthermore, Senior (1836, 1965, p. 92) claims that proprietors of natural agents would be themselves gifted individuals: "There will therefore be little danger of obscurity if we consider the word 'possess,' when applied to the proprietor of a natural agent, as implying the receipt of the advantages afforded by that agent, or, in other words, of rent. Talents, indeed, often lie idle, but in that case they may be considered for economical purposes as not possessed. In fact, unaccompanied by the will to use them, they are useless."
66 Senior (1836, 1965, pp. 128–134).
67 Idem.
68 Say (1821, 1971, p. 74).
69 Idem.
70 Say (1821, 1971, pp. 77–78).
71 Say (1821, 1971, pp. 85–89). Say defines labor as follows: "continuous action, exerted to perform any one of the operations of industry, or a part only of one of those operations."
72 Say (1821, 1971, Book II, Chapters 7, 8, 9).
73 Say (1821, 1971, p. 364).
74 Say (1821, 1971, pp. 360–361): "In the present, we are to inquire, wherein consists the peculiar profit of land itself, independent of that accruing from the industry and capital, devoted to its cultivation; and to consider the profit of land in the abstract, and whence it originates, without any inquiry as to who may be the cultivator, whether the proprietor himself, or a tenant under him."
75 Say (1821, 1971, pp. 360–364).
76 Say (1821, 1971, p. 366).
77 Mill (1871a, p. 29).
78 Mill (1871a, p. 126).
79 Mill (1871a, pp. 30–33).
80 Mill (1871a, p. 33).
81 Say (1821, 1971, p. 65).

82 Mill (1871a, pp. 525–531).
83 Mill (1871a, pp. 34–35).
84 Mill (1871a, pp. 547–586).
85 For instance, Senior (1836, 1965, p. 128) describes rents as "the revenue spontaneously offered by nature or accident."
86 Mill (1871a, pp. 37–53).
87 Idem.
88 As we have seen before, Mill proposed that human work could generate three forms of utility. See previous chapter and Mill (1871a, pp. 55–56).
89 Senior (1836, 1965, p. 26).
90 Senior (1831, 1966, p. 48).
91 Idem. The fuel could be used, for instance, for cooking or warming cold houses in harsh winters.
92 For instance, Mill (1948, p. 104): "These characteristics of depravity do not apply to the English workmen who have received an education, but attach to the others in the degree in which they are in want of it. When the uneducated English workmen are released from the bonds of iron discipline in which they have been restrained by their employers in England, and are treated with the urbanity and friendly feeling which the more educated workmen on the Continent expect and receive from their employers, they, the English workmen, completely lose their balance: they do not understand their position, and after a certain time become totally unmanageable and useless."
93 Say (1821, 1971, p. 85).
94 Say (1821, 1971, p. 81).
95 Say (1821, 1971, p. 86).
96 Senior (1831, 1966, p. iv): "the rate of wages depends on the extent of the fund for the maintenance of labourers, compared with the number of labourers to be maintained."
97 Say (1821, 1971, pp. 314–315).
98 Mill (1871a, pp. 491–493).
99 Mill (1871a, p. 419).
100 See, for instance, Ekelund and Hébert (1997), Brue (2000), Kurer (1998), Gordon (1973).
101 As seen earlier, Smith and Ricardo also were concerned that wages, workers conditions and their reproduction were connected. However, they did so from the perspective of work-based theories.
102 Say (1821, 1971, p. 333): "If the wages of the lowest class of labour were insufficient to maintain a family, and bring up children, its supply would never be kept up to the complement; the demand would exceed the supply in circulation; and its wages would increase, until that class were again enabled to bring up children enough to supply the deficiency." Senior (1836, 1965) considered as an elementary proposition of the science of political economy "That the Population of the world, or, in other words, the number of persons inhabiting it, is limited only by moral or physical evil, or by fear of a deficiency of those articles of wealth which the habits of the individuals of each class of its inhabitants lead them to require."
103 Mill (1871a, pp. 446–448).
104 Say (1821, 1971, pp. 333–337).
105 Mill (1871a, p. 445) or "call into existence swarms of creatures who are sure to be miserable, and most likely to be depraved" (Mill, 1871a, p. 438).
106 Mill (1871a, p. 438).
107 Mill (1871a, pp. 438–438).
108 Mill (1871a, p. 465).
109 Mill (1871a, p. 470). Recall that Mill, as his father, was employed by the East India Company. Senior (1831, 1966) also advocates sending working poor to the colonies: "The only immediate remedy for an actual excess in one class of the population, is

the ancient and approved one, coloniam deducere. It is of great importance to keep in mind, that not only is emigration the sole immediate remedy, but that it is a remedy preparatory to the adoption and necessary to the safety of every other."

110 Becker (1962, 1964, 1996, 2008), Goldin (2001, 2016).
111 Becker (1962, 1964, 1996, 2008), Goldin (2001, 2016).
112 Say (1821, 1971, pp. 325–220), Senior (1836, 1965, pp. 139–154), Mill (1871a, pp. 471–489).
113 See, for instance, Mill (1971a, pp. 564–570), Senior (1836, 1965, pp. 153–174), Say (1821, 1971, p. 76).
114 See, for instance, Mill (1871a, pp. 568–574).
115 Eatwell (2019).
116 Sraffa (1960), Eatwell (2019).
117 Say (1821, 1971, p. 76).
118 Senior (1836, p. 93).
119 The same would apply to multinational company directors receiving massive salaries and monetary prizes.
120 Carlyle (1849), Mill (1850).
121 Mill (1871a, pp. 306–310).
122 Mill (1871a, pp. 310–312).
123 Mill (1850).
124 Idem.
125 Idem: "If labour is wanted, it is a very obvious idea to import labourers; and if negroes are best suited to the climate, to import negroes."
126 Harris (1964).
127 Major (2012), Logan (1956).
128 Richards (2002).
129 Rocha (2000).
130 Idem.
131 Rocha (2000), Hodgson (1823), Lisboa (1844).
132 Remond (2014a, 2014b), Dubois (2011), Brown (2011).
133 Remond (2014a, 2014b), Dubois (2011). Although at the time some argued that their condition had not suffered such a great change.
134 Remond (2014a, 2014b), Dubois (2011).
135 Sismondi (1819), de Lamennais (1840). Makintosh (1840).
136 Makintosh (1840, p. 87).

References

Backhouse, R. (2002). *The Penguin History of Economics*. London: Penguin.

Becker, G. (1962). Investment in human capital: A theoretical analysis. *Journal of Political Economy*, 70(1), 9–49.

Becker, G. (1964). *Human Capital*. New York: Columbia University Press.

Becker, G. (1996). *The Economic Way of Looking into Behaviour: The Nobel Lecture*. Essays in Public Policy, 69. Stanford, CA: Hoover Institution, Stanford University.

Becker, G. (2008). Human capital. In *The Concise Encyclopedia of Economics*. Library of Economics and Liberty. Online at: https://www.econlib.org/library/Enc1/HumanCapital.html.

Bentham, J. (1787, 1818). Defence of usury. In Bentham, J. (Ed.) *Defence of Usury; Shewing the Impolicy of the Present Legal Restraints on the Terms of Pecuniary Bargains; in Letters to a Friend. To which is Added a Letter to Adam Smith, Esq. LL.D. On the Discouragements Opposed by the Above Restraints to the Progress of Inventive Industry; and to Which Is Also Added, a Protest Against Law-Taxes*. London: Payne and Foss.

Boutillier, S. and Uzunidis, D. (2014). L'empreinte historique de la théorie de l'entrepreneur. Enseignements tirés des analyses de Jean-Baptiste Say et de Joseph Aloïs Schumpeter. *Innovations*, 3, 97–119.

Brown, C. L. (2011). Abolition of the Atlantic Slave trade. In Heuman, G. and Burnard, T. (Eds.) *The Routledge History of Slavery*. New York: Routledge.

Brue, S. (2000). *The Evolution of Economic Thought*. Mason, OH: Thomson/South Western.

Cantillon, R. (1755, 2011). *Essai de la nature du commerce en général*. Paris: Institute Coppet.

Carlyle, T. (1849). Occasional discourse on the negro question. *Fraser's Magazine for Town and Country*, 40, 670–679.

Da Costa, A. and Saraiva, L. (2012). Hegemonic discourses on entrepreneurship as an ideological mechanism for the reproduction of capital. *Organization*, 19(5), 587–614.

de Lamennais, F. (1840). *Modern Slavery*. London: J. Watson.

Dodd, S. and Anderson, A. R. (2007). Mumpsimus and the mything of the individualistic entrepreneur. *International Small Business Journal*, 25(4), 341–360.

Dubois, L. (2011). Slavery in the age of revolution. In Heuman, G. and Burnard, T. (Eds.) *The Routledge History of Slavery*. New York: Routledge.

Eatwell, J. (2019). Cost of production and the theory of the rate of profit. *Contributions to Political Economy*, 38(1), 1–11.

Ekelund, R. and Hébert, R. (1997). *A History of Economic Theory and Method*. 4th Edition. New York: McGraw-Hill Companies.

Fayolle, A. (2007). *Entrepreneurship and New Value Creation: The Dynamic of the Entrepreneurial Process*. Cambridge: Cambridge University Press.

Filion, L. (2011). Defining the entrepreneur. In Dana, L. (Ed.) *World Encyclopedia of Entrepreneurship*. London: Edward Elgar Publishing.

Goldin, C. (2001). The human-capital century and American leadership: Virtues of the past. *The Journal of Economic History*, 61(2), 263–292.

Goldin, C. (2016). Human capital. In Diebolt, C. and Haupert, M. (Eds.) *Handbook of Cliometrics*. London: Springer.

Gordon, S. (1973). The wage-fund controversy: The second round. *History of Political Economy*, 5(1), 14–35.

Harris, A. L. (1964). John Stuart Mill: Servant of the East India company. *Canadian Journal of Economics and Political Science*, 30(2), 185–202.

Harvey, D. (1990). *The Condition of Postmodernity: An Inquiry into the Origins of Cultural Change*. Oxford: Basil-Blackwell.

Hodgson, A. (1823). A letter to M. Jean Baptiste Say on the comparative expense of free and slave labour. In Hodgson, A. (Ed.) *Remarks During Journey Through North America in the Years 1819, 1820 and 1821*. New York: Samuel Whiting.

Jones, C. and Murtola, A. (2012). Entrepreneurship and expropriation. *Organization*, 19(5), 635–655.

Jones, C. and Spicer, A. (2009). *Unmasking the Entrepreneur*. London: Edward Elgar.

Knight, F. (1921). *Risk, Uncertainty and Profits*. London: School of Economies.

Kao, R. W. (1993). Defining entrepreneurship: Past, present and? *Creativity and Innovation Management*, 2(1), 69–70.

Kurer, O. (1998). Mill's recantation of the wages-fund doctrine: Was mill right, after all? *History of Political Economy*, 30(3), 515.

Levy, D. and Scully, M. (2007). The institutional entrepreneur as modern prince: The strategic face of power in contested fields. *Organization Studies*, 28(7), 971–991.

Lisboa, J. (1844). *Considerações sobre as doutrinas econômicas de M. João Batista Say*. Minerva Brasiliense, 15th set.

Long, W. (1983). The meaning of entrepreneurship. *American Journal of Small Business*, 8(2), 47–59.

Logan, F. A. (1956). The British East India company and African slavery in Benkulen, Sumatra, 1687–1792. *The Journal of Negro History*, 41(4), 339–348.

Major, A. (2012). *Slavery, Abolitionism and Empire in India, 1772–1843*. Liverpool: Liverpool University Press.

Makintosh, T. (1840). *An Inquiry into the Nature of Responsibility, as Deduced from Savage Injustice, Civil Justice, and Social Justice, Etc.* Birmingham: James West.

Mill, J. S. (1844, 1948). Of profits, and interest. In Mill, J. S. (Ed.) *Essays on Some Unsettled Questions of Political Economy*. London: London School of Economics.

Mill, J. S. (1848, 1820). *Principles of Political Economy with Some of Their Applications to Social Philosophy*. London: Longmans and Green and Co. Online. Mill, J. S. (1848). *Principles of Political Economy with Some of Their Applications to Social Philosophy*. London: Longmans and Green and Co.

Mill, J. S. (1850). The negro question. *Fraser's Magazine for Town and Country*, 41, 25–31.

Mill, J. S. (1871a). *Principles of Political Economy with Some of Their Applications to Social Philosophy*. Volume 1. 7th Edition. London: Longmans and Green, Reader and Dyer.

Mill, J. S. (1871b). *Principles of Political Economy with Some of Their Applications to Social Philosophy*. Volume 2. 7th Edition. London: Longmans, Green, Reader and Dyer.

Nodoushani, O. and Nodoushani, P. (1999). A deconstructionist theory of entrepreneurship: A note. *American Business Review*, 17(1), 45.

Paganelli, M. (2003). In medio stat Virtus: An alternative view of usury in Adam Smith's thinking. *History of Political Economy*, 35(1), 21–48.

Parker, S. (2018). *The Economics of Entrepreneurship*. Cambridge: Cambridge University Press.

Ravix, J. (2014). Jean-Baptiste Say et l'entrepreneur: la question de la filiation avec Cantillon et Turgot. *Innovations*, 45(3), 59–76.

Reinert, H. and Reinert, E. (2006). Creative destruction in economics: Nietzsche, Sombart, Schumpeter. In Backhaus, J. G. and Drechsler, W. (Eds.) *Friedrich Nietzsche (1844–1900). The European Heritage in Economics and the Social Sciences*. Volume 3. Boston: Springer.

Remond, R. (2014a). *L'Ancien Regime et la Révolution 1750–1815: Introduction à l'histoire de notre temps*. Paris: Points.

Remond, R. (2014b). *Le XIX Siécle 1815–1914: Introduction à l'histoire de notre temps*. Paris: Points.

Richards, J. (2002). The opium industry in British India. *The Indian Economic and Social History Review*, 39(2–3), 149–180.

Rocha, A. P. (2000). As observações de Jean-Baptiste Say sobre a escravidão. *Estudos Avançados*, 14(38), 181–212.

Saint-Simon, H. (2016). *Henri Saint-Simon, (1760–1825): Selected Writings on Science, Industry and Social Organization*. Oxon: Routledge.

Sánchez, J. (2011). Entrepreneurship as a legitimate field of knowledge. *Psicothema*, 23(3), 427–432.

Say, J.-B. (1815, 1826). Catéchisme d'Économie Politique. In Say, J-B. (Ed.) *OEuvres de Jean-Baptiste Say*. Volume 4. 3rd Edition. Paris: Publiée du vivant de l'auteur.

Say, J.-B. (1821, 1971). *A Treatise on Political Economy or The Production, Distribution and Consumption of Wealth*. New York: Augustus M. Kelley Publishers.

Say, J.-B. (1828–1829, 1852). *Cours complet d'économie politique pratique*. 3rd Edition. Paris: Guillaumin.

Say, J.-B. (1841, 2011). *Traité D'économie Politique ou Simple exposition de la manière dont se forment, se distribuent et se consomment les richesses*. 6th Edition. Paris: Institut Coppet.

Schumpeter, J. (1934). *The Theory of Economic Development*. MA: Harvard University Press.

Schumpeter, J. (1954). *History of Economic Analysis*. Edited from the manuscript by Schumpeter, Elizabeth Boody. New York: Oxford University Press.

Screpanti, E. and Zamagni, S. (2005). *An Outline of the History of Economic Thought*. 2nd Edition. Oxford: Oxford University Press.

Senior, N. (1831, 1966). *Three Lectures on the Rate of Wages*. New York: Augustus M. Kelley Publishers.

Senior, N. (1836, 1965). *An Outline of the Science of Political Economy*. New York: Sentry Press.

Sismondi, J. (1819). *Nouveaux príncipes D'economie politique, Ou De la richesse dans ses Rapports avec la population*. Paris: Delaunay.

Smith, A. (1776, 1999). *An Inquiry into the Nature and Causes of the Wealth of Nations (The Wealth of Nations) (Books I-III)*. London: Penguin.

Sraffa, P. (1960). *Production of Commodities by Means of Commodities: Prelude to a Critique of Economic Theory*. Cambridge: Cambridge University Press.

Steiner, P. (1997). La théorie de l'entrepreneur chez Jean-Baptiste Say et la tradition Cantillon-Knight. *L'Actualité économique*, 73(4), 611–627.

Togati, T. (2019). How can we restore the generality of the general theory? *Cambridge Journal of Economics*, 43(5), 1397–1415.

Turgot, A. (1766, 1913–1923). Réflexions sur la formation et la distribution des richesses. In Schelle, G. (Ed.) *Oeuvres de Turgot et documents le concernant*. Volume II. Paris: F. Alcan, 533–601.

Verin, H. (1982). *Entrepreneurs, entreprises, histoire d'une idée*. Paris: Presses Universitaires de France.

14 Human commodity framework origins and its possible elimination

14.1 Introduction

As exhibited, the human commodity framework appears in two different theory types, which are quite often classified as the same theory for value, production and existence. "*Classical Economics*" is the expression that has often described them. However, this expression is not fit to address the human commodity framework because it entails two theory types that have opposed each other, namely: (i) work-based theories formed after Adam Smith's system and (ii) hedonist economic theories formed after Jeremy Bentham's utilitarianism. In economics and affiliated disciplines, these are still the two leading propositions from which the human commodity framework is derived.

Relativism from social constructivism, poststructuralism or postmodernism would be most unhelpful to address these theoretical formulations or provide workable alternatives. Take, for example, the claim of many relativists deemed as postmodernists. Allegedly, they would be reacting to modifications carried in the enlightenment (generally poorly defined) when modernism would have been established. Indeed, Smith and Bentham could be situated as enlightenment thinkers. However, their economic theories are quite different. Moreover, part of Smith's and Bentham's proposals are connectable to systems proposed by ancient philosophers who lived thousands of years before. To a great extent, Smith's system was based upon Aristoteles's economic and societal ideas and virtue moral system. Bentham's system was partially inspired by ancient hedonist philosophers such as Epicurus and Lucretius, although Bentham presented a much less sophisticated version. Some ancient hedonist philosophers expressed concern in distinguishing among different pleasures and different pains, advising his followers to avoid some hurtful desires, and in addressing virtue. Bentham's version consists in a crude quantitative hedonism. Nevertheless, hedonisms suffer from systematic problems, as we have explained. Undeniably, however, Smith's and Bentham's writings were developed at times of industrial revolution and great turbulence on the planet, with processes such as technological developments, empire expansions and contractions over territories, new country formation, human impacts on the biosphere, social tensions and several armed conflicts. Yet, Smith's and Bentham's theories contain many elements reenacting ancient debates.

Furthermore, contemporary relativists quite often repeat themselves olden arguments where they would be on the side of ancient relativists. Moreover, David Hume, a friend to Adam Smith, also partially endorsed ancient Sophist and Skeptic[1] arguments (though later in life he has recanted part of them). Contemporary relativists would be on the side of Protagoras and other Sophists who declared man to be the measure of all things ("*of the existence of things that are, and of the non-existence of things that are not*"[2]). As in the ancient monetary societies of Greece and Rome, this view would suit well current versions in which all things would be socially constructed by human languages and methods. Interpretative communities would be the measure of all existing and non-existing things. Yet, thousands of years ago, anti-relativist philosophers showed that relativism is incoherent and self-defeating. Furthermore, relativism leads to dangerous societal relativism forms such as moral relativism, which can be used to enhance many evils and abuses.

Likewise, suggesting that work-based and hedonist theories have operated merely through versions of local relativism would be preposterous, that is, under the banners of different paradigm, episteme, research program, final vocabulary, regime of the production of truth, and other designations. It is correct that proponents of these work-based and hedonist theories have meaning variance in some concepts, for instance, the definition of utility or purpose of production. However, both theories have common elements. Moreover, as explained by intangible flow theory, both theories are constrained by the reality they try to explain. They are both related to tangible phenomena such as occurred monetary flows and intangible but perceivable phenomena such as workflows. Furthermore, proponents of both theoretical types knew each other well and spent plenty of time socializing, writing and debating. Evidence that many researchers have been treating these theoretical types as the same theory demonstrates that there are many common elements among them. Moreover, Parts 1 and 2 have explained that relativists should not be expected to articulate consistent alternative theories. Paradoxically, although appearing otherwise, relativists' work generally reinforces dominant theories and social groups. Besides being impotent to present systematic alternatives, relativism tends to reinforce the human commodity framework.

14.2 Synthesis of labor theories of value, production and existence after Smith's system and Ricardo's reformulation

Adam Smith, a moral philosopher, presented an economic system organizing many ideas that were dispersed in the 18th century. He was concerned with societal harmony and how natural order could emerge in human societies. To him, in mercantile societies, harmony would arise out of conflicts among different social classes, natural law and the Divine Providence, which would be connected to his popular but often misconstrued invisible hand metaphor. Nonetheless, Smith's invisible hand metaphor is connected to the sense of touch (a definition of tangibility). It differs from intangible flow theory's definition of intangible flows as flows that cannot be identified with precision (another definition of tangibility). Smith invokes an elusive sense of touch to reach the invisible. For intangible flow theory, flows remain intangible only until humans find manner to identify them with precision.

Panel A: Smith's system

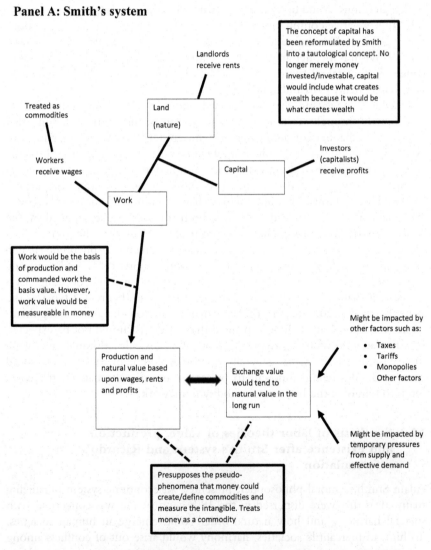

Figure 14.1 Work theories of production, value and existence in Smith's system and Ricardo's reformulation

Nonetheless, although contemporary economics' foundations have commonly been attributed to Smith, he did not support any self-regulating market myth. Curiously, furthermore, in Smith's system we find many themes that currently we tend to associate with Marxism. His system organized a work-based theory of production, value and existence, which is summarized in Figure 14.1 (Panel A). Smith's system is to a great extent derived from the ancient philosopher Aristoteles's economic ideas. At the core of the system is Aristoteles's distinction between natural use of money (for addressing life necessities like eating, drinking or finding shelter) and nonnatural use of money (for reasons of enrichment through abusive trade or usury, namely, through unjustifiable profits or interest rates). As Aristoteles, Smith has adopted a commodity theory of money. Correspondingly, Smith has embraced a distinction between natural

Panel B: Ricardo's reformulation

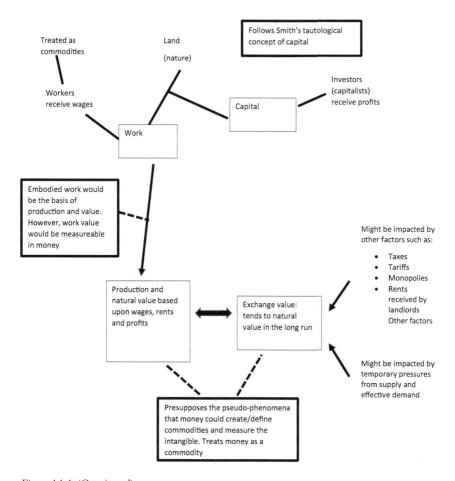

Figure 14.1 (Continued)

and exchange value of commodities. However, Smith lived through different times, where trading activities and monetary loans were more acceptable. Still, he manifested a certain suspicion about some of these activities when they could go against public interest.

Smith accepts that commodity values could be temporarily influenced by exchange pressures from supply and effective demand or other factors such as tariffs, taxes or monopolies. However, his system argues that exchange values tend to their natural value in the long run. To explain what that natural value would be, Smith proposed a rather different formulation from Aristoteles, who lived in a slave-based society where waged work was less frequent. According to Smith, natural value would be explained by the manner products would be produced. Henceforth, his system suggests connecting production, value and existence.

Smith divides human beings into three social classes who would participate in production and value at mercantile societies: (i) capitalists who apply capital to production and receive profits; (ii) landowners who lease land (and other properties) for production and receive rents; and (iii) workers who contribute work and receive wages. Yet, Smith transformed the meaning of the word capital. The previous meaning, which is still applied in plenty of business and management contexts, equates capital with money invested or investable in productive ventures. After Smith in economics and other social sciences, capital becomes elements where money has been invested to participate in production and create wealth. For example, instead of capital being money invested in a machine, the machine itself becomes capital. Likewise, humans could conceptually become capital. Still, Smith has brought upon a tautological definition of capital that pertains in economics and other social sciences: Capital creates wealth because it is what creates wealth.

Regarding landowners, Smith took several agrarian examples perhaps because the economy of his time was essentially agrarian. However, his system could be applicable to other forms of rents as those over mines, houses or other properties. Indeed, his general lessening of the biosphere and biophysical world into land can be quite restrictive. The pseudo-phenomena involving money creating or defining other commodities is a major pathway for workers to be treated as commodities that would reproduce according to their monetary wages (a view commonly attributed to Malthus). As work would be reflected in monetary flows (for instance, wage flows), workers and their workflows would be treated as akin to commodities.

Smith identifies that human work is at the core of any form of human production. Hence, according to him, it follows that work must also be the focal point of commodities' natural value. Rents and profits would likewise gravitate towards work. However, Smith understands that work among humans can immensely vary, which can happen for several reasons: workers' motivations, their skills, temperaments, type of work, contexts and so forth. Therefore, it would be difficult to precisely identify exact work that could have been exerted. Moreover, investors measure the work commanded (by paying wages), as they could not be sure of the precise work that could have been produced by their monetary outflows. In any case, however, although Smith defines human work as the basis of natural value, such value would be expressible in money. Hence, given that human work is to great extent intangible, money would be a measure for the intangible. Treatment of money as a measure for the intangible becomes henceforth generalized in economics and affiliated disciplines.

As noted, many factors could deviate commodities' exchange values from their natural values, such as taxes, tariffs, monopolies and pressures from supply and demand. However, Smith believes that in the long run commodity prices tend to their natural values, which would be based on natural values of profits, rents and wages, occurring out of societal harmony among the three productive social classes. Far from preaching a self-regulating market, Smith is afraid that some unscrupulous investors may associate with members of governments to increase their own wealth, generating very negative consequences to the rest of society. For instance, governments could increase investors' profits by creating tariffs that make importing competing commodities more expensive or by regulating the creation of monopolies that could protect specific national producers at the expense of the rest of society. Smith is frontally against these types of government interventions in trading and producing activities.

Yet, Smith praises investment and organizational activities with moral standards. He identifies an archetype of good investor, namely, the frugal investor who reinvests accumulated profits into further production. Moreover, Smith's system does not endorse any artificial dialectics between states and markets. On the contrary, Smith identifies that governments are necessary for the existence of markets by providing, for instance, security, regulations and laws, protection for property, or even money, without which the existence of markets would not be possible. Moreover, governments can contribute with education of the population or with building important infrastructures. As another example, governments could create laws restricting abuses in the concession of loans (usury laws).

David Ricardo's reformulation of Smith's system is summarized in Figure 14.1 (Panel B). Ricardo accepts most features of Smith's system, recommending also a work-based formulation. However, Ricardo contests that landowners could actively contribute to production. He does not deny that rents will impact exchange prices of commodities because rents such as taxes or tariffs tend to be shifted to buyers at the prices paid for products. Still, Ricardo has many doubts that landowners could be considered as productive agents, rather that exploitative agents collecting rents out of production. Often, Ricardo has in mind landowners who descended from traditional aristocracy in a period of great societal turbulence. Nevertheless, Ricardo engages in a discussion of productive types of lands and rents, already partially addressed by Smith.

Production with impact on commodities' natural values, Ricardo claims, must be based upon the actual work exerted to produce commodities, that is, the embodied labor that has been incorporated in products. Here we have another important divergence from Smith, who has based his system on labor commanded instead of embodied labor. However, as in Smith's system, embodied labor would also be expressed in monetary terms, whereby money could measure the intangible. Ricardo admits exceptional cases in which commodity values could diverge from their natural values in the long run, such as in goods deriving their value from scarcity alone (Ricardo exemplifies with rare statues and pictures, scarce books, or rare wines), goods produced under a monopoly, paper money, or goods entering international trade. Likewise, he admits the difficulty of applying this theory to cases where there are differences in workers' labor quality, distinct capital-labor ratios among different industries, and high variability of incomes among workers, capitalists and landowners. However, Ricardo dismisses these problems as minor, and he is happy to state that for the general case a work-based theory would apply.

Although diverging in several aspects, both Ricardo and Smith hold cost-based theories of value, where work is the key element. Ricardo did discuss finding a universal measure of value (and production) setting the standard to appropriately measure any commodity's value. It is, however, unclear whether he did take such matters seriously or merely as a speculative hypothesis. Still, he seems to imply that embodied work, as a commodity, could approximately operate as universal standard of value. However, once again, one must not fail to note that embodied labor would be expressed in monetary values, which makes us return to the systematic problem of having money considered an adequate measure for the intangible (a paradox).

Before and after Smith's writings, Europe observed the rise of several social writers of production, value and existence. It would be difficult to identify causes for those events or to limit them to Smith and Ricardo, whose writings some of the social relations writers contested. Among the many possible causes might be verifiable social conflicts in production and distribution of products and monetary flows, ongoing industrial revolution, the misery and plight of many workers and their families which have been compared by Sismondi as worse than that of the slaves, many tensions caused by the post-French Revolution, and empires' expansions and contractions around the planet. Diverse social relations writers have begun contesting status quos of owners of means of production and other moneyed persons in comparison to deplorable conditions many wage workers faced in factory production, as well as the misery and decrepitude their families could experience. Furthermore, some of those writers have presented theoretical alternatives. Moreover, several social movements partially inspired by these writers have started demanding alternatives and causing significant social agitation in the most industrialized countries. While formulated sensibly at the same time, thus, before the advent of Marxism, hedonist economic theory makes a description of owners of means of production and other moneyed persons that is much more favorable to the one that could be derived from work-based theories. However, hedonist theory will maintain important elements of Smith's system, also agreed upon by Ricardo.

14.3 Synthesis of hedonist theory of value, production and existence

Hedonist writers have identified relevant problems in work-based theories, for instance, the difficulty of isolating direct and indirect work that might have been involved in production or that production requires not only human work as it needs materials and energy from nature (thus, the biosphere and biophysical world) and employs technology. Furthermore, distinguishing an investor, a landlord and a worker might in several events be difficult because the same person can perform two or three activities connected to these categories. Indeed, investments in land or mines may have similar characteristics to investing in organizations. Moreover, workers might be quite different among themselves. Entrepreneurs and persons of knowledge may give relevant contributions to economic and societal production. Furthermore, in monetary societies, sooner or later we will all be consumers, for we will need to buy something. Undeniably, these are problems in work-based theories. However, hedonist writers allege that their hedonist prejudices could address them.

We have studied six writers who have developed hedonist economic theory, namely, Jeremy Bentham, John Maitland, Thomas Malthus, Jean-Baptiste Say, Nassau Senior and John Stuart Mill. Their writings would be crucial to form the self-regulating market myth, which we can find in contemporary mainstream economics. According to this myth, hedonist equilibrium would address most if not all problems of our frail human condition. Nonetheless, to great extent, Maitland and Malthus have anticipated John Maynard Keynes's position, who, as many of his orthodox and heterodox followers in economics, would not fully endorse this myth while, however, accepting most of its theoretical postulates.

Hedonist writers have justified pseudo-phenomena of hedonist calculus (in money) with actual phenomena that were known much before Bentham's writings: that prices of most products in monetary societies, though not all, tend to negatively impact the traded quantity. Luxury products might increase trading with higher prices, and basic products as water or bread might maintain trade levels despite of small price variations. However, empirically observable price–quantity traded relations for most products do not necessarily require hedonist explanations. Figure 14.2 (Panel A and B) describes key components of the hedonist theory of value, production and existence. Making a break with previous work-based theories, a new concept of market has been brought forward. It is based on the abstraction of hedonist utility, which later will be foundational to mainstream economics' hyper-mathematization. Demand represents abstract consumers, who hold monetary means to exchange and are looking out for potential hedonist utility (either final or intermediate). Supply is the abstraction of hedonist utility on offer within products by eventual producers, constrained by scarcity and costs. Consumers and producers are separated into two blocks, who would meet at this figurative market, feebly situated in time

Panel A – Hedonist market parable

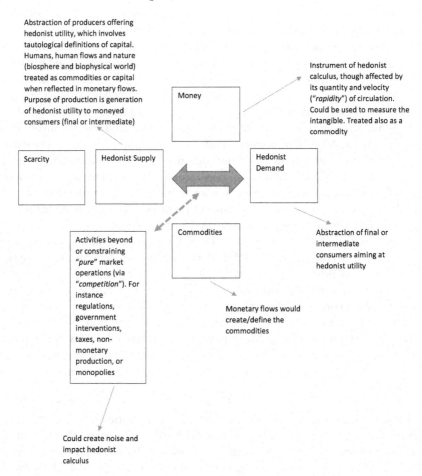

Figure 14.2 Hedonist utilitarian economic theory of production, value and existence: The market as the social mechanism for hedonist calculus

and space. One block would not exist without the other. Despite an apparent matching among buyers and sellers, economists are essentially concerned with monetary relations. Most other human interactions are discarded, even when they impact prices and trade flows. Moreover, hedonist economists pay little attention to social structures, functions of money, trade and markets. When economic and societal production is not reflected in monetary flows, such production becomes generally indiscernible to hedonist-based research.

It is therefore quite a different view of things to Smith, Ricardo and several social relations writers, who were trying to explain the relevance of human

Panel B – Dialectic form of hedonist economic theory

Thesis: Construction of hedonist market parable as the ideal form of production	**Antithesis:** Other forms of production as government and communal production (Condemned to fail due to hedonist prejudices)

Synthesis: Hedonist market parable is better than any other form of production and could address the human condition. Other forms of production should occur only when hedonist markets would not be available.

However, this synthesis must be deconstructed. It is only possible due to invoking several pseudo-phenomena. This synthesis neglects that governments are necessary for the existence of money and markets and that markets are embedded in human societies. The monetary flow is merely a micro flow of production and delivery of products to humans.

Furthermore, this synthesis ignores many relevant flows that are not reflected on monetary flows.

Other forms of production (e.g., governmental or communal) can indeed be poorly managed and fail, but their failures are not excused by hedonist theory as hedonist market constructions' failures are.

Figure 14.2 (Continued)

toil to the occurrence of production. Although hedonist writers certainly have discussed the division of labor,[3] its relevance becomes much diminished when consumers turn out to be the producers or use value equates exchange value. In Adam Smith's famous example of a pin factory,[4] he identifies 18 different operations required to produce pins, such as when: "*One man draws out the wire, another straights it, a third cuts it, a fourth points it, a fifth grinds it at the top for receiving the head; to make the head requires three distinct operations,*"[5] and so forth. Smith concludes that these factory workers were able to produce thousands more pins each day than if each worker were to produce complete pins by him-/herself. Several advantages arise from the division of labor such as increase in workers' skills and dexterity, saving time, or renewed potential for inventing new machines.[6] Smith was also concerned about how the methods of production affected workers' livelihood and dignity.[7] Instead, hedonist utility theory brings about an abstraction of production and consumption, which to a great extent impairs concerns about how flows are produced in economic and societal production. For instance, it obfuscates how things get done, how things are delivered to human users, what are the impacts upon those humans who participate in economic and societal production, and what are the impacts to the biosphere. On the other hand, hedonist utilitarian theory can be advocated to situate holders of large amounts of money, as investors or landlords, in much more beneficial settings in comparison to work-based theories.

Society, as suggested by Bentham, would be a fiction beyond the cumulative sum of pleasures and pains of affiliated humans. Hedonist supply and demand, in the famous graphic representation of the market in economics is but the figurative drawing of this theory. Supply would represent producers offering hedonist utility contained somewhere within the products. Demand represents potential consumers, either final or intermediate, with monetary means to aim at obtaining hedonist utility. Money would be the instrument of hedonist calculus allowing supply to match demand. The hedonist quantitative theory of money is a complementary theory to the market parable. That is, money could only be used for proper hedonist equilibrium if it were to operate as a neutral commodity. If governments or other institutions such as banks could take measures affecting quantity and/or rapidity of money circulation, hedonist calculus would be disturbed. Likewise, if governments could intervene in the so-called market, or if competition among producers or consumers could be disturbed (for instance through a monopoly), markets would not be able to find mystical hedonist equilibrium. Hence, when constructions of hedonist equilibrium fail (for instance, in crises, conflicts, war and misery), blame would be shifted elsewhere.

Initial versions of hedonist theory developed by Say, Malthus, Maitland and Senior could approximate economics to a science of hedonist exchange. Demand would be dependent on subjective utility, for no hedonist consumer would buy a product if expected utility was to be lower than price. Likewise, supply would be constrained by labor and other costs, for no producer would be keen to produce when selling prices were lower than costs. However, costs of production would also be formed out of hedonist market exchanges. Nonetheless, J.S. Mill integrated a fragment of labor theories into supply, namely, by claiming that labor and other costs would remain even if values were not defined in exchange. However, Mill was a foremost proponent of quantitative hedonism in economics. Although he may have advanced elsewhere a slightly more sophisticated qualitative hedonist version, to address economic matters he mostly endorsed quantitative hedonism. In this regard, Mill follows Bentham and the other hedonist economic writers. Mill proposed that the relation between supply and demand could be represented by an equation (instead of a ratio). By several decades, he anticipated Alfred Marshall, Francis Edgeworth and other economists often defined as neoclassical, who would draw the graphs carrying the famous visual representation of economic hedonism. Humans, our contribution to economic and societal production, and nature would need to fit somewhere along those graphs; otherwise, we were to be ignored or discarded by economics and affiliated social sciences. There is no demonstration, however, that such hedonist supply and demand exist or that hedonist market formulations are adequate descriptions of how flows of products and money occur. Foremost hedonist economists can sometimes assume that their suppositions and models could not be entirely realistic. However, they do not display much concern about it.

Blurring the distinction between costs and profits (or interests) was an important contribution to the market parable. In work-based theories, profits are revenues out of investments, which are computed after costs of production are subtracted. Thus, sooner or later, profits can be understood as a surplus. Thereby, profits would help explaining why investors would be motivated to move along different investment opportunities. However, in hedonist theory, profits would be akin to costs that pay services of capital to hedonism, or the abstinence of investors in not engaging in hedonist pleasures. Every element participating in production and exchange would be turned into commodity and/or capital (or asset or resource). Even nature is conceptually transformed into capital and/or commodity. By treating everything as a cost, there can no longer exist coherent theories of costs or of rates of profits. Commodities (including human commodities), would mysteriously appear in hedonist markets. As in labor theories, humans and our related flows would keep being described as commodities. However, the biosphere, humans and our flows would also become both capital and commodities to produce hedonism; otherwise, we would be irrelevant.

The hedonist economic theory is dialectic in explaining production, value and existence. It has a thesis-antithesis-synthesis formulation. The hedonist market parable would be the ideal production type. Other forms of production would be the antithesis (or binary opposite), for instance, those of governments or communal production, which by hedonist prejudice would be condemned to fail when in comparison to hedonist markets. Alternative forms of production would be allowed only when hedonist markets did not cover for them. However, a realistic deconstruction is necessary towards this artificial dialectic, which is based on invoking several pseudo-phenomena. As explained by Smith, the very existence of markets is dependent on several features that are only possible after being enabled by governments such as laws, regulations, money, institutions, justice systems, security and infrastructures. Moreover, this hedonist dialectic ignores many relevant flows that are not reflected in monetary flows. Monetary flows are just micro moments in the production and delivery of most outputs. Although markets are created by humans and integrated within human societies, markets as micro moments cannot cope with the existence of the entire humankind. Furthermore, market-based, government-based, and communal production can be better or poorly managed, and they can all succeed or miserably fail.

Before the advent of Marxism, however, hedonist theory addressed perilous claims against owners of the means of production and other moneyed persons. Social relations writers and social movements had claimed that moneyed persons could be establishing lazy classes depending on and exploiting the hardships of the working poor. Or they would not provide beneficial contributions to production. These implications could also be derived from Smith's and Ricardo's writings. However, hedonist theory would theoretically (and rhetorically) put moneyed persons at the command of economic and societal production. Money would be the instrument of hedonist calculus, which would underlie human production, value and existence. Hedonist calculus would be commanded by those who have money (without clearly studying their money and its origins). Hedonist markets would be mystical constructions to be worshiped. Those who had money were not entirely responsible for their decisions or actions because they would be constrained by the preternatural forces regarding mechanisms for societal equilibrium, namely, hedonist markets. Suffice it to say that none of these fabulous claims has ever been empirically demonstrated.

Hedonist theory has disguised a moral philosophy within the discipline of economics. Instead of addressing economic and societal production, mainstream economics is preaching utilitarian hedonism. According to this philosophy, humans would be mostly driven by pleasure and pain. Societies would merely be the sum of their members' pains and pleasures. Money could be the instrument for hedonist calculus in measuring pleasures and pains, as advocated by Bentham. Hedonist economic theory, as developed by Maitland, Malthus, Say, Senior and J.S. Mill, constructs the market as the social mechanism for hedonist calculus. The self-regulating market myth, as developed by Senior, Say and Mill, suggests that markets could by themselves reach hedonist equilibrium, a formidable hedonist utopia only possible out of several mystical constructions.

Contrary to what has been suggested, for instance, by Amartya Sen and others,[8] there is no disconnection between ethics and mainstream economics. Indeed, neutrality of the discipline of economics has been claimed by Senior and J.S. Mill. This important assertion would later be followed by several Nobel Prize winners in Economics. However, Senior and Mill were two major contributors to the self-regulating market myth, which is derived from the moral philosophy of utilitarian hedonism. Recent efforts to create a deontological code for economists indeed have merit.[9] Furthermore, one may notably aim at distinguishing ethics in economics, ethics of economics and ethics of economists.[10] However, while mainstream economic theory is to be based on unverified hedonist constructions in the market parable, mainstream economics and affiliated disciplines will be propaganda channels for the moral philosophy of utilitarian hedonism. Irresponsibly, they will theoretically disintegrate humans, human flows, the biosphere and the biophysical world upon monetary flows. Furthermore, they will support social positions of moneyed persons, regardless of their contributions to human societies and our integration on the biosphere.

For sure, some wealthy individuals will have quite beneficial contributions to economic and societal production. However, not necessarily all of them will.

14.4 Elements of intangible flow theories to creatively eliminate the human commodity framework

Intangible flow theory must avoid falling upon a local relativism ambush: considering itself an absolute rupture to previous theories, thereby forming a different paradigm, episteme, research program, final vocabulary, regime of the production of truth, or any other similar designation.[11] As local relativism (subjectivism) claims that truth exists only in relation to local systems of validity, it overemphasizes breaks, discontinuities and differences. However, common elements of continuity among methods and language forms are necessary to identify those breaks, discontinuities and differences. Furthermore, identification of validity systems and social group require non-relativist truth statements. As explained in Parts 1 and 2, relativism smears new theories and reinforces dominant theories and social groups. It operates as a rhetorical device to preventively sabotage new theories. However, new theories have continuity elements to previous ideas, methods, language forms, problematics and contexts. On close inspection, local relativist theses come to nothing.

Intangible flow theory has common elements to work-based theories, particularly, the concern with relevance of human work to production. However, the new theory pays attention to broader and more complex phenomena. Human work integrates a larger dynamic array of human-related tangible and intangible flows. Moreover, the new theory is not only limited to economic production. It expands the analysis into societal production. Furthermore, the new theory accepts the relevance of several difficulties raised by hedonist writers regarding work-based theories. Those include the difficulty of precisely identifying work involved in production or that human work can be highly heterogeneous. Moreover, economic and societal production does not depend only on human-related flows. It requires resources and energy from the biosphere and biophysical world. It relies on technology. Furthermore, as the 20th century would demonstrate, it can be highly problematic to classify human beings into homogeneous groups of workers, capitalists and landowners. For research purposes, we may classify humans according to common features. However, we must be very careful in not treating human beings as homogenous beings. Likewise, intangible flow theory accepts the relevance of innovation, knowledge, money and human agency. In some cases, moneyed persons can beneficially contribute to economic and societal production, as a poor person is not necessarily a kind one. Likewise, as identified by hedonist writers, humans easily become consumers in monetary societies when, sooner or later, we need to buy something for us or our families.

Furthermore, the new theory must be open to cooperate with other theoretical frameworks, which have been making relevant contributions albeit often ignored or sent to the fringes. Likewise, although most dominant economic ideas since the 18th century were developed in the Occident, the new theory must be open to learn from ideas and contributions developed in other parts of the planet. Intangible flow theory is not an absolutist theory that would prevail over all other theories. In this book, several other theoretical frameworks were referred to and employed to help build the argument.

It is necessary, however, to abandon Smith's unsubstantiated system in which production would explain value, and vice versa, and both would explain human existence. As explained in Part 2 (See Figure 2.1), mere occurrence of a single tangible monetary flow might be dependent on very complex, intangible and not perceivable flows, many of which have not temporal coincidence to the monetary flow. Theories that claim to be able to explain value, however, would lead us to some precise measurement. Nevertheless, it is simply not possible, at this stage, to find explanations for precise value as ambitioned by Smith's system or by hedonist calculus. Value is necessarily socially constructed and dependent on many flows that cannot be identified with precision. Likewise, it is necessary to abandon the commodity theory of money that Smith has obtained in Aristoteles, which would later be continued in hedonist theory. Aristoteles may have confused money with a commodity because at his time money had mostly a physical form. Coins were a relatively recent technological development in ancient Greece. However, Aristoteles could not be aware of monetary forms that would arise in the following thousands of years. Nevertheless, the money commodity theory invokes pseudo-phenomena.

Likewise, the hedonist explanatory systems addressing both production and value through hedonist calculus must likewise collapse. Hedonist calculus in money further entails petitions to pseudo-phenomena. Contrary to Bentham's view deeply ingrained in mainstream economics, there is no demonstration whatever that money would always operate as a hedonist instrument. The hedonist market parable must be revealed as a mystical construction, sacrificing humans, human flows and the biosphere to the cult of hedonism. As noted, price–quantity traded relationships remain quite pertinent. However, they precede hedonist theory and do not necessarily require hedonist explanations.

Hedonist market parable breakdown leads to elimination of an artificial binary opposition between hedonist market and non-market production. The latter is generally represented by state production, though it could include other forms such as not-for-profit or communal production. What are called markets are but occurrences of monetary flows, which are micro moments of all flows necessary for economic and societal production. Likewise, humans who are consumers in those moments cannot have their entire existence defined by monetary flows. As understood by Smith, governments are necessary for the existence of markets. As explained by Polanyi, markets are embedded in human societies. Intangible flow theory demonstrates the intangible flow dynamics of tangible flows such as flows of money and commodities. The occurrence of tangible flows must not be taken for granted. These phenomena merit themselves attention and investigation.

Indeed, the market-state dialectic is but a pseudo binary opposition created by hedonist writers to defend their market parable. Recall how Bentham advocated government's quietism to support his utilitarianism. However, this pseudo binary opposition led opponents of hedonist theory to fall upon another rhetorical trap: By defending governmental production in opposition to market production, they are indeed reinforcing the market–state pseudo binary opposition. Furthermore, they were led to defend governmental production as always adequate, efficient and efficacious. Yet, plenty examples demonstrate that it is possible for government production to fall upon cronyism, corruption and waste of public resources. When no control systems are in place, a small group of people can get hold of state apparatus and divert resources to their families, friends and associates.

Furthermore, there can be bad and good for-profit management. Many firms can be appallingly managed and go bankrupt. Likewise, there can also be good and bad public management. That several opponents of hedonist writers were to defend governments as some form of idyllic production form is but a temporal victory of economic hedonism. It represents the acceptance of the binary imposture described here. Quite a few contemporaries to the earlier hedonist writers fell upon the error of considering that because hedonist writers did support monetary societies and moneyed persons, hedonist writers could understand and explain them. Often, this error persists. Hedonist theory cannot explain any of that. Money is a quite complex social technology, which cannot be captured by the many pseudo-phenomena in the commodity theory of money and hedonist calculus.

As seen in Parts 1 and 2, currently, human organizations are the major mechanisms capable of producing and delivering flows of products to members of human societies. In the process, they generate tangible monetary flows. Thus, organizations must be better researched and understood. How are these flows created and improved? How can different organizations be better managed? How do organizations evolve, grow and die? How are economic and societal production fundamentally reliant on the biosphere? How do monetary resources become significant for organizations in monetary societies? These questions, among others, are vital to study economic and societal production. Any writer trying to find alternatives to contemporary economic and societal production must first carefully try to better understand how they work.

Nevertheless, a necessary modification might be considered as shocking by some readers: abandoning the description of economic systems as capitalist or the term capitalism altogether. Indeed, to return to the original meaning of capital as money invested or investable in organizations is important advice,[12] which has been followed by the new theory. However, defining capital as money dispenses the use of a word as capitalism. Moreover, the latter would be rightly associated with the problematic concept of capital in work-based and hedonist economic theories. Smith introduced a tautological concept that remains in economics and affiliated disciplines: Capital would be what participates in production. As a result, capital would produce outputs and create wealth (value) because capital would be what produces outputs and creates wealth. Capitalism would be the term used to describe societies where this vacuous notion of capital would apply. Furthermore, capitalism is a term used and abused by many relativists. However, the human commodity framework, with its human commodities, assets, capital or resources, is highly reliant on this tautological concept. Furthermore, the poorly defined idea of capitalism obscures actual phenomena regarding tangible flows of commodities and money. Hence, we must replace capitalism with another expression that could more precisely capture what has been going on in the most technologically advanced human societies.

Nowadays, monetary flows are demonstrable to be associated to many instances of economic and societal production. Perhaps, therefore, it could be preferable to refer to our societies as monetary societies instead of describing them as capitalist. Our societies have many differences from the ancient monetary societies of Greece and Rome regarding institutions, technologies, cultures, knowledge, values, organization, production methods, work regimes, conflicts, space arrangements, formal slavery, and so forth that they are barely comparable. However, in employing monetary technologies, shared elements may exist to problems faced by ancient Greeks and Romans. Certainly, there are many other motives at stake. However, use of monetary technologies could eventually help explain why the leading economic theories in the 20th and 21st centuries have so much commonality with ancient Greek and Roman philosophies, as we have seen, work-based theories with Aristoteles' ideas and utilitarianism with ancient hedonist systems (that were much more sophisticated). Some relativists claim to be the next big thing for declaring the end of theory. However, they repeat many arguments formulated by ancient Sophists and Skeptics, who charged money for their services of instructing how to defend moneyed persons and dominant social groups. The many dissimilarities between ancient and contemporary monetary societies must never be undercut if one is to try understanding what they have in common. Yet, mutual elements between ancient and contemporary monetary societies can lead to the collapse of the contemporary relativist thesis that the enlightenment (poorly defined) would have been such a rupture, thereby creating a modernism to which postmodernism would be reacting. However, ancient Sophists' and Skeptics' arguments are recurrent on contemporary relativist writings. How then could relativism be a total rupture to the enlightenment or ancient monetary societies? Simply, it could not.

To study monetary and non-monetary human societies, we need to reject several pseudo-phenomena that are constantly promoted in economics and allied disciplines. These pseudo-phenomena include the alleged capacity of using money to measure the intangible, the reference to money as a mystical commodity that could create and/or define commodities and hedonist calculus in money. These pseudo-phenomena undermine studying the formidable social technology we human beings have created as money and moreover studying important innovations in this social technology. Examples are several breakthroughs in societies caused by innovations such as coins, checks, promissory notes and bills, paper money, organized banks and financial institutions, fiat money, digital money and credit cards, digital and body recognition payment systems, financial exchanges, online currencies, multi-country currencies or indexed currencies.

Alterations to monetary technologies can bring about impressive societal consequences. New institutional frameworks can be created to organize, support and eventually profit from them. Money has generally operated with reference to an authority as a state, government, or sovereign, with powers of supervision and control.[13] Nevertheless, taxes have also been collected through monetary flows.[14] Digital money modalities have enabled those in charge with forceful means of monitoring what citizens and organizations do. However, we must be careful to not invoke another falsehood arising from the market–state pseudo binary opposition: to claim that money would simply depend on a market–government dialectic. Money can only function when endorsed and accepted by members of that human society. Moreover, we must not take our contemporary monetary technologies as settled or historical determined. Historic events demonstrate they can be reformulated and eventually improved. Likewise, we may eventually find better social technologies for addressing many challenges of our human condition. Although alternative social technologies might only be created in a faraway future, contemporary monetary technologies are not inevitably forever.

Glorification of money as a mystical commodity in economics and allied disciplines is done with tacit support from relativism. It takes precedent from the human commodity framework. Moreover, it formulates an artificial separation of economic and societal production from the biosphere and biophysical world. Furthermore, it leads to neglecting or discarding many important human-related flows not reflected in monetary flows. These are formulations intangible flow theory tries to creatively eliminate. In future works, we will continue studying the human commodity framework and alternative theories that may assist our argument. Furthermore, we will introduce more proposals from the new theory, which does not represent the final theory of all theories. Intangible flow theory is instead a demonstration that to address the reality we humans are immersed within, new theories remain possible.

Notes

1 Refers to specific ancient relativist schools with this name, not to a healthy dose of skepticism.
2 Plato (2013, p. 45).
3 For instance, Say (1821, 1971, Book1, Chapter VIII), Mill (1871a, p. 110), Senior (1836, 1965, p. 59).
4 Chandra (2004), Crowley and Sobel (2010), Galizzi (2014), Pratten (1980), Vincent-Lancrin (2003). According to Pratten (1980), Smith may have obtained the pin factory example from Diderot's Encyclopedia and other French writers from the 18th century.
5 Smith (1776, 1999, pp. 109–101).
6 Smith (1776, 1999, pp. 109–101), Chandra (2004, p. 787).

7 In fact, there is an ongoing debate on whether Smith has anticipated Marx's and Hegel's view of workers' participation in production and their eventual alienation. See, for instance, West (1969), Waszek (1985), Henderson and Davis (1991), Lamb (1973).
8 Sen (1988, p. 78): "It is arguable that a closer contact between ethics and economics can be beneficial not only to economics but even to ethics." See also Blommestein (2006), Dutt and Wilber (2010), Little (2002).
9 Barker (2016), DeMartino (2011), Dow (2016).
10 Dolfsma and Negru (2019, pp. 2–3).
11 This relativist ploy is real. Your writer fell on it at the theory's initial formulations.
12 As suggested by Hodgson (2014).
13 See, for instance, Ingham (1996), Lawson (2016), Peacock (2017), Skidelsky (2018).
14 Idem.

References

Barker, D. (2016). Ethics and social justice. In Searing, E. and Searing, D. (Eds.) *Practicing Professional Ethics in Economics and Public Policy*. Dordrecht: Springer.

Blommestein, H. (2006). Why is ethics not part of modern economics and finance? A historical perspective. *Finance Bien Commun*, 1, 54–64.

Chandra, R. (2004). Adam Smith, Allyn Young, and the division of labor. *Journal of Economic Issues*, 38(3), 787–805.

Crowley, G. and Sobel, R. (2010). Adam Smith: Managerial insights from the father of economics. *Journal of Management History*, 16(4), 504–508.

DeMartino, G. (2011). *The Economist's Oath: On the Need for and Content of Professional Economic Ethics*. Oxford: Oxford University Press.

Dolfsma, W. and Negru, I. (2019). Introduction. In Dolfsma, W. and Negru, I. (Eds.) *The Ethical Formation of Economists*. Oxon: Routledge.

Dow, S. (2016). Codes of ethics for economists, pluralism, and the nature of economic knowledge. In DeMartino, G. and McCloskey, D. (Eds.) *The Oxford Handbook of Professional Economic Ethics*. Oxford: Oxford University Press.

Dutt, A. and Wilber, C. (2010). *Economics and Ethics: An Introduction*. London: Macmillan.

Galizzi, M. (2014). Bringing Adam Smith's pin factory to life: Field trips and discussions as forms of experiential learning. *Journal of the Scholarship of Teaching and Learning*, 14(5), 27–47.

Henderson, J. and Davis, J. (1991). Adam Smith's influence on Hegel's philosophical writings. *Journal of the History of Economic Thought*, 13(2), 184–204.

Hodgson, G. (2014). What is capital? Economists and sociologists have changed its meaning: Should it be changed back? *Cambridge Journal of Economics*, 38(5), 1063–1086.

Ingham, G. (1996). Money is a social relation. *Review of Social Economy*, 54(4), 507–529.

Lamb, R. (1973). Adam Smith's concept of alienation. *Oxford Economic Papers*, 25(2), 275–285.

Lawson, T. (2016). Social positioning and the nature of money. *Cambridge Journal of Economics*, 40(4), 961–996.

Little, I. (2002). *Ethics, Economics, and Politics: Principles of Public Policy*. Oxford: Oxford University Press.

Mill, J. S. (1871a). *Principles of Political Economy with Some of Their Applications to Social Philosophy*. Volume 1. 7th Edition. London: Longmans and Green, Reader and Dyer.

Peacock, M. (2017). The ontology of money. *Cambridge Journal of Economics*, 41(5), 1471–1487.

Plato. (2013). *Theaetetus: Translated by Benjamin Jowett.* The Project Gutenberg EBook. Online at: https://www.gutenberg.org/files/1726/1726-h/1726-h.htm.

Pratten, C. (1980). The manufacture of pins. *Journal of Economic Literature*, 18(1), 93–96.

Say, J.-B. (1821, 1971). *A Treatise on Political Economy or The Production, Distribution and Consumption of Wealth.* New York: Augustus M. Kelley Publishers.

Sen, A. (1988). *On Ethics and Economics.* Oxford: Basil-Blackwell.

Senior, N. (1836, 1965). *An Outline of the Science of Political Economy.* New York. Sentry Press.

Skidelsky, R. (2018). *Money and Government: A Challenge to Mainstream Economics.* Milton Keynes: Penguin.

Smith, A. (1776, 1999). *An Inquiry into the Nature and Causes of the Wealth of Nations (The Wealth of Nations) (Books I-III).* London: Penguin.

Vincent-Lancrin, S. (2003). Adam Smith and the division of labour: Is there a difference between organisation and market? *Cambridge Journal of Economics*, 27(2), 209–224.

Waszek, N. (1985). Miscellanea: Adam Smith and Hegel on the pin factory. *The Owl of Minerva*, 16(2), 229–233.

West, E. (1969). The political economy of alienation: Karl Marx and Adam Smith. *Oxford Economic Papers*, 21(1), 1–23.

Acknowledgements

I acknowledge some financial support from the Advance Research Center from ISEG, University of Lisbon, which is funded by FCT – Fundação para a Ciencia e Tecnologia (Portugal), national funding through research grant UIDB/04521/2020.

Index

Note: Page numbers in *italics* indicate figures; page numbers in **bold** indicate tables.

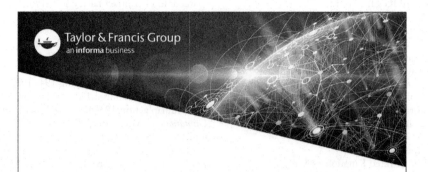

Printed in the United States
By Bookmasters